This Book

presented to the

CHURCH
LIBRARY
IN MEMORY OF

Neal Murrell

BY

Birdville Baptist Church

Code 4386-23, No. 3, Broadman Supplies, Nashville, Tenn. Printed in USA

EXPLORING THE PSALMS

VOLUME ONE

EXPLORING THE PSALMS

VOLUME ONE: *Psalms 1—41*

JOHN PHILLIPS

LOIZEAUX BROTHERS
Neptune, New Jersey

FIRST EDITION, July 1985
SECOND PRINTING, April 1987

A publication of LOIZEAUX BROTHERS, Inc.

*A Nonprofit Organization Devoted to the Lord's Work
and to the Spread of His Truth*

Library of Congress Cataloging in Publication Data
Phillips, John, 1927-
  Exploring the Psalms: Volume 1 (1—41).

  1. Bible. O.T. Psalms—Commentaries. I. Title.
BS1430.3.P46 1985   223'.207   85-6784
ISBN 0-87213-684-1

PRINTED IN THE UNITED STATES OF AMERICA

To

JEAN

the loved friend and companion of my life
my wisest human counselor
my most faithful advisor
and my best example in goodness and Godliness

CONTENTS

8   *Contents*

INTRODUCTION

THE PSALMS are rich in human experience. At times they ring with
the din and noise of battle, at other times they take us with
hushed hearts into the inner sanctuary, into the immediate presence of God. At times they set our hearts aflame and our feet dancing
for joy, at times we turn to them when our face is drenched with tears.

For the psalms touch all the notes in the keyboard of human
emotion. Here we have love and hate, joy and sorrow, hope and fear,
peace and strife, faith and despair. This is the stuff of which life is
made. No wonder God's saints in all ages have felt the tug of the
psalms. The book is a vast storehouse of human experience.

In times of trouble, especially, we turn to this book. When Jonah
found himself in what he called "the belly of hell" he prayed and his
short prayer is saturated with quotations from the psalms. Jesus loved
them. He went from the upper room with the strains of the psalms
still sounding in His soul. They enabled Him to face Gethsemane. He
endured Golgotha, quoting from the psalms. On the day of Pentecost,
Peter turned instinctively to the psalms to find words to explain vital
truth to the stricken Jewish people in Jerusalem. Paul, in summarizing
the Holy Spirit's great indictment of the human race in Romans 3,
found the language he needed in the psalms.

There is a sameness in the psalms, as anyone who has tried to
preach through them consecutively has soon discovered. Yet there is
an astonishing variety in them, too. The sameness is that of the waves
rolling in from the depths of a vast ocean to break upon the sands
of the shore—the same, yet each one slightly different.

It is not surprising that there is a similarity about them. They
nearly all came out of a relatively few historical molds. Some were
born during David's fugitive years in the days of Saul; others were
wrung out of his soul during the Absalom rebellion. Some he wrote
when firmly enthroned as Israel's king, reigning in the affections of
his people. Some he penned in the terrible days that followed his sin
with Bathsheba. Hezekiah wrote a fair number of psalms during the
days of the Assyrian invasion. Some psalms seem to relate to the
experiences of Israel during their Babylonian captivity and others to
the travails of the remnant who returned to claim again the Promised
Land for the coming Messiah. The psalms seem to have been plucked
on relatively few strings of the harp.

Yet none are quite identical. I was particularly struck, for instance,
with the seeming sameness of Psalms 14 and 53. Yet the differences

between them appear at once upon closer investigation. So marked is this dichotomy I was led to handle them in quite different ways. I took Psalm 14 with me into the great courtroom scene of Romans, and Psalm 53 into the dramatic theater of Revelation.

This is one feature of this particular exposition which should appeal to general reader and student alike. I have been very much aware that often a given psalm could be handled in several ways. I have tried, therefore, to vary the approach to the psalms. Sometimes I have thrown a psalm back into its historical setting and expounded it in the light of the author's own experiences—David's circumstances, Hezekiah's dilemma, Moses' experience. Sometimes I have touched but lightly on the historical mold and emphasized the way a psalm relates to the life of a struggling soul today.

Sometimes for the sake of variety, I have taken the prophetic aspect of a psalm and handled it in the light of the coming great tribulation or the millennial reign of Christ. Many commentaries completely overlook, or only lightly acknowledge, the prophetic features in the psalms. Some psalms, however, are full-length prophecies revealing an astonishing picture of coming events.

Prophecies in the psalms anticipate both comings of Christ. They foretell His birth; His life; His character; His death, burial, and resurrection; His ascension; and His coming again. Some anticipate the horrors of the dreadful days when the Antichrist will rule the earth, others dwell with joyful anticipation on the glories of the golden age. In highlighting many of the prophecies in the book of Psalms I have discovered that there is probably as much, if not more, clear-cut prophecy in the psalms as in many of the more obvious prophetic books of the Bible.

One problem many have found in approaching the psalms relates to their complicated structure. They seem to be especially difficult to analyze structurally and put in preachable form. As in all my other books, I have given with each psalm a complete alliterated outline. I have been careful never to "sacrifice the sense for the sake of the sound." The outlines will be found to be true to the text and a useful tool for preachers and Bible teachers.

HEBREW PSALM TITLES
AND HEBREW WORDS IN THE PSALMS

Note: The psalms identified below are the psalms as printed in the standard King James text of the Bible. It should be pointed out that more often than not these titles belong as subscriptions to the previous psalm rather than as superscriptions to the psalms as normally printed. It is in this light that they have been handled in this exposition. However, they are listed here as they traditionally appear in most editions of the Bible. Where they are treated as belonging to the subscription of the previous psalm, this is noted in parentheses.

Aijeleth Shahar: "The day dawn." Psalm 22 (21)

Al Alamoth: "Relting to maidens" (young, unmarried women), a song for the sopranos. Psalm 46 (45)

Al-taschith: "Destroy not." Psalms 57; 58; 59; 75 (56; 57; 58; 74)

Gittith: "The winepresses." This is taken to be a reference to the Feast of Tabernacles which took place in the fall of the year. 8; 81; 84 (7; 80; 83)

Higgaion: "A soliloquy" or a meditation. 9:16; 19:14; 92:3. It is rendered *higgaion* in Psalm 9, *meditation* in Psalm 19, and *solemn sound* in Psalm 92.

Jeduthun: A personal name, the name of one of the three "chief musicians" or music directors of the temple worship (1 Chronicles 16:41-43; 25:1-6; 2 Chronicles 5:12; 35:15). He was a Levite, a descendent of Merari (1 Chronicles 26:10). It is thought by some that Ethan and Jeduthun are the same person (1 Chronicles 15:17-19). Psalms 39; 62; 77 (38; 61; 76)

Jonath Elim Rechokim: "The dove in the far off terebinth trees." Psalm 56 (55)

Mahalath: "The great dance." Psalm 53 (52)

Mahalath Leannoth: "The great dancing and shouting." Psalm 88 (87)

Maschil: "Understanding" or "teaching," particularly public instruction. Psalms 32; 42; 44; 45; 52; 53; 54; 55; 74; 78; 88; 89; 142

Michtam: "An engraving," hence, a permanent writing, a golden poem. All were written by David and refer to the days of his rejection. Psalms 16; 56; 57; 58; 59; 60

Muth Labben: "The death of the champion." Psalm 9 (8)

Neginoth: "Smitings." Psalms 4; 6; 54; 55; 61; 67; 76 (3; 5; 53; 54; 60; 66; 75)

11

Nehiloth: "The great inheritance." Psalm 5 (4)

Psalm: A translation of "Mizmor." Psalms 3; 4; 5; 6; 8; 9; 12; 13; 15; 19; 20; 21; 22; 23; 24; 29; 31; 38; 39; 40; 41; 47; 49; 50; 51; 62; 63; 64; 73; 77; 79; 80; 82; 84; 85; 98; 100; 101; 109; 110; 139; 140; 141; 143

Selah: "to pause and lift up"; it can be freely rendered: "There! What do you think of that?" Occurs once: Psalms 7; 20; 21; 44; 47; 48; 50; 54; 60; 61; 75; 81; 82; 83; 85; 143; occurs twice: Psalms 4; 9; 24; 39; 49; 52; 55; 57; 59; 62; 67; 76; 84; 87; 88; occurs three times: Psalms 3; 32; 46; 66; 68; 77; 140; occurs four times: Psalm 89

Sheminith: "the eighth." Psalms 6; 12 (5; 11)

Shiggaion: "a loud cry." Psalm 7

Shoshannim: "lilies." This is taken to be a reference to the Passover feast which occurred in the spring of the year. Psalms 45; 69 (44; 68)

Shushannim Eduth: Shushannim refers to the spring festival, as above, and *eduth* to "testimony." Psalm 80 (79)

Shushan Eduth: same as above only *Shushan* is the singular. Both the above are thought to have some reference to the keeping of the Passover in the second month of the year instead of the regular first month (Numbers 9:10-11; 2 Chronicles 30:1-3). Both psalms where it occurs have to do with the land being invaded by enemies. Psalm 60 (59)

Song; a translation of *shir.* Psalms 18; 45; 46; and 120; 121; 122; 123; 124; 125; 126; 127; 128; 129; 130; 131; 132; 133; 134 (a song of degrees)

Authors of the Psalms

David: 3; 4; 5; 6; 7; 8; 9; 11; 12; 13; 14; 15; 16; 17; 18; 19; 20; 21; 22; 23; 24; 25; 26; 27; 28; 29; 30; 31; 32; 34; 35; 36; 37; 38; 39; 40; 41; 51; 52; 53; 54; 55; 56; 57; 58; 59; 60; 61; 62; 63; 64; 65; 68; 69; 70; 86; 101; 103; 108; 109; 110; 122; 124; 131; 133; 138; 139; 140; 141; 142; 143; 144; 145

Asaph: 50; 73; 74; 75; 76; 77; 78; 79; 80; 81; 82; 83

Sons of Korah: 42; 44; 46; 47; 48; 49; 84; 85; 88

Solomon: 72, 127

Heman the Ezrahite: 89

Moses: 90

Psalms to the Chief Musician

The following list shows the psalms which have a reference to the chief musician appended as a subscription (in most editions of the Bible the ascription is included as a superscription to the following psalm): 3; 4; 5; 7; 8; 10; 11; 12; 13; 17; 18; 19; 20; 21; 30; 35; 38; 39; 40; 41; 43; 44; 45; 46; 48; 50; 51; 52; 53; 54; 55; 56; 57; 58; 59; 60; 61; 63; 64; 65; 66; 67; 68; 69; 74; 75; 76; 79; 80; 83; 84; 87; 108; 138; 139.

Those wishing to study these matters further, without getting into too many technicalities, should consult *The Companion Bible.*

Psalm 1

THE SAINT AND THE SINNER

I. THE GODLY MAN (1:1-3)
   A. His Path—He Is Separated from the World (1:1)
   He does not:
   1. Listen to the Ungodly Man
   2. Linger with the Sinful Man
   3. Laugh at the Scornful Man
   B. His Pleasure—He Is Satisfied with the Word (1:2)
   God's Word has:
   1. Captured His Full Affection
   2. Claimed His Full Attention
   C. His Prosperity—He Is Situated by the Waters (1:3)
   1. His Prominence
   2. His Permanence
   3. His Position
   4. His Productivity
   5. His Propriety
   6. His Perpetuity
   7. His Prosperity
II. THE GODLESS MAN (1:4-6)
   A. He Is Driven (1:4)
   B. He is Doomed (1:5)
   C. He Is Damned (1:6)

THE HEBREW HYMNBOOK begins with two "orphan" psalms, that is, with two psalms the authors of which are not given. In the New Testament the second psalm is adopted and ascribed to David (Acts 4:25). But during the entire Old Testament period, like its companion it stood fatherless on the sacred page. There they are, two psalms without author or inscription, owning no stated author but God.

There is something fitting in the grand isolation of these first two Hebrew hymns, for the first has to do with *law,* the second with *prophecy.* The Law and the prophets! On these two great hinges all Old Testament revelation hangs. On these same two hinges all the vast themes which make up the psalms are suspended as well.

They have other points in common. Psalm 1 is emotional. It begins with an overflowing rush of emotion: "Oh the happiness of the man who delights in the law of God." Psalm 2 is intellectual. It deals with a moral problem. It begins with the word "Why?"

Psalm 1 begins with a blessing and ends with a curse; Psalm 2 begins with a curse and ends with a blessing. Psalm 1 is essentially a psalm of Christ; Psalm 2 is essentially a psalm of Antichrist. Psalm 1 shows the meditation of the godly; Psalm 2 shows the meditation of the ungodly. These two psalms form the introduction to the Hebrew hymnbook and they summarize for us the content of the whole.

Psalm 1 obviously divides into two parts. We have the godly man (1:1-3) and we have the godless man (1:4-6). The first half of the psalm gives us a picture of the saint, the second half gives us a picture of the sinner.

I. THE GODLY MAN (1:1-3)

When I was young I was required to take music lessons. I have forgotten almost everything my teacher taught me, but one thing I do remember is where to find "middle C." Everything flows up and down from that mysterious middle C. Though I never did learn why the musical alphabet doesn't start with "A," I did learn that middle C is the starting point, the dividing line, as it were, between treble and bass.

But God doesn't start the music of Heaven with middle C. God finds a high note and begins there! The book of Psalms begins with the word "blessed," or as it can be more colloquially rendered, "happy." In the original it is not in the singular but in the plural. We can render the first word of the Psalms: "Oh the blessednesses of the man," or even more colloquially, "Happy, happy is the man," or: "Oh the happinesses of the man." God does not dole out His blessings one at a time, He pours them out in the plural.

A. The Godly Man's Path
He Is Separated from the World (1:1)

"Happy, happy is the man who walks not in the counsel of the ungodly, who stands not in the way of sinners, who sits not in the seat of the scornful." Modern psychology tells us to emphasize the positive; God begins by emphasizing the negative. The happy, happy man is marked by the things he does *not* do, the places to which he does *not* go, by the books he does *not* read, by the movies he does *not* watch, by the company he does *not* keep. Surely that's a strange way to begin!

God begins this book not with the power of positive thinking, but with the power of negative thinking! In other words, a man who would be a happy, happy man begins by avoiding certain things in life, things which make it impossible for happiness to flourish because they are poisonous, destructive, and counterproductive.

1. He Does Not Listen to the Ungodly Man

"Blessed is the man who walketh not in the counsel of the ungodly."

A Christian becomes involved in a car accident which clearly is his fault and does considerable damage to the other person's car. The attending police officer writes a citation and hands him a summons to appear in court. The man consults a lawyer who is none too scrupulous and who goes over the citation carefully and finds a clerical error. He goes into court to crossexamine the police officer:

"Where did this accident happen, officer?"

"At the corner of Twenty-third and Main."

"You made out this citation?"

"Yes sir."

"What is the date on this citation, officer?"

"April 24. The time 5:30 P.M."

The lawyer turns to the judge: "Your honor, according to this police officer, my client is supposed to have been involved in this accident on April 24. My client was not even in the city on the 24th of April. He was not even in the country." The judge says: "Case dismissed." The man gets off on a technicality. He is guilty, the police officer knows he is guilty, and the injured party knows he is guilty. However, following "the counsel of the ungodly," he is able to get off.

Many people would think something like that very clever; really it is very crooked. It is the counsel of the ungodly. How far do you think that Christian would get in offering a tract or a word of testimony to the police officer or the other motorist?

2. He Does Not Linger with the Sinful Man

"Blessed is the man who . . . standeth not in the way of sinners." There is nothing wrong with being friendly with lost men and women, of course. Jesus was. He made friends with all kinds of people, but He did so in order to lead them to a higher, holier way of life. They called Him "a friend of publicans and sinners." This verse teaches we are not to stand in the *way* of sinners; we are not to participate in their sinful activities.

Abraham stood in the way of sinners when he went down to Egypt to escape the famine in Canaan, where he told Pharaoh that Sarah was his sister, and lost his testimony. Lot stood in the way of sinners when he listened to the king of Sodom instead of the king of Salem, went back to Sodom, and lost his family. Peter stood in the way of sinners when he warmed himself at the world's fire during the trial of Jesus and consequently denied his Lord with oaths and curses.

3. He Does Not Laugh at the Scornful Man

"Blessed is the man who . . . sitteth not in the seat of the scornful."
The ungodly man has his counsel; the sinner has his way; the scornful
has his seat. Note the progression in wickedness—the ungodly, the
sinner, the scornful; and the corresponding progression in backslid-
ing—walking, standing, sitting. As the company gets worse sin in-
creases its hold.

What the Psalmist called the "seat" referred to what we would call
the "chair" of the scornful. We speak, for instance, of the professor's
chair; the Hebrews would speak of their seat: "The scribes . . . sit in
Moses' seat" (Matthew 23:2), that is, they were professors of the law.
The happy, happy man avoids the seat of the scornful, he avoids the
classroom of the atheist and humanist who delight to shred the faith
of the unlearned. Our colleges are full of them today and even our
seminaries are not free from them.

I know a young man who went to just such a seminary. He came
from a fine home, his parents were missionaries, his father translated
the Bible into a native tongue, his brother became an outstanding
evangelist. As a young man he went to seminary to prepare for the
ministry but he chose the wrong school and soon found himself
sitting with the scornful. His faith was systematically undermined and
destroyed.

He was taught that the Bible is not divinely inspired, that it is full
of gross errors and superstitions, and that it is a collection of myth,
folklore, and fable. He was taught to deny the deity of Christ and to
write off as nonsense the beliefs that had sent his father as a pioneer
missionary to Africa. He was taught to deny the virgin birth of Jesus,
the miracles, the Lord's atoning death, resurrection, and ascension,
and to repudiate the blessed hope of Christ's coming again. Jesus,
after all, was simply "the flower of evolution." He was assured that
the New Testament documents are unreliable.

Worse still, all this was poured into his young mind day after day
with wit and charm and with convincing but wholly one-sided and
biased insistence. He simply did not have the expertise to counter it.
He emerged from that school several years later more equipped to
be a Marxist than a minister. His Bible and his boyhood faith had
been torn to shreds. He had been sitting in the seat of the scornful.

The godly man is separated from the world. He avoids the perils
and pitfalls which lie along the path trodden by those who have no
love for the Lord.

B. The Godly Man's Pleasure
He Is Satisfied with the Word (1:2)

1. The Word of God Has Captured His Full Affection

"His *delight* is in the law of the LORD." He has a different counselor than the ungodly man, he finds different company than the sinful man, he has a different cause than the scornful man. His first love is for the Word of God.

2. The Word of God Has Claimed His Full Attention

"And in His law doth he meditate day and night." He does not pour over the books of the scornful; he pours over the Scriptures.

By "meditation" the Bible does not mean so-called transcendental meditation, which is nothing but a trap for the unwary, Hinduism masquerading as science. Beware of any philosophy which teaches how to disengage the mind from deliberate and normal thought processes so it can be free to receive impressions from elsewhere. That kind of thing leads to demonic suggestion.

The meditation the Psalmist advocates deliberately engages the conscious mind with the truths of God's Word. We come into God's presence, open Bible in hand, and say, "Speak, Lord, thy servant heareth." Then we read the Bible in a methodical, meaningful, meditating way, seeking to understand and appropriate its truths. We ask the following questions, for instance, when pondering the sacred page: Is there any sin here for me to avoid? Is there any promise for me to claim? Is there any victory to gain? Is there any blessing to enjoy? Is there any truth I have never seen before about God, Christ, the Holy Spirit, about man, sin? What is the main thing I can learn here? *That's* meditation, especially keeping a note pad and pen handy and writing down what the Holy Spirit brings to mind as we thus ponder God's Word. For writing maketh an exact man. If we cannot verbalize it, we haven't learned anything.

C. The Godly Man's Prosperity
He Is Situated by the Waters (1:3)

In the symbolism of Scripture, water for *cleansing* invariably represents the *Word* of God; water for *drinking* symbolizes the *Spirit* of God. Meditation in Scripture releases the river of God's Spirit so that our lives are refreshed and revitalized.

The Psalmist notes seven things which mark the life of the man who is situated by the river.

His Prominence: he is like "a tree."

His Permanence: he is like a tree "planted." Unlike the grass, which is mowed down in successive harvests, a tree sends its roots down deep into the soil. It has a deep, hidden life.

His Position: he is planted "by the rivers of water." The droughts which bring bleakness and barrenness to others do not affect him. He has an unfailing source of life.

His Productivity: he "brings forth fruit." His branches run over the wall, he is a blessing to everyone.

His Propriety: he brings forth his fruit "in his season." He is not a freak. There are times for fruit-bearing just as there are times for growth and times for rest. So long as we are abiding in the Spirit we need not worry about the fruit. It will come in its season.

His Perpetuity: "his leaf also shall not wither." There are two trees outside my window. One has little rust-red leaves on it just now. They look very pretty, but soon they will fall to the ground. The other tree has fresh, green pine needles. It is an evergreen. That's what we are to be like—not affected by the winter or the weather—always the same.

His Prosperity: "whatsoever he doeth shall prosper." Everything will prosper—his family life, his business life, his church life, his personal life. Such is the godly man, the happy, happy man.

II. The Godless Man (1:4-6)

This is the person who leaves God out of his life. The "ungodly"— that is the mildest description of the lost man in the Bible. By definition a man is either married or unmarried, he is either happy or unhappy, he is either thankful or unthankful, he is either godly or ungodly. Everything about the ungodly man in this psalm sets him in stark contrast with the godly man. The ungodly man is driven, doomed, and damned.

A. He Is Driven (1:4)

Having described the godly man, the Holy Spirit, with studied and deliberate contrast, introduces the ungodly man: "The ungodly are not so." In the Septuagint version there is a much more pungent way of expressing the double negative of this verse: "Not so the ungodly, not so." In contrast with the towering tree, with its roots deep in the soil, nourished by a perennial stream, the ungodly is likened to "the chaff which the wind driveth away." The unsaved man is at the mercy of forces he does not see and which he cannot control.

Here is a ship, its engines broken, its steering out of order, caught in the grip of a gale. It is being driven by wind and tide toward the jagged rocks that guard the coast. Gripped by forces beyond its control, it is being driven straight to disaster.

Such are the forces at work in the life of the ungodly. They are satanic forces, wielded by "the prince of the power of the air, the spirit that now worketh in the children of disobedience." The unsaved man doesn't believe in Satan or in evil spirits. His education has taught him to believe only in what he can test with his senses; but these are invisible forces and the pressure they exert is secret pressure.

The ungodly man is not the master of his own soul, the captain of his own destiny. He is being relentlessly driven. He is as powerless against these forces as the chaff is before the wind. That is how God describes the ungodly.

B. He Is Doomed (1:5)

"Therefore the ungodly shall not stand in the judgment, nor sinners in the congregation of the righteous." The sinner has no standing in the day of judgment. He will be summoned to the great white throne there to find that the heaven and the earth have fled away. Everything familiar will be gone. Everything he has sought to build, everything in which he has invested his time and his talents—gone! He has nowhere to stand. He has built his house upon the sand and the judgment has swept it all away.

Britain's illustrious Queen Elizabeth launched the ships which smashed the power of Spain and saved England from the papacy and the Spanish Inquisition. She set Britain on the road to empire, inaugurated a golden age, and reigned in pomp and splendor for forty-five years. Though she was a staunch Protestant one wonders how much she knew of the true salvation of God.

The historian tells how she died, propped up on her throne, a haggard old woman of seventy, frantically hanging on to life, desperately fighting off the last enemy. Her last words have rung down the centuries: "All my possessions for a moment of time." But death came, bore away her soul, and left her clutching fingers riveted to the arms of her deserted throne.

C. He Is Damned (1:6)

"For the LORD knoweth the way of the righteous; but the way of the ungodly shall perish." There are only two ways. There is the way of the cross, the way that leads by Calvary to glory. And there is the way of the curse, the broad and popular way that leads to a lost eternity.

By nature and by practice our feet are set on the broad way. "We have turned every one to his own way," the prophet declares. But, by deliberate choice, we can make the change. We come to Jesus, "the way, the truth, the life," the One who says, "No man cometh unto the Father but by Me." We take Him as Saviour and become numbered with the godly. We are no longer driven but directed. The lost man, on the other hand, can no more fight his end than the chaff can fight the gale. "The way of the ungodly shall perish." That is the Holy Spirit's sobering, closing word in this first great Hebrew hymn.

Psalm 2

REBELS OF THE WORLD, UNITE!

I. GOD'S GUILTY SUBJECTS (2:1-3)
   A. The Formality of their Rebellion (2:1)
   B. The Force of their Rebellion (2:2)
   C. The Focus of their Rebellion (2:3)
II. GOD'S GREAT SCORN (2:4-6)
   A. He Speaks in Derision (2:4)
   B. He Speaks in Displeasure (2:5)
   C. He Speaks in Determination (2:6)
III. GOD'S GLORIOUS SON (2:7-9)
   A. His Sonship (2:7)
   B. His Sovereignty (2:8)
   C. His Severity (2:9)
IV. GOD'S GRACIOUS SPIRIT (2:10-12)

THERE ARE FOUR SPEAKERS in this psalm. That is its key.

David, the Psalmist (2:1-3), whom God promised that one day his son and Lord would sit upon his throne ruling the tribes of Israel and all the nations of mankind. Yet, looking down the corridor of time he sees the opposite. He sees the nations massing in rebellion against the Lord's anointed. Like many another saint, puzzled over this seeming inconsistency, he asks the age-old question, *why?*

God, the Father (2:4-6), answered David's question with a peal of laughter. The rebellion of the nations is ludicrous from the standpoint of Heaven. When men united against God's Son at His first coming all Heaven *wept;* when they unite against Him at His second coming all Heaven *laughs.*

God, the Son (2:7-9), assures David that He indeed will reign. He is already acclaimed on high as God's beloved Son so David need have no doubts about the ultimate outcome.

God, the Holy Spirit (2:10-12), upholds the sovereign claims of Christ and has a warning for the nations. It is not too late to lay down the arms of rebellion, but they had better submit—or else.

That is how this interesting psalm, which introduces the second great theme of the Psalter, unfolds. The first psalm underlines the law; this one underlines prophecy.[1] And what prophecy! It carries us on to the end times and brings into focus the ultimate triumph of Heaven over earth.

The psalm, as we have seen, divides into four equal parts, each part with a separate speaker.

The voice of David sets before us:

I. God's Guilty Subjects (2:1-3)

David sees the world in a state of outright rebellion. There has always been rebellion against God on earth ever since Adam and Eve took the forbidden fruit. But here we have united and universal rebellion against God, a federation of nations drawn together in a common hatred of God. We note three things about this coming rebellion.

A. The Formality of Their Rebellion (2:1)

"Why do the heathens rage and the people imagine a vain thing? The kings of the earth set themselves and the rulers take counsel together." There are several important words in this statement.

The word "imagine" we have already seen in Psalm 1 where the godly man is said to find his delight in the law of the Lord in which law he *meditates* day and night. The word "meditate" is the same as the word "imagine." The godly man uses his imagination to meditate upon the things of God; the godless nations use their imagination to find ways to rid mankind of God.

This is what our courts call *premeditated* crime. This is not a crime of passion, but a crime of purpose; one which has been planned and carried out by deliberate design.

The next important word is "set": "the kings of the earth *set* themselves." The word literally means to take one's stand, in other words, the nations take up position. They decide they have had enough of religion, especially the Judeo-Christian religion, and they take their stand against it.

When Antiochus invaded Egypt the desperate Egyptians, who had suffered at his hands before, appealed to Rome. The Romans sent one of their ablest and most determined tribunes to confront the haughty and ambitious Syrian with an ultimatum. Antiochus prevaricated, hoping to gain by guile what he could not win by war. He told the Romans he needed time to think over the senate's demands. The tribune took an immediate stand. Swiftly he drew a circle around Antiochus in the sand: "Decide before you step out of that circle."

Now a mightier Roman, the last of the Caesars indeed, takes his stand, a stand against God, and he has the backing of the world. He

---

[1]There is probably more direct and indirect prophecy in the psalms than anywhere else in the Bible. *All* of the psalms contain a prophetic element; some are clearly Messianic; some portray Christ's first coming, some His second coming.

tells God, in effect, to get out of mankind's affairs and stay out forever.

The third expression worth noting says that "the rulers take coun-sel together" against the Lord. It can be rendered "the rulers have gathered by appointment." The decision to do away with God is a United Nations' resolution, put to the vote and passed unanimously without abstentions and without vetos. The world is formally and firmly united in its desire to get rid of God.

B. The Force of Their Rebellion (2:2)

Notice the various conspirators he mentions: "Why do the *nations* rage and the *people* imagine a vain thing? The *kings* of the earth set themselves and the *rulers* take counsel together against the LORD." This rebellion is not something imposed on the masses of mankind by the masters of the world. It is a popular, grass-roots movement which embraces everyone—princes and people alike. It is a mass movement which has popular support. The world is of one mind. It may have its different political systems, different ideas about econom-ic and social structures, about education and national goals, but it is united in this: get rid of God!

C. The Focus of Their Rebellion (2:3)

The nations convene to get rid of Christianity and the Jews, to get rid of the Bible and God. They "take counsel against the LORD [Jeho-vah] and against His Anointed [Christ], saying, Let us break their bands asunder and cast their cords from us." The focus is twofold.

It is against the hated *Person* of God. It is against Jehovah (God as He is known among the Jews) and it is against the Christ (God as He is known among Christians). The rebellion is against God as He is revealed in the Judeo-Christian world, against the God of the Bible. Satan hates both Judaism and Christianity because it is in the Jewish Old Testament and in the Christian New Testament that God has revealed Himself to men. The focus of the rebellion is the *person* of God.

The rebellion is also against the hated *precepts* of God. Men want to get rid of God's "cords" and "bands," the restraints which the Bible imposes on society. The moral and ethical teachings of the Bible are repugnant to the rebellious human heart. The precepts of the law of Moses and the sermon on the mount aggravate the fallen nature of men.

The Psalmist sees a world in which time-honored Bible restraints are thrown off. Men have a new system of morality, a morality which lets them do as they please without being faced with the warnings and wooings of God. Modern man finds wholly unacceptable what the Bible has to say about the sanctity of marriage, sexual purity, respect for parents, reverence for those in authority; about sin, salvation, and coming judgment.

So the rebellion finds its focus in universal hatred of God's Person and God's precepts. The world is already getting ready for this final rebellion. Atheistic communism dominates the lives and destiny of a billion people on this planet while humanism, atheism, and secular-ism rule much of the rest of the world. Atheistic propaganda is becoming more and more blatant and abusive while organized hatred of God is a common phenomenon today. This is only the beginning, for the Holy Spirit is still here as the Restrainer and the worst manifes-tations of God-hate are yet to come.

So David has a word about God's guilty subjects.

II. GOD'S GREAT SCORN (2:4-6)

A. He Speaks in Derision (2:4)

"He that sitteth in the heavens shall laugh; the Lord shall have them in derision." That is God's answer. God simply sits back on His throne and fills the universe with peal after peal of terrible, spine-tingling laughter. Men are such fools! How can puny man hope to win against Almighty God?

Modern man is like the French revolutionary who had helped storm the Bastille. He had scaled the Cathedral of Notre Dame, torn the cross from the spire and dashed it into fragments on the pave-ment of Paris far below. He said to a peasant: "We are going to pull down all that reminds you of God!" "Citizen," was the calm reply, "then pull down the stars!"

As though man, who has successfully orbited some hardware in space, using material God has supplied, and who has put a feeble footprint on the moon—as though man can compete with a God who has orbited a hundred million galaxies! As though man, who has solved some of the subtleties of the atom, and managed to scare himself half to death in the process, can compete with a God who stokes the nuclear fires of a billion stars! No wonder He that sits in the heavens simply laughs. Man—for all his technology and talents, for all his science and skill, for all his inventions—is still man—mere mortal man. And God is God—eternal, uncreated, self-existent, om-nipotent, omniscient, omnipresent, infinite, infallible, holy, high, and lifted up, worshiped by countless angel throngs.

God laughs at men for being such fools. "He that sitteth in the heavens shall laugh: the Lord shall have them in derision."

B. He Speaks in Displeasure (2:5)

When that last peal of chilling laughter dies away it is replaced by a rising tide of fearful, holy wrath. "Then shall He speak unto them in His wrath, and vex them in His sore displeasure." God looks at a conference of kings, and listens to its communiqué: "We decree the banishment of God together with His principles, and His people from the face of the earth." "Is that so?" says God, "Here, Michael—take half a dozen angels and go down and pour out My wrath on that planet."

C. He Speaks in Determination (2:6)

"*Yet* have I set My king upon My holy hill of Zion." *Zion* is a poetical and prophetical name for Jerusalem, which is mentioned as such thirty-eight times in the Psalms.

Jerusalem is at present in Hebrew hands but it will not remain there. Saudi Arabia and the Arabs have demanded that it be handed back to them, and Iran has vowed to "liberate" Jerusalem. It will be seized by the Beast who will use it as a convenient place from which to revile God. Jerusalem will be "trodden down of the Gentiles until the times of the Gentiles be fulfilled," as Jesus said.

The fact that God foreknows the fate of Jerusalem does not change God's mind about the city. He calls down to men His holy determina-tion: "*Yet* have I set My king upon My holy hill of Zion." He speaks in the past tense. It is already done as far as He is concerned.

III. GOD'S GLORIOUS SON (2:7-9)

The actual speaker in this section is Jesus Himself.

A. His Sonship (2:7)

"I will declare the decree: The LORD has said unto Me, Thou art My son; this day have I begotten Thee." Now of course Jesus was *eternally* the Son of God, from everlasting to everlasting; He was *incarnately* the Son of God when He came down to that Bethlehem stable to be born as a Man among men; He was *manifestly* the Son of God when He came back from the dead in invincible power; He is *gloriously* the Son of God, as God's own chosen King. The Lord has a word to say about His Sonship. All the atheists and cultists in the world are not going to change the fact that Jesus is God's unique Son.

B. His Sovereignty (2:8)

"Ask of Me, and I shall give Thee the heathen for Thine inheri-tance, and the uttermost parts of the earth for Thy possession." Satan said to Jesus, "Ask those kingdoms of me. I will give them to you—at a price." Jesus adamantly refused to ask Satan to give them to Him, but He does ask them of His Father. And God will give them to Him in due time.

C. His Severity (2:9)

"Thou shalt break them with a rod of iron; Thou shalt dash them in pieces like a potter's vessel." One moment the Beast will be strutting across the world and the armies of mankind will be drawn to Megiddo to oppose Christ's coming again. The next moment the Beast and his armies will be gone and Jesus will reign "from the river to the ends of the earth." He will reign with a rod of iron, determined that man's wickedness shall be properly curbed.

IV. GOD'S GRACIOUS SPIRIT (2:10-12)

God's Holy Spirit yearns over lost mankind. God takes no pleasure in judging men, He would much rather save them than judge them. That is why He adds this last word: "Be wise now therefore, O ye kings; be instructed, ye judges of the earth. Serve the LORD with fear, and rejoice with trembling. Kiss the Son, lest He be angry, and ye perish from the way, when His wrath is kindled but a little. Blessed are all they that put their trust in Him."

God offers man peace, not war. But He will not force His love and mercy upon those who are determined to rebel. Before waging war He offers conditions of peace. The arms of rebellion must be put down. He must be trusted. He offers, indeed, to make of men the happy, happy people we met in the previous psalm.

One of the great chores of my schoolboy days was trying to memorize the names and dates of all the English kings. The list seemed endless. We started with William the Conqueror (1066–1087), then came William Rufus (1087–1100), followed by Henry I (1100–1135). The list went on and on. But there was one king who always sparked the interest of even the dullest boy: Richard the Lionheart (1189–1199), and almost as interesting was Richard's graceless brother John.

How we all loved Richard! Richard was a born leader of men—general, fighter, wrestler, runner, poet, and the courtliest knight who ever put on shining armor. He was thirty-two when he came to the throne. He led the Third Crusade determined to take to the East the most powerful and best-equipped army which had ever crossed the seas.

But while he was away trouncing Saladin, his kingdom fell on hard times. His chancellor abused his office and rode roughshod over the people, and Richard's brother John plotted to seize the throne. John was selfish and cruel, crafty and cynical, lustful and false. He had none of the Plantagenet good looks, was irreverent and blasphemous, devoid of wisdom, and knew nothing of statecraft.

When news came to England that Richard had been imprisoned and was being held for ransom by his old enemy, Leopold of Austria, John was delighted. He entered into treasonable correspondence with the King of France and planned to seize England for himself while the people suffered and longed for the return of the king. But Richard's coming was delayed.

Then one day Richard came. He landed in England and marched straight for his throne. Around that coming many tales are told,

woven into the legends of England. John's castles tumbled like nine-
pins. Great Richard laid claim to his realm and none dared stand in
his path. The people shouted their delight. They rang peal after peal
on the bells of London. The Lion was back! Long live the king!

One day a greater King than Richard will lay claim to a greater
realm than England. Those who have abused His absence, seized His
vast estates, mismanaged His world, will all be swept aside. "And
every eye shall see Him, and they also which pierced Him." As the
hymn writer says:

> The Heavens shall glow with splendour
>   But brighter far than they
> The saints shall shine in glory,
>   As Christ shall them array;
> The beauty of the Saviour
>   Shall dazzle every eye,
> In the crowning day that's coming
>   By and by.

"Be wise, now, therefore. . . . Be instructed. . . . Kiss the Son lest
He be angry. . . ." This world has not seen the last of Jesus. Jesus is
coming again, and He's coming back in sovereign, omnipotent power,
backed by the armies of Heaven. Today, by His Holy Spirit, He is
offering terms of peace and we can come and embrace Him and be
saved for all eternity. The amnesty, however, is not forever and will
one day be withdrawn. Then men will face Christ as God's avenging
King.

Psalm 3

DAVID AT MAHANAIM

I. DAVID'S TRIAL (3:1-2)
   A. The Multiplicity of His Foes (3:1)
   B. The Malignity of His Foes (3:2)
II. DAVID'S TRUST (3:3-4)
   A. His Assurance in God (3:3)
   B. His Appeal to God (3:4)
III. DAVID'S TRIUMPH (3:5-8)
   A. David's Vision (3:5-6)
   B. David's Victory (3:7-8)

A S WE STEP ACROSS THE THRESHHOLD of this psalm we are aware at once that there are new features not met in the previous psalms. This is the first psalm with a *historical title*. This is a psalm of David "when he fled from Absalom his son." What a flood of light that sheds upon it. It is evidently a morning hymn. It could not have been written on the first dreadful morning after the hasty flight from Jerusalem the night before. That was spent in getting David's little company safely across Jordan (2 Samuel 17:15-22). It could have been written the following morning after a night's refreshing sleep. In any case, we are with David the fugitive king on the high road to Mahanaim where old Barzillai came out to meet David with the bravery and the bounty of a king.

Then this is the first psalm in the Hebrew hymnbook that is actually entitled "a psalm." The word comes from the Hebrew *mizmor,* which has to do with the pruning or cutting off of superfluous twigs. We can see how appropriate this descriptive word is in Psalm 3, a song made up of short sentences. A man might use flowery phrases when making a speech, but when he's in trouble, he will not waste time with fine words and nicely turned expressions, but will come right to the point. David was in trouble. In this psalm he prunes away wordy speech.

Then, too, this psalm has a *subscription* at the end, as well as a *superscription* at the beginning. This fact is not visible in the ordinary printed texts of the Bible, but some scholars believe that the words: "To the chief Musician on Neginoth" (from the next psalm) really

27

belong as a footnote to this one. Psalms which have the phrase: "To
the chief Musician" in their subscription were set apart for use in
public worship, either in the temple services in a general way, or on
special occasions in the corporate worship of the Hebrew people.

The word *Neginoth,* which also occurs in the subscription, is a
Hebrew word meaning "smitings," and has reference to the subject
matter of the psalm. David had been smitten by the words of his
enemies who were saying, "There is no help for him in God!" He was
about to be smitten by the swords of his enemies, for Absalom's
armies were mobilizing not far away. And he had been smitten by
God. As the smitings of a hand upon a stringed instrument produce
music, so the smitings of God's hand produced songs in the soul of
His servant. David had entered fully into a blessed truth, that God
chastens only His sons. The smitings of God were proof that God was
at work in his soul.

One other word needs comment before we look at the beauty of
this lovely hymn—the word "Selah." This significant little word is
inserted into this psalm three times. It is one of the commonest words
in the psalms, but is found in Scripture in only one place outside the
psalms—in Habakkuk 3; which is, itself, a little psalm inserted by the
prophet in the middle of the problem he is seeking to solve. It is
generally believed that the word Selah has something to do with
music. This is why the word does not find its way into the Old
Testament prophecies, which were spoken and not sung.

Selah means "to lift up" and so it is thought to be a kind of
crescendo mark in the music. There has been a soft accompaniment
up to a certain point and then David makes a note for the musicians—
Selah! Boom it out! Pull out the stops! There is a roar of music to draw
attention to the sentence being sung, a kind of musical punctuation
mark.

Another explanation is that the word means, "There, what do you
think of that!" Or, as we would say today: "Print that in italics! Print
that in capital letters!" Selah!

Look at David's use of the word in this psalm:

"There is no help for him in God. Selah." What do you think of
that?

"I cried unto the LORD . . . and He heard me out of His holy hill.
Selah." What do think of that?

"Salvation is of the LORD. . . . Selah." What do you think of that?

It doesn't always happen, but in this psalm the three uses of the
word *Selah* divide the whole hymn.

I. DAVID'S TRIAL (3:1-2)

Let us picture the scene. David is in full flight from Jerusalem. His
favorite son Absalom has seized the throne and is contemplating
David's execution. David has had a dreadful twenty-four hours, but

now he has had a good night's rest and his spiritual bouyancy has reasserted itself. He looks at his faithful friends, companions in many a previous tramp over the hills of Judah in those far-off outlaw days. There's Joab, his commander-in-chief. If there's to be a fight, then thank God for men like Joab!

There's Benaiah, son of Jehoiada, a valiant man and the son of a valiant man. Courage flowed like quicksilver through Benaiah's veins. David felt a special kinship to him. In their youth the pair of them, each by himself, had slain a lion. Thank God for Benaiah!

And there's Abishai, the son of Zuriah and brother of Joab. Both Joab and Abishai were David's cousins. Abishai had once killed three hundred men with a spear in hand-to-hand combat.

David looked from one to another of his mighty men, his noble thirty! It wanted only Uriah the Hittite to make up the whole. But Uriah was dead and now David was reaping what he sowed in that terrible affair.

But David had slept well, despite his troubles. A night on the hills beneath the stars brought back memories of his shepherd days and of the fugitive years when Saul had hunted him like a partridge from hill to hill.

The sentry on the ridge had his eye peeled towards Gilead, the direction from which the attack would come. Would Absalom lead the legions of Israel or would he send Ahithophel? Of the two, Ahithophel was the far more dangerous man. May God turn the counsel of Ahithophel into foolishness! So David, encouraging himself in the Lord, seizes his pen and begins to jot down the thoughts that come crowding into his mind. Joab yawns, sits up, and casts a fierce eye around the camp to make sure the guard is awake and alert. He glances over at the king. There he sits, propped up on his bedroll, writing away as though he were safe in his study at home. "What's he doing now?" wonders Joab. He sees a smile on the face of the king and catches a word or two as David finishes with a flourish and throws down his pen: "For the chief Musician on Neginoth."

Joab's jaw drops. The fugitive king has been writing a hymn—and with Absalom's forces mustering by the thousand only a hill or two away! Just then David glances up and catches Joab's eye. David's smile broadens. "Here, Joab, listen to this: 'LORD, how are they increased that trouble me!' " He reads to Joab the stanzas of what has been handed down to us as the third psalm. Such is the scene.

A. The Multiplicity of His Foes (3:1)

"LORD, how are they increased that trouble me! many are they that rise up against me." David had failed to win over the nation's youth. The older people who remembered all that David had done for Israel were not so impressed with Absalom, but the young people—clever, charming, handsome Absalom had won their hearts. The army—

made up, no doubt, as most armies are, of the vigorous youth of the nation—had opted for Absalom. David was aware of the multiplicity of his foes.

B. The Malignity of His Foes (3:2)

"Many there be which say of my soul, There is no help for him in God." Probably David had Shimei in mind when he wrote that. Shimei, "a reptile of the house of Saul," had cursed David as David fled from the city, crossed the Kidron, and hurried over Olivet. Shimei's resounding curse boiled down to this: "No help for him in God." The word "help" can be rendered "salvation." David's enemies were really saying: "There is no salvation for him."

David knew it to be a lie. "No salvation of God for him!" He wrote it into the psalm. Then he wrote *Selah* right after it. "There, what do you think of that?"

No salvation in God! No one to wash away his sin! No one to clothe him with righteousness! No one to present him faultless before the throne! No blood! No altar! No sacrifice! No great high priest! No Christ! No Calvary! No cleansing! No conversion! No help in God! Such will be the last despairing wail of a Christ-rejecting sinner, launched bankrupt and alone into a lost eternity to wail out his torments forever, beyond the pale of mercy and hope. No salvation in God!

Think of François Marie Arouet, better known as Voltaire. He died in France on November 21, 1694. He was eighty-three and he died after a round of pleasure which overtaxed his strength. His wraithlike body and wrinkled grin had been a well-known sight in the glamorous courts of Europe. He entertained his guests with the liveliest talk on the Continent. He surrounded himself with people who had reverence for nothing save wit, pleasure, and literary talent.

"My trade," said Voltaire, "is to say what I think." What he thought ran into ninety-nine volumes of plays, poems, novels, and articles, and some eight thousand letters written to famous people. One of his works has been translated into more than one hundred languages. Censors banned his books and closed his plays with the result that fashionable Paris thronged the opening nights and gleefully memorized his most stinging lines.

Fourteen years after his death godless French revolutionaries brought Voltaire's body to Paris, laid him out in triumph on the ruins of the Bastille, and made him their patron saint. A quarter of a million people pressed between lines of guards to pay homage to his remains. Then his body was given a state burial in the French Pantheon.

His admirers have sought to blunt the edge of Voltaire's vigorous infidelity, but with little success. When Voltaire was overtaken by a stroke and knew he had not long to live he sent for a priest and sought reconciliation with the church. But reconciliation with Rome is not reconciliation with God. His infidel friends crowded his chambers to prevent their idol from recanting his writings, but he cursed them and turned them out on the street. Then, hoping to allay the terrible anguish of his soul, he prepared a written recantation and signed it before witnesses. But it was no use. He had sinned away the day of grace. *There was no help for him in God.*

For two long months the wretched man was tormented with such agony of soul that he was seen to gnash his teeth in rage against God and man. At other times he would whimper like a kitten. He would turn his face to the wall and cry out: "I must die—abandoned of God and of men." As his end drew near, his spiritual condition became so frightful that his unbelieving friends feared to approach his bed, but still they mounted their guard so that others might not see how dreadful was the end of an infidel. His nurse declared: "Not for all the wealth of Europe would I ever see another infidel die." *There was no help for him in God! Selah.*

But David was no Voltaire. David was a man who knew God. He was a failing, stumbling saint but he knew God and he knew the salvation of God.

II. DAVID'S TRUST (3:3-4)

"There is no help for him in God!" sneered David's foes, but David knew there was.

A. His Assurance in God (3:3)

"But Thou, O LORD, art a shield for me; my glory, and the lifter up of mine head." David knew God and he appealed to Him under the name of "The LORD"—i.e. *Jehovah*—the God who keeps His Word, the God of covenant. David leaned hard on that. His assurance was based on God's Word, not on his circumstances or his feelings—both of which might easily overwhelm him. God had pledged to him the throne, and God would not give that throne now to rebel Absalom. The God who had put David on the throne once was quite able to put him on it again.

B. His Appeal to God (3:4)

"I cried unto the LORD with my voice, and He heard me out of His holy hill. Selah."

David was going back to the past, to the day when Nathan had come to accuse him of adultery and murder. David had known only too well the extent of his guilt—Bathsheba was shamed and her husband was dead.

David had flung himself down and moaned out his repentance and remorse. "Have mercy on me, O God ... wash me ... cleanse me ... my sin is ever before me." Nathan, moved by the depths and reality of the king's agony, had said, "The Lord hath put away thy sin."

"There is no hope for him in God," sneered his foes. "I cried unto the LORD"—sinful man that I was, says David. "I cried unto the LORD with my voice, and He heard me out of His holy hill." *Selah!* Think about that. Over against the vengeful sneers of his foes David set one glorious fact—I cried, He answered!

III. DAVID'S TRIUMPH (3:5-8)

Trial. Trust. Triumph. That's always the way it is.

A. David's Vision (3:5-6)

"I laid me down and slept; I awakened; for the LORD sustained me. I will not be afraid of ten thousands of people, that have set themselves against me round about." It was a settling and sustaining vision.

In the midst of torment, torture, and treachery David smiled up into the face of God. "Good night, LORD!" he said, "I have done what I can. I have put as much distance as possible between us and the foe. I have posted a guard. Now do Thou sustain our cause." And with that he went to sleep.

There were ten thousands of foes, for Absalom had the numbers, but David had God. That was David's vision.

B. David's Victory (3:7-8)

"Arise, O LORD; save me, O my God: for Thou hast smitten all mine enemies upon the cheek bone; Thou hast broken the teeth of the ungodly."

It was a new day with God. David invoked the words of Israel's marching song, "Arise O Lord!" The critical battle with Absalom and with the armed forces of Israel was still in the future, but David had no doubt about the outcome. Actually God had already drawn the fangs of his foes. David did not know it, but away in Absalom's council chamber the sage advice of Ahithophel was already being discounted by the would-be king and the counsel of Hushai the Archite, David's secret agent in the palace, was being espoused in its place.

> Ye fearful saints fresh courage take,
> The clouds ye so much dread;
> Are big with mercy and shall fall
> In blessings on your head.

David had one more word. It sums up the psalm: "Salvation is of the LORD. Thy blessing is upon Thy people. Selah." "There, what do you think of that?"

Salvation is of the Lord! Salvation is not the personal property of a preacher or a priest or a pope. Salvation is only of the Lord.

Take the case of Henry II, the first of the Plantagenets, father of Richard the Lionheart, greatest of all of England's kings. Henry had appointed his friend, Thomas à Becket, to be archbishop of Canterbury, hoping to find an ally against Rome, but Becket flung the weight of his office against the king. Then, as a result of a chance word, Becket was murdered by Henry's aides and the king had to face the wrath of the pope.

The pope placed England under interdict, a terrific fate in those far-off days, for people believed that salvation was of the pope. The bishops of England donned the robes of mourning usually reserved for Good Friday and entered their churches to the funeral tolling of bells. Shrines and crucifixes were covered, the relics of saints were removed, the wafer was solemnly burned. Throughout the land the bishops of Rome declared England to be under the ban of the church. Torches and candles were extinguished and England was plunged into the dark. There could be no marrying and no burying. There was no salvation for any soul in England. The church had withdrawn its light. The fear of interdict entered every home and every heart.

Before long, Henry, strong as he was, buckled. He prostrated himself, he kissed the stones where Becket had fallen, he went to the martyr's crypt and lay all night before the tomb. He bared his royal back to the lash and allowed each high officer of Canterbury to smite him five times and each of the monks to smite him three—thus receiving in his royal person hundreds of lashes. He lay bruised, broken, bleeding in silence before the martyr's tomb. He walked across Canterbury in his bare feet. He did all this to persuade the pope to relent.

But it was all a giant fraud. Had Henry II read his Bible, had he known God half as well as David knew Him—he would have known this simple, satisfying truth: Salvation is of the Lord. And he would have read that word *Selah* which follows it. There, what do you think of that? Salvation is of the *Lord*.

Salvation is not in ourselves. It is not in crying and tears, in promises and resolves, in charities and good works. It is not in the church. It is not in creeds, baptisms, communions, rituals, and ceremonies. Salvation is of the Lord. God shuts us up to Him. Selah. What do you think of that?

We have no idea what Joab thought of it all when David looked up from reading this hymn. But we know what David thought of it. He added a postscript: *"This is for the chief Musician!"* It has to do with *smitings*. It has to do with One who was to be smitten of God and afflicted that we might forever go free!

Psalm 4

AN EVENING HYMN

I. SALVATION (4:1-2)
   A. Personal Salvation (4:1)
   B. Practical Salvation (4:2)
II. SANCTIFICATION (4:3-4)
   A. Personal Godliness (4:3)
   B. Personal Goodness (4:4)
III. SACRIFICE (4:5)
   A. The Burnt Offering
   B. The Meal Offering
   C. The Peace Offering
IV. SONG (4:6-7)
   A. The Tragedy of a Joyless Life (4:6)
   B. The Triumph of a JoyfulLife (4:7)
V. SECURITY (4:8)

WE NOTE FROM THE SUBSCRIPTION appended to this psalm that it had to do with one's inheritance. That's what the word *Nehiloth* means. David had been driven out of his inheritance by Absalom but David knew that his true inheritance was spiritual, not material. His true inheritance was in the Lord. Nobody could drive him out of that.

The circumstances of this psalm are similar to those of Psalm 3. However, things had simmered down, for Absalom failed to follow up his initial advantage and David had time to recruit forces of his own. He warned his enemies to reflect upon their beds before committing themselves. Rotherham takes this to be a sarcastic jab at them for being asleep at their posts and not following up their attack while they had the chance. The future was still full of peril but it was much better than it had been for the past twenty-four hours, so David composed himself for sleep.

We look a thousand years into the future from David's day to Christ's. We see the Lord Jesus, in those closing days of His life coming and going between Bethany and Jerusalem. The days were spent in Jerusalem seeking to awaken the conscience of the nation which had rejected Him, the nights spent with His friends at Bethany and in restful trust in God. When reading Psalm 4 we should keep that picture before us, too.

The psalm has a perennial message for David deals with five basic issues. The psalm speaks to our needs whether as *penitent sinners* or *pilgrim saints*.

I. SALVATION (4:1-2)

The salvation David had in mind was salvation from adverse circumstances, but we can translate that to our own need of salvation from sin.

A. A Personal Salvation (4:1)

"Hear me when I call, O God of my righteousness: Thou hast enlarged me when I was in distress; have mercy upon me, and hear my prayer." That's the kind of salvation we need—personal salvation.

We can be philosophical enough about matters of belief until we see our utter lostness. That is what makes it personal. The story is told of two men at the beach, one was sitting on the sand soaking up the sunshine, the other was in the water. Suddenly the one in the water, wading in what he thought was the shallows, stepped off a hidden ledge into the deep. "Help! Help," he called, "I can't swim." The fellow on the bank replied: "Neither can I, but I'm not making a fuss about it!" The one knew he was lost, the other had no sense of need. It's when we get into deep water that we feel our need of salvation.

What David wanted was a *personal* salvation. "Hear *me* when I call . . . have mercy upon *me* and hear *my* prayer."

B. A Practical Salvation (4:2)

"O ye sons of men, how long will ye turn my glory into shame? how long will ye love vanity, and seek after [lies]? Selah." David wanted his salvation to be so thorough, so complete, so beyond question that it would shut the mouths of the enemies of God.

That's the way it was with George Mueller of Bristol. Before he was ten he was already an accomplished thief. The night his mother died he was wandering the streets more than half drunk after a wild night with his friends. He disgraced himself in one school after another. Even in divinity school, training to be a minister of the gospel, he was no better. He was constantly in debt and up to all tricks and schemes to supply his lack of funds. Aware that no church was likely to call him to a pastorate in his dissolute condition, he tried in vain to reform.

Then God saved him, transformed him, and gave him a ministry. Mueller determined to establish a group of orphan houses and to do so in a way which would strike dumb the voices of atheism in England. He would keep his financial needs a secret between himself and God alone. "If I, a poor man, could get means to carry on an orphan house," he said, "it would demonstrate that God is faithful and still hears prayer."

He succeeded. When he died, a very old man, Bristol went into mourning. Business houses closed and employees from companies all over the city lined the streets to witness the passing of one of the greatest men the city had ever known. On churches and cathedrals flags flew at half-mast and the bells were rung with muffled peals. The Bristol *Times* said: "Mr. Mueller was raised up to show us that the age of miracles is not past." Professor Rendle Short, one of Bristol's foremost surgeons of the next generation, said: "My father used to say that during the days of George Mueller agnosticism did not dare to raise its head in Bristol."

That was what David wanted—a practical salvation that would shut the mouth of the foe. That is the kind of salvation God still offers—a salvation that makes drunken men sober, crooked men straight, profligate women pure.

That's the first theme of this psalm. *Salvation,* however, is always followed by *sanctification.*

II. SANCTIFICATION (4:3-4)

There is nothing mysterious about sanctification. It is just the practical outworking in the life of the eternal, irrevocable, majestic work that salvation does in the soul.

A. Personal Godliness (4:3)

"But know that the LORD hath set apart him that is godly for Himself: the LORD will hear when I call unto Him." Sanctification is separation *from* ungodliness and separation *to* God. First, God makes a person *godly,* then He sets that person apart for Himself. Being set apart for God makes us love the things that once we loathed and makes us loathe the things that once we loved.

A lady once said to D. L. Moody: "Mr. Moody, I wish you'd tell me how to be a Christian, but I don't want to be one of *your* kind."

"I didn't know I had any particular kind," he said. "What is the matter with my kind?"

"Well, I have always gone to the theater. Indeed I am far better acquainted with theater people than I am with church people. I don't want to give up the theater."

Said Mr. Moody: "When have I ever said anything about theaters? We have reporters here every night. Have you seen anything in the newspapers I have said against theaters?"

"No."

"Then why did you bring up the subject?"

"I supposed you would be against theaters."

"What made you think that?"

"Why," she said, "Do you ever go?"

"No."

"Why don't you go to the theaters?"

"Well," said Mr. Moody, "I have something better. I would sooner go out on the street and eat dirt than do some of the things I used to do before I was a Christian."

"I don't understand."

"Never mind," said D. L. Moody. "When Jesus Christ has the preeminence in your life you will understand it all. He didn't come down here to tell us we couldn't go here or couldn't go there and lay down a lot of rules. He came to give us new life. Once you love Him you will take delight in pleasing Him."

"But Mr. Moody, if I become a Christian can I continue to go to the theater?"

"Yes," he said, "You can go to the theater just as much as you like if you are a real, true Christian so long as you can go with His blessing."

"I am very glad you are not a narrow-minded Christian, Mr. Moody."

"Well," he concluded, "Just so long as you can go to the theater for the glory of God. If you are a Christian you will want to do whatever will please Him."

Said Mr. Moody: "I really believe she became a Christian that day." But just as she was leaving him at the door she said: "But I am not giving up the theater, Mr. Moody."

A few days later she came back.

"Mr. Moody, I understand now all that you said about the theater. I went the other night with a large party but, when the curtain lifted, everything looked different. I told my husband: 'I am not going to stay here.' He said, 'Don't make a fool of yourself. Everyone has heard that you have been converted at the Moody meetings. Please don't make a fool of yourself here in front of our friends.' But I said, 'I have been making a fool of myself all my life.' And, Mr. Moody, I got up and left."

In telling the story, Moody added: "What had changed? Had the theater changed? No! But she had gotten something better."

That's it! "If any man be in Christ he is a new creature. Old things are passed away, behold all things are become new." The Lord sets apart him that is godly for Himself. He changes us inside. We begin to love the things that once we loathed—the prayer meeting, the worship service, the Bible class, and we begin to loathe the things that once we loved. That's *sanctification*. It works its way through all the areas of our lives—not just the area of worldly amusements.

David was thinking about *personal godliness* and *personal goodness*.

B. Personal Goodness (4:4)

"Stand in awe, and sin not: Commune with your own heart upon your bed, and be still." David saw sanctification working two things in his life.

It brought a new *quality* of life: "Stand in awe and sin not." That's the missing dimension in much of our spiritual life today—awe—awe of God! We need an awe-inspiring vision of the holiness and purity of God such as makes sin a horror and a shame.

It brought a new *quietness* to life: "Commune with your own heart upon your bed, and be still." The word translated "still" could be translated "silent." "Be quiet!" Hull uses an even stronger expression. He says it means "shut up." God would have us shut up, be silent, get off the treadmill and listen to what *He* has to say.

III. Sacrifice (4:5)

"Offer the sacrifices of righteousness and put your trust in the Lord." The "sacrifices of the righteous" are *not* the kind a person could offer while he was in a state of rebellion against God. They are a very special kind of sacrifice.

There were two basic kinds of sacrifice the people of the Old Testament could bring to the altar, a sweet savor offering or a sin offering. The first was the sacrifice of a *righteous saint,* the second was the sacrifice of the *repentant sinner.* David had in mind the sweet-savor sacrifice—the kind offered by the righteous saint.

There were three such offerings.

A. The Burnt Offering

The burnt offering was all for God. It was a picture of Christ's *passion.* The smoke of the sacrifice ascended to God and was accepted by Him as an act of worship. The burnt offering spoke of Christ offering Himself to God in unswerving devotion, wholly and unreservedly—obedient unto death even the death of the cross.

B. The Meal Offering

The meal offering, consisting of flour, even and smooth and pure, was a picture of Christ's *perfection.* The flour had been evenly ground until it was flawless in texture. As such it pictured the life of the Lord Jesus. No matter where we touch that life we find this amazing, supernatural evenness. His life displayed nothing but perfection.,

C. The Peace Offering

The peace offering brought the worshiper and God together in communion and it was the basis for God and the worshiper to join in a ceremonial meal. The peace offering pictured Christ's *presence.*

The celebration of this sacrifice was not only a holy occasion, it was a happy occasion.

"Now then," said David, "Offer the sacrifices of the *righteous.*" Offer the burnt offering, the meal offering, the peace offering. What does the Lord's *passion* mean to us? In the light of Calvary, how should we then live? Surely we should live a *crucified* life, presenting our bodies a living sacrifice, holy, acceptable unto God which is our reasonable service!

What does the Lord's *perfection* mean to us? In the light of that marvelous, flawless, perfect life of the Lord Jesus, how should we then live? Surely we should live a *corresponding* life, allowing His indwelling Holy Spirit to make us like Himself.

What does the Lord's *presence* mean to us? He has made it plain that He desires to meet with us and enjoy our fellowship, how should we then live? Surely we should live a *communing* life, not just at the Lord's table but every day we should offer the sacrifices of the righteous.

IV. SONG (4:6-7)

If there is one thing which should characterize the life of the believing person it is song. A Christian should be a happy person. Everything's going his way, adverse circumstances notwithstanding.

A. The Tragedy of a Joyless Life (4:6)

"There be many that say, who will show us any good? LORD, lift Thou up the light of Thy countenance upon us." No doubt there were some in David's camp who were casting gloomy looks all around. The conspiracy with Absalom was very strong. Perhaps some were looking at the circumstances and thinking they'd made a mistake. "Who will *show* us any good?"

They wanted to *see* rather than believe. That doesn't call for much faith. David was such a spiritual giant and they were such pygmies because David could do something they found impossible. David could *sing* even with tears running down his cheeks. All they could say was *"show us."* While they were saying that, David was writing psalms.

B. The Triumph of a Joyful Life (4:7)

In contrast with the gloomy pessimists who were beaten by their circumstances, David says: "Thou hast put gladness in my heart, more than in the time that their corn and their wine increased." David was thinking of the annual harvest festival in Israel, the great feast of tabernacles. What a happy, boisterous time it was! The barns were nearly bursting, the wine vats were filled to overflowing. Everyone was on holiday. It was a rollicking good time with rich religious overtones when the nation flocked to Jerusalem to raise their harvest hymns of praise to God. David's joy exceeded that! And here he was destitute and reduced to accepting charity.

But David's spirits soared. After all, what had he lost? A palace, a loaded table, money—mere material things. And what did he have left? God! His joy was in God, not in goods. Goods could come and go—but as long as he had *God,* he had everything.

Salvation! Sanctification! Sacrifice! Song!

V. Security (4:8)

Absalom's forces were massing for what they hoped would be the knockout blow. The armies of Israel, armies David had trained him-self and honed to a fine edge for war, were with Absalom. Ahitho-phel, whose counsel was as the very oracle of God, was with Absalom.

What did David do? He went to sleep! He enjoyed *personal* peace: "I will both lay me down in peace and sleep." He enjoyed *perfect* peace: "For Thou Lord only makest me to dwell in safety."

David was secure. Not an arrow could touch him so long as he was in the arms of the Lord. When he went to sleep in his palace, armed men tramped up and down the corridors and watched at his gates. Here on the hills he was even safer; his security was in God.

One morning in 1875 Canon Gibbon of Harrogate preached from the text: "Thou wilt keep him in perfect peace whose mind is stayed on Thee." The Hebrew is "peace peace" rather than "perfect peace." Bishop Bickersteth took up the thought and wrote one of the great hymns of the Church, a hymn in which the first line is a question and the second line is the answer:

> Peace, perfect peace? In this dark world of sin?
> The blood of Jesus whispers peace, within.

Peace! Perfect peace! David could say "Amen!" to that.

Psalm 5

GOOD MORNING, LORD!

I. DAVID ASKS THE LORD TO LISTEN (5:1-7)
He wants to talk to Him about:
A. The Situation (5:1-4)
1. God Is a Hearing God (5:1-3)
a. Holy Boldness
b. Heavy Burdens
c. Harmonious Beginnings
2. God Is a Holy God (5:4)
B. The Sinner (5:5-6)
1. He Has No Footing (5:5)
2. He Has No Future (5:6)
C. The Sanctuary (5:7)
II. DAVID ASKS THE LORD TO LEAD (5:8-9)
III. DAVID ASKS THE LORD TO LEGISLATE (5:10-12)
A. The Destruction of the Rebel (5:10)
B. The Delight of the Redeemed (5:11-12)
1. No Foe Can Daunt Him (5:11)
2. No Fear Can Haunt Him (5:12)

PSALMS 3, 4, AND 5 stand together in the Hebrew hymnbook and very likely they stand together in the history of David. Psalm 3 is evidently a morning prayer, Psalm 4 an evening prayer, and Psalm 5 another morning prayer. Possibly they were written in that order, one right after the other. There seems no doubt that all three relate to the time of Absalom's rebellion. Psalm 3 clearly seems to come first. Psalm 5 seems to have been written later because in Psalm 4 David was pleading, as it were, *with* the rebels, but in Psalm 5 he is pleading *against* them, realizing his foes are determined to pursue their rebellion to the bitter end.

The possible sequence of these psalms could be as follows: David, having left Jerusalem under cover of the night, had conveyed his people across the Jordan and had marched hard all day toward the north to put distance between himself and his foes. Then, worn out and exhausted, he had flung himself down and slept for the first time in many hours. He awoke refreshed and wrote Psalm 3.

41

The next day was spent in crossing the Jabbok and continuing northward to Mahanaim, where David hoped to win to his side his mountain clansmen. David knew only too well what a desperate battle lay ahead. That evening he wrote Psalm 4 acknowledging God's goodness and provision.

The next morning he wrote Psalm 5. He was going forth to face treacherous and powerful foes and he prepared for such a day with prayer. The psalm should thus speak to our own hearts for, as G. Campbell Morgan reminds us, we face no day which is not filled with danger.

I. DAVID ASKS THE LORD TO LISTEN (5:1-7)

Imagine that! What holy daring to ask God to listen, as though he who hears the very murmur of our thoughts needs such an admonition! But David had something very important to say to the Lord and he wanted to be sure he had the Lord's undivided attention. He was going to talk to the Lord about three things.

A. The Situation (5:1-4)

If ever David needed to be sure God was paying heed to his prayers it was now. In his far-off fugitive days, when an outlaw on these selfsame hills, ever only a hairbreadth away from death at the hands of Saul's executioners, David often prayed. But in those days he did not have the seduction of Bathsheba on his conscience, nor the murder of Uriah. Sin haunts us—even forgiven sin. When God forgives he forgets, but we don't. So David wanted to make sure the Lord was listening to what he had to say.

1. God is a Hearing God (5:1-3)

"Give ear unto my words O LORD, consider my meditation. Hearken unto the voice of my cry, my King, and my God. . . . My voice shalt Thou hear in the morning, O LORD; in the morning will I direct my prayer unto Thee, and will look up." The words used by David teach us three principles about prayer. First, *holy boldness* is a great aid to prayer. David used two words here which are really astonishing when we think to whom he was speaking: "*Give ear* unto my words, O LORD." The Hebrew word for "give ear" literally means "to broaden" the ear with the hand, as when a deaf man cups his hand behind his ear to hear better what is being said to him. That's the expression David used to God: "Lord put Your hand behind Your ear so You can hear better what I have to say."

"*Hearken* unto the voice of my meditation, my King and my God." The word "hearken" is even more daring. It is a Hebrew word which means "to prick up the ear," as when a dog suddenly cocks his ear to listen to a sound that escapes the human ear. That's what David asked God to do—His *King,* mind you, and his *Creator!* The use of such language surely tells us that, without being flippant and irreverent, we must approach God with holy boldness.

A second great aid to prayer is a *heavy burden.* Prayer becomes much more fervent when something is really bothering us, when we desperately need the Lord's help. All of a sudden prayer becomes imperative and importunate.

Here again, David uses two interesting expressions. "Consider my meditation." The word for meditation is found only here and in Psalm 39:3. It hints at unspoken prayer, at the aching longing and yearning of the innermost being. We have all experienced times when our sorrow and our situation is so beyond us that it is like a gnawing toothache in the soul. But David immediately dropped that word and picked up another: "Consider my meditation, hearken to the voice of my cry." He used a Hebrew word which refers especially to a call. Sometimes we cannot put our prayers into words, they are simply a cry. But the Lord interprets that cry. He understands.

A *harmonious beginning* is a great aid to prayer: "I will *direct* my prayer unto Thee." The Revised Version renders that: "I will order my prayer." The word is used to depict the setting in order of pieces of wood upon an altar of sacrifice. We read that Abraham at Mount Moriah "laid the wood in order, and bound Isaac his son" (Genesis 22:9). It's the same word. When David said: "I will direct my prayer unto Thee," that's the word he used.

It is all very well to be bold and burdened in prayer, but that is no excuse for laziness. We have to put our petitions in order, to have a harmonious beginning. We need to think through carefully what we are going to say to God. What Scriptures are we going to employ? Exactly what is it we want God to do? Have we really thought through in a rational, sensible way what our needs are? How and why do we expect the Lord to supply those needs?

That is how David prayed. He talked to the Lord about his situa-tion. His heart was heavy. He was bold and importunate. But he was methodical and orderly in his approach. He knew exactly what he wanted of God.

But if God is a *hearing* God there is something else to consider.

2. God Is a Holy God (5:4)

"For Thou art not a God that hath pleasure in wickedness: neither shall evil dwell with Thee." The word David used for "wickedness" means "lawlessness." Absalom and his friends had lawlessly driven him from the throne upon which God had set him. David knew that God could not bless that kind of thing. The word he used for God is not *Elohim* but *El,* a contraction which emphasizes God's power. It was God's power that made the difference for David.

B. The Sinner (5:5-6)

David talked to God about the wicked man, the lawless man, and those who take sides with him against the Lord's anointed. David can clearly see that such a man has:

1. No Footing (5:5)

"The foolish shall not stand in Thy sight: Thou hatest all workers of iniquity." The "foolish" man was the boaster, the arrogant, proud man. His name was Absalom. The "workers of iniquity" were those who were vain, empty, nothing; again Absalom. He had no footing. He had nothing upon which to base his claim to the throne of David except his own conceit and arrogance. He was handsome, he had personal charm and charisma, he was a good talker and an able politician. But the throne he had usurped was *God's* throne and he had neither the calling, the character, nor the competence to fill that throne.

Outwardly it looked as if the tide was running full for Absalom. David knew better. He knew that the tide had already crested and that soon it would ebb out beyond recall. The sinner has no footing.

2. No Future (5:6)

"Thou shalt destroy them that speak [lies]: the LORD will abhor the bloody and deceitful man." Again, that is exactly what Absalom was. He had already committed one murder, and a particularly nasty, bloody, and deceitful murder it was—the murder of his brother. He had committed fratricide and, without any sense of repentance or remorse, he was planning patricide and regicide. There was no future for him.

C. The Sanctuary (5:7)

"But as for me, I will come into Thy house in the multitude of Thy mercy: and in Thy fear will I worship toward Thy holy temple."

I can well remember the bleakest period in my life. I had been in the British Army for several years and was near Haifa on my way home. Conditions were highly explosive and Haifa was posted out of bounds to British servicemen except when on active duty. Not far away, halfway up the slopes of Mount Carmel, was a small assembly of believers where I had enjoyed the sweetest fellowship for a couple of years. But it was now inaccessible. So the weeks came and went without any opportunity for fellowship with the people of God. I think those were among the longest weeks of my life. The army provided food, clothes, and shelter, snackshops and entertainment, books, newspapers and magazines, work, and exercise. It even provided us with religion—Roman Catholic, Protestant, or Jewish. But there was one thing it could not supply—fellowship with God's people in God's house.

That's how David felt. He was cut off from the sanctuary and he felt it keenly. He looked forward to the day when he could once more enter the Lord's house as a worshiper. He tells the Lord so in prayer.

II. DAVID ASKS THE LORD TO LEAD (5:8-9)

"Lead me, O LORD, in Thy righteousness because of mine enemies; make Thy way straight before my face. For there is no faithfulness in their mouth; their inward part is very wickedness; their throat is an open sepulchre; they flatter with their tongue."

That is how Absalom had stolen the hearts of the men of Israel. Suppose an embassy were to come to David from Absalom and Ahithophel, offering conditions of peace, how could he trust them? He couldn't.

Their speech was characterized by falsehood, foulness, and flattery. Perhaps some latecomer to David's cause had brought him news of Ahithophel's counsel that Absalom publicly rape each and every one of David's wives still remaining in Jerusalem. No wonder David speaks of their throat being "an open sepulchre." The foul things Absalom and his crowd were saying and suggesting were proof enough of the corruption of their hearts. David prayed that the Lord would lead his steps and protect him from their evil schemes.

III. DAVID ASKS THE LORD TO LEGISLATE (5:10-12)

"Destroy them, O God!" he cries as he thinks of the massed might of the foe.

A. The Destruction of the Rebel (5:10)

"Destroy Thou them, O God; let them fall by their own counsels; cast them out in the multitude of their transgressions; for they have rebelled against Thee." This was not a prayer for revenge against his foes; the spirit of David rose far higher than that. Within a few days David would withhold his hand from executing even Shimei who cursed him so vehemently. He would plead too with Joab and his generals to deal gently with Absalom. David's heart was not tainted with sordid desires for revenge.

But an attack upon his throne was an attack upon God. Rebellion against the king was rebellion against God who had made him king. These passages in the Psalms which seem to breathe out a vengeful spirit must be regarded in the light of that. David was merely assenting to what he knew God's justice would demand.

Absalom's rebellion failed in the end because he took the counsel of Hushai (David's secret agent) instead of the counsel of Ahithophel. He listened to the wrong man. Absalom the great deceiver was himself deceived. It is an instance of the poetic justice of God.

B. The Delight of the Redeemed (5:11-12)

"But let all those that put their trust in Thee rejoice; let them ever shout for joy, because Thou defendest them; let them also that love Thy name be joyful in Thee." In other words, *no foe can daunt him!* "For Thou, LORD, wilt bless the righteous; with favour wilt Thou compass him as with a shield." In other words: *no fear can haunt him!*

The word David used for shield here signifies a buckler, a large shield made to protect the whole body and usually twice the size of the ordinary shield.

To all outward seeming, David was vulnerable. His forces were thin and some of his followers were wondering already if maybe they'd made a mistake. But David was not looking at them, he was looking at the Lord. The Lord was his buckler.

That's where the word *Neginoth* comes in, in the subscription to the psalm. The word means "smitings." Some have taken it to mean the striking of the strings of some musical instrument, but more likely it refers to the circumstances of the Psalmist. The enemy was striking at David. Absalom had struck at him viciously with words and was now arming his troops for a massive blow against him. David's buckler was the living God. That was ample, abundant protection. Nothing could touch him without God's express permission.

"There!" said David. "Send that to the chief Musician."

Then he adds a word which has puzzled many: "To the chief Musician on Neginoth upon *Sheminith.*" Most are agreed that the word "sheminith" is a Hebrew word which means "the eighth." According to 1 Chronicles 15:21 David set apart a certain group of men to lead the male choir. The Talmud suggests that, since circumcision in Israel was on the eighth day, the Sheminith were a class of true Israelites, circumcised the eighth day and "Israelites indeed."

David was surrounded with foes. Never had his fortunes been at a lower ebb, humanly speaking. But a new day had dawned for, having talked things over with the Lord, David took his stand firmly on ground where no foe could daunt him and where no fear could haunt him. "Sheminith! The eighth!" The number is associated in Scripture with a *new beginning*.

Absalom could have his wicked ones, his armies, his advisers, and his vain ambitions. As for David, he was in touch with *the Chief Musician* Himself! His soul was filled with song. The smitings would soon be over. David would yet stand with the Sheminith—the Israelites indeed—and make the courts of the Lord ring with songs of loudest praise.

What a way to start a difficult day!

Psalm 6

A DARK NIGHT

I. DAVID'S SAD CONDITION (6:1-7)
   A. He Speaks About His Excuse:
      1. His Plight (6:1-3)
      "I Am Weak" (6:1-5)
         a. Along Spiritual Lines
         b. Along Physical Lines
         c. Along Moral Lines
      2. His Plea (6:4-5)
         a. Along the Line of Mercy
         b. Along the Line of Memory
   B. He Speaks About His Exercise:
      "I Am Weary" (6:6-7)
      1. He Was Worn Out (6:6)
      2. He Was Waxing Old (6:7)
II. DAVID'S SUDDEN CONFIDENCE (6:8-10)
   A. His Fears Are Stilled (6:8-9)
   B. His Foes Are Stopped (6:10)

THIS IS THE FIRST of seven *penitential psalms*. The others are psalms 32; 38; 51; 102; 130; 143. The first seven verses of this psalm are one great cry of anguish. There is no confession, as such, just a hopeless wail, wrung out of a tortured soul in the darkness of the night. What we have here is not conscious, orderly, systematic laying out before God one's sins and shortcomings. This is a soul on fire, on the rack of torment, suffering the dreadful pangs of awakened conscience, crying out for release. His distress is so great he cries all night long. There can be little doubt from the first few verses of the psalm that David is suffering from the results of divine visitation.

David's sin with Bathsheba was a hideous thing. She was the wife of one of his mighty men, one of the men who had marched with him across the bleak Judean hills in the old fugitive days. David had seduced her and then arranged with Joab for Uriah's murder. Finally, to cover up the consequences of his sin, David had hastily married the woman and tried to bluff the whole thing.

The evidence of this psalm is that before David repented he had to be very severely punished by God. The punishment seems to have taken the form of a frightful illness. The historical records are silent about this but the conclusion is inescapable from David's psalms. Moreover, what David said in the psalms about this sickness suggests that at first David could easily conceal it from his servants and friends. The implication is that David became a leper!

In his excruciating mental anguish at this discovery David wept out loud until the very echoes of the palace corridors resounded with his cries. It sounded like an animal in pain. David's servants spread the word and it leaked out into the city until David's enemies picked up the news. "There's something wrong with the king! He refuses to allow his valet near him. He wakes up in the night sobbing and screaming. There's something wrong with the king!" As Rotherham says, this explains many a statement in this and other of David's psalms.

David's agony, as expressed in this psalm, had several sources. There was, of course, the fearful gnawings of conscience over unconfessed sin. There was the knowledge that he was under the stroke of God—the evidence being printed plainly in his flesh. There was the growing evidence that he had numerous foes, some of them actually present at court. There was the knowledge that news of his condition had leaked out and that his foes would most certainly take advantage of it.

Such are the ingredients in this, the first of the penitential psalms. We could wish that the historians had told us something about David's illness. It would have helped in dating this psalm. But such cries of the soul as are voiced here need no date. They are the universal experience of all with whom God has begun to deal concerning some secret sin or great wrong as yet unconfessed and uncleansed.

I. DAVID'S SAD CONDITION (6:1-7)

David began by rehearsing before God the deplorable condition in which he found himself. Remember, here was a man who for years had been one of the sweetest and noblest saints of God. The Holy Spirit calls him "a man after God's own heart." But he had fallen and worse still, he persisted in pretending, publicly at any rate, that nothing was wrong. We all know what that is like.

A spiritual man knows when he's out of touch with God; when the flames have died out of the fire, when prayer becomes a mere mouthing of words. We know when we have unconfessed sin on the conscience how quickly it blights spiritual life.

David, in reviewing his sad condition, had two things to say.

A. He Spoke About His Excuse (6:1-5)

"I Am Weak!"

1. His Plight (6:1-3)

"O LORD, rebuke me not in Thine anger, neither chasten me in Thy hot displeasure. Have mercy upon me, O LORD; for I am weak: O LORD, heal me; for my bones are vexed. My soul is also sore vexed: but Thou, O LORD, how long?"

He voiced his plight along three lines—spiritual, physical, and moral.

a. Along Spiritual Lines

We note in the very first verse the essential spirituality of David, even though he was in a terrible state. He did not ask the Lord not to rebuke him; he well knew that he deserved whatever punishment the Lord saw fit to send. He only pleaded that God would not punish him in anger and in hot displeasure.

When I was a boy I loved to read stories by Richmal Crompton about a boy and his friends and the scrapes in which they were always embroiled. In one story, after a series of adventures in which William had earned certain punishment when his father came home, he received some good advice from his older brother: "Go to bed before father comes back." "William inwardly agreed. There was something to be said for being in bed and asleep when his father came home. Explanations put off to the following morning are apt to lose the keeness of their edge." Tomorrow, if his father decided to exact punishment from him for what he had done, it would not be in fierce anger nor in hot displeasure. His wrath would have had time to cool down.

David took this human characteristic and applied it, in a figure of speech, to God. He deserved severe chastisement, indeed the stroke had already fallen upon him, but he pleaded with God not to go on smiting him in anger and hot displeasure. He prayed for the Lord's anger to cool.

b. Along Physical Lines

"Heal me; for my bones are vexed"—a poetic way of describing his physical condition. He was shaken to the core of his being. "Heal me! Heal me!"

Not all human sickness is the direct result of human sin, but some is and David saw a direct link between his fearful affliction and his dreadful sins. Since there is no actual confession of sin in this psalm it would seem he had not yet learned that, until he confessed the sin which was the cause of his sickness, no healing was possible for him.

This is the principle which lies behind that controversial healing passage in James: "Is any man sick, let him call for the elders of the church." When a man is sick, he calls for the doctor. But, in the case being reviewed by James, the elders of the church are to be called because evidently the sickness, a result of sin, has been brought on by church discipline. When the sin is confessed and canceled, then the anointing oil and the prayer of faith will heal the sickness. In other words, to heal the sickness without dealing with the sin that caused it would be like putting a bandaid on a cancer. The Great Physician insists on going to the real cause of the sickness, in this case—sin. Put that right and the sickness—which after all, was only a symptom— would disappear of itself.

c. Along Moral Lines

"My soul is sore vexed." The word translated "sore vexed" literally means "troubled" or "dismayed exceedingly." Only one thing causes this kind of soul trouble—sin. Then David added: "But Thou, O LORD , how long?" He stopped suddenly as though words failed him.

This sudden stopping, as though overwhelmed in the middle of a sentence, is a figure of speech called *aposiopesis* (sudden silence). It occurs several times in the Scriptures, for the first time in connection with the fall of man. God had just clothed Adam and Eve in skins. His eye ran to and fro through the Garden of Eden, lighting upon the ravished tree of knowledge and upon the remaining tree of life. He took counsel with Himself over the disaster which had overtaken the world: "And the Lord God said: Behold the man is become as one of Us, to know good and evil: and now, lest he put forth his hand and take also of the tree of life and eat and live for ever. . . ." There is sudden silence as though the thought overwhelms God Himself; as though words fail even Him at such a thought—that man, in his sin and folly, should perpetuate himself forever in a lost condition and thus place humanity beyond all hope of redemption. What a preg- nant sudden silence! For man to live forever in his sins!

Aposiopesis occurs again right after the making of the golden calf, when Moses came down from the mount with the tables of the law in his hand and saw what the people were doing. As he flung himself upon his face before God, in abasement and anguish, he cried: "Oh, this people have sinned a great sin, and have made them gods of gold. Yet now, if Thou wilt forgive their sin. . . ." There is sudden silence. Moses finished, as soon as he could get his choking emotions under control: "And if not, blot me, I pray Thee, out of Thy book" (Exodus 32:31-32).

And the figure of speech occurs here in Psalm 6: "But Thou O LORD , how long?" Then sudden silence as the horror of his situation sank into his soul. Suppose God should never see fit to heal him! Suppose the sentence of death in his body were to be confirmed, the horrible thing which had overtaken him were to be allowed at last to over- whelm him. Words failed him.

2. His Plea (6:4-5)

As his plight was multiple, so was his plea.

a. Along the Line of Mercy

"Return, O LORD, deliver my soul: oh save me for Thy mercies' sake." The word "mercy" is a favorite word in the psalms; it is really the word "loving-kindness." God extends to us not just kindness, but *loving*-kindness. It was this aspect of the character of God upon which David, with true spiritual intuition, laid hold. Surely, God is holy, just, and righteous, and it was in keeping with His holiness, justice, and righteousness that David was being punished. But God is also gracious, kind, and merciful. It was in keeping with God's grace, mercy, and kindness that David should be pardoned. That is always a potent argument with God. Appeal to Him along the line of mercy.

b. Along the Line of Memory

"For in death there is no remembrance of Thee: in the grave who shall give Thee thanks?" (As Spurgeon remarked, "Churchyards are silent places.")

In Old Testament times the grave had not been flooded with light by the resurrection of Christ. It was cold, dark, and silent for the Hebrews did not have the revelations we have about the life beyond. David, using every argument he can think of, tells God that if He wants praise from His servant He'd better heal Him so he can do it while he's still alive!

So much for David's *excuse:* "I am weak." But in reviewing his sad condition, David spoke not only about his excuse.

B. He Spoke About His Exercise (6:6-7)

"I am weary!" He told the Lord two things.

1. He Was Worn Out (6:6)

"I am weary with my groaning; all the night make I my bed to swim; I water my couch with my tears." The phrase "all the night" can be rendered "every night."

Somehow he managed to put on a good front during the day. He would get up and bathe his inflamed eyes, comb his hair, brush his beard. He would put on his robes, acknowledge the greetings of his servants, and attempt to eat his breakfast. He would go about his business of the day, hiding the growing proof in his body of the mark of God upon him. He would do his best to pay attention to the cases being brought before him for adjudication. His closest advisers, however, would notice a strange inattention, a vagueness about the king who was usually so fair and swift in his decisions. He would listen in a desultory way to his advisers on the affairs of state and make a few remarks. Then he would face the entertainment of the evening, pretending to be amused or interested. As soon as decency would permit, he would dismiss the guests and performers and flee to his bedroom, brushing off the services of his slaves. As soon as the door was bolted he would fling himself on his bed, and cry as though his heart would break. "Every night." No wonder he was weary. This was pay day indeed for half an hour's sin.

2. He Was Waxing Old (6:7)

"Mine eye is consumed because of grief; it waxeth old because of mine enemies."

It was becoming increasingly clear to David that he was fooling nobody. His enemies were beginning to take note. His sleeplessness and sorrow were evident on his face. His eyes, particularly, were betraying him. The eyes are the windows of the soul; the look of the eye is often a sure indication of the condition within. David was visibly aging before his courtiers. Much more of this kind of anguish and he'd be in his grave. *That* was David's *sad condition.*

But almost without warning, the emotional pendulum swung.

II. DAVID'S SUDDEN CONFIDENCE (6:8-10)

The transition is abrupt, like the flipping of a coin. One moment David was overwhelmed with tragedy, the next he was marching forward in triumph.

A. His Fears Were Stilled (6:8-9)

He had no assurance as yet that his health was going to get better, but he was absolutely confident that his enemies were not going to get the best of him. "Depart from me, all ye workers of iniquity; for the LORD hath heard the voice of my weeping. The LORD hath heard my supplication; the LORD will receive my prayer."

Tears are an eloquent argument with God. Spurgeon called them "liquid prayers." They need no interpreter, and carry enormous weight at the throne of grace. David had sudden peace in his soul, an inner conviction that God had heard him. The rainbow shone upon the downpouring tears.

B. His Foes Were Stopped (6:10)

"Let all mine enemies be ashamed and sore vexed: let them return and be ashamed suddenly." David had found his vexation to be a highway back to God. His bones had been vexed, his soul had been vexed. What had been so good a medicine for himself he now prescribed for his foes.

Well might we sing with Moore and Hastings:

> Joy of the desolate
> Light of the straying,
> Hope of the penitent, fadeless and pure.
> Here speaks the Comforter
> Tenderly saying
> Earth has no sorrow that Heaven cannot heal.

Psalm 7

A LOUD CRY

THE SUPERSCRIPTION of this psalm, "Shiggaion of David, which he sang . . . concerning the words of Cush the Benjamite," gives us a clue as to when the psalm was originally sung by the composer. The subscription notes that the psalm was handed over "to the chief Musician upon Gittith," suggesting when the psalm was ordinarily sung by the congregation.

According to some the word *shiggaion* comes from a root meaning "to wander" so it might be inferred that the poet simply allowed his mind to wander when composing this particular song—that is, a rambling poem. Others think the word refers to David's wanderings during his fugitive days. Others think the word *shiggaion* comes from a word meaning "to roar," used to denote a loud cry of either danger or joy. *Shiggaion* points to a time of stress when David was under the influence of strong emotion.

The reference to "the words [the matter or business] of Cush the Benjamite" is an additional clue concerning the composition of this psalm, though we do not know who Cush was. The name means "black." Some infer that this man was a kinsman, or at least a tribesman, of King Ṣaul, that he was a member of Saul's court and had been slandering David to the king. Some say Cush was a poetic name for King Saul himself. Whether the name Cush was real or symbolic we do not know. Certainly the individual involved was a black-hearted villain. Whoever he was, David is most indignant against this Cush and much of his prayer is concerned with this individual's mistreatment of him.

The subscription of the psalm shows that eventually this psalm was included in the repertoire of the temple choir. It was sung upon *Gittith*, meaning "winepresses." Certainly David was in the winepress during those hazardous days when Saul's executioners and blood-hounds were ever on his trail. The Gittith psalms were used in the annual fall festivities in Israel, the joyous feast of tabernacles. There are three Gittith psalms in the Hebrew hymnbook—Psalms 7, 80, and 83.

No doubt, as David, in his later years as the crowned king of Israel, looked back over the collection of psalms he had written during his outlaw years, he could not help but be impressed with God's amazing goodness to him. The Lord had helped, protected, and crowned him with goodness and glory. Handing this particular psalm over to the chief musician for use in public worship he could well have added this note: "*Gittith*—appropriate for the harvest festival."

The psalm divides into three parts—Justification, Judgment, Jubilation.

I. JUSTIFICATION (7:1-5)

A. Trusting (7:1-2)

"O LORD [Jehovah] my God [Elohim], in Thee do I put my trust: save me from all them that persecute me, and deliver me." Jehovah the covenant God, and Elohim the creator God! Jehovah the God of *love,* and Elohim the God of *power!* David in his need marries the two titles of God. As we would sing:

> How good is the God we adore
> Our faithful, unchangeable Friend—
> Whose love is as great as His power
> And knows neither measure nor end.

B. Triumphing (7:3-5)

David's enemies were numerous enough. But one of them was conspicuous above the rest, namely the man called Cush, who had slandered David to the king.

Cush had accused David of iniquity (7:3). The word translated "iniquity" is *aval,* a word used primarily to denote injustice, that which is unfair, sin as deceitful and dishonest, unfairness in one's dealings with other people. If ever there was a man in Israel in those days whose personal integrity was beyond reproach, that man was David. It must have been especially hard on him to be accused of deceitful, dishonest dealings.

Cush had also accused David of rewarding evil to a man who was at peace with him (7:4). The word for "evil" is *ra'a,* which comes from a root meaning "to break up," especially to break up that which is good and desirable. In the Greek translation of the Old Testament this word was rendered *poneros* (from which comes our word pornography). The word is used to depict depravity, corruption, lewdness. Cush had accused David of that.

1. Positive Assurance

"*If* I have done this; *if* there be iniquity in my hands; *if* I have rewarded evil unto him that was at peace with me; (yea, I have delivered him that without cause is mine enemy:) *let* the enemy persecute my soul, and take it; yea, *let* him tread down my life upon the earth, and lay mine honour in the dust."

David indignantly repudiates the charge of *duplicity* and *depravity,* urged against him at Saul's court and evidently thoroughly believed by Saul.

It is a great thing to have a clear conscience, to be able to come to God and say: "I am innocent of these charges, Lord. You know it. If I have ever done these things—then hand me over to my enemies. I rest my case."

2. Positive Assertion

Having reminded the Lord that, far from doing these kinds of things, he had actually delivered Saul from peril, David adds that significant word, *Selah!* "There! What do you think of that?"

Slander is one of the most difficult things to fight. A man's good name and reputation can be destroyed by a lying, jealous tongue and his whole life laid in ruins. Slander is one of Satan's favorite weapons. It is done in secret and usually behind the back of the victim. The more a slanderous charge is denied the more it seems to be true in the minds of those who have been poisoned by it. David realized that, so he took the slander to the Lord: "Lord, you know these things are untrue. You vindicate me. You justify me because it is impossible for me to justify myself."

II. JUDGMENT (7:6-16)

David wanted God to deal with his enemies. Twice Saul was in his hands, twice David could have killed him, but both times David had refused to strike the Lord's anointed. He always left Saul's case with God.

A. David's Desire (7:6-8)

He wanted God to act in judgment, to judge the sinner, and then to judge the saint. It is a bold man who invites the judgment of God! But in those days David was a bold man, bold because he was a good man, a man after God's own heart.

1. Judge the Sinner (7:6-7)

"Arise, O LORD, in Thine anger, lift up Thyself because of the rage of mine enemies: and awake for me to the judgment that Thou has commanded. So shall the congregation of the people compass Thee about [i.e., gather round Thee to hear judgment pronounced]: for their sakes therefore return Thou on high." Some render that last phrase as "sit on high."

David asked the Lord to come into the judgment room and to come, not dispassionately with the cold, calm, aloofness required of a human judge, but to come storming into the courtroom wrapped in His anger. What a terrible thing to have a judge come into court having already privately nursed his anger against the accused. Moffat's translation of this is: "Bestir Thyself in anger O Eternal, in bursts of fury against our foes." That's how keenly David felt the injustices done against him by Doeg, by Saul, and by all those sycophant courtiers who encouraged Saul in his rage against David. It is not the kind of language we use in prayer meeting today, but it is language quite consistent with David's day and with David's circumstances.

2. Judge the Saint (7:8)

"The LORD shall judge the people: judge me, O LORD, according to my righteousness, and according to mine integrity that is in me." Having asked the Lord to come into court in all the fearfulness of His anger to judge the sinner, David then invited Him to turn His fiery eye upon the saints and particularly himself.

Such prayers and pleas of David underline a moral problem. Wickedness seems to triumph on the earth, the forces of ungodliness go from one outrage to another and God seems apparently unconcerned. David felt this keenly, especially since he was the persistent subject of such injustice. Why did God not arise in judgment?

God often allows wicked people to work out the evil that is in them. Everyone has a birthright as a moral, responsible creature—the right of moral freedom, the right to make his own choice. Too often that choice is to do wickedness. To see wickedness triumph is a great trial to godly people.

The eye of faith, however, sees that since God is God and since He is holy and righteous, then He must be storing up His anger and wrath. There must also be times when that wrath overflows. God's timetables, however, are not the same as ours.

A certain agnostic farmer once wrote to the editor of the local paper of an experiment he had made: "In defiance of your God I plowed my fields this year on a Sunday, I harrowed and fertilized them on a Sunday, I planted them on a Sunday, I cultivated them on Sundays, and I reaped them on Sunday. This October I had the biggest crop I have ever had. How do you explain that?" The editor replied: "God does not always make full reckoning in October."

David's desire was to see God act in judgment—and in hot, furious judgment at that. David invoked that judgment on the sinner and he invited that burning eye to be turned upon God's people too, and upon himself in particular. It was a very bold prayer.

B. David's Defense (7:9-13)

David explained how God works when at last He does rise up in judgment.

1. How God's Judgment Works in Principle (7:9-10)

"Oh let the wickedness of the wicked come to an end; but establish the just: for the righteous God trieth the hearts and reins. My defense is of God, which saveth the upright in heart." The phrase, "Oh let the wickedness of the wicked come to an end," can be translated: "O let evil make an end of the wicked." That is how God's judgment works in principle. The punishment of the wicked invariably springs from his own misdeeds.

Thus we see Haman being hanged on the gallows that he prepared for Mordecai. We see Jacob being cheated by his uncle in the same ways that he had cheated his father and his brother. We see David, later on in life, laying down with his own hands the paving stones along which the retribution of God followed. The principle of God's judgment is summed up in the sobering words: "Whatsoever a man soweth *that* shall he also reap." It is a law of the *soil;* it is also a law of the *soul.*

2. How God's Judgment Works in Practice (7:11-13)

"God judgeth the righteous, and God is angry with the wicked every day. If he turn not, He will whet His sword; He hath bent His bow, and made it ready. He hath also prepared for Him the instru- ments of death; He ordaineth His arrows against the persecutors." God is not asleep after all. Even as time passes and wickedness flourishes, God is making ready the instruments He plans to use to strike it down.

What a solemn statement: "God is angry with the wicked every day." The King James text does not give us the force of the original. The word for anger in this verse is *zo'am,* which comes from a verb meaning "to foam at the mouth." Even the best day that dawns on a sinner is still a day with the curse of God resting upon it. He goes about his business as though God did not exist. He indulges his lusts and God is angry with him. The sinner may have many a self-satisfying day, but he never has a safe day. God "foams at the mouth," as the Hebrews say. Between the sinner and the wrath of God is nothing but the beating of his heart; the only thing that keeps *that* going is God's sovereign grace, for God would much rather see a sinner enrolled among the redeemed than cast into the lake of fire.

C. David's Discernment (7:14-16)

He concludes this discussion of God's anger against sin with three illustrations which help explain God's moral government of the universe. They describe how God allows sin to work itself out and bring its own inevitable consequences upon the unrepentant.

1. Sin in Its Process: Like a Birth (7:14)

"Behold, he travaileth with iniquity, and hath conceived mischief, and brought forth falsehood." The illustration is that of a pregnant woman. The sinner conceives wickedness in his heart and it grows within him until he is full of it. He is then at pains to carry it out.

The father of sin is *Satan,* the mother of sin is *self.* The devil, that fallen and monstrously wicked spirit, is the ultimate author, origina-tor, and father of sin. Self is its mother—our own inner, bent, and twisted perverseness. That is the word David uses. The word "mis-chief" comes from a word often translated "perverseness" in the Old Testament. Satan knows how to impregnant the innate perverseness of fallen human nature with his own diabolical spirit. Some form of wickedness then begins to grow and develop in the soul.

Wickedness had already grown to full development in the soul of Cush. We do not know what facet of perverseness Satan quickened in that man's heart. It might have been ambition or jealousy or malice or even cowardice. Whatever it was, it swelled up in this man's soul and when he could hold it no longer he brought it forth in malicious lies about David, lies that later came to full and dreadful maturity.

2. Sin in Its Plan: Like a Bait (7:15)

"He made a pit, and digged it, and is fallen into the ditch which he made." This is another aspect of sin—cold-blooded, calculating, premeditated, deliberately executed wickedness. The picture here is not that of a man who speaks a hasty word or a lie in a moment of pressure or passion. The picture here is of a man who thinks through the best way to ruin, rob, or revile somebody and who then deliber-ately executes his plan. David sees that such people eventually get caught in their own plots. This end result of deliberate wickedness may not be obvious to us but God never fails eventually to take a man in his own snares.

3. Sin in Its Punishment: Like a Boomerang (7:16)

"His mischief shall return upon his own head, and his violent dealing shall come down upon his own pate." Thus, for instance, God caused the dogs to lick the blood of Ahab in the midst of the vineyard of Naboth whom he had murdered and whose property he had stolen.

The explorers who first went to Australia found that the wild aborigines had a very curious weapon, a curved throwing stick which they used for war and hunting. It was curved at an angle of about ninety degrees or more, it weighed about eight ounces, and it was from eighteen to twenty-four inches in overall length. The skilled hunter could throw that boomerang for more than one hundred yards, at which point, if it missed its target, it curved around and came back to him.

David knew nothing about the Australian boomerang. If he had he would surely have used it here to illustrate his point because sin, in its punishment, is just like a boomerang. A person can throw his wickedness at other people but he had better watch out. That very wickedness will obey higher laws than those the sinner can control. God will watch over that wickedness until it finally comes home to punish the one who threw it—either in this life or the next. We do not control the factors of time and space. We cannot retain control over the wrongs we do once they have been launched upon their way. But God can and does. "With what measure ye mete, it shall be measured to you again" is God's sure and certain word.

It is not surprising that this psalm which begins with justification and which is largely taken up with judgment should end the way it does.

III. JUBILATION (7:17)

"I will praise the LORD according to His righteousness: and will sing praise to the name of the LORD most high." There is something very satisfying to the soul to know that, evil as this world undoubtedly is, God has not lost control of things—whether they be the affairs of the individual or of the nations.

David refers to God here as *Jehovah Elyon.* Jehovah, the God of *covenant,* is also Elyon, the God of *control.* The name "Elyon," "most high" occurs thirty-six times in the Bible and here for the first time in the book of Psalms. Its first use in Scripture is in Genesis 14 where Abraham learned this name for God when he returned from the battle against the kings of the East. As he sat there at the table with Melchizedek, with the bread and the wine on the table before him, Abraham learned that God was *Elyon:* "the Possessor of Heaven and earth."

Elyon, then, is God as the One who dispenses blessings to men and who is the Possessor of all things. David can sing now! His circumstances are dire but God is still on the throne. God is in control. Men may curse, but no one can really curse one whom God has blessed!

"There!" says David. "Send that to the chief Musician! Here's something to sing about at the feast of tabernacles"—the feast which was a foreview of the coming millennial reign!

Psalm 8

DEATH OF A CHAMPION

I. THE LORD'S POSITION (8:1)
II. THE LORD'S POWER (8:2-3)
   David saw the Lord as:
   A. Conqueror of the World (8:2)
   B. Creator of the World (8:3)
III. THE LORD'S PRESENCE (8:4-8)
   The Mystery of It! That He should:
   A. Come to Us the Way He Does (5:5a)
   B. Care for Us the Way He Does (5b-8)
IV. THE LORD'S PORTION (8:9)

T HE STORY OF DAVID AND GOLIATH is one of the most exciting stories
in the Old Testament. The Philistine champion would come out
every morning, march to the brow of the hill, and look across
the valley of Elah to the camp of Israel. Then, to the amusement of
the Philistines and the discomfiture of Israel, he would begin his daily
mockery of Israel. David listened in astonishment to Goliath. "Where's
the king?" he thought. "Why doesn't Saul fight him? He's nearly as
big as he is!" Or, "Why doesn't Jonathan fight him?" Or, "Why
doesn't Shammah or Eliab fight him?" Since no one else would do
so, David decided to fight the giant himself. Everyone thought Goliath too big to fight; David thought he was too big to miss. Saul
objected: "Thou art not able . . . thou art but a *youth!*"

But David was able and down came Goliath with his blasphemies
cut off in his throat. Soon afterward David was appointed court
musician and given the task of trying to charm the king out of his dark
moods with the music on his harp.

It was probably about this time that David wrote this psalm. The
clue is found in that word *Muthlabben:* "To the chief Musician upon
Muthlabben." The note often appears at the head of Psalm 9, but it
really seems to belong as a footnote to Psalm 8. Later, when David
was king and was arranging music for the royal choir he included this
psalm with the note: "Muthlabben," a Hebrew expression which
means, "the death of the champion." The tradition that refers it to
Goliath is as old as the Targum. There it is paraphrased: "Concerning

the death of the man who went forth between the camps." Scholars
tell us that this is a direct reference to the story of David and Goliath
for in 1 Samuel 17:4 the Hebrew word for champion is "the man of
the space between the camps"—that dread no-man's land between
Israel and the Philistines dominated by Goliath of Gath.

Psalm 8 is prophetic and anticipates the coming of the Lord Jesus
Christ at the end of the age. The world will have found itself another
champion, the beast, and Israel will be powerless before him. He will
be the one who "stands between the camps" to defy God and fight
His people. But great David's greater Son will come, "the stone cut
without hands," and He will fight against that blasphemous and
defiant champion. Down he will go! It will all be over in a moment,
in the twinkling of an eye, and Satan's strong man will be no more.

This lovely little Davidic psalm was written by David, the champion
of champions, and was sung perhaps before King Saul to subdue the
demon that flared from his jealous eye.

I. THE LORD'S POSITION (8:1)

"Oh LORD our Lord, how excellent is Thy name in all the earth!
who hast set Thy glory above the heavens." Jehovah's name is not
yet acknowledged in all the earth. Half a billion Moslems place Allah
on the throne of their hearts, a quarter of a billion Buddhists bow
down to the graven image of Buddah, half a billion Hindus grovel at
the feet of countless idols, millions of communists and atheists deny
there is any God at all. But to those who have come to know Him,
His is the name above all names—the saving, sovereign name: "Oh
LORD our Lord how excellent is Thy name in all the earth!" Yes, even
today, when God's glory is hidden, His Name *is* excellent in all the
earth! Millions own that Name. We know it now as Jesus. In Old
Testament times that name was Jehovah! David sang, "Oh LORD
[Jehovah] our Lord, how excellent is Thy name in all the earth!"

When Goliath saw David and realized that the Hebrews were sending a stripling against *him,* the mighty giant of Gath, he "cursed David
by his gods." David replied, "Thou comest to me with a sword, and
with a spear, and with a shield: but I come to thee in the name of the
LORD [in the name of Jehovah] of hosts" (1 Samuel 17:45). The Lord's
name is excellent in the earth and a glory set above the heavens.

II. THE LORD'S POWER (8:2-3)

David saw that power demonstrated in two dimensions.

A. The Conqueror of the World (8:2)

"Out of the mouth of babes and sucklings hast Thou ordained
strength because of Thine enemies, that Thou mightest still the enemy
and the avenger." A cynic once said, "God is on the side of the big

battalions." That is not so. God does not need armies at all. All God
needs is a babe!

To humble mighty Pharaoh's empire, God did not summon Assyr-
ia or mobilize Macedonia. He sent a baby to a Hebrew home. The
babe was hidden among the bulrushes and was found by Pharaoh's
daughter. As the princess looked at the handsome little boy he cried.
A tear ran down his cheek and Almighty God wrote the downfall of
a kingdom. That tear sped like an arrow to the royal lady's heart and,
disdaining court decrees, she raised him as her own. She called him
Moses and, in the fullness of time, Moses humbled Egypt to the dust.
"Out of the mouths of babes and sucklings hast Thou ordained
strength because of Thine enemies, that Thou mightest still the enemy
and the avenger."

B. The Creator of the World (8:3)

"When I consider Thy heavens, the work of Thy fingers, the moon
and the stars, which Thou hast ordained."

David was a shepherd boy. He had watched the stars wink awake
night after night. He knew some of their names, Orion perhaps and
the Pleiades. He knew the moon and the nearer planets, which changed
their positions from month to month and from year to year. He knew
from his Bible that God had created them, counted them, and called
them by their names. He knew enough to be awed at the might, the
majesty, and the mystery of God as creator of the worlds of space.

David's awe should be totally eclipsed by ours. When Galileo Galilei
first turned a telescope on the sky and announced to an astonished
world that the earth was not the center of the universe an outraged
pope ordered him to recant. But it was no use: the secret was out.
There was far more to outer space than man had ever dreamed.
There were empires out there—empires in bewildering number, of
staggering dimensions, traveling at inconceivable speeds, reaching
further and even further into unimaginable depths. It is all a tribute
to the Lord's power—the work of His *finger.*

III. THE LORD'S PRESENCE (8:4-8)

David faced a double mystery—that God should *come* to us the way
He does and that God should *care* for us the way He does.

A. Come to Us the Way He Does (8:4-5a)

"When I consider Thy heavens, the work of Thy fingers, the moon
and the stars, which Thou hast ordained: What is man, that Thou art
mindful of him? and the son of man, that Thou visitest him? For Thou
hast made him a little lower than the angels." How wonderful! God
is more interested in *people* than He is in *planets,* more interested in
souls than He is in *stars,* more interested in *us* than He is in the *universe!*
And because He is interested in us He *visits* us.

There are four Hebrew words for man, three of them have a bearing on this psalm. There is the word *gibber.* The Philistine champion Goliath was "the *man* in between." The word used in 1 Samuel 17 is *ishlabben* from which comes *muthlabben,* the key word at the foot of this psalm. But after David slew Goliath he was no longer "the man of the space between the camps." He is referred to instead as the "champion," *gibber,* "the strong man."

Two words for man are used here in Psalm 8. "What is *man* that Thou art mindful of him?" That is not *gibber* but *enosh,* which means "mortal man," man in his weakness. God is mindful of us in our weakness.

The other word for man is in this same verse: "And the son of *man* that Thou visited him." There is no article in the Hebrew. It is not "the son of man," it is simply "son of man," literally "son of Adam." The word comes from *adamah* which means "dust." God comes to visit us as before the fall He came to visit Adam.

The expression "son of man" is a typical Old Testament expression for man as a natural descendant of Adam. It occurs about one hundred times, for instance, in Ezekiel: "Son of man hast thou seen this?" It is used to contrast the prophet, poor son of Adam that he was, with the mighty cherubim.

In the New Testament the expression changes. It is no longer "son of man," now it is "the Son of man." In the New Testament it always has the article. Without the article the expression refers to a mere human being, with the article it refers to Christ as the second Man, the last Adam, taking the place in the universe forfeited by Adam.

The God who visited man occasionally in the Old Testament is now revealed as the Son of man, the rightful Heir to Adam's forfeited estates, and successor to the dominion of the earth. In the Person of Jesus Christ God has visited the earth and in the Person of Jesus Christ He is coming back—coming back to stay!

It was also a mystery that God should:

B. Care for Us the Way He Does (8:5b-8)

"And hast crowned Him with glory and honour. Thou madest Him to have dominion over the works of Thy hands; Thou hast put all things under His feet: All sheep and oxen, yea, and the beasts of the field: The fowl of the air, and the fish of the sea, and whatsoever passeth through the paths of the seas."

The writer of Hebrews relates this statement to Jesus. He, the second Person of the Godhead, came down from the pinnacle of glory to be born in that Bethlehem barn. He was "made flesh," "made a little lower than the angels," that He might redeem ruined mankind.

The present queen of England was a teenager at the outbreak of World War II. As soon as she was old enough she asked her father, King George VI, to allow her to join the armed forces and serve

Britain as others were doing. Her father finally allowed her to join the Auxiliary Territorial Service as a *private*. She had a superior officer who took pleasure in bossing and bullying her. It was, "Private Windsor do this, Private Windsor do that!" "Yes, sergeant! Yes, sergeant," was all Elizabeth could say. She was made a little lower than the noncommissioned officers for the sake of her service to her people. But then, on February 6, 1952, she received word that her father was dead. From that moment on she was Queen of England. She was no longer "Private Windsor," to be baited and badgered by a small-minded noncommissioned officer. She was "Her Royal Majesty, Queen Elizabeth II." She had entered into the position for which she had been born, a position resigned temporarily for the call of duty. Never again did that sergeant address her as "Private Windsor."

Our glorious Lord has assumed again His throne on high. He has carried humanity with Him for there, in glory, He sits enthroned in a battle-scarred body of flesh! And we, the redeemed of Adam's race, are to share that glory for all eternity.

In the meantime we are "a little lower than the angels." But that is only a temporary rank. We are under tutors and schoolmasters, but all that is going to end. Then we, too, shall be exalted higher than the highest archangels of glory, joint heirs with Christ of the ages to come.

"A little lower than the angels" is God's estimate of the human race. We are not "a little higher than the beasts"; we are "a little lower than the angels." Charles Darwin described man as "the most efficient animal ever to emerge on earth." What a degrading view of man! Man is not just an efficient animal; he was made by an act of God, and made in the image and likeness of God. When the Son of God stepped off the throne of the universe to enter into human life He did not become "an efficient animal," He became a man.

God has delivered into human hands dominion over the planet. Thou "hast crowned him with glory and honour. And madest him to have dominion over the works of Thy hands; Thou hast put all things under his feet . . . the fowl of the air, and the fish of the sea, and whatsoever passeth through the paths of the seas." Six things are listed in the psalm. In David's day man's dominion was displayed in his power over animals, power to domesticate and tame them and turn them to his use.

Today man's dominion is demonstrated in his ability to subjugate the forces of nature. The atom smashers have unleashed and harnessed the energy of the universe. The code breakers have unraveled the mysteries of DNA and RNA. Psychologists have explored the workings of the human brain. The marks of man's genius are everywhere despite the fall. Man is "a little lower than the angels," not an efficient anthropoid ape. The Lord having created us, companions us and crowns us and commissions us. It is almost too wonderful for words!

VI. THE LORD'S PORTION (8:9)

"O LORD our Lord how excellent is Thy name in all the earth!" The first and last verses are exactly the same. We call it "an envelope psalm" because the opening and closing statements wrap up the truth which lies between.

Now it may be that someone challenges: "You say, 'O Jehovah our Lord, how excellent is thy name in all the earth.' Very well—prove it!" David offers two lines of proof. There is the evidence of God's *greatness*—look at the moon and stars. They are the work of God's *fingers,* not His hand. The Bible speaks of God's arm, it speaks of God's hand, and it speaks of God's fingers. There is far less power in a finger than there is in an arm. To create stars and satellites and suns God needed only His fingers! That's how great He is.

But there is the evidence of an even greater magnitude, His *grace.* God, who can orbit the Milky Way, the Andromeda galaxy, and a hundred million universes and toss them into space as mere handfuls of stardust—this God loves and cares for us! "O LORD [Jehovah] our Lord, how excellent is Thy name in all the earth!"

God has no more to say. If we still want to argue He will simply bring us back to verse 1. "Very well, let's go over it again." The psalm begins where it ends, ends where it begins, and completes the cycle endlessly and forever. "'How excellent is Thy name in all the earth!'"

Psalm 9

THE FALL OF THE BEAST

PSALMS 9 AND 10 BELONG TOGETHER, so much so that in some ancient versions they appear as one single psalm. They are linked together by a broken but continuing acrostic. In Psalm 9 the first ten letters of the Hebrew alphabet are used to emphasize the various stanzas (except for the fourth letter of the alphabet, which is left out on purpose); Psalm 10 carries on the acrostic, with a number of equally significant omissions. We shall leave the reason for the broken and incomplete acrostic until we examine Psalm 10.

As the outline reveals, this psalm is one of the great prophecies of the Old Testament.

I. THE DELIGHT OF THE PROPHET (9:1-2)

David was a prophet as well as a king, and many of his prophecies are immortalized in his psalms. Unless we recognize that we shall never get beyond the surface of many of them. The Psalms stand in the same relation to the historical books of the Old Testament as the Epistles do to the Gospels in the New Testament. The Epistles, which are chiefly concerned with theology, go deeper than the Gospels, which are concerned mainly with history. The Psalms are the same, going beyond the historical books to give us theology. Much of the theology of the Old Testament is couched in song, as much of the theology of the New Testament is embodied in letters.

In Psalms 9 and 10 David looks at the end times. Seven times in these two psalms he makes reference to "the lawless one" (9:5,16; 10:2,3,4,13,15), the same described by Daniel and by Paul—the man of sin, the beast, the devil's messiah.

David was victorious over all his foes; his trials and tribulations were all swallowed up in triumph. So it will be with the people over whom he ruled. Israel through great tribulation will one day enter into the Millennial kingdom. This psalm is written as though from the other side of the great tribulation. David shows God's troubled saints how to:

A. Praise the Lord Freely

"I *will* praise the LORD," he says, "I *will* praise the LORD . . . I *will* show forth all Thy marvellous works. I *will* be glad and rejoice . . . I *will* praise Thy name." That is the kind of victory that infuriates the hosts of hell. What can Satan do with a man who turns a prison into a palace, a crucifixion into a coronation, a torture into a triumph?

Next David shows God's troubled saints how to:

B. Praise the Lord Fully

"I will praise the LORD with my whole heart." David was no theorist—most of his psalms were written in times of great affliction. There is a tremendous difference between praising with the lips and praising with the heart; between mechanically singing a hymn and singing it from an overflowing soul.

We used to have a little black dog called Sambo. When Sambo misbehaved we would tie him to a tree. He would sit there with his head hanging, advertising his dejection to all the world. When the front door would open Sambo would perk up a little and give a token wag of his tail. He acknowledged us, but half-heartedly. But when we let him off the leash he would yelp and bark and dash around the house at full speed, tossing his head, racing back and forth, with his eyes dancing, and his tail going like a fan. With his whole heart he was expressing gratitude and praise.

That is what God wants from us—not just a token wag of the tail, so to speak, but wholehearted, unstinting, spontaneous praise.

II. THE DESTRUCTION OF THE BEAST (9:3-6)

David's vision of the end times was clear enough but he did not always have events in their right order. This is quite characteristic of Old Testament prophecy.

A. The Lord's Presence (9:3-4)

First we *sense the thrill with David*: "When mine enemies are turned back, they shall fall and perish at Thy presence." When the beast is first unveiled he will seem to be a veritable messiah to the Jews, who will make a seven-year pact with him. In return he will hold off their enemies and give his support to the building of their temple. However, after the lapse of only 1,260 days, he will throw off the mask of friendship and reveal himself as their most inveterate foe. His chief propagandist, the false prophet, will set up an image of the beast in the rebuilt temple and will demand that everyone worship it. All people must also receive the mark of the beast. Throughout the world the slogan will be "No seal, no deal." The great tribulation will begin and the Jews in particular will suffer. Anti-Semitism will flourish from pole to pole and from sea to sea. It will become a global nightmare.

Then suddenly it will be over. The sign of the Son of man will appear in the sky. Such Jews as are still alive will weep as they "look on Him whom they pierced" and as they realize, at last, that Jesus is indeed the true Messiah.

The beast and the false prophet will be hurled into the lake of fire. The Psalmist senses the thrill of it. The mere manifestation of the Lord's *presence* will be all that is needed to break the devil's stranglehold on this planet.

Next we *see the throne with David:* "For Thou hast maintained my right and my cause; Thou satest in the throne judging right." The Lord will set up a throne of judgment on the Mount of Olives where He once spoke the parable of the sheep and the goats. The nations will be assembled before Him, the surviving and converted remnant of the Jews in the valley of Jehoshaphat, perhaps better known to us as the Kidron Valley, which the Lord crossed on His way to Gethsemane. From the assembled Gentiles gathered before Him, the Lord will select "the sheep"—those who showed kindness to the persecuted Jews during the great tribulation and thus expressed their opposition to the beast and their belief in God. These will be made to stand on His right hand, over against Jerusalem.

Those remaining will be "the goats"—those who persecuted the Jews during the beast's reign and who sided with the beast and received his mark. These will be made to stand on His left hand near Tophet, the dread valley of Hinnom where the flames were never quenched and where the worms never died. David did not see all this in sharp focus, but he saw it and he identified himself with his remote descendants in that coming day: "For Thou hast maintained my right and my cause; Thou satest in the throne judging right."

B. The Lord's Power (9:5-6)

These two verses concentrate on the destruction of the beast himself. First, his destruction will be *personal*: "Thou hast rebuked the heathen, Thou hast destroyed the wicked [the wicked one]." The verse refers to the Antichrist, the beast who will have once bestrode the earth like a colossus but who will then make his bed in hell.

His destruction will be *permanent*: "Thou has put out their name for ever and ever. O thou enemy, destructions are come to a perpetual end." The beast will glory in his name. He will even reduce it to a number and force people to wear that number embossed on their hands or foreheads. But what is his name? We do not know! God does not consider it worth recording. It is a name so abhorrent to God that He does not even record it in the Apocalypse and during the millennium it will disappear from the languages of men. Moffat renders the second half of verse 5: "Thou hast curbed the pagans, crushing the ungodly, blotting out their name for all time." God will obliterate the name of the beast. His destruction will be both personal and permanent.

It will also be *proper*: "And Thou has destroyed cities; their memorial is perished with them." Like previous world conquerors the beast will leave a trail of destruction behind him. What he did to others, will be done to him—his very name will be obliterated.

III. The Dawn of the Millennium (9:7-8)

The destruction of the beast and the banishment of the lost from the earth will lead directly to the millennial reign of Christ. David did not have the same light as we have, but he did catch glimpses of the coming golden age. With true spiritual insight David underlined the two features which make the millennial reign a true golden age.

A. The Lord's Invincible Majesty (9:7)

"But [in contrast with His foes] the LORD shall endure for ever: He hath prepared His throne for judgment." What a throne! What an empire! What a King!

When I think of kings and empires and thrones, my mind goes instinctively to Britain and my native land. The British throne goes back over a thousand years into the mists of recorded time. But the British throne, long and illustrious as has been its history, has known dynastic change and now it is a mere shadow. Magna Charta was the first constitutional chip hammered from the British throne and now the kings of England are constitutional kings—kings only in name. Once the British Empire spread from pole to pole and from sea to sea. The kings of England had empire thrust upon them by restless, disinherited, younger scions of nobility. Lord Clive gave India to England; Wolfe scaled the heights before Quebec and in a dramatic fifteen minutes seized Canada from the French and handed that to England; Cecil Rhodes donated North and South Rhodesia; missionaries and explorers added other parts of Africa; Captain Cook contributed empires in the east.

The empire was tossed away almost as casually as it was collected. George III threw away America for the sake of a tax on tea. After World War II leftist-leaning socialists dismembered much of what remained.

What a contrast is the Lord's crown and throne and empire! "The LORD shall endure for ever."

B. The Lord's Inviolate Ministry (9:8)

"And He shall judge the world in righteousness, He shall minister judgment to the people in uprightness." There will be no more graft in government, no more corruption in the courts, no more injustice, no more unfairness. No longer will truth be on the scaffold and wrong on the throne. The Lord's ministry will be inviolate. He will sit on His throne and the twelve apostles will occupy thrones with Him, judging the twelve tribes of Israel. Israel—regenerated, filled, and anointed with the Holy Spirit—will administer the King's justice around the world with an impartial righteousness.

IV. THE DURATION OF THE TERROR (9:9-14)

David saw, with awed fascination, the great tribulation. Its dark scenes held him as a snake's eye holds it prey. He described three things about this dreadful period.

A. The Place of Refuge (9:9-10)

"The LORD also will be a refuge for the oppressed, a refuge in times of trouble [the great time of trouble]. And they that know Thy name will put their trust in Thee: For Thou, LORD, hath not forsaken them that seek Thee." The word for "refuge" is sometimes rendered "a high tower." David was no stranger to trouble. He had spent most of his youth and early manhood hiding in the hills, forests, wastelands, and foreign countries from Saul's executioners. Often he had longed for a high tower, a place of security into which he could run and hide, secure from his foes. He found such a refuge in the Lord. The persecuted tribulation saints (those who obey the Lord's instructions in Matthew 24) will find just such a high tower in the Lord.

B. The Period of Rejoicing (9:11)

"Sing praises to the LORD, which dwelleth in Zion: declare among the people His doings." The time of tribulation will be sharp, but it will also be short. Once it is over the world will resound with song, the very trees will clap their hands, and the brooks will cease their mournful murmur to babble with bliss.

C. The Process of Retribution (9:12-14)

"When He maketh inquisition for blood, He remembereth them: He forgetteth not the cry of the humble." The word "humble" signifies those bowed down by their sorrows. Inquisition for blood! God takes a serious view of murder. In Noah's day He legislated that the death penalty be the punishment for taking a human life. Under the Mosaic law, the execution of the sentence was entrusted to the next of kin, to "the avenger of blood," whose sacred duty it was to track down and execute the man who had murdered his relative. Now that the Lord has become next of kin to the human race He has become the Avenger of blood. Mistrials of justice here and sentimental softness toward the murderer do not close the books. The Lord is to come back as the Avenger of blood.

The primary reference seems to be the great tribulation but in its broadest application the statement looks on to the great white throne. Again the perspective changes.

V. THE DAY OF THE LORD (9:15-18)

It is all over! The tribulation is finished!

A. Something That Needs to be Perceived (9:15-16)

"The heathen are sunk down in the pit that they made: in the net which they hid is their own foot taken . . . the wicked is snared in the work of his own hands. Higgaion. Selah."

Haman is hanged on the gallows he prepared for Mordecai. The kings of Sodom and Gomorrah fall into the very slimepits into which they hoped to trap Amraphel. Such is the poetic justice of God. God sees to it that *whatsoever* a man sows, *that* he also reaps. It is as much a law of the *soul* as it is a law of the *soil*.

Selah means: "There, what do you think of that!" Higgaion (soliloquy of meditation) means: "Think about it for a while!" These are things of God would not have us forget or treat lightly.

Sometimes we have to ponder the poetic justice of God because it is not always obvious and it does not always take place swiftly. It is none the less sure, something David discovered before his days were done. When he seduced Bathsheba and murdered Uriah he laid with his own hands the foundation along which retribution eventually came. Selah! Higgaion!

B. Something That Needs To Be Proclaimed (9:17-18)

1. God's Attitude Toward the Nations (9:17)

"The wicked shall be turned into hell, and all the nations that forget God." That needs to be proclaimed, but it needs to be proclaimed in context: the great tribulation and the battle of Armageddon.

Years ago I used to speak occasionally in a large city at a very small church right across from a large, ornate Catholic church. The little church was located on a long, narrow lot and butted almost wall-to-wall with the house next door. On its property line, right near the neighbor's front door, the church erected a sign reading: "Evil pursueth sinners," and on the other side it declared: "The wicked shall be turned into hell." No wonder that church had no success in reaching its neighborhood for Christ. "The wicked shall be turned into hell, and all the nations that forget God." These words are true and we need to proclaim them, but we need to speak that truth in love and in context. In Psalm 9 the context points to the last days when the nations will unite against the Lord and His anointed.

2. God's Attitude Toward the Needy (9:18)

"For the needy shall not alway be forgotten: the expectation of the poor shall not perish for ever." Moffat renders that: "One day the needy will be remembered, the hopes of the downtrodden will not always be disappointed." It is a remarkable fact that Jesus did not launch a campaign against poverty when He was here. On the contrary, He was poor Himself. Judas was able to cloak his final act of treason by pretending to minister to the poor in Christ's name: "the poor ye have always with you," Jesus said. The presence of the poor gives God's people opportunity to exhibit their faith in a practical way. Solomon would one day write, "He that hath pity upon the poor lendeth unto the LORD" (Proverbs 19:17). And God always pays His debts!

In a coming day, however, Jesus will abolish poverty. During the millennium every man will dwell beneath his own fig and his own vine. Earth's wealth will be distributed fairly so that all men will be increased with goods and have need for nothing.

Now comes the end of the psalm. David has shown us the destruction of the beast; the dawn of the Millennium; the duration of the terror, and the day of the Lord.

VI. THE DOCTRINE OF THE PSALM (9:19-20)

"Arise, O LORD; let not man prevail: let the heathen [the nations] be judged in Thy sight. Put them in fear, O LORD: that the nations may know themselves to be but men." Nations have arisen in our day to mass collective consciousness and modern communications and technology have increased tension and competition between them. The nations are more arrogant, more resentful, more aggressive than ever before. David prayed that the nations might learn their utter mortality. The word for "man" here, at the end of this psalm, is *enosh,* mortal man. That is the doctrine of this psalm. God is God and the nations are but mortal. They are only collections of men. It is worth remembering. Man can be very clever, very cruel, very crafty. But man is only man. And God is God! Well might we sing:

> Under the shadow of Thy throne
> Thy saints have dwelt secure;
> Sufficient is Thine arm alone
> And our defense is sure.

That's the doctrine of this psalm.

Psalm 10

THE LAWLESS ONE

I. THE LORD IS CONCEALED
When the Wicked Flourish (10:1-11)

The Wicked Man's:
A. Seeming Blessing (10:1)
B. Sinful Behavior (10:2)
C. Scornful Boasts (10:3)
D. Stubborn Bias (10:4)
E. Spiritual Blindness (10:5)
F. Swelling Bigotry (10:6)
G. Spoken Blasphemies (10:7)
H. Secret Brutalities (10:8-10)
   1. His Cruelty (the Bandit) (10:8)
   2. His Confidence (the Lion) (10:9a)
   3. His Cunning (the Hunter) (10:9b-11)

II. THE LORD IS CONCERNED
What the Wicked Forget (19:12-15)

God's eye is on:
A. The Wicked Man's Scornfulness (10:12-13)
B. The Wicked Man's Spitefulness (10:14)
C. The Wicked Man's Sinfulness (10:15)

III. THE LORD IS CROWNED
What the Wicked Face (10:16-18)

A. The Lord Will Subdue the Heathen (10:16)
B. The Lord Will Support the Helpless (10:17-18)

PSALM 10 IS A CONTINUATION of Psalm 9. As we have noted, the two psalms are linked together by an irregular acrostic, begun in Psalm 9 and concluded in Psalm 10. In Psalm 9 the emphasis is on the enemy *outside* the nation of Israel, in Psalm 10 on the enemy *inside* the nation of Israel. In all, no less than seven letters are dropped out of the alphabetical acrostic. Also, in Psalm 10 there is a gap of nine verses (10:3-11) where the acrostic vanishes altogether. The irregular acrostic is a literary way of emphasizing the broken and troubled times the Psalmist is describing in his song.

Psalm 9 takes us through the first half of the Hebrew alphabet; Psalm 10 completes the alphabet. The alphabetical structure of these two psalms is intended to depict governmental order—order which is broken by a gap of six letters near the beginning of Psalm 10. From verses 3-11, we have the boastings and blasphemies of the wicked man and the Holy Spirit drops the acrostic as He records this. The fact that there are six letters omitted is suggestive: the number six is the number of man, and preeminently it is the number of the devil's man, the man of sin (666). As soon as God comes back into view (10:12) the alphabetical acrostic is resumed and carried on to the end.

In Psalm 9 only one letter of the alphabet is missing from the eleven which make up the first half of the Hebrew alphabet—the fourth letter, *daleth*. Four in Scripture is the number of earth and is particularly the number of world order. It is this fourth letter that is so significantly dropped from Psalm 9, leaving ten letters, ten being the number of human responsibility (the Ten Commandments, for instance).

Psalms 9 and 10 are both prophetic in character, and both look down the ages to the coming of the lawless one. Psalm 9 is mostly concerned with Israel and the nations, particularly with the beast. Psalm 10 is concerned more with the troubles within the nation itself. In Psalm 9 the individuality of David is clearly to be seen; in Psalm 10 that individuality disappears. Psalm 9 is a paean of praise—the Psalmist has no doubt about the outcome when it is merely a matter of confrontation between Israel and the nations. In Psalm 10 that triumphant note vanishes because the nation itself is corrupted. The waters outside a ship can do it no harm, but when the water gets in, that's a different matter.

The devil is to have two men on earth in a coming day, the beast and the false prophet. The beast, the coming world ruler, will be a *Gentile;* he will come up out of the *sea* and be purely and simply a wild beast. The second beast, the false prophet, appears to be a *Jew,* for he comes up out of the earth and has the outward appearance of a lamb. It is this danger from within which so frightens the prophet. That a wild beast should arise and threaten Israel—well, that was to be expected; but that he should have an accomplice within the nation itself—that was something else, cause for urgent alarm. Yet David does not lose sight of the Lord, even when contemplating all the evil that is yet to befall the people of Israel.

While the psalm is prophetic in character it nevertheless has practical truth for the troubled saint today. How often it looks as though God is remote and unconcerned—especially when the enemy comes right into the sanctuary, right into the Church. The Lord seems to be concealed but He is concerned and He will be crowned. We examined Psalm 9 from the prophetic standpoint so we shall keep the same perspective in mind in Psalm 10.

I. The Lord is Concealed

When the Wicked Flourish (10:1-11)

The writer wrestled with the perennial problem of the apparent prosperity of those who hate and reject the Lord.

A. The Wicked Man's Seeming Blessing (10:1)

"Why standest Thou afar off, O Lord? Why hidest Thou Thyself in times of trouble?" The time of trouble, in its ultimate prophetic focus, will be the time of *Jacob's* trouble—that dreadful period of persecution yet to come upon mankind and especially upon the Jews known as the great tribulation. If ever history seems to declare that God is unconcerned, it will be during the great tribulation. The beast will have the world in his grasp and the false prophet will direct the worship of the world to the beast, to his image, and to Satan himself.

God will be strangely silent. The expression "standest afar off " is used by David in Psalm 38:11 as well as here. In that psalm he was lamenting the terrible catastrophe which had overtaken him and was telling how his lovers and friends stood aloof from him. They were fair-weather friends. The same expression is used here. David is asking God if He, too, is just a fair-weathered Friend. Or at least he is putting that language prophetically into the lips of those who will be living in the days of the great tribulation.

The wicked man seemingly is enjoying blessing, carrying everything before him. God has gone into hiding and the heavens are as brass. God does not answer when His persecuted people cry. The reason, of course, is that the hour of wrath has come and Israel must be brought to her knees before the Lord Jesus Christ.

B. The Wicked Man's Sinful Behavior (10:2)

"The wicked in his pride doth persecute the poor [i.e., the oppressed ones]: let them be taken in the devices that they have imagined." The word for "wicked" is the Hebrew word for the lawless man. That, of course, is the great name for the beast. In 2 Thessalonians 2 he is actually described as "that wicked" or "that lawless one." In this section of the psalm (verses 1-11) no less than twenty-six things are listed concerning the character and career of this individual. The expression "the lawless one" occurs seven times in Psalms 9 and 10 (9:5,16; 10:2,3,4,13,15) and throughout it is used in the singular. It has to do not just with lawless men in general, but with the lawless one in particular. It refers to the beast and also to the false prophet, his soul twin, the second person in the coming satanic trinity.

David could see the lawless one persecuting "the poor." The word "poor" literally means "the wretched." It is the same expression which is used in Proverbs 14:21: "He that hath mercy on the poor [the afflicted ones], happy is he." During the great tribulation some will do just that, they will defy the beast and his international campaign to exterminate the Jews. Some will hide and shelter the wretched fugitives, at great risk to themselves. Those who do so will be "the sheep" of Matthew 25. David says: "Happy is he that hath mercy on the afflicted ones" because this will be the criteria of judgment in that day. "Inasmuch as ye have done it unto one of the least of these My brethren, ye have done it unto Me" (Matthew 25:40).

"The wicked in his pride doth persecute." Pride will be the supreme characteristic of the beast. Nothing but satanic pride will make him think that he can win in thus throwing down the gauntlet to God by seeking to exterminate His people.

C. The Wicked Man's Scornful Boasts (10:3)

"For the wicked boasteth of his heart's desire, and blesseth the covetous, whom the LORD abhorreth." The word "covetous" is inadequate; the Hebrew implies something much stronger than mere coveting. It carries the thought of appropriating by violence or injustice. Thus Hitler looted the Jews. The wretched victims exploited by the gestapo were told to bring their wealth with them when embarking for "resettlement." They were systematically robbed along the way— even their gold teeth being legitimate loot for the reichbank. Adding up the total cost of the holocaust to the Jews of Europe, one author came up with the figure of 55.5 billion dollars. The beast, in the expressive language of David, will "bless the covetous," that is, he will wholeheartedly endorse the systematic expropriation by violence and injustice the wealth of the Jews worldwide.

D. The Wicked Man's Stubborn Bias (10:4)

"The wicked, through the pride of his countenance, will not seek after God; God is not in all his thoughts." A man's face is the index of his soul. Abraham Lincoln was once asked to appoint a certain man to an important position. He said: "I don't like his face." "But the man isn't responsible for his face," argued the person putting forth the candidate's name. Said Abraham Lincoln: "Every man over forty *is* responsible for his face." What a face the lawless one will have! Written all over it will be sneering contempt, ambition, vanity, and incomparable pride. The sin of Satan will saturate his soul. Like Pharaoh of old he will cry, "Who is the Lord that I should obey His voice? I know not the Lord."

E. The Wicked Man's Spiritual Blindness (10:5)

"His ways are always grievous; Thy judgments are far above out of his sight: as for all his enemies, he puffeth at them." The lawless one will be so infatuated with his own importance that he will be blind to all else. Far above and beyond him, on a throne high and lifted up, will sit the eternal God, swaying His scepter across vast empires in space, pursuing His eternal purposes from everlasting to everlasting. His judgments are infallible and invincible, but the wicked one will be blinded to that. The possibility of retribution will never enter his head. As for his enemies, in the expressive language of the King James text, "he puffeth at them." Everything will seem to be going his way: Europe at his feet, the western hemisphere under his control, Russia swept away, and China, India, the East have made their peace with him. Enemies? Pooh!

F. The Wicked Man's Swelling Bigotry (10:6)

"He hath said in his heart, I shall not be moved: for I shall never be in adversity." He will believe he is invincible. John tells us that the world will say: "Who can make war with the beast?" It seems clear from Revelation 13 and 17 that the beast in his final manifestation will be a resurrected man.

The phrase: "I shall never" is translated in the Revised Version as, "to all generations": "He has said in his heart, I shall not be moved. To all generations I shall not be in adversity." He will think he can live forever in the power of endless supernatural, resurrection life and that he is therefore invincible. He will forget in his spiritual blindness and in his swelling bigotry that he is able to be cast alive into the lake of fire.

G. The Wicked Man's Spoken Blasphemies (10:7)

"His mouth is full of cursing and deceit and fraud: under his tongue is mischief and vanity." The word "deceit" is in the plural, "deceits." It expresses the abundance and the variety of his deceptions. With the coming of the lawless one men will be given over to what Paul called "the strong delusion." They will believe the lie. The beast will thoroughly deceive them with great lies all laced with swelling blas-phemies against the living God.

H. The Wicked Man's Secret Brutalities (10:8-10)

He describes him in a threefold way. He is a *bandit;* that depicts his *cruelty:* "He sitteth in the lurking places of the villages: in the secret places doth he murder the innocent: his eyes are privily set against the poor [the weak ones, the helpless]" (10:8).

He is a *lion;* that depicts his *confidence:* "He lieth in wait secretly as a lion in his den" (10:9a). As the lion lurks for its prey, and is strong and fierce, bloodthirsty and terrible, so is the lawless one. He is a true child of the devil, a true offspring of the old lion.

He is a *hunter;* that depicts his *cunning:* "He lieth in wait to catch the poor: he doth catch the poor, when he draweth him into his net. He croucheth, and humbleth himself, that the poor may fall by his strong ones [ruffians]" (10:9b-10). Again and again it is the poor he snares—the oppressed of verse 2, the weak ones of verse 8—prey to the craft of the lawless one.

All throughout this long section dealing with the lawless one, the Lord is concealed. Where is He? There is no sign of Him. The lawless one goes from one triumph to another and the saints of God are counted as sheep for the slaughter, as fuel for the fire. But then the tempo of the psalm changes. We have seen how the wicked flourish because the Lord is concealed. But no more! The Psalmist strikes a new note.

II. THE LORD IS CONCERNED
What the Wicked Forget (10:12-15)

God is not dead, He is not asleep, He has not gone on a vacation, He is not deaf nor blind. He is not remote and distant and uncon-cerned.

A. The Wicked Man's Scornfulness (10:12-13)

"Arise, O LORD; O God, lift up Thine hand: forget not the humble. Wherefore doth the wicked contemn [spurn] God? he hath said in his heart, Thou wilt not require it." This is a continuing problem—how a person can persist in unbelief. It is a problem which will become even greater at the end of the age when the devil's messiah is en-throned, blaspheming and ridiculing God.

But the acrostic is resumed and a new staccato beat is introduced into the psalm. God is suddenly brought back into the picture to give the lie to the wicked man's scorn.

Towards the end of the nineteenth century there emerged in Eu-rope a man who did more than any other single individual to pave the way for the coming Antichrist. His name was Friedrich Nietzsche. He was born into the home of a Saxony clergyman and both his father and mother came from a long line of Protestant ministers. His father died while he was still young and the boy grew up in a home dominated by women—mother, sister, grandmother, and aunts. By the time he was twelve he had rejected the orthodoxy of his parents. He blasphemously redefined the Trinity as God the Father, God the Son, and God the devil. This was the first step in a lifelong revolt against the beliefs imbibed at home. His philosophies were radical, violent, and disastrous both to himself and to society. He died a lunatic. His teachings led directly to nazism and the concentration camps. His great cry was for the coming of a superman. His book, *The Will to Power,* had a tremendous influence on men like Hitler. Nietzsche taught that Christianity was "the one great curse . . . the one immoral blemish of mankind." He hammered away at the lie of lies: "God is dead! God is dead! God is dead!" He called for the abolition of all morality. His most famous and diabolical work was *The Antichrist,* in which he called upon the world to recognize its true god and to fall at his feet.

God silently watched this wicked man's scornfulness. He judged him by having him locked up in a madhouse.

When the great philosopher died, one astute observer penned this couplet:

> "God is dead." (Signed) Nietzsche
> "Nietzsche is dead." (Signed) God

"Wherefore doth the wicked [spurn] God? he hath said in his heart, Thou wilt not require it." In the end the lawless one will learn what Nietzsche learned: God always has the last word.

B. The Wicked Man's Spitefulness (10:14)

"Thou hast seen it; for Thou beholdest mischief and spite, to requite it with Thy hand: the poor [the weak one] committeth himself unto Thee; Thou art the helper of the fatherless." Again and again the Psalmist sees the poor and the helpless as the ultimate victims of the lawless one. He will despise, detest, and exploit all weakness. His, indeed, will be "the will to power" so vehemently preached by Nietzsche. Power he will understand, respect, use, and exploit, but poverty and weakness he will ruthlessly trample down out of sheer malice and spite. This too God sees. "Thou hast seen it!" says David, "Thou [wilt] require it."

C. The Wicked Man's Sinfulness (10:15)

"Break Thou the arm of the wicked and the evil man: seek out his wickedness till Thou find none." Again the word for "the wicked" denotes the lawless one. The word for "evil" here (the "evil man") comes from a Hebrew word signifying the breaking up of all that is good and desirable. The corresponding Greek word is *ponoros* from which comes our English word "pornography," which speaks especially of moral depravity, corruption, and lewdness. These are the kinds of things the lawless one will promote.

David can clearly see, however, that even though He will allow wicked man to prosper, the Lord is concerned. David prays that God will break his arm, that God will render him powerless! He prays too that God's intervention will be so complete that by the time He is through not the slightest vestige of the lawless one's wickedness will be found on the globe. David's prayer will be answered during the millennium.

III. THE LORD IS CROWNED

What the Wicked Face (10:16-18)

God is still on the throne! One of these days that fact is going to be obvious even here on earth, the scene of His rejection.

A. The Lord Will Subdue the Heathen (10:16)

"The LORD is King for ever and ever: the heathen are perished out of His hand." We know how it will happen. The heathen nations will be drawn to Megiddo. The Lord will descend from the sky and His foes will be swept into a lost eternity. The lawless one and the false prophet will be flung into the lake of fire. Satan will be locked up, and Jesus will reign. He is going to subdue the heathen.

B. The Lord Will Support the Helpless (10:17-18)

"LORD, Thou hast heard the desire of the humble: Thou wilt prepare their heart, Thou wilt cause Thine ear to hear: to judge the fatherless and the oppressed, that the man of the earth may no more oppress." The "man of the earth" is the lawless one, but then his day will be done. Then the Lord Jesus will reign, He who said: "Suffer little children and forbid them not, to come unto Me: for of such is the kingdom of heaven" (Matthew 19:14). The Lord Jesus will reign— He who met the widow of Nain with the tear-drenched eyes, on the way to the graveyard to bury her only son, and turned her tears to joy. The Lord Jesus will reign—He who found poor blind Bartimaeus, with his beggar's bowl and his blind man's stick, and sent him away seeing and singing! Jesus will reign! "The LORD is King for ever and ever!"

"There!" said David, "send that to the chief musician." That is something worth singing about!

Psalm 11

WHY NOT RUN AWAY AND HIDE?

I. Fear is Conquered (11:1-3)
   A. David's Determined Trust (11:1)
   B. David's Developing Troubles (11:2-3)
II. Facts are Considered (11:4-6)
   A. Where the Lord Sits (11:4a)
   B. What the Lord Sees (11:4b-5)
   C. What the Lord Sends (11:6)
II. Faith is Confessed (11:7)

WE HAVE LITTLE DIFFICULTY in dating this psalm. It is a psalm of David and fits easily and naturally into his life when he served in the court of Saul after slaying Goliath.

David's early life was in three parts: *in the country,* the *formative* years; *in the court,* the *fateful* years when he never knew from one day to the next if he would still have a head on his shoulders; then *in the cave,* the *fugitive* years when he was chased from one end of the country to the other with Saul's bloodhounds ever at his heels.

In the *country,* David learned *worship;* how to *love God;* the country made him into a *saint.* In the *court* David learned *widsom;* how to *limit self;* the court made him into a *sage.* Again and again in this period "he behaved himself wisely," "he behaved himself more wisely," "he behaved himself more wisely than all the servants of Saul"—so much so that Saul feared David as much for his prudence as for his populari- ty. In the *cave* David learned *warfare;* how to lead men, to be a *soldier.*

Of the three periods into which those early years divide, the short- est by far was the period spent at court. He was hired first so that his harp might charm away the black, sullen moods which fell upon King Saul. Saul brooded on the thought that his dynasty would end with himself. David was later hired to be the king's errand boy, kept where Saul could keep an eye on him and send him on risky errands. Saul hoped that David would be killed on one of these expeditions.

It was at this time that David was married to Saul's daughter, Michal; that Saul's son Jonathan became his firm friend; and when the nation cheered louder for David than it did for the king. All these things increased Saul's suspicions and spite. More than once he threw a javelin at David in a fit of demonic hate.

It was during this dangerous, nerve-racking period in his life that David wrote Psalm 11. It is an appropriate psalm for those who are facing some great crisis in life and who may be tempted simply to run away and hide. The psalm is in three parts.

I. FEAR IS CONQUERED (11:1-3)

The Psalmist deals with his situation.

A. David's Determined Trust (11:1).

"In the LORD I will put my trust: how say ye to my soul, Flee as a bird to your mountain?" A bird is a very apt picture of a man who seemingly has no refuge save in flight.

Some years ago we had a little black dog named Sambo. Sambo's first self-imposed task every morning was to race around the house and clear every bird off the lot. As he came yelping, off they'd go, making for the branches of the trees, their refuge.

It was like that every morning—except one. As usual, he launched himself off the front steps with a preliminary yelp to announce that he was on the way. Around the house he came, expecting to experience his usual morning ecstasy of seeing birds fly off in every direction—expecting to return wagging his tail in triumph. But the impossible happened. A colony of blue jays dive-bombed him! They screamed and whirled about his head, made fierce dashes at his face, and pecked at his back legs. Sambo gave one frightened howl and headed for the shelter of the neighbor's porch. There he cowered, looking out between his paws until he was sure the coast was clear. Then he headed for home. But one of the jays was still watching for him. As soon as Sambo appeared this bird harassed him every step of the way!

David could have done what those blue jays did. He was a popular man in the land. He had slain Goliath of Gath. The women of Israel had chanted his praises far above and beyond the praises of Saul. David had a charismatic personality and he could have easily organized a revolt against the throne. Some urged him to flee like a bird to the mountain. He did neither for he was controlled by a *determined trust:* "In the LORD put I my trust: How say ye to my soul, flee as a bird to the mountain?" To flee at that time, without God's permission, would have been an act of mistrust in God.

B. David's Developing Troubles (11:2-3)

"For, lo, the wicked bend their bow, they make ready their arrow upon the string, that they may privily shoot at the upright in heart." The word "privily" can be translated "in the dark." They "shoot in the dark at the upright in heart." The bow and arrow is a coward's weapon. A person can conceal himself and destroy another person without his victim even knowing from whence the shafts are coming.

David is referring here to the malicious and spiteful stories which were being circulated about him at court. Saul did not have a more loyal supporter than David but Saul felt inferior to David. In his soul there rankled the shame and disgrace of Elah, when he had trembled in his tent while Goliath had boasted and blasphemed. He remembered how all Israel had looked to him, their own giant of a king. He remembered how this stripling had come whistling into camp with rations for his brothers and a merry laugh at Goliath. He remembered how this youngster had stood before him offering to fight Goliath and how, in desperation, he had allowed him to go. He remembered how ridiculous David had looked standing in Saul's armor—about six sizes too big for him and so heavy he could hardly move in it. He remembered David's asking them to take it off, and sauntering out of the tent swinging a slingshot in his hand.

Saul remembered his inner struggle of resentment, fear, admiration, jealousy, hope, and annoyance as David went singing into the valley. He remembered the sudden surge of wrath when the women of Israel sang, "Saul hath slain his thousands and David his tens of thousands." What more could David have than the kingdom? From that moment Saul's rage and resentment took root, growing into a tangled jungle in his soul. Eventually it would choke out every decent feeling in his heart.

Then, to have this fellow for a son-in-law and to have Jonathan infatuated with him! Didn't Jonathan know that David was his rival to the throne? Saul's soul was fertile soil for the whisperers, the backbiters, and the social climbers at court who could see in David only an upstart who threatened their own ambitions.

These are the men who shot the arrows barbed with poisonous suggestions for the ear of the king: "Watch out for that fellow David! One of these days he'll seize your throne! He's as sly as a fox, as slippery as an eel. . . ." "For lo, the wicked bend their bow, they make ready their arrow upon the string that they may shoot in the darkness at the upright in heart." David knew about their insinuations and lies, all poisonous and all aimed at destroying him and his destiny.

"If the foundations be destroyed, what can the righteous do?" David cried. The word "foundations" comes from a Hebrew word meaning "the settled order of things." David likened society to a building. The foundation of society is law and order, justice and truth. If law and order, justice and truth are undermined in a society then what can the righteous do? In the original text the form of the question is such that David can find no answer.

These are the very foundations which are being destroyed in western society today. Law, order, truth, justice, morality, decency, integrity. Humanist and libertarian views prevail in our schools, our courts, our government, and in the media. A determined attack is being mounted against everything decent, moral, and Christian in our society. The foundations are being destroyed to make room for the coming reign of the man of sin.

In his day, David's question amounted almost to a cry of despair. He could see the throne, the establishment, if you like, being undermined by unscrupulous and vicious men. What could he do? No nation could last where those in power listened to lies. David's personal fear was conquered, but he was greatly disturbed by the social and political implications for the nation. Israel was surrounded by enemies and King Saul was no match for any of them. The one man in the nation who could deal with Philistines was David and he was systematically isolated, insulted, and intimidated by men at court concerned only with their own political advantage. "What can the righteous do?" It is a cry of many a believer today.

II. FACTS ARE CONSIDERED (11:4-5)

David comes back to his basic position—he has put his trust in God. No matter what the problem, be it an individual or an international problem—God is sufficient. Facts are now considered, facts ignored by those who would destroy David.

A. Where the Lord Sits (11:4a)

"The LORD is in His holy temple, the LORD's throne is in heaven." It is so easy to judge by the appearances of the moment. Often it looks as though God has abdicated His throne, He is so strangely silent. Evil men and seducers wax worse and worse. But God is in His Heaven, that is where He sits and He has no end of options for dealing with wicked men.

Take for instance two alternatives which could be in God's mind for dealing with the situation today. The first option could be *revival.* There is nothing like an old-fashioned, Holy Ghost revival for cleaning up a corrupt society. The devil has never learned how to cope with revival for the simple reason he is no match for the Holy Ghost! One really good, soul-saving life-transforming, earth-shaking revival could put righteousness, morality, integrity, and faith back into every phase of human life and society.

In the eighteenth century, for instance, especially following the French and American revolutions, there was such a decline in vital Christianity that many concluded that Christianity's influence was about finished. But then in the nineteenth century came four great revivals which made an enormous impact upon society throughout Europe and the English-speaking world. Christianity again became a force to be reckoned with in human affairs. Enlightened legislation was enacted by governments, the world was invaded by missionaries and evangelists, social and family life were purged. It could happen again in the late twentieth century, should the Lord so decree.

Another option God has could be *ruin*. God could just as easily rapture the Church and let the wickedness work itself out to its logical conclusion in the coming of the Antichrist and the horrors which will attend his reign.

B. What the Lord Sees (11:4b-5)

"His eyes behold, His eyelids try, the children of men. The LORD trieth the righteous: but the wicked and him that loveth violence His soul hateth." God is not dead, He is not blind, He is very much alive and alert.

The reference to God's "eyelids" is interesting. When we want to look at something very narrowly we narrow our eyelids, half closing our eyes. Far from being indifferent to what was happening to David, the Lord narrowed His eyes, taking a sharp look at it. He was using the situation at Saul's court—just as He uses the situation in today's world—to try both the sinner and the saint. God puts men in the crucible in order to make them reveal themselves either as dross or silver.

C. What the Lord Sends (11:6)

"Upon the wicked He shall rain snares, fire and brimstone, and an horrible tempest: this shall be the portion of their cup." This prayer for divine retribution upon the wicked is not a vindictive, personal thing but a conscious realization that God and sin cannot continually coexist. God must punish sin or He must cease to be holy.

In the Old Testament the outstanding example of God's wrath being outpoured was the destruction of Sodom and Gomorrah. The judgment of the flood was more extensive, but the overthrow of Sodom and Gomorrah in the flaming fire was more intensive. Moreover, it is the Old Testament type of the judgment to come—judgment by fire. David could clearly see that sins which corrupt the very foundations of society simply cannot be ignored by God. And since He has pledged Himself never again to drown the world in water, the next time He acts in summary judgment it will be in flaming fire.

"Upon the wicked He shall rain snares," said David. God will first so entangle the wicked with their own wickedness they will not be able to escape the descending judgment of God. Thus it was that Pharaoh's heart was eventually hardened by God Himself. Thus Balaam was snared finally by his own lusts and perished with the people of Moab. Thus Haman was hanged on the gallows he had prepared for Mordecai. Thus the vile men who hammered at Lot's door were smitten with blindness by the avenging angels just before the wrath of God fell.

Thus *fear was conquered,* and *facts were considered.*

III. Faith is Confessed (11:7)

"For the righteous LORD loveth righteousness; His countenance doth behold the upright." Or, as some prefer to render that last clause: "The upright shall behold His face."

Whatever happens, the righteous person will win in the end. His final and everlasting reward will be to gaze upon the lovely face of the Lord in glory. Present circumstances may be dark but the future is magnificent. We shall see His face! It is the crowning bliss of glory. Thus truth, which became very precious to David, has been immortalized in the lovely hymn of William Cowper:

> Ye fearful saints fresh courage take,
> The clouds ye so much dread
> Are big with mercy and shall fall
> In blessings on your head.
>
> Judge not the Lord by feeble sense
> But trust Him for His grace.
> Behind a frowning providence
> He hides a smiling face.

So David wrote this lovely little psalm and sent it later to the chief musician for the temple choir. He adds this note: *upon Sheminith,* which means "the eighth." In 1 Chronicles 15:20-21 we read of the singers appointed by the chief Levites under David's direction and of certain ones who were to sing with psalteries "on Alamoth." We read of others who were to sing with harps "on Sheminith." The *Alamoth* were young women—those who sang the high notes. The Sheminith seem to be the young men—who sang the low notes. But what class of young men? What is the significance of "the eighth"? Old Jewish authorities suggest that the expression refers to a true class of Israelites—those circumcised on the eighth day as demanded by the Mosaic law.

So then here is a hymn to be sung by the young men because it called for special skill in handling the low notes. It was to be sung by those who were truly covenant members of the company of the people of God. The high notes are easy to sing, but only those who have been brought into a true spiritual relationship with God can properly sing the low notes of life. Can we?

Psalm 12

THE DECEITFUL MAN

I. DAVID'S APPEAL (12:1-4)
A. The Man of God Is Gone from the Earth (12:1)
B. The Man of Guile Is Great on the Earth (12:2-4)
1. His Deceitfulness (12:2)
2. His Downfall (12:3)
3. His Defiance (12:4)
II. DAVID'S ASSURANCE (12:5-6)
A. Its Greatness (12:5)
B. Its Guarantee (12:6)
III. DAVID'S ARMOR (12:7-8)
A. The Nature of It (12:7)
B. The Need for It (12:8)

THIS PSALM begins with the land being depopulated of its godly and faithful remnant. It ends with the lawless and the vile on the increase. Its great theme is deception and its author is David. But when did he write it? That's a question not even the scholars can settle.

Some think he wrote it during his days as a *minister under suspicion,* that is, during those trying days when his duties kept him chained to King Saul's courtroom—kept there really so that Saul could eye him, feed his resentments, and seek ways to kill him. Others think he wrote it during his days as a *man without a country,* that is, during those days when he fled here, there, and everywhere—now in the wood, now in the wilderness, now in the cave, now on Carmel, now in Moab, now in Gaza—but with his footsteps dogged and his movements ever reported to Saul. There are those who think he wrote it during his days as a *monarch in exile,* that is, during the days when Absalom seized the throne by stealth and drove him across the Jordan.

David certainly knew enough about deception. Constant lies were told about him at court. People he had befriended betrayed him as soon as his back was turned—the treacherous and ungrateful citizens of Keilah, for instance, and the Ziphites who cold-bloodedly planned to sell him to Saul. His own son Absalom deceived him and plotted against him and stole the hearts of his subjects. Ahithophel, his counselor and friend, betrayed him in such a monumental way he is etched upon the page of the Old Testament as a type of Judas Iscariot. Certainly David knew enough about deception, but what particular deception it was that prompted this psalm we do not know.

I. DAVID'S APPEAL (12:1-4)

David is conscious of deceit and the pervasive power of evil all about him.

A. The Man of God Is Gone from the Earth (12:1)

"Help, LORD; for the godly man ceaseth; for the faithful fail from among the children of men." The word for "help" is simply "save" and the word "ceaseth" can be translated "is no more." Save, Lord! For the godly man is no more. So said the prophet Isaiah in his day: "The righteous perisheth, and no man layeth it to heart: and merciful men are taken away, none considering that the righteous is taken away from the evil to come" (Isaiah 57:1).

This whole psalm can be viewed prophetically as referring to the coming Antichrist. Before he can come, however, as we learn from 2 Thessalonians 2, the godly must be taken from the earth in what we call the rapture. There is a hint of this great event here. Of course the Old Testament saints knew nothing about the rapture, but the Holy Spirit possibly hints at it here. "Help, Lord! for the godly man is no more. The righteous is taken from the evil to come." That is what is going to happen at the rapture. The deceptions of the last days cannot come to fruition until the godly are removed from the earth. From where we stand today that is certainly the next item on God's prophetic program.

David, of course, could not see this. David could only see, in his day, that wickedness and deception were on the rise and that it was becoming increasingly difficult to find a godly person. In all ages there have been those who have said with Elijah, as he stood in lonely isolation far from the haunts of men and pursued by the threats of Jezebel: "I, even I only am left." Such was David's first observation— the man of God is gone from the earth.

B. The Man of Guile Is Great on the Earth (12:2-4)

David tells us three things about this man.

1. His Deceitfulness (12:2-4)

"They speak vanity every one with his neighbour; with flattering lips and with a double heart do they speak." The Hebrew for "a double heart" is interesting—literally, a "heart and a heart." Woe betide the man who puts his trust in that kind of a person. He says one thing and means another and makes promises he has no intention of keeping. It is easy enough to understand the person who, under some great pressure, tells a lie and who afterward feels sorry about it and tries to put matters right. But the man who will sit down and tell a string of calculated lies is a man who has a heart and a heart. He is what we call today a "con man." Pity the person who falls into the snares of such a person.

Of all the double-hearted deceivers this world will ever know the coming man of sin will be the chief. He will be of his father the devil, a past master of deceit and, in the expressive language of Daniel, he will "make craft to prosper." He will be the author of *the* big lie.

Modern history gives us an example. "The greater the lie the more chance it has of being believed," said Adolf Hitler in *Mein Kampf.* The manipulation of truth was an essential part of Nazism. Behind the scenes, manipulating the media, orchestrating the propaganda for the Nazis was Josef Goebbels, the greatest liar of them all. He was the tactical genius behind the clever promotion of the party, the myth-maker, the creator of that halo of infallibility which allowed a petty politician by the name of Adolf Schicklgruber to become *Der Führer.* Goebbels with his personal courage, his tireless mental energy, his unfailing flair for propaganda, and his hatred of the human race perhaps did more than any person other than Hitler to foist Nazism on the German people. They were a pair well met—Hitler the politician and Goebbels the propagandist—and they were put on stage by Satan as a dress rehearsal for the coming staging of the beast and the false prophet.

Deception is to be Satan's masterpiece for the end of the age. The parable of the wheat and the tares shows three stages in the development of the coming great lie. There is to be a sowing, a growing, and a mowing. The very word "seed" implies life. The seed sown in the second of the mystery parables is the word not of God but of men. Christ sows His men into the field, the world (Matthew 13). Satan sows his men and both grow together toward harvest. The tares are beginning to reveal themselves in all their ugliness today. Why doesn't the Lord root out those tares? It's not yet time, the growing is still going on. Why doesn't Satan tear up the wheat? He can't. God has denied him that power. So what does Satan do? He does not try to persuade people that wheat is not wheat. They know better. So he imitates, he sows something into the world which looks so much like the wheat while it is growing that people find it difficult to tell the true from the false. When the growing is complete, however, the tares will be revealed, for their black crowns will stand out conspicuously against the bowed, golden heads of the wheat of God.

The *sowing* took place right at the very beginning of the church age, but the *growing* has been going on ever since. Satan's master plan for obstructing the Church and for hindering the work of the Holy Spirit can be summed up in one word—deception; especially religious deception. In the New Testament the word "deception" occurs nineteen times, always in connection with the devil and his work.

All the unregenerate, of course, are lost, but the *children* of the devil are apostates and false teachers and those who have given themselves over to the evil one to further his work. Jesus did not say that all the unregenerate were children of Satan. It was to the religious leaders of His day, those who were seeking to oppose Him and who were plotting His death, that He said: "Ye are of your father the devil." These are the kinds of people Satan is sowing in the world today, apostles of deception.

David catches just a glimpse of this. He sees the man of guile great on the earth. He sees his deceitfulness, that he has a "heart and a heart," a double heart, a deceitful heart. He sees him building his life on lies and deliberately, systematically, persistently deceiving. There were men like that in his day. He met them at each stage of his career and they were a source of great perplexity to his own open, transparent soul.

2. His Downfall (12:3)

"The LORD shall cut off all flattering lips, and the tongue that speaketh proud things." James quotes this verse on the sins of the tongue (James 3:5). In the end, lies and deception are always found out. D. L. Moody used to say: "Lying covers a multitude of sins— temporarily." Luther declared: "A lie is a snowball; the further you roll it, the bigger it becomes." Sir Walter Scott said:

> Oh what a tangled web we weave,
> When first we practice to deceive.

God never allows lies to prosper in the end. The man of guile eventually makes one false move too many. Whatever may be the appearance of the hour, God has emphatically declared that He will cut off the man of guile in the end. Such will be the doom of the Antichrist.

3. His Defiance (12:4)

"Who have said, "With our tongue will we prevail; our lips are our own; who is lord over us?" In David's case, the reference seems to apply to some who supported Saul or Absalom. They were putting David down so as to put themselves up. Both Saul and Absalom were susceptible to flattery.

This psalm, however, looks beyond David's time to the day when the man of guile will be boasting and blaspheming on the earth. With what sarcasm and scorn he will ridicule God in Heaven and His beloved Son! Men utter appalling blasphemies today, but no man who has ever lived will use invective and vilification like the beast. This then, is *David's appeal:* "Lord! The man of God is gone from the earth. The man of guile is great on the earth!"

II. DAVID'S ASSURANCE (12:5-6)

Now the Lord speaks, and with the sound of the Lord's voice comes assurance.

A. Its Greatness (12:5)

"For the oppression of the poor [i.e. the wretched], for the sighing of the needy, now will I arise, saith the LORD. I will set him in safety from him that puffeth at him." Now! The moment for action has come. God is never in a hurry, His patience is well-nigh inexhaustible, but now, now He is going to act. He arises from His throne and now there will be no sitting down again until He has made a clean sweep of His foes. All that man has been able to do, all that the enemy has been able to accomplish, all that the Antichrist will be is summed up in one contemptuous phrase—"him that puffeth"!

In creating the various creatures to inhabit our planet, the Lord seemingly did so with a mind to our spiritual and moral instruction. Consider the toad, for instance. What an ugly creature it is—squat, clumsy, covered with rough warts, a denizen of two worlds. Its skin carries poisonous liquid which it exudes when attacked. Its chief weapon of offense is its tongue which is attached to the front of its mouth. When the toad sees its prey it sticks out its tongue with a motion too fast to be seen. But, what is of special interest about the toad is a balloonlike sack attached to its throat. When it wishes to trumpet its presence, it fills this fleshy bag with air which it then forces across its vocal chords, making them vibrate. That is the bellowing one can hear at night near a lake. What a picture of man in his sin! Is not this the picture David has been painting for us in this psalm? Man, engineered by God for two worlds, but fallen and squat and ugly in his sin, full of poision so quickly released when attacked, and with a tongue swift and ready to seize upon others and destroy them.

As God on His throne looks down He sees the man of guile, particularly the coming man of guile, the beast, and He sees a toad. He sees a denizen of two worlds, a man with a heart and a heart, a man with a human origin as "the beast of the sea" and a man with a hellish origin as "the beast out of the abyss." He sees a man full of poison and with a deadly tongue. But He also sees a bloated windbag. "He puffeth!" That is God's assessment of this one who takes the world by storm.

That is the first part of David's assurance. Our attention is drawn to its greatness, which lies in the fact that it is *God Himself* who is finally going to act.

B. Its Guarantee (12:6)

"The words of the LORD are pure words: as silver tried in a furnace of earth, purified seven times." Such is the Word of God in contrast with the words of men. Men may deceive. God *cannot* deceive. His words are like a molten, shining river of silver, white hot in intensity, purified again and again. His Word is beyond all possibility of *any* taint or dross. Silver purified seven times has no trace of alloy; such are the words of God. We have a God who is utterly dependable, whose Word is thoroughly reliable. We can rest fully upon anything He says. It is here that David brings his faith to rest. And so may we.

III. DAVID'S ARMOR (12:7-8)

After God speaks, David speaks again. He puts on the whole armor of God.

A. The Nature of That Armor (12:7)

"Thou shalt keep them, O LORD, Thou shalt preserve them from this generation for ever." David's slanderous enemies have not yet gone away. They are still there armed with hate, but David does not worry about them any more. He has God's Word that He will act and in that armor David can sally forth to fight a giant even greater than Goliath. He has to fight the malicious, lying whisperer who has the ear of the king. Thus in a coming day those who know their God during the reign of the beast will be able to clothe themselves in a similar coat of mail. God has much to say about this period, many of the psalms relate to it. God has already issued His directives for that battle and the armor His own will need is already in His Word.

B. The Need for That Armor (12:8)

"The wicked walk on every side, when the vilest men are exalted." This is an observable fact in our day and age. We are entering a phase of life where a Sodomite society is emerging and where vile men are achieving public office; as a result, vile men everywhere are encouraged and emboldened.

This closing verse of the psalm cannot be exhausted by reference to either David's day or to ours. It looks ahead to the coming of the lawless one, the man of guile. Scholars tell us that the Hebrew of this verse is full of interest. The word translated "vilest" is really a feminine plural and comes from a root meaning "to shake" or to "be loosed"; that is, loosed or loose in morals. But why the use of the feminine plural to describe the vile men who will take over the earth in the days of the beast? Who can they be but Sodomites?

David sees a coming world culture akin to that of Sodom. No

wonder God is going to judge the world with an outpouring of His wrath such as has never before been seen on earth, not even in the days of Noah and Lot. The beginnings of this ultimate and final corruption of the race are upon us today.

But let us not leave it there. God says: "Now will I arise!" And so He will. The Lord will arise at any moment now to take us home; then He will deal with the world as it deserves!

Psalm 13

HOW LONG? HOW LONG? HOW LONG?

I. SORROW (13:1-2)
   A. His Seeming Abandonment (13:1)
      It seemed that God had:
      1. Forgotten Him
      2. Forsaken Him
   B. His Sorrowful Abasement (13:2)
      He has been brought low by:
      1. His Feelings
      2. His Foes
II. SUPPLICATION (13:3-4)
   He tells the Lord he is:
   A. Overwhelmed By His Emotions (13:3)
   B. Overwhelmed By His Enemies (13:4)
III. SONG (13:5-6)
   He is singing because of:
   A. God's Salvation (13:5)
   B. God's Sufficiency (13:6)

D AVID WROTE THIS PSALM when he was exhausted and depressed. His troubles with King Saul had gone on year after year and he was dispirited and discouraged. He had already been driven to desperate human expedients to escape his relentless foe. This psalm was wrung out of the extremity of his soul. He simply could not go on, not for another day, not for another hour, not for another minute.

Most of us have been right there at some time or another. It may be a long drawn out sickness or a financial problem of great severity or long standing, difficult, tangled, seemingly hopeless. It may be a wayward son or daughter, an alcoholic spouse, an unsaved loved one. It may be a situation at work, a demanding, unreasonable boss; a jealous, spiteful fellow worker. We'll probably find ourselves in David's shoes over and over again.

But man's extremity is God's opportunity. When we are at our wit's end, without resources, at a loss for a way, perplexed and desperate—*that* is usually when we see God begin to work. But before

97

He does anything about our *situation* He wants to do something about *ourselves,* and that is where we begin to hedge. We want God to *deal with our complication;* He wants to *develop our character.* We want Him to change our circumstances; He wants to change us first. That is why He allowed the circumstances. We cry: "Hurry up, Lord!" He says: "It's your move. I won't move until you do." That is what this little psalm is all about.

The psalm falls easily into three divisions. The keynote of the first division is the cry, "How long?" The keynote of the second division is the word "lest." The keynote of the third division is the word "but." We have *sorrow* (13:1-2); *supplication* (13:3-4); and *song* (13:5-6). Here we have the story of a man taken out of a horrible pit and from the miry clay, his feet set upon a rock, and a new song put into his mouth—all within half a dozen verses which can be read in less than a minute.

I. SORROW (13:1-2)

"How long? How *long?* How LONG? That is how this psalm begins. It starts with two interesting figures of speech. The first is called *erotesis*—asking questions without waiting for or expecting an answer. When driven into a corner by our circumstances we have all used this figure of speech in prayer, audible or unexpressed. How we love David for baring his innermost soul to us in this way! We have been there so often ourselves and have expostulated with God over His seemingly endless delays in the same way.

The second figure of speech is *anaphora*—repetition of the same word at the beginning of successive sentences. Its purpose is to add emphasis to statements and arguments by calling repeated attention to them. How long? How long? How long? How long? It is David's rhetorical way of saying, "Here, Lord! I'm talking to You. I'm trying to get through to You!"

When I worked in Chicago sometimes I would try to phone home. With a wife and three teen-age girls in the house, and one telephone, my chance of getting through was about one in four million! Many a time I put down the receiver in exasperation. You know what it's like! A busy signal. You call the operator and she tells you that your phone *is* in good working order and "No, sir, I can't disrupt a conversation unless it is an emergency." Nothing short of death, disaster, fire, famine, flood, earthquake, war, or pestilence is an emergency!

That is how David felt. How long? How long? How long? It was like getting a busy signal from God. So he uses this figure of speech to go around, as it were, and hammer at Heaven's door. Bang! Bang! Bang!

Notice two things which emerge from a study of David's spiritual frustration at this time.

A. His Seeming Abandonment (12:1)

It seemed to David that God had *forgotten him*: " How long wilt Thou forget me, O Lord? for ever?"

How swifty time flies when we are having a good time! We can hardly believe it when we look at the clock and realize that an hour, two hours, five hours have gone. But when we are in trouble—then time seems to creep by on leaden feet. And we cry "How long? How long?" Is this vain repetition?

Come for a moment to an olive yard, near the oil press in a garden at the foot of the hill called Olivet about half a mile from Jerusalem. It is late at night. The central Figure has three men with Him, His other eight friends He has left some distance away. One of His friends is at that moment rounding up a band of ruffians, in keeping with his bargain with the evil men who have bought his loyalty for the price of a slave. That central One, the Lord Jesus, speaks to His three friends: "Wait here, watch and pray." He walks on "a stone's cast" (the distance of death) silently and alone. He has come to Gethsemane. He prays, "Father if it be possible, let this cup pass from Me, nevertheless, not My will but Thine be done." Sweat covers His brow and His groans fill the garden, but Peter, James, and even John are sound asleep. Even human sympathy is denied Him in His hour of need.

The long night drags on. An angel comes from Heaven to strengthen Him for the anguish. He prays more earnestly. He is in agony and His sweat becomes as it were great drops of blood falling down to the ground. At last He goes to His disciples and they are fast asleep. He wakes them and urges them to pray.

Again He withdraws Himself that somber distance, about fifty yards, and again He prays, "saying *the same words.*" The moments creep by as He gazes into that dreadful cup. It is not the thought of death that crushes Him, but the thought of being abandoned by God. Here in Gethsemane, He is taking His first three sips of that dreadful cup.

Once more the lonely Man seeks out His human friends. It almost seems as though they are in a stupor. They blink at Him in the darkness. The Holy Spirit tells us that "they knew not what to answer Him." He leaves them to their sleep and walks silently, slowly, in utter isolation back to the worn, tear-drenched spot where He wrestled with God alone. And He prays again the third time *"saying again,"* the Holy Spirit records, "the same words."

When we find ourselves *there* let us remember that *He*, our great High Priest, knows the spot well—the place where it seems as though God has abandoned us.

David felt the Lord in heaven had forgotten him. Worse, he thought that the Lord had *forsaken him*: "How long wilt Thou hide Thy face from me?"

One thing we have to learn is that God is never in a hurry. The kind of work He wishes to accomplish in our souls can be accomplished only if sufficient time is given to allow His plans to ripen and mature.

Some time ago a friend took me through a plant where they make cars and trucks. Everything was geared to automation. The designers had done everything that human ingenuity could suggest to speed up the process of making a motor vehicle. The flow of materials was timed with mathematical precision, nothing moved out of sequence, even the men and women who handled the elaborate tools were trained to perform a single function, each one a specialist. One man knew how to put in windshields; another specialized in windshield wipers. As a result, cars rolled off the assembly line in a steady stream. Yet every vehicle moved at a snail's pace through the factory. It didn't matter if they were assembling the chassis or putting on doors or installing the dashboard—the car moved along from one process to the next at an exasperatingly slow pace. I watched the cars being painted and going from the painting room to the drying room. The engineers who designed that plant knew down to the second how long it would take for the paint to be fully dry; not until that exact moment was the car allowed out of the furnace heat. It went into the painting process dull and drab. It came out, at length, a gleaming thing of beauty. Everything was geared to speed, but at the same time everything was geared down to a snail's pace. A car was not forsaken at any stage. On the contrary, each stage was the result of the highest engineering skill.

Our seeming abandonment by God, when we hammer at Heaven's door, does not mean that we have been forgotten or forsaken. God knows what He is doing. The intensity of our trial is controlled from on high. He has something to teach us. He has an end product in mind. Things are moving forward but so slowly, from our impatient viewpoint, that we cannot see it. But He can.

B. His Sorrowful Abasement (13:2)

David had been brought low by his feelings: "How long shall I take counsel in my soul, having sorrow in my heart daily?"

If we have ever been through some great trial we know what David was talking about. If we haven't been there yet, we will be. Job said, "Man is born to trouble as the sparks fly upward." David was talking about that knot in the stomach, that lead-weight in the breast that makes the thought of food nauseating, that blights every joy as a cool winter's blast withers the summer's flowers. We can't sleep, can't eat, can't settle to anything. Every time we try to get our mind on some-thing else, back it comes—that gnawing ache inside.

At this point in his spiritual pilgrimage, David was no longer the master of his emotions, *his feelings* had brought him low. He had also been brought low by *his foes*: "How long shall mine enemy be exalted over me?" It seemed as though Saul was bound to win. He had the means and he had the power. The resources of the nation were being harnessed, not to fight the Philistines, but to hound and hunt David. The heat was on.

David was learning by experience the spiritual side of the law of thermodynamics—the greater the heat, the greater the expansion. Saul was a physical giant. David was fast becoming a spiritual giant.

II. SUPPLICATION (13:3-4)

In the first two verses, David had been crying out, almost incoherently and certainly emotionally. Now he turned to deliberate, rational, thoughtful prayer.

A. Overwhelmed by His Emotions (13:3)

"Consider and hear me, O LORD my God: lighten mine eyes, lest I sleep the sleep of death." He was so worn out with his long drawn out emotional drain that he was afraid it would bring him to an early grave.

But then he nailed his emotions to a glorious truth: he called upon God as *Jehovah my Elohim!* Jehovah—the God of promise; Elohim—the God of power. For Saul could never win! Had not Samuel the prophet taken the holy, anointing oil and anointed David as Israel's next king? David was going to reign no matter what Saul could do! In other words, David nailed emotions to the Word of God. Supplication brought a new dimension into the picture.

B. Overwhelmed by His Enemies (13:4)

"Consider . . . lest mine enemy say, I have prevailed against him; and those that trouble me rejoice when I am moved."

A speaker gave a graphic illustration in a totally different context at the Moody Bible Institute Founder's Week conference some years ago. When he was young he considered *himself* the world's greatest checkers player but there was an old man in town who was looked upon by the townsfolk as being the greatest. Our preacher friend was convinced that this was because he had never played *him*.

Well, one day this old fellow was sitting on the porch of his home when the young man went by. The old gentleman challenged him to a game. The young man dusted his hands. He'd show him! They put the pieces on the board; the young fellow made a couple moves and so did the old man. Then the younger player saw an opening and snapped up one piece after another of his opponent's men. He thought to himself: "Doesn't this fellow know he can't win by losing men like this? He's a pushover."

Then it happened. Suddenly the old man leaned over the board and—click! click! click! click! click!—five of the boy's pieces were swept away. The man had come all the way down the board. "Crown me!" he said. With a crestfallen look the young man crowned the old man's piece. Then—click! click! click! click! click!—with that one piece the old man took every checker the young player had remaining on the board. He learned the value of losing a checker or two as long as he was heading for king territory.

What a lesson there is in that for us today. We can afford to give up a few things in life if we are going for a crown. We don't have to have everything we want. We can give up a few liberties, such as watching hours of TV a night, or going to places of worldly amuse-ment, especially when we tell the Lord we don't have time to ponder and to pray. We don't have to have two jobs. We expect our mission-aries to live by faith. Why should they have to when we don't? We can give up a few loyalties. The devil is very clever. He will get us all wrapped up in good things, good activities, good commitments and see to it that these things take up our time, time that belongs first and foremost to Christ, secondly to our children, or to the church.

How much time do we really spend with the Lord? If our children have reached a point of rebellion and rejection, surely we need to spend a proportionate amount of time talking to the Lord about them, looking for answers in the Word, and seeking to build bridges to them. The greater part of any loyalty we have left should be devoted to building up the Church and particularly the local church where we find our fellowship.

David was fretting that the enemy might rejoice if he was moved, that the enemy might say, "I have prevailed against him!" What God was teaching him was the value of being utterly in His will. Then the moves, even when they looked like losses, would be eternal and glorious gains.

III. SONG (13:5-6)

David had moved to the final stage of the soul's experience in a time of trial and testing. He had come through tears to truth and through truth to triumph. Some people have wondered how David could swing so swiftly from gloom to gladness. The secret is found in the middle section of the psalm where he gets his eyes firmly fixed on the Lord his God, Jehovah his Elohim.

His song is in two parts:

A. He Can Sing Because of God's Salvation (13:5)

"But I have trusted in Thy mercy; my heart shall rejoice in Thy salvation." Is this salvation from sin? Probably that is included. Is this salvation from self? Probably that is included too. Is this salvation from Satan? Surely that is included. But probably this salvation is also salvation from Saul. David is standing now on the victory side. So can we, for our salvation includes salvation from situations—in the Lord's good time and way.

B. He Can Sing Because of God's Sufficiency (13:6)

"I will sing unto the Lord, because He hath dealt bountifully with me." Have David's actual immediate circumstances changed? No. Has Saul called off his bloodhounds and his bullies? No. Is Saul dead? No. Has David received a new shipment of arms? No. Nothing has changed. But David can sing because God hasn't changed!

Notice that David put everything in the past tense: "He hath *dealt* bountifully with me." The change in his situation is so sure David reckons it as already having happened. No wonder he could sing!

Psalm 14

THE DEPRAVITY OF MAN

I. THE SUMMONS (14:1-3)
  A. The Case of the Prosecutor (14:1)
     Man is guilty:
     1. In His Innermost Being
     2. In His Iniquitous Behavior
  B. The Calling of the Witness (14:2)
     1. His Person
     2. His Perception
  C. The Conclusion of the Judge (14:3)
     Man stands convicted because of:
     1. His Total Departure
     2. His Total Defilement
     3. His Total Depravity
II. THE SUMMATION (14:4)
  A. Man's Iniquity
  B. Man's Ignorance
  C. Man's Intolerance
  D. Man's Indifference
III. THE SENTENCE (14:5-6)
  A. The Fear It Registered (14:5a)
  B. The Folly It Revealed (14:5b)
  C. The Facts It Rehearsed (14:6)
IV. THE SUSPENSION (14:7)
  A sudden, unexpected:
  A. Note of Hope
  B. Note of Happiness
     is injected into the Psalm

I ONCE LOCKED MYSELF out of the house and, not having a second key, was obliged to force an entry by breaking a window. The frustrating thing was that my wife had a hidden key available if I'd only known where to look . That's the way it is with Psalm 14. It is easy enough to break and enter this psalm, but the best way in is to find the hidden key.

It is an observable fact that Psalms 14 and 53 are, at least on the surface, almost identical. However there are real differences between the two which become obvious when they are carefully compared. Psalm 53, for instance, is a *maschil* psalm, that is, it was intended for *instruction;* its purpose is somewhat different than that of its near-identical twin.

Psalm 14 is personal; Psalm 53 is private; Psalm 14 is pragmatic; Psalm 53 is prophetic; Psalm 14 is about the *past;* Psalm 53 is about the *future;* Psalm 14 was written by David; Psalm 53, while still an original Davidic composition, seems to have been edited somewhat (probably by Hezekiah) to suit the dark days in which he lived.

Psalm 14 has its roots in the *past.* David had received cruel treatment himself, so his sense of justice had been greatly honed and sharpened by the injustices done to him. The psalm's theme is the universal corruption of the human race, especially in the days before the flood, before the judgment at Babel, prior to the destruction of Sodom, and also in the terrible defiance of God exhibited by Pharaoh at the time of the Exodus. However, the actual key is not really found in Genesis and Exodus, but in Romans. It is there, in Romans 3, that the Holy Spirit shows us the best way to use the half-dozen verses of Psalm 14.

In Romans 3 we have God's court case against the human race. Paul's Spirit-inspired handling of that case is simply an elaboration of Psalm 14. The key to this psalm is a court case in which the eternal God presses home His charges against mankind. There are four movements.

I. THE SUMMONS (14:1-3)

The human race is hauled into God's court and accused of *total depravity.* Total depravity does not mean that each and every human being is a murderer or a sex pervert, nor does it mean that the worst of men cannot at times exhibit kindness and generosity. Total depravity, in the Bible, means that even the best men are tainted with sin. Sin is like leprosy: a leper may appear to be well and whole; his leprosy may be hidden at first, but the disease is entrenched in his body and it contaminates his very touch. Thus sin contaminates the whole man, taints all society. As a thrice-holy God looks at our lives He sees the sin that permeates our being. Even our best deeds are tainted by the fact that in our inner and essential beings we are sinners.

A. The Case of the Prosecutor (14:1)

In cases brought before human judges, the prosecutor begins with what we have said and done. That is all a human court can deal with—the actual words and deeds of the accused. The divine Prosecutor begins with what we *think!* No human prosecutor would think of resting his case by asserting: "This is what the accused *thinks.*" The heavenly Prosecutor does because He, the Holy Spirit, *can* read the thoughts and intents of every human heart. So the trial begins. The Prosecutor calls the accused before the bar and opens the trial. Man stands accused on two counts.

1. Guilty in His Innermost Being (14:1a)

"The fool hath said in his heart, There is no God." Two words here need explanation. The first is translated "fool." The Hebrew word is *nabal,* which denotes moral perversity rather than weakness of intellect. It is obvious that man is a brilliant creature. Along certain lines his achievements are astounding. He has developed the technology to put a man on the moon and to denature plutonium. But the unregenerate man is cursed with an ingrained moral perversity. He is a fool in his thinking toward God.

Also needing explanation is the word for *God* in verses 1, 2, and 5. In the original, the word is the usual one for God. Ancient Hebrew scholars, known as the Sopherim, say the name here was changed from *Jehovah* to *El.* In the original text, the name was *Jehovah.* "El" stands for God the Omnipotent, "Jehovah" stands for God in covenant with His people, God as He reveals Himself to men.

The full scope of the charge is not just that men say that there is *no God,* it is that they say there is *no Jehovah.* The person who says "There is no God" denies the *reality* of God; the person who says "There is no Jehovah" denies the *revelation* of God. The one becomes a *rationalist;* the other does not go that far, but he denies the evidence of the Bible as to the true nature of God and he substitutes his own concepts and creeds for divine truth and becomes a *religionist.* In other words, man is guilty in his innermost being of harboring wrong thoughts about God in spite of the fact that, as *Jehovah,* God has revealed to us just what He is really like.

In Montreal there is a replica, on a reduced scale, of the famous St. Peter's in Rome. While in that church some years ago I watched a devout woman lighting a candle to a dead saint in the hope that the saint would take an interest in her needs. I saw a well-dressed man in a business suit crawling on his knees from one carved statue to another, pouring out his petitions to the blocks of shapen stone. Both these people were undoubtedly sincere, but they were both guilty of approaching God in a way which He has condemned. There is no excuse for either of them for God has revealed His mind on these matters. The man in the business suit, for instance, would have to read less than eighty pages of the Bible in order to discover that God has expressly forbidden the making or worshiping of any kind of graven image.

"There is no Jehovah!" "There is no revealed God." "I have my own ideas about religion. Don't bother me with the Bible." Man is guilty in his innermost being of entertaining wrong thoughts about God.

2. Guilty in His Iniquitous Behavior (14:1b)

"They are corrupt, they have done abominable works, there is none that doeth good." The word translated "corrupt" is the same word used four times in Genesis 6 to describe the world of Noah's day—a world so vile that God had to inundate it under the judgment waters of the flood.

There are men whose works are vile even by human standards. A man who would take little children and sexually abuse them, get them hooked on drugs, or pollute their little minds is not fit to live. Jesus said it would be best for that man if a millstone were to be hung around his neck and he be cast into the depths of the sea. But there are people whose behavior is *virtuous* by human standards who are nevertheless pronounced corrupt by God and whose "goodness" God repudiates.

When I was a boy in school our work was graded on a numerical system. When we wrote an essay, the teacher would assign so many points out of a possible hundred for composition, so many for spelling, so many for handwriting, so many for originality, so many for grammar, so many for neatness, so many for factual accuracy. A perfect score was 100. Points were deducted for failure in each area being tested. Each student knew exactly where he stood when he received his mark. Usually the teacher would write some appropriate comment on the paper, according to the grade—"Fair" "Weak" "Very average" "Disgraceful." Only those who received a perfect score would have the comment "Good!"

Teachers in the United States often grade papers by letter rather than by number. This gives a lot more leeway. An "A" might be anything between 90 and 100, "B" between 80 and 90, "C" between 70 and 80. The final year's grade might be averaged in much the same way. Another system is called "grading on the curve," in which the highest in the class receives "A" and the lowest a failing mark, with the others where they fit relatively in between. This system often gives the under-achieving students a better chance to pass.

Well, *God does not grade on the curve.* God's standards are absolute. He has only two grades: "good" for absolute perfection and "failure" for anything else. That is why He says that there is "none that doeth good," that we have "all done abominable works." That's the case of the *prosecutor.*

B. The Calling of the Witness (14:2)

"The LORD looked down from heaven upon the children of men, to see if there were any that did understand and seek God." It is as though the Prosecutor says: "I need call only one Witness. When *He*

takes the stand it will be enough. I shall rest my whole case on Him.
I am confident that once He takes the stand, all defense will crumble.
I shall not even need to cross-examine Him. I draw the court's atten-
tion to two things about this Witness."

1. His Person (14:2a)

The Witness who corroborates God's charges against humanity is
the Lord, that is, *Jehovah:* the *Jehovah* of the Old Testament, the *Jesus* of
the New Testament. "The LORD looked down from heaven." His is
the eye of omniscience, the eye of One who sees everything. Nothing
is hidden from Him. All things are "naked and open before the eyes
of Him with whom we have to do."

David said "The LORD *looked down* from heaven." We would say
"The Lord *came down* from Heaven." We know what the result of that
was. Men nailed Him to a cross.

So this awesome Witness takes the stand, as it were, and all eyes
are fixed upon Him. He rests His hands upon the rail and it is seen
at once that those hands are *pierced.* This Witness knows whereof He
speaks when called upon to testify as to the guilt of man.

1. His Perception (14:2b)

"The LORD looked down from heaven upon the children of men,
to see if there were any that did understand and seek God [Jehovah]."
An ordinary witness on the stand may deliberately lie, even under
oath, or he might get confused under cross-examination. He may be
honestly mistaken in reporting what he saw, he might have seen only
a part of what happened, and of course he cannot possibly know the
motives or the hidden factors in the case.

But *this* Witness is infallible in His perception. He has all the attributes of deity. He is omniscient, omnipotent, and omnipresent. He
cannot be mistaken, He cannot lie, He cannot be intimidated. He
knows every man, woman, and child. He knows every thought, word,
and deed. He knows the time when, the place where, the how of
everything that has ever happened. He knows the motive and the
manner. He knows the intent, the impact, and the influence of everything we have ever thought or said or done. There never was a
Witness like this!

Indeed, so dreadful, so awesome is this Witness and so convinced
is everyone that the moment He speaks it will be to expose completely every human heart, *the case is not even tried.* There is no more to be
said. The Prosecutor rests His case.

C. The Conclusion of the Judge (14:3)

Since no defense is possible, since it is obvious that man is guilty,
the Judge now gives His verdict. And a terrible verdict it is. No

wonder the average unregenerate man hates the Bible! But attacking the Bible because it tells the truth is like kicking an X-ray machine because the picture reveals an internal cancer.

The Judge concludes that man is guilty on three counts.

1. Man's Total Departure (14:3a)

The human race is guilty individually and inclusively. The race as a whole, and man as an individual, have turned away from God and His Word. False religious systems, far from being expressions of man's desire to know God, are expressions of his departure from God. One and all they slander His real character.

Dr. Wilbur M. Smith, the well-known Bible teacher and author, once went into a drugstore. The man behind the counter was reading a book. Being an avid reader himself, Dr. Smith asked the man what he was reading. The man was embarrassed and tried to avoid the question. Finally he said: "This book cost me fifty dollars—this thin little book. Moreover, I had to make a statement to the United States Government that I was researching Hinduism before I could even get it into the country." It was with reluctance that he let Dr. Smith see the volume—a book of photographs of Hindu temple carvings with accompanying explanations. The pictures were so vile and the explanations so obscene that the United States Government, at the time, would not allow the book to be brought into the country without a sworn statement that it was needed for research. It was a religious book, but it was obscene and pornographic. That is but one illustration of how man has "gone aside."

2. Man's Total Defilement (14:3b)

"They are all together become filthy." That word "filthy" means "tainted." Sometimes my wife will open the refrigerator and say, "I think there's something bad in there," and she'll find a piece of leftover meat that has become tainted. It gives a bad smell! God says we are all tainted, guilty of total departure, of total defilement.

3. Man's Total Depravity (14:3c)

"There is none that doeth good, no, not one." Some years ago a doctor friend came to a home Bible class I taught. He was a decent, cultured, and educated individual. However, he had been raised in a godless home and knew nothing of spiritual things. One night he took exception to teaching regarding man's lost condition and inability to do anything good enough for God. He became angry. He refused to believe that the Bible said that he was not a good man. "I'm doing the best I can," he said. "I don't see how God can expect any more than that."

"Robert," I said, "You are condemned by your own religion. You

say you are doing your best, but that is not really true. Think of the
last time you gave a few dollars to charity. You could have given ten
times as much. You did not do your best, all you did was give a tip
to get the canvasser off your back. There has *never* been a time when,
if you had tried a little harder, you could not have done a little
better." He did not like it at the time but not long afterward saw the
truth and became a Christian.

"There is none that doeth good!" God's standards are absolute.
The only Person who ever lived who was truly good, whose whole
life could be summed up in the statement of one of His best friends,
"He went about doing good," was Jesus. He alone lived a truly *good life*
and He was arrested, was given a mock trial by three human courts,
and was crucified on Golgotha's hill.

II. THE SUMMATION (14:4)

The Judge sums up. His astonishment and His grief are very evident in what He has to say, for human sin is a dreadful thing. It not
only breaks God's *laws,* it breaks God's *heart.* God wrings His hands,
as it were, over our *iniquity:* "Have all the workers of iniquity no
knowledge? who eat up my people as they eat bread, and call not
upon the LORD" (14:4) It is almost as though God Himself were
astonished at man's state of soul. The word used for "iniquity" is
especially connected in the Old Testament with idolatry—the final
act of religious folly. He wrings His hands over our *ignorance* for, in
spite of all God has done to reveal Himself, we persist in thinking
wrong thoughts about God. He wrings His hands over our *intolerance,*
over man's persistent persecution of His prophets and His people. He
wrings His hands over our *indifference:* "They call not upon the
LORD," He says.

III. THE SENTENCE (14:5-6)

David is now acting as court reporter. He makes note of events
connected with the sentence rather than recording the actual sentence itself, for the sentence is a foregone conclusion. The law has
already demanded the maximum penalty.

A. The Fear It Registered (14:5a)

"There were they in great fear." The Hebrew text says: "They
feared a fear." Man is very bold and brazen in his unbelief as he struts
across the stage of time. But he will be gripped with stark, naked
horror when he stands doomed at the great white throne.

B. The Folly It Revealed (14:5b)

"For God is in the generation of the righteous." That word "generation" can be translated company, class, or circle. That is the

ultimate folly of the ungodly. For God is to be found easily enough. The Lord Jesus has promised: "Where two or three are gathered together in My name *there am I* in the midst of them." He can always be found in the circle of a company of His people.

C. The Facts It Rehearsed (14:6)

"Ye have shamed the counsel of the poor, because the LORD is his refuge." The wicked always underestimate those who are in the special care of God—the weak, the downtrodden, and the oppressed. The attitude people take toward life's unfortunate ones is an accurate measure of the attitude they take toward the Lord Himself. This, of course, will be the very criteria of judgment in a coming day in the valley of Jehoshaphat. "What did you do for the poor, the naked, the sick, the stranger, the imprisoned?" (Matthew 25:31-46) If we don't have a *faith that works,* then we don't have a *faith that saves.*

The case is over. The sentence is passed, the reactions are recorded, the court is being cleared, and the accused are being marched away to execution. But what's this? There is *another verse!* It seems out of place, *but thank God for it.* David adds a postscript.

IV. THE SUSPENSION (14:7)

A new fact has come to light and the court is hastily reconvened. A new and wonderful truth has been injected into the trial, and it is the *Witness* who brings it to the attention of the court.

A. A Sudden Note of Hope (14:7a)

"Oh, that the salvation of [God] were come out of Zion!" The Witness has dropped a bombshell! He has quietly reminded the court that God has a salvation for men, that He has devised a means whereby His banished be not expelled from Him. It is not just a *millennial* salvation (as the context indicates), it is a *personal* salvation. The court must take that into account.

B. A Sudden Note of Happiness (14:7b)

"When the LORD bringeth back the captivity f His people, Jacob shall rejoice, and Israel shall be glad." Again the emphasis is *millennial* but the application is *universal.* The same Saviour who will transform Israel *nationally* then, can save men *individually* now. God has a Saviour for sinners. The Witness has spoken sharply and to the point.

So all proceedings are suspended. The court will now wait while those who wish to avail themselves of this salvation step forward and file their claim. The suspension, that stay of execution, is still in force today.

Psalm 15

A GUEST IN THE LORD'S HOUSE

I. DAVID'S WORSHIP (15:1)
   A. A Pilgrim Worshiper
   B. A Permanent Worshiper
II. DAVID'S WALK (15:2-4)
   A. His Works (15:2a)
   B. His Words (15:2b-4)
      1. His Secret Words (15:2b)
      2. His Spoken Words (15:3-4)
         a. Restrained (15:3a)
         b. Righteous (15:3b)
         c. Respectful (15:4a)
         d. Reliable (15:4b)
III. DAVID'S WAYS (15:5)
   A. They Were Fair (15:5a)
   B. They Were Fixed (15:5b)

THIS PSALM stands in sharp contrast with its next door neighbor. In Psalm 14 we have the *polluted* man; in Psalm 15 we have the *perfect* Man. In Psalm 14 we have the *sinner;* in Psalm 15 we have the *Saviour.* Here in this lovely little psalm of David we have a beautiful portrait of the Lord Jesus. You will recall that Psalm 14 brings us into court and finds us guilty and under the dread sentence of a Holy God. But there was a stay of execution in that psalm, for a *Saviour* had stepped forward. Well, here He is in Psalm 15, in all His perfection and beauty.

There are good reasons for thinking the Lord Jesus used this psalm as the text for the Sermon on the Mount. The same subjects are treated and in more or less the same order as the brief outline at the end of this exposition shows. This is the first great fact connected with this psalm—it is David's "sermon on the mount."

Scholars believe that this psalm is closely related to Psalm 24, which was written to celebrate the bringing of the sacred ark of the covenant to Jerusalem. When David finally brought the ark into the city he placed it in a special tent constructed for it (2 Samuel 6:17). The arrival of the ark at Jerusalem would vest the city with special significance and sanctity. Such a solemn occasion might well prompt the writing of Psalm 15 with its probing inquiry into what kind of conduct should be expected of those into whose very midst Jehovah himself had come to dwell. That is the second great fact connected with the psalm—it celebrates the settling of God's ark in the city of Jerusalem.

There is another fact worth noting. For centuries the Church has linked this psalm with Ascension Day. Christ, having lived a perfectly holy life, passed into the presence of God, there to sit down on God's throne, at God's right hand.

Thus before we begin to analyze and explore the psalm we are confronted with a threefold truth indicating what God's people should be:

A Happy People. The bringing up of the ark was a happy occasion. We can visualize great crowds of people lining the streets as the ark entered the city, as they did centuries later when the Lord Jesus, the true Ark of God, entered Jerusalem amid the hallelujahs and hosannahs of the people. The people did not cower in dust as the ark made its way through the city. They saw David dancing before the Lord with all his might and were conscious that this was a *happy* occasion. God's people should be a happy people. This truth is underscored by the fact that at least four other psalms were written to celebrate the same great event (24, 68, 87, 105).

A Holy People. If this psalm was indeed the text for the Sermon on the Mount, no more need be said. Selfward, manward, and Godward, in character, conduct, and conversation we are to be holy. "Be ye holy for I am holy, saith the LORD."

A Heavenly People. The Church has linked this psalm with the Lord's homegoing to glory. That is where He is now, where we shall be soon, and where, positionally, we already are—in Heaven!

This psalm divides into three parts. The psalm itself grew out of David's feelings but its fulfillment was in David's greater Son. He alone fulfilled the moral and spiritual requirements expressed by David. The voice is the voice of David; but the vision is the vision of Christ.

I. DAVID'S WORSHIP (15:1)

"LORD, who shall abide in Thy tabernacle? who shall dwell in Thy holy hill?" These are two opposite concepts here.

A. Pilgrimage

"LORD, who shall abide in Thy tabernacle?" The word for "tabernacle" is "tent" and it refers to the tent David had just pitched for the ark on Mount Zion. A tent is a symbol for something transient and temporary. A tent is easily struck, is a movable house, the very symbol of pilgrimage in the Old Testament. Abraham, Isaac, and Jacob lived in tents although they were wealthy men and could easily have built palaces fit for a king. They were content, however, to live in tents, ready to move in a moment at the call of God.

God had become a Pilgrim down here. He pitched His tent on Zion. David longed to come into that tent, even though he knew that the massive ramparts of the Mosaic law were reared like a barrier to keep him out. Rotherham rephrases the first statement of this psalm. Instead of "LORD, who shall abide in Thy tabernacle?" he has: "Jehovah! who shall be a guest in Thy tent?" What a wonderful way to think of God. David saw Him as a Host, the kind of Host who would have none but noble guests. The rest of the psalm describes the kind of person who can expect to be God's guest. Let us remember we are God's invited guests at His table.

B. Permanence

"Who shall dwell in Thy holy hill?" A hill is a symbol for something permanent. David wanted to build something much more permanent for God than a tent on Mount Zion, He wanted to build Him a temple on Mount Moriah. He said to Nathan: "See now, I dwell in an house of cedar, but the ark of God dwelleth within curtains" (2 Samuel 7:2). A delighted Jehovah promised David that, for having such a good and generous thought, his house, his dynasty, should last forever.

So we approach God aware of these opposite truths of pilgrimage and permanence. We who have no lasting roots here can have them in God's holy hill. True worship withers our roots down here and establishes our foundation up there. The wheat dies downward as it ripens upward; the stalk and the roots are dead as the grain is ripe. As transient as wheat, we are passing rapidly from the earth in successive harvests. Pilgrimage is our lot down here; permanence awaits us over there.

"Who shall be a guest in the house of Jehovah? who shall dwell in Thy holy mountain?" David now answers his question.

II. DAVID'S WALK (15:2-4)

Alas, we know too much about David's life. We know he strayed from the straight and narrow path he now describes. But not so our Lord. The walk that David traced, Jesus trod. It is sad that we often see much more of the truth of God than we practice. David describes the *walk* of a man who would be the guest of the living God.

A. His Works (15:2a)

"He . . . walketh uprightly and worketh righteousness." The word "uprightly" is interesting. Here, for instance, is an Israelite who wants to bring a special burnt offering to God. He finds a fine, full-grown ram, one of his prize breeding stock, the very best in his flock. He runs his eye and hand over it to make sure it has no hidden blemish. He takes it to the priest who also gives it a careful examination. The ram is then slain and the priest exposes all the inward parts, sharply watching for an imperfection. But it is a perfect sacrifice, a ram "without blemish." That is exactly what the word "uprightly" means here. Translated into spiritual terms, the man who would be a guest in God's house must be without blemish; he must be blameless. His works must stand the test of the scrutiny of God.

B. His Words (15:2b-3)

David has much to say about this for here is where our blemishes reveal themselves most quickly. The Epistle of James has a remarkable test for a perfect man: "If any man offend not in word, the same is a perfect man, and able also to bridle the whole body" (James 3:2). The word James uses for "perfect" means something which has reached its end; something finished; there is nothing beyond. God is going to have no loose talk at His table.

1. His Secret Words (15:2b)

"[He] speaketh the truth in his heart." This is the first time the word "truth" occurs in the Psalms. The priest's dissecting knife is about to open up our inmost parts to inspection—our thoughts, desires, motives. He is looking for a man who not only speaks the truth but whose whole inner life is truth.

Have you ever had to meet someone you really dislike; someone against whom you had a grudge; someone who perhaps owes you money but who won't pay. You don't like this person but you have to meet him. You shake hands, you smile, you say all the right things: "How are you? How's your family? It's a lovely day, isn't it?" But down in your heart you are saying: "You thief, why don't you pay your debts?" The Lord is looking for truth in the heart.

God considers not only our secret words but also our innermost, hidden thoughts.

2. His Spoken Words (15:3-4)

"He ... backbiteth not with his tongue, nor doeth evil to his neighbour, nor taketh up a reproach against his neighbour. In whose eyes a vile person is contemned ... he that sweareth to his own hurt, and changeth not." The Lord here puts His unerring finger on four areas where we can sin with words. The man who would be a guest at the Lord's table must be marked by words that are *restrained:* "He that backbiteth not with his tongue" (3a). We have one modern word for that sin—gossip! And we have one modern instrument which is a handy tool for the spread of gossip—the telephone!

In that terrible catalog of sins, which forms the backbone of God's indictment of the human race in Romans 1, there are two kinds of people who are made to stand side by side, surrounded by murderers, fornicators, and homosexuals. They are (as the King James puts it) "whisperers and backbiters" or, as J. B. Phillips translates it, "whisperers-behind-doors, stabbers-in-the-back." That's the backbiter, a man or woman who stabs you in the back.

Backbiters murdered David Livingstone's wife as surely as if they had plunged a knife in her heart. They were never brought into court for it, for where is the human court which could convict a person of murder on the ground of gossip? Imagine an indictment reading: "The Accused: Gossips. The victim: Mary Livingstone. The Place: The vast solitudes of Africa. The time: April 27, 1862—sometime during the evening. The Weapon: Human tongues."

But they killed her as surely as if they had put arsenic in her tea. Mary Livingstone was never strong enough to be the constant companion of a pioneer. For years she struggled through the African bush, surrounded by hardships, seeing none but savage women. But with little children hanging on her skirts she could struggle on no more. She gave up and stayed home with her little ones to pray for her husband as he continued valiantly on. Then the gossips at the white settlements got busy. "Why would a man want to leave his wife and plunge into the interior save the desire to be as far from her as possible?"

Hearing the scandal that was being bandied about, Livingstone sent for his wife. She came, but the unhealthy climate of the river country with its fevers and malaria proved too much for her, and she died after being reunited with her beloved David for only three months. "Oh, my Mary, my Mary!" wept the brokenhearted man at her lonely graveside; but the gossips at the coast did not hear that. They had done their deadly work months before. God heard the desolate cry of His servant, however, and He gathered up those tears and put them in His bottle to await the judgment day.

The man who would be a guest at the Lord's table must also be a man whose words are *righteous:* "Nor doeth evil to his neighbour." The word "evil" comes from a root which implies the breaking up of all that is good and desirable. The Greek equivalent is the word *poneros* (from which we derive our word "pornography"). The word is used especially of moral depravity, corruption, and lewdness. The Lord doesn't want anyone at His table who tells dirty jokes: "He doeth no evil [pornography] to his neighbour." It is astonishing that even some professing Christians tell unclean stories. It reveals an unclean heart. The man who would be the Lord's guest must be one whose words are *respectful:* "In whose eyes a vile person is contemned [contemptuous], but he honoureth them that fear the LORD."

The word for "vile" is interesting. A silversmith or a goldsmith heats the metal until it is molten. The scum, the dross, rises to the surface and the smith treats it with contempt. He scoops it off and throws it away. It is worthless. That is the idea here.

The man who would sit at the Lord's table as His guest feels that way about the vile person, whose whole manner of life is contemptible. But in contrast he honors the godly man. He speaks of him with the greatest respect.

When I arrived at this point in the psalm I asked myself: "Who, in all the wide circle of my acquaintances is a man like that? A man whose whole life exemplifies this principle of speaking well of the Lord's people? Who, if not in the circle of those I have met in person, who of those I have met in my reading?" And I thought almost at once of Harold St. John. His daughter tells how he would not speak ill of any of the Lord's people or judge unless it was his business to do so. She has recorded two illustrations.

A group of young men once began to discuss in front of him a brother who had been causing a great deal of trouble. Mr. St. John remained silent. One of them finally turned to him and said, "Tell us honestly, Mr. St. John, what do you think of Brother So-and So?" The thoughtful brown eyes twinkled. "What do I think of Brother So-and-So? I think he has a perfectly charming wife."

On another occasion, when the conversation drifted to others who were causing controversy, someone spoke critically of them. Mr. St. John spoke out, "I have heard that some of these men have been much used of the Lord in evangelistic work in days gone by and were a great help to the saints of God. Shall we bow our heads in prayer." Then the conversation was shifted to a better subject.

The man who would sit as the Lord's guest must also be a man whose words are *reliable*. "He that sweareth to his own hurt, and changeth not" (15:4b).

I remember hearing Jim Vaus speak years ago at an annual Bible conference at Prairie Bible Institute. Arrangements had been made for him to speak at a little church in Gardena, California. A little later he received an invitation to speak on the same date at a large meeting in Boston and he was tempted to cancel the meetings at the smaller church. However, he felt that although he had "sworn to his own hurt" (or so it seemed), he must keep his word.

Sometime afterward he was interrogated by the FBI. "We have some bad news for you," one of the agents said, "We've orders from Washington to pick you up." Jim Vaus stared at them. "What for?" "Armed robbery." "Armed robbery? Where? When?" "Boston. January 17," the men said.

The FBI believed that Jim Vaus had pulled off one of the most famous robberies in the United States—the Brink's robbery. "We've been notified by Washington that you are one of the few men in the country who could have planned the job," said the FBI man. "You were in Boston on January 17, weren't you?" Jim Vaus pulled out his diary. "No," he said, "I was clear across the country in Gardena, California. It is true I was invited to be in Boston to speak at a rally there, but I turned it down. I was in Gardena and I have hundreds of witnesses." Jim Vaus had honored his word even though it seemed at the time to be to his own disadvantage—and it was a good thing he did.

III. DAVID'S WAYS (15:5)

There are two things said about the ways of the man who would be a guest in God's house.

A. They Were Fair (15:5a)

"He that putteth not out his money to usury, nor taketh reward [bribes] against the innocent." Bribery and usury are the two most common and flagrant sins against justice in the East. The wheels of justice never move in Eastern countries unless they are well oiled— then they move in favor of the highest bidder. The man who is greedy of gain and who is not too scrupulous about what he does to make money has no place as God's guest in His house and at His table; his ways must be fair.

B. They Were Fixed (15:5b)

"He that doeth these things shall never be moved." The man who lives according to the dictates of Psalm 15 will be God's guest, assured of a permanent welcome. Rotherham renders that closing clause: "He that doeth these things shall not be shaken to the ages." In other words, he will have a welcome, not only as the Lord's guest *here,* but He will be the Lord's guest *hereafter.* "I shall dwell in the house of the Lord forever!" said David in Psalm 23.

But where can we find such a man—the man who qualifies to be God's guest? Well, we shall have to cross over into the New Testament to find Him. The only Man who ever walked uprightly, working righteousness; whose innermost thoughts and whose every spoken word met the approval of God; whose words were restrained, righteous, respectful, and reliable; whose ways were always fair and whose path was firmly fixed was *Jesus.* He preached the Sermon on the Mount and then—under the all-seeing eye of God, and exposed to public scrutiny—He practiced what He preached. Then He passed His righteousness on to you and me. His righteousness has become our righteousness so that now we, even though we stumble, can come into His house and be a guest at His table. What was the gracious word of Paul's? "Let a man examine himself and so let him eat."

APPENDIX TO PSALM 15
THE PSALM AND THE SERMON ON THE MOUNT

Psalm 15 *The Citizen of Zion*	Matthew 5—7 *The Citizen of the Kingdom*
15:1 Introduction	5:3-12 Introduction
15:2 "He that walketh uprightly, and worketh righteousness, and speaketh the truth in his heart"	5:13-16 Walking in the light 5:17-20 Righteousness to exceed that of the scribes 5:21-6:34 Truth in the heart Heart hatred (5:21-26); heart adultery (5:27-32); heart generosity (6:1-4); heart prayer (6:5-15); heart fasting (6:16-18); heart treasure (6:19-21); heart service (6:22-24); heart rest (6:25-34)
15:3 "He that backbiteth not . . . nor taketh up a reproach against his neighbor" "Nor doeth evil to his neighbor"	7:1-5 "Why beholdest thou the mote that is in thy brother's eye?" 5:43-48 "Love your enemies"
15:4 "In whose eyes a vile person is contemned; but he honoureth them that fear the LORD. He that sweareth to his own hurt, and changeth not."	7:15-23 "Beware of false prophets. Ye shall know them by their fruits" 5:33-37 "Let your [word] be "Yea, yea; Nay, nay"
15:5 "Putteth not out his money to usury. . . . He that doeth these things shall never be moved."	5:38-42 "Give to him that asketh thee" 7:24-27 The wise man whose house is built upon the rock.

Psalm 16

SATISFIED

DAVID'S LIFE was always in danger during those turbulent years when he fled from King Saul. There were times when the danger was active and menacing but on the two notable occasions when David deliberately spared Saul's life, Saul called off the hunt and left David in peace. He was still an outlaw, cut off from his family, from his inheritance in the land, and from the religious life of the nation but his dangers were passive rather than active. Probably Psalm 16 was written during some such period. Danger there was, for as long as Saul reigned, subject to fits of insanity and goaded by courtiers who played on his suspicions, David would never be safe. But for the time being the danger has receded.

On the second occasion when David spared Saul's life, he retreated to an adjacent hilltop and called across the valley to the king. He held up Saul's spear and the flask of water which had stood beside his bed—graphic evidence that, but for his mercy, his enemy would even now be dead. Then David remonstrated with Saul and the language he used (1 Samuel 26:19-20) is echoed in this psalm (16:4-6), which seems to have been written about that time.

It is a *michtam* psalm. There are six psalms which bear this description, all are by David and all were written during the time of David's
rejection. The other five are Psalms 56—60. The word *michtam* has
been explained in various ways. Some think it comes from a word
meaning to engrave, or sculptured writing. Applied thus, the thought
would be that here something is preserved that should never be
forgotten. Interestingly enough, each of the *michtam* psalms preserves
the thought of resurrection. Some think the word *michtam* is mystical
in nature, "a psalm of hidden, mysterious meaning." Others say the
word means "a golden psalm." *Michtam* suggests that this psalm was
one of David's golden meditations, dealing with truth so significant
it should be preserved forever, although originally a personal, private
meditation.

No study of this psalm can be complete unless we see, somewhere
in its shadows, the glorious Person of great David's greater Son. It is
cited both by Peter and by Paul as referring to Christ. "Thou wilt not
leave my soul in hell, neither will Thou suffer Thine Holy One to see
corruption" (16:10) is clearly a prophecy of the resurrection of the
Lord Jesus.

We are going to look at the psalm, however, more in light of what
it meant to David and what it ought to mean to us.

I. THE PRACTICE OF THE GODLY MAN (16:1-4)

The first three verses give us three glimpses of the godly person.

A. Living in the Lord's Presence (16:1-2)

"Preserve me, O God; for in Thee do I put my trust. O my soul,
thou hast said unto the LORD, Thou art my Lord; my goodness
extendeth not to Thee." David uses three words for God in these two
short sentences. He is *El,* He is *Jehovah,* and He is *Adonai.*

He is EL. EL is an abbreviated form of the great name Elohim, God
the Creator. EL is God as the omnipotent, the all-powerful One. EL
stands for God in all His strength and might. David is living in the
light of that.

He is the LORD, that is, he is JEHOVAH, the God of Covenant. He is
the God who deigns to enter into a saving contract with men. David
is living in the light of that.

He is ADONAI, the Lord, or "my Lord." Rotherham renders the
name as "my Sovereign Lord" or, as we would say, "my King." David
is living in the light of that.

Let us bring the three names EL, Jehovah, and Adonai together.
We might say that "EL" is God *my Maker,* Jehovah is God *my Mediator,*
and Adonai is God *my Master.* Here is the protection of the godly man.
He is living in the Lord's presence so no fear can haunt him and no
foe can daunt him.

Note how David expresses it: "Thou art my Lord; my goodness

extendeth not to Thee." The word translated "extendeth" is in italics in the King James Version which means that the translators have supplied some words to make the sense. "Thou art my Lord. You do not need my goodness" is the way the Hebrew scholars who trans-lated the Old Testament into the Greek Septuagint handled it, and that is a wonderful way to render it.

Years ago, in a European kingdom, there was a poor widow who had a very sick child. She needed fruit for the child, but it was winter and fruit was costly and she was poor. One day she noticed fruit in the royal greenhouses but it was as inaccessible as fruit for sale in the stores. It so happened that the princess saw the widow gazing wistful-ly at the fruit and a few brief questions told her the whole story. In a moment the princess cut a large bunch of grapes and gave them to the widow, who offered a few pennies in payment. But the princess said: "I cannot take your money. My father is a king, and he does not need your coins. You can have these grapes freely or not at all." This is the thought which lies behind the Septuagint version of this verse: "Thou art my Lord. You do not need my goodness." Wonderful!

But other translators have rendered it in a different way. Rother-ham: "My sovereign Lord art Thou, for my well-being goeth not beyond Thee." The Revised Version: "I have no good beyond Thee." In other words, David confesses he has no well-being apart from God-Jehovah, his Sovereign Lord.

A wealthy Roman had a faithful and capable slave named Marcel-lus and also a son who was a disappointment to him. The Roman died and when his will was opened, it was found he had left all his estate to Marcellus, the slave. His will decreed, however, that his son could choose one item and only one from the estate before the will was settled. "I'll take Marcellus!" he said. By taking him he took all. That is the thought here: "I have no good beyond Thee." I have Him and I take all!

We follow the Septuagint and we find in our Lord the One who *saves:* "Thou art my Lord, You do not need my goodness." Or we follow the others and we find in our Lord the One who *satisfies:* "Thou art my sovereign Lord. I have no well-being beyond Thee." As the hymnwriter puts it:

> All that I need is in Jesus
> He satisfies, joy He supplies
> Life would be worthless without Him
> All things in Jesus I find.

The godly man is seen Living in the Lord's presence.

B. Living for the Lord's People (16:3)

"The saints that are in the earth . . . the excellent, in whom is all my delight." David had discovered by experience that it was better to find his delight in the Lord's people than to cultivate the great ones of earth. Jonathan, the king's own son, professed friendship for David and once indeed came out to meet him in the wilds to "strengthen his hand in God." But, immediately afterward, we read: "And David abode in the wood, and Jonathan went to his house" (1 Samuel 23:18). Jonathan, one of the great ones, was a broken reed after all.

The word translated "saints" means "holy ones" or "separated ones." It first occurs in Exodus 3:5 where God, speaking to Moses out of the burning bush, said: "[Remove] thy shoes from off thy feet, for the place whereon thou standest is holy ground." The same Hebrew word is translated "saints" elsewhere in the Bible. David, then, was not only living in the Lord's presence; he was living for the Lord's people. They were his delight. Are they ours? One of the first marks of a born-again believer is this: "Hereby we know that we have passed from death unto life because we love the brethren."

C. Living by the Lord's Precepts (16:4)

David was kept from evil aspirations: "Their sorrows shall be multiplied that hasten after another god: their drink offerings of blood will I not offer, nor take up their names [upon] my lips."

David knew about idolatry, he had been down to Gath and had looked at Dagon, the weird half-man, half-fish god of the Philistines. He had been down to Moab and had seen Chemosh, the bloodthirsty idol of the Moabites. The idolatrous times of the judges were still very much alive in everyone's memory in David's day. King Saul kept pagan men like Doeg the Edomite on his payroll. David wanted no part with that kind of thing. He was living by the Lord's precepts and this practice kept him from evil aspirations and associations. It will do the same for us.

II. THE PORTION OF THE GODLY MAN (16:5-6)

It is a double portion. David had a portion:

A. In the Lord (16:5)

"The LORD is the portion of mine inheritance and of my cup: Thou maintainest my lot." David was excluded by Saul's watchdogs from his share in the family inheritance. Each family in Israel had its territory assigned to it by line and lot by Joshua in the original distribution of Canaan among the tribes. The inheritance stayed in the family. David's share was in the farms and fields of Bethlehem but so long as Saul sat on the throne there was no hope he could enjoy his inheritance. His own parents were fugitives in Moab. "Never mind," says David. "I have a better inheritance. I have the Lord."

A beautiful story is told of King George VI of England, a born-again believer who, before his accession to the throne, used to visit a small brethren assembly in London and enjoy the weekly Bible readings. After he became king he had to discontinue this practice but he remained a devout believer in the Lord Jesus. In the course of his duties George VI came to Canada and his official visit took him to British Columbia. It was thought by the Canadian officials that King George might like to meet a native-born Indian chief. The one chosen for the honor was a well-known and influential Indian known as Chief Whitefeather. Chief Whitefeather was told to sing something for the king and, needless to say, the officials supposed he would sing a native war song. But the Chief was a Christian and had something else in mind. One can picture the surprise of the officials, when Chief Whitefeather began to sing:

> I'd rather have Jesus than silver or gold,
> I'd rather be His than have riches untold,
> I'd rather have Jesus than houses or land,
> I'd rather be led by His nail-pierced hand—
> Than to be the king of a vast domain
> Or be held in sin's dread sway;
> I'd rather have Jesus than anything
> This world affords today.

The stunned officials waited to see what King George VI would do. They did not have long to wait. The king went over, took Chief Whitefeather by the hand and said: "I'd rather have Jesus, too."

Said David, "The Lord is my portion." He also had a portion:

B. In the Land (16:6)

"The lines are fallen unto me in pleasant places; yea, I have a goodly heritage." David was a fugitive when he wrote that, with no home, with the moss for a mattress and the caves and forests for his shelter. How could he say: "The lines are fallen unto me in pleasant places; yes, I have a goodly heritage"?

But David was not forgetting. This was the language of faith. Years ago the prophet Samuel had visited the farm in Bethlehem, had poured the holy anointing oil of God on David's head, had told him he would one day be Israel's king. Nothing Saul could do could prevent that. Not just the Bethlehem farm—but all of Judah, all of Benjamin and Dan, all of Gilead and Goshen—all was his. Present appearances to the contrary notwithstanding, the lines had fallen unto him in pleasant places. And they have to us, too! If we suffer with Christ we shall also reign with Him. We have God's Word for it.

III. THE PROSPECTS OF THE GODLY MAN (16:7-11)

David's prospects were twofold. There were his prospects in *this* life (16:7-9), and his prospects in *that* life (16:10-11). They are the godly man's prospects.

A. In This Life (16:7-9)

1. Guided by God (16:7)

The godly man has the best of both worlds. He has three things in this life the unsaved person does not have. He can know what it is to be *guided by God:* "I will bless the LORD, who hath given me counsel: my reins [thoughts] also instruct me in the night seasons" (16:7).

Nearly all the old guidelines have been broken down today. Old restraints, old moral standards have been swept away and people are frightened, confused, lonely, and at their wit's end. They run to professional counselors for help as never before in history. They turn to the dark world of the occult and devour the prognostications of people like Jeanne Dixon, ignoring the fact that some of her guesses never come true. They are looking to eastern religions hoping to find answers there, all in vain. The Christian has it all over them. He can know what it is to be guided by God. In this life!

2. Guarded by God (16:8)

We can know too what it is to be *guarded by God:* "I have set the LORD always before me: because He is at my right hand, I shall not be moved" (16:8). In the old days when people fought with swords, a soldier defending another would naturally stand on his right. David could see the Lord standing on his right to defend him from his foes. That is something the unsaved man doesn't have.

3. Gladdened by God (16:9)

Then, too, the godly man can know in this life what it is to be *gladdened by God:* "Therefore my heart is glad, and my glory rejoiceth: my flesh also shall rest in hope" (16:9). Come what may, the godly man can lift up his heart and voice in song. In this life! Guided! Guarded! Gladdened! And these are just the fringe benefits of being a believer. These are things God gives us for this life. Even if there were no life to come, it would be worth being a believer just to have the peace, the rest, the joy God gives here and now to His own. But there's more to it than this life. Think of the prospects of the godly man:

B. In That Life (16:10-11)

Here the psalm takes a giant leap into the unknown—into that which cannot be known by human reasoning but only by divine revelation. David speaks of things that transcend reason. He puts his finger unerringly on two truths which had to await New Testament revelation to be properly grasped.

1. The Truth of Resurrection (16:10)

First, there was *the truth of resurrection:* "For Thou wilt not leave my soul in hell; neither wilt Thou suffer Thine Holy One to see corruption" (16:10). David could say: "My flesh shall rest in hope" because he could anticipate resurrection.

Old Testament believers did not have much light on the subject of death. They knew that hades claimed the soul and that the grave claimed the body. David believed that neither the triumph of the tomb over his flesh, nor the hold of hades over his soul, was final. Why? Because he had been such a godly man? Because he had accumulated enough merit to ensure his deliverance from death? No indeed! His faith leaps forward again, this time to Christ: "For Thou wilt not leave my soul in hell; nor suffer Thine Holy One to see corruption."

Great a saint as David was, he certainly was not God's "Holy One," the ideal Israelite. Only the Lord Jesus Christ can claim that title "the Holy One of God." The wages of sin is death, but Jesus was sinless so death and hades had no power over Him. His soul went down into hades so that He could proclaim in those dark regions the mighty triumph of His cross. His body lay for three days and nights in Joseph's tomb but corruption and decay could not touch Him. Then:

> Up from the grave He arose
> With a mighty triumph o'er His foes:
> He arose a Victor from the dark domain
> And He lives forever with His saints to reign.

There it is! David, with the eye of faith, with keen unerring vision, was able to see the truth of resurrection. He would live beyond the grave because of what the Holy One would do when He would bear away in triumph the very gates of death.

2. The Truth of Rapture (16:11)

David's prospects however reached beyond that, for David foresaw also *the truth of rapture:* "Thou wilt show me the path of life: in Thy presence is fulness of joy: at Thy right hand there are pleasures for evermore" (16:11). The path of life begins at the very lowest point in the dark regions of the underworld. But it leads up, out of hades, out through the portals of the tomb, up to the heights of Heaven, up to the right hand of God. That is the ultimate prospect of the godly man! Where is the Lord Jesus now? At God's right hand! Where are we going to be? At God's right hand! Where is there fullness of joy? Where are those "pleasures for evermore"? At God's right hand!

The Bible does not disclose what kind of pleasures they are except in barest outline. When I was a boy my father often went away on business trips. If he was to be away for only a few days he would often promise to bring us something when he came home. We would pester him. "What's it going to be? Is it going to be this? Is it going to be that?" Dad would usually reply: 'You'll have to wait and see!"

For the most part God simply says the same.

Psalm 17

LEST I FORGET GETHSEMANE

I. LORD, HEAR ME! (17:1-6)
   A. I Want You to Examine Me (17:1-2)
   B. I Want You to Exonerate Me (17:3)
      You know:
      1. My Wishes (17:3a)
      2. My Words (17:3b)
      3. My Works (17:4)
   C. I Want You to Exercise Me (17:5-6)
II. LORD, HIDE ME! (17:7-9)
   For You know how to be:
   A. Merciful (17:7a)
   B. Mighty (17:7b)
   C. Moved (17:8-9)
III. LORD, HELP ME! (17:10-15)
   Lord, I am going to:
   A. Tell You about My Circumstances (17:10-12)
   B. Trust You in My Circumstances (17:13-15)
      1. Lord Save Me! (17:13-14)
      2. Lord Satisfy Me! (17:15)

THIS PSALM is called "a prayer of David." David and his friends were being hard pressed by their foe but one enemy in particular stands out as a very lion for the ferocity and boldness of his attack. That enemy undoubtedly was King Saul.

A basic approach to a psalm is to ask what sort of man appears to have written it, under what circumstances, with a view to what dangers (if any), and with what feelings? With this psalm instead of asking who could have best *penned* it, we will consider who could have best *prayed* it. For this psalm is preeminently a prayer. The answer to these questions about its author leads us to a dark night, some two thousand years ago, to a garden called Gethsemane, and to the bowed form of One who, throughout a night of woe, wept out His heart to God. Now we do not know for sure that Jesus prayed this prayer that night. But we know He *could have*. Indeed, He is the only One who ever could have used some of the statements we find in this anguished cry.

Thinking through this psalm in the light of Jesus' long and lonely vigil in Gethsemane will give us a better understanding not only of the psalm, but of the heartache and pain of Christ's agony. Gethsemane was "the beginning of sorrows" for Him. Let us try to understand those sorrows.

I. LORD, HEAR ME! (17:1-6)

The sufferer begins by asking God to do three things.

A. Lord, Examine Me. (17:1-2)

"Hear the right, O LORD, attend unto my cry, give ear unto my prayer, that goeth not out of feigned [deceitful] lips." The first indispensable condition of real prayer is a good conscience. We cannot hope to get anywhere with God if we come to Him "tongue in cheek," as it were, simply putting on a show. He knows us too well. The Bible says, "If I regard iniquity in my heart, the Lord will not hear me." If we come to God with unconfessed sin in our heart or with the deliberate intention of doing something contrary to His mind and will, we might as well save our breath.

Lord, examine me. "Hear the right, O LORD!" That word "right" is the word for "righteousness." The brokenhearted Suppliant in the Garden knew the righteousness of His life squared exactly with the righteousness of God. Every line of His life matched the divine blueprint. The word for "cry" denotes a shrill, piercing cry that rends the night when an animal is stricken by its foe. It says something for the soundness of John's and Peter's sleep in Gethsemane that they were able to sleep through that piercing cry of anguish and pain. Lord, examine me! That was the first petition. It is followed swifty by a second one:

B. Lord, Exonerate Me. (17:3-4)

"Thou hast proved mine heart; Thou hast visited me in the night; Thou hast tried me, and shalt find nothing." The Lord Jesus is the only One who could ever have prayed such words as those. He opens up His life for inspection. He says, "Look at my life from all angles and exonerate me," even the thoughts that came to Him in the dead of night, when so often we find *our thoughts and desires* wandering off down forbidden paths. The Lord Jesus asks God to look and see if ever He entertained an impure, improper, impatient, impious thought. "Thou hast tried me!" He says. The word for tried literally means "proved," a word associated with the refiner.

Some years ago a friend of mine visited a gold mine in South Africa. He described the refining process as the gold was dug out of the darkness of the mine and prepared for the markets and bank vaults of the world. First, the gold ore was crushed as great machines took the alluvial rock which contained the precious metal and ground it to powder. The resulting mixture of gold and dross was given a chemical bath to dredge out as much as possible of the worthless deposits. Then it was put into a furnace where the fierce heat made the gold rise to the surface and the unwanted rock deposits sink to the bottom. The refiner skimmed off the semirefined gold and at once put it into another crucible to be heated again to the same fierce heat. When that was finished the refiner came and examined the gold. "It's pure," he said.

But then the assayer took the gold. He too put it into a furnace just as fierce as the gold had been through before. My friend told of his astonishment at this procedure. "Why is he doing that?" he asked the guide. "The original fire was to *purify* the gold," he was told, "the assayer's fire is to *prove* it."

There are some who believe that Jesus could have sinned and He was tempted by Satan to see if He would. Nonsense! In His incarnation, Jesus assumed everything that was essentially human, but He relinquished nothing that was essentially divine. God cannot sin. Jesus went through temptation—through fires and furnaces hotter than anything we could have faced—to *prove* it! He was sinless. He was pure.

But more! "I am purposed that my mouth shall not transgress." The word for "transgress" literally means "to pass beyond." This is probably the most common sin of the tongue—to say more than was meant, more than was wise, more than was necessary. Jesus never did that. Never once did He have to apologize for anything He said. "Lord," He says, "You know *My words.*"

He says, You know *My works:* "Concerning the works of men, by the word of Thy lips I have kept me from the paths of the destroyer" (17:4). The Lord Jesus lived His life according to the precepts of the Word of God. Every step He took was in complete obedience to the known and revealed will and Word of God. No wonder He could pray in Gethsemane, "Lord, I want You to *examine* Me and I want You to *exonerate* Me."

C. Lord, Exercise Me. (17:5-6)

"Hold up my goings in Thy paths, that my footsteps slip not. I have called upon Thee, for Thou wilt hear me, O God: incline Thine ear unto me, and hear my speech." The word for "goings" literally means "to go straight ahead"; "paths" means "tracks" or "ruts," "footsteps" comes from a root which means "to tap" and describes the rhythmic beat of a march.

Let us see how the Lord could have used words like this in Gethsemane. Before Him lay the greatest trial of all, a trial so dreadful that the Gospel records reveal that three times Jesus prayed that, if it were possible, some other way might be found, some other path, some other road. He knew that from Gethsemane the road pointed directly to Gabbatha and from thence on to Golgotha, where things were to happen to Him which made His holy soul shudder with horror.

Now look afresh at the Lord as He prays, perhaps, the words of this prayer: "Hold up My going in Thy paths! Help Me to go straight ahead! Let Me not swerve aside. Hold up My goings in Thy paths. Lord, I have made it the fixed habit of My life to obey You. It is a path I have beaten so often it has become a holy rut, worn deep and undeviating through all the years. Now, hold My feet in that blessed rut, right through to the end." There is the value of a holy habit. The Lord, in the last great crisis of His life kept in step with His Father. His obedience was such a fixed thing that not for one beat of the march did His foot falter.

We can see our Lord as the sweat covers His brow. He is looking down the road. He knows what lies ahead. "Lord!" He prays, "Examine Me! Exonerate Me! Exercise Me! Let nothing turn me aside from Thy will. Let me carry it through, right to Golgotha and the grave. Yea, and on to glory too!" Surely we should pray like that—that doing God's will might become an instinctive, intuitive thing in our lives, even in the face of testing, temptation, and trial. There are times in life when the enemy's attack is so pernicious, so persistent, so pressing that nothing but holy habit keeps us from disaster. That is the first part of this "Gethsemane prayer"—Lord *hear me!*

II. LORD, HIDE ME! (17:7-9)

We now draw near to the deepest mystery of Gethsemane. Like Moses at the burning bush we would remove the shoes from off our feet for the place whereon we stand is holy ground. We would draw near and hear our Lord pleading with His father to shield Him from the cross: "If it be possible, let this cup pass from Me." He knew that His prayer could not be answered, but He prayed it just the same. *That* is the mystery of Gethsemane!

Three reasons are given in the psalm why God should hide His suffering servants. First, hide me for You know how to be *merciful:* "Shew Thy marvellous loving-kindness" (17:7a). Nobody knew the Father like Jesus. He knew His Father was a merciful God, that His mercy was displayed not just in kindness but in the loving-kindness of God. But oh, the mystery of it! That marvelous loving-kindness had to be withheld from Him. "He saved others, Himself He cannot save," mocked the priests as they ridiculed the Christ on the cross. They did not know how squarely their arrows hit the target.

Hide me for You know how to be *mighty:* "Shew Thy marvellous loving-kindness, O Thou that savest by Thy right hand them which put their trust in Thee, from those that rise up against them" (17:7b). It takes us nineteen words to say but there is an astonishing brevity in the Hebrew where the whole verse contains just six words.

God saves by His right hand, the hand of power. This is the hand that held back the Red Sea for Israel, that guides the galaxies, that lights the evening star. The hollow of that hand can hold the waters of the seven seas but that hand could not be stretched out to save our Lord. Rather it would be lifted up to smite. No wonder Jesus wept and prayed. The writer of Hebrews refers to His midnight agony as "strong crying and tears." Hide me! Thou art a merciful God, Thou art a mighty God.

Hide me for You know how to be *moved:* "Keep me as the apple of the eye, hide me under the shadow of Thy wings, from the wicked that oppress me, from my deadly enemies, who compass me about" (17:8-9).

The Lord could see Judas leading the mob toward Him. His eye could see that crowd even then shuffling through alleys of Jerusalem toward the Golden Gate and the Valley of the Kidron. He could see them leading Him away, down the valley, across the Jericho Road, up the adjacent Valley of Hinnom, back to the city, and to the house of Caiaphas. He could see them all—His deadly enemies, Judas, Caiaphas, Pilate, Herod, the Sanhedrin, the soldiers. "Keep me as apple, daughter, eye" (as the Hebrew puts it) or, "Keep me as the little one of the eye." The phrase is one of great tenderness and endearment. Jesus used a similar term when He appealed to God as "Abba," a word which literally means: "Daddy!" We hear Him thus appealing to the tender depths of the Father's heart.

The same thought comes through in the cry: "Hide me under the shadow of Thy wings." It is a favorite Old Testament picture—a brood of little chicks running at full speed from that which has frightened them to a safe, warm shelter under the wings of the mother hen. There in Gethsemane, the Lord Jesus fled for refuge to the heart of God. He longed to hide Himself there from the appalling horrors now marching through the night toward Him. But there was no hiding place for Him.

III. LORD, HELP ME! (17:10-15)

The prayer now takes on a more dispassionate note, a new note of calm appraisal. It is as though the shaking sobs have ceased, as though all emotion is spent, as though now the great sufferer can calmly assess what lies ahead. He is still in prayer, still appealing to God, still wanting help but He is calm now. The seas are still running high but the fierce gales have subsided.

A. Lord, I Am Going to Tell You about My Circumstances (17:10-12)

He points to His enemies and says: "They are inclosed in their own fat." In other words, they are *prosperous.* "With their mouth they speak proudly." They are not only prosperous, they are *proud.* "They have now compassed us in our steps; they have set their eyes bowing down to the earth; like as a lion that is greedy of his prey, and as it were a young lion lurking in secret places." They are not only prosperous and proud, they are *persistent.* The Lord Jesus knew that His real foes were not the common people but the elite of the nation. And behind them was Satan, the lion, greedy for its prey.

There, in the presence of His Father, the Lord reviews the forces set against Him and assesses the mighty power of the foe. Prayer, in the garden, brought Jesus to the place where circumstances, threatening and fearful as they undoubtedly were, were simply put in their place.

B. Lord, I am Going to Trust You in My Circumstances (17:13-15)

In other words, nothing can happen that is not God's will. "Not My will but Thine be done" was the very prayer of Jesus in Gethsemane. He trusted God in His circumstance even though that "good and acceptable and perfect will of God" included a cross and a tomb. *That's* the way to deal with circumstances which are beyond us.

There in Gethsemane Jesus asked for the impossible. "If it be possible, let this cup pass from Me." God allowed Him to drink that cup to its bitterest dregs; but Calvary, the greatest tragedy in man's dealings with God, became the place of the greatest triumph in God's dealings with man.

Jesus prayed, "I am going to *trust You* in My circumstances." He prayed: *Lord, save Me* (17:13-14). "Arise, O LORD, disappoint him, cast him down: deliver my soul from the wicked, which is Thy sword [i.e., God uses even wicked men to accomplish His purposes]; from men which are Thy hands, O LORD, from men of the world which have their portion in this life" (17:13-14).

The Lord, now, on top of His circumstances, calmly assesses the men already on their way to arrest Him and the men already gathering in the house of Caiaphas to judge Him. He calls them "men of the world." The word "men" is an unusual one, literally meaning "full grown" men. The word for "world" means "age," literally "that which glides swiftly by."

Look at just one of those men—Judas. He was a man "full grown." In him wickedness and treachery had come to the full. Satan had entered into him and he was about to commit an act which would shame him for all the rest of time. He was about to betray Jesus with a kiss. He was a man of the world, a man of the age. He was riding the crest of the wave, but his moment was sliding swifty by. Jesus would be dead by three o'clock the coming afternoon; Judas would be dead before nine o'clock that very morning.

And, of course, Jesus did "disappoint" the men who plotted His death; when they had nailed Him to the tree, and then planned callously to smash His legs, He deliberately dismissed His Spirit and frustrated their wicked scheme.

The psalm ends with the plea: *Lord, satisfy Me!* "As for me, I will behold Thy face in righteousness: I shall be satisfied, when I awake, with Thy likeness" (17:15). Death was not the end! The full and glad assurance of resurrection lay just three days and three nights beyond the darkness of the tomb.

It was as a man already standing by faith on resurrection ground that Jesus confronted His foes when finally they crowded into the garden. "Whom seek ye?" He demanded. "Jesus of Nazareth," they said. "I AM," He replied. And they fell backwards before Him. It was a solemn warning to them of what they were doing. They took Him to the trial, to the tormentors, to the tree, and to the tomb. But:

> Death can not hold its prey, Jesus my Saviour!
> He tore the bars away, Jesus my Lord!
> Up from the grave He arose,
> With a mighty triumph o'er His foes.

As David puts it, Jesus awoke satisfied. He awoke bearing forever the likeness of God. The glory He had with the Father before the world began, the glory He had laid aside for a few, short moments of time, that glory He took again! He marched triumphantly out of Gethsemane, to Gabbatha. He marched victoriously from Gabbatha to Golgatha. He went majestically from Golgotha to the grave. He came magnificently up from the grave and on into glory! The sobs, the sighs were over! The future was in His Father's hands. God was in absolute control.

"There!" says David. "Send that to the chief Musician!" Let us have no more sobs and sighs. Let us now have nothing but songs!

Psalm 18

GREAT DAVID'S GREATER SON

I. The Rejected Prophet (18:1-19)
   A. Trusting at all Times (18:1-3)
   B. Travailing on the Tree (18:4-15)
      We see:
      1. A Tormented Person (18:4-6)
      2. A Tottering Planet (18:7-8)
      3. A Terrible Presence (18:9-11)
      4. A Terrified People (18:12-15)
   C. Triumphing over the Tomb (18:16-19)
II. The Royal Priest (18:20-31)
   A. His Authority (18:20-24)
   B. His Activity (18:25-27)
   C. His Ability (18:28-31)
III. The Returning Potentate (18:32-50)
   A. Reclaiming the Kingdom for God (18:32-42)
   B. Ruling the Kingdom with God (18:43-48)
   C. Restoring the Kingdom to God (18:49-50)

WE KNOW JUST WHEN David wrote this psalm. The title tells us this is "a psalm of David, the servant of the LORD, who spake unto the LORD the words of this song in the day that the LORD delivered him from the hand of all his enemies, and from the hand of Saul." At long, long last the outlaw years were ended. The civil war between David and Ishbosheth, too, was at an end. A united kingdom had crowned David at last, and David's enemies on every hand, those within the kingdom and those across the frontiers, had all bowed before his footstool. Nathan the prophet had come too with a wonderful word from God—because of David's love and loyalty to Him, the Lord would establish David's throne for ever.

This psalm is found twice in the Bible—twice because the Holy Spirit wants to emphasize it. It is found in the *history book* of Israel in 2 Samuel 22 and it is here in the *hymnbook* of Israel. There are a few minor changes, changes no doubt made by David's own hand when, with the Spirit's leading, he edited the former work and submitted the psalm to the chief musician as a piece for the temple choir.

David describes himself as the "servant of Jehovah," a title used of only a handful of people in the Bible. Moses, who led the people *out,* and Joshua, who led the people *in,* were both honored with this title. Preeminently, however, it is a title of the Messiah. He is the true Servant of Jehovah. It is thus that Isaiah describes Him and it is thus that Mark portrays Him. David calls this writing "a song," indicating that this composition, right from the start, was intended to be sung. It is the first of some fifty psalms so called. All the psalms thus inscribed seem to be psalms of victory.

There is one other item of interest in this superscription to the psalm. David tells us the song was written when it became obvious that never again would Saul's shadow fall upon him: "In the day when the Lord delivered him from the hand of . . . Saul." The word he used for "hand" is most interesting; literally it is "paw." We recall what David said when first he had stood before Saul, the day he went down into the valley to smite Goliath of Gath. Saul had looked him up and down and told him he was no use, he was just a stripling. David then recounted two secret victories and concluded; "The LORD that delivered me out of the *paw* of the lion, and out of the *paw* of the bear, He will deliver me out of the hand of this Philistine" (1 Samuel 17:37). He uses the same word "paw" here. Saul had become a wild animal in his persecution of David. God had delivered David out of Saul's paw!

So, then, we can look upon this psalm as a magnificent poem of David's triumph over all his foes and of his exaltation to the throne. However that view is the *history book* version and is best studied in 2 Samuel 22 as a review of David's life. Here we are in the Hebrew *hymnbook* so we are going to look at this psalm not as history but as prophecy. Instead of treating it as a review of David's life, we are going to see it as a revelation of Christ's life.

If we are going to look at this psalm from the historical viewpoint we would outline it as follows:

I. DAVID THE CONTENTED WORSHIPER (18:1-6)

II. DAVID THE CONFIDENT WARRIOR (18:7-45)

    A. The Providential Side to a
       Life of Victory (18:7-19)

    B. The Personal Side to a
       Life of Victory (18:20-45)

III. DAVID THE CONVINCING WITNESS (18:46-50)

Instead we are going to divide the psalm quite differently and see in it the life of great David's greater Son.

I. The Rejected Prophet (18:1-19)

When Jesus came to earth He came as that Prophet of whom Moses spoke. In His messages and in His miracles Jesus was indeed a prophet, a man "mighty in deeds and words." And, like all the prophets, He knew what it was to be rejected and slain. In this psalm David gives us a glimpse of all this.

A. Trusting at All Times (18:1-3)

No matter what happened to Him, no matter what people said about Him, our Lord's unfailing trust in His Father enabled Him to walk with confidence. "I will love Thee, O LORD, my strength." The word for "love" here is not the usual word for love. It means "to yearn over" and actually carries the thought of fondling. If we can say it reverently, the word suggests that the Lord wanted to hug God. We might paraphrase the verse: "Fervently—with yearning, with a desire to hug You—do I love Thee, O LORD." Have we ever felt like that? felt a surge of spiritual emotion come over the soul to a point where we wish we could just put our arms around the Lord? Mary tried to do that, on the resurrection morn, just simply hug Him!

Having told the Lord he wanted to hug Him, the Psalmist exhausts his vocabulary in telling Him all that He has been to him: "My strength, my rock, my fortress, my deliverer, my shield, the horn of my salvation, my high tower." Nine times He uses the word "my," which brings things where we are. While all like to use the possessive pronoun it is one of the first words a little child learns to use. It is "my" truck and "my" doll and "my" kitty and "my" everything. In this regard the Lord would have us become as little children—only He would have us elevate the possessive pronoun to the spiritual plane and say that the Lord is "my" strength and "my" fortress and "my" deliverer and "my" salvation and "my" high tower.

Jesus was a prince of the prophets because He knew how to trust God at all times. No matter how unfair and bitter the criticism, no matter how fierce and caustic the opposition, no matter how frowning and fearful the circumstances—He trusted at all times. "I will call upon the LORD, who is worthy to be praised; so shall I be saved from mine enemies" (18:3). His trust was always expressed in prayer.

There were seven great crises in the life of Christ—His birth, His baptism, His temptation, His transfiguration, His crucifixion, His resurrection, and His ascension. Study them and you will see the Lord in close communion with Heaven. He knew what it was to call and conquer, trusting at all times!

Next see the Rejected Prophet:

B. Travailing On the Tree (18:4-15)

History does not record a crime ever perpetrated with such high-handed injustice against so illustrious and sublime an individual, or ever carried out with such callous and calculated cruelty as the crucifixion of Jesus, the Son of the living God, by sinful men.

What David describes here is a great thunderstorm or some great convulsion of the earth. That is the historical setting for these verses, but when we think of the psalm prophetically our minds go straight to Calvary. We see three things.

1. A Tormented Person (18:4-6)

"The sorrows of death compassed me, and the floods of ungodly men made me afraid. The sorrows of hell compassed me about: the snares of death [confronted] me. In my distress I called upon the LORD ... and my cry came before Him, even into His ears." Prophetically this depicts the Lord's death.

In *Pilgrim's Progress,* when Christian and Hopeful came at last in sight of the Celestial City a deep, wide river barred their way. The sight of this river stunned the pilgrims who began to inquire if there were no other way to the city. They were told, "Yes, but only two, Enoch and Elijah, had been permitted to tread that path since the foundation of the earth." The pilgrims then asked if the waters were the same depth all the way across. "You shall find it deeper or shallower as you believe in the king of the place," they were told. So the pilgrims waded into the water and at once Christian began to sink. "I sink in deep waters," he cried, "and the billows go over my head." His companion said, " Be of good cheer, my brother; I feel the bottom and it is good." What Pilgrim experienced, however, was nothing compared with what the Lord experienced at the river, as described here in this psalm.

The word translated "sorrows" in verse 4 ("the sorrows of death") is rendered "breakers" by Rotherham: "there encompassed me the breakers of death." The breakers, the surging seas of death, came rolling in and swept over the tormented One we see in this psalm. Like Bunyan's pilgrim, the Lord cried out—a desperate, dreadful cry. It pierced through the atmosphere of earth, sped outward to the fringes of the solar system, on out beyond the stars, and echoed around the high halls of Heaven until it came to the ears of God. The only answer was silence. For the Lord there was *no* bottom.

2. A Tottering Planet (18:7-8)

"Then the earth shook and trembled; the foundations also of the hills moved and were shaken, because [of His wrath]. There went up a smoke out of His nostrils, and fire out of His mouth devoured: coals [of fire] were kindled by it." Historically this is probably a reference to the marshaling by God of the armaments of Heaven to rescue David from his relentless foe. However we are not looking backward but forward, not at history but at prophecy. Again we are brought to Calvary.

All nature was convulsed when men murdered their Maker. The darkness came down, the rocks rent, the graves burst open. We remember the portents that supposedly heralded the death of Julius Caesar. Shakespeare puts these words in Casca's mouth:

> O Cicero
> I have seen the tempests when the scolding winds
> Have riv'd the knotty oaks; and I have seen
> The ambitious ocean swell, and rage, and foam
> To be exalted with the threatening clouds:
> But never till tonight, never till now
> Did I go forth through a tempest dropping fire.
> Either there is a civil war in Heaven;
> Or else the world, too saucy with the gods,
> Incenses them to send destruction.
> Act I, Scene III

The portents which Shakespeare says surround the death of mighty Caesar were nothing compared with the portents which surrounded the death of Christ. God put His hand upon the *sun* and upon the *sanctuary* and upon the *stones* and upon the *sepulcher* and upon the *soldiers*. The planet earth tottered through space shaken to its very foundations. The sun in the sky hid its face in shame.

3. A Terrible Presence (18:9-11)

"He bowed the heavens also, and came down: and darkness was under His feet. And He rode upon a cherub, and did fly: yea, He did fly upon the wings of the wind. He made darkness His secret place; His pavilion round about Him were dark waters and thick clouds of the skies."

Here we approach the deepest mystery of the cross. The living God came down, not to *save* but to *smite* as, on the cross, the Lord Jesus became sin for us. The Psalmist hints at three things here. First he speaks of *the terrible majesty of God's coming*. He bows the heavens, He comes down from the realms of light to plunge the world into darkness.

He hints at *the terrible ministers of God's court*. The cherubim are His chariots. The cherubim are associated in Scripture with God's creatorial and redemptive rights. As the Shekinah glory in the Temple rested over the cherubim, so here God is described as coming down, riding upon a cherub. The sanctuary of sanctuaries in the Heaven of heavens is brought down, as it were, to that skull-shaped hill where men were crucifying their Creator. God's vengeance must surely fall— either upon the sinners or upon the Saviour.

The Psalmist speaks of *the terrible mystery of God's curse,* of the thick darkness. The Gospels tell us more. Out of that darkness came Emmanuel's orphan cry when Jesus was accursed for us.

4. A Terrified People (18:12-15)

"He sent out His arrows, and scattered them; and He shot out His lightnings, and discomfited them." These flaming fires of vengeance which played around the cross would have made short work of the multitudes who, moments before, had been mocking their Maker. God's thunderbolts of wrath, however, burst instead upon Jesus. At last the darkness lifted and the multitudes hurried away beating their breasts, humbled, awed, and terrified. They left behind them a battered form hanging lifeless on a tree.

The Psalmist gives us one more look at this *Rejected Prophet.* We have seen Him *trusting at all times* and we have seen Him *travailing on the tree.*

C. Triumphing Over the Tomb (18:16-19)

"He sent from above, He took me, He drew me out of many waters. He delivered me from my strong enemy . . . He brought me forth also into a large place; He delivered me, because He delighted in me." Death was the strong enemy, the strong man armed that kept fast his goods. Death had met its match in Jesus! Let the Romans seal the tomb and post their armed guard! God raised Him from the dead and sent His angels to fling open the tomb in defiance of priest and procurator alike—not to let Christ out but to prove that He was gone! So much for the *Rejected Prophet.*

II. THE ROYAL PRIEST (18:20-31)

We see this Priest in the place of power, seated there by virtue of His sinless life. We see Him controlling all that happens on earth, forcing men to face the consequences of their behavior. We see Him reaching out to save and secure a people for His Name. The Psalmist says three things about this Royal Priest. The language here, of course, goes far beyond anything David could say about himself.

A. The Royal Priest's Authority (18:20-24)

It is an authority based solidly upon the experiences He had as a man among men, and from the impeccable life He lived. His authority to function on high stems from His sinless life: "The LORD rewarded me according to my righteousness; according to the cleanness of my hands . . . . For I have kept the ways of the LORD . . . . I was also upright before Him . . . . Therefore, hath the LORD recompensed me according to my righteousness." Tested He was and tried, tempted in all points as we are, yet without sin. He can act with authority as a priest because He knows from firsthand experience what it is like to be a man living in a sin-cursed world.

B. The Royal Priest's Activity (18:25-27)

He is not remote and unconcerned about world affairs. He is actively engaged in the lives and actions of all men, be it the sinister lords of the syndicate, the strategists of the Kremlin, the prelates of some false religious system, or the man who runs the corner store: "With the merciful Thou wilt shew Thyself merciful; with an upright man Thou wilt shew Thyself upright; with the pure Thou wilt shew Thyself pure; and with the [perverse] Thou wilt show Thyself [perverse]. For Thou wilt save the afflicted people; but wilt bring down high looks."

If His *authority* as a priest rests on His humanity there can be no doubt His *activity* rests on His deity. Who but God can know the thoughts, words, and deeds of every man, woman, and child on the face of the earth? Who but God can control and overrule the consequences of all that men think and say and do? The Psalmist here pictures One in Heaven who is watching out to safeguard the interests of His own, One who counters all the moves of men with absolute assurance and with infallible results.

Most of us have played dominoes. You put down a six, I put down a six; you put down a two, I put down a two. The point of the game is to match perfectly the other person's play. That is what Jesus does. We call it *poetic justice*. The Bible is full of it. We see Haman being hung on the gallows he had built for Mordecai; we see Laban cheating Jacob who himself had cheated Esau; We see David reaping murder and adultery in his own family after he himself had seduced Bathsheba and murdered her husband.

When the Lord plays dominoes on a galactic scale it becomes far too complicated for us to follow. That is why we don't always see the principle of poetic justice at work; but we can be quite sure that "*whatsoever* a man soweth, *that* shall he also reap." Jesus, the Royal Priest, is insuring that all are treated with mercy and with judgment. In the end He will see that the law of poetic justice is impartially applied to all.

C. The Royal Priest's Ability (18:28-31)

However, the great activity of this Royal Priest focuses not so much on His *goodness* or His *government* as on His *grace*. We see Him imparting *newness of life* to men: "For Thou wilt light my candle: the LORD my God will enlighten my darkness." This Royal Priest reveals to men their lostness and lights the lamp of the Spirit in their innermost beings. He can impart newness of life.

We see Him imparting *nobility of life:* "For by Thee I have run through a troop; and by my God have I leaped over a wall." He not only gives us *eternal* life, He gives us *victorious* life. He makes us *warriors,* and He makes us *worshipers.* The word "God" in verse 31 is *Eloah*—the God who is to be worshiped.

III. THE RETURNING POTENTATE (18:32-50)

Yesterday Jesus was the *Rejected Prophet,* today He is the *Reigning Priest,* tomorrow He is coming as the *Returning Potentate,* the mighty Prince of Peace.

A. Reclaiming the Kingdom for God (18:32-42)

The speaker, of course, is David; the language is that of great David's Greater Son: "It is God that girdeth me with strength. . . . He teacheth my hands to war, so that a bow of steel is broken by mine arms. . . . I have pursued my enemies and overtaken them: neither did I turn again till they were consumed . . . . For Thou hast girded me with strength unto the battle. . . . They cried, but there was none to save them: even unto the LORD, but He answered them not. Then did I beat them small as the dust before the wind: I cast them out as the dirt in the streets." The word David uses here for "God" is El, the Almighty, God the Omnipotent, God in the concentration of His power.

Some have objected to this kind of language. They say David was exulting in war and that, after the crash and chaos of the house of Saul, he might have been more charitable. That is a slander on the character of David. Nobody was more charitable than David to his enemies. Did he not say: "Is there not yet left any of the house of Saul, that I might show unto him the kindness of God?" Of course he did!

This is not the language of pride, this is the language of *prophecy.* What we have here is a foreview of Armageddon. It pictures the day when the Lord will turn His hands to war, and cast His enemies out as dust. David foresees the day when the mighty *El* will skill His hands to a new and a dreadful work. The hands that will take and break man's weapons of war are pierced hands, hands pierced by men. We see Him, then, reclaiming the kingdom for God, and doing so not by converting the world but by forcibly subduing His foes.

B. Ruling the Kingdom with God (18:43-48)

"Thou has delivered me from the strivings of the people; and Thou hast made me the head of the heathen: a people whom I have not known shall serve me. As soon as they hear of me, they shall obey me: the strangers [the sons of the foreigner] shall submit themselves unto me." For:

> Jesus shall reign where'er the sun
> Doth his successive journeys run;

His kingdom stretch from shore to shore,
Till moons shall wax and wane no more.

C. Restoring the Kingdom to God (18:49-50)

"Therefore will I give thanks unto Thee, O LORD, among the heathen, and sing praises unto Thy name. Great deliverance giveth He to His king; and sheweth mercy to His anointed [His Messiah], to David, and to his seed for evermore." The Lord Jesus is David's seed. He it is who will restore the kingdom to God. The dark reign of sin will be over, Satan will be imprisoned in the abyss, the beast and the false prophet will be in the lake of fire, the world will be purged of the ungodly, and the remnant will bow the knee to Jesus. He will lead them back to God.

"There!" says David, "Send *that* to the chief Musician."

Psalm 19

THE HEAVENS DECLARE THE GLORY OF GOD

I. GOD'S REVELATION OF HIMSELF IN THE SKY (19:1-6)
  A. An Unmistakable Witness (19:1)
  B. An Untiring Witness (19:2)
  C. An Understandable Witness (19:3-6)
II. GOD'S REVELATION OF HIMSELF IN THE SCRIPTURES (19:7-14)
  A. God's Word Is Precious (19:7-10)
    1. It Challenges Us (19:7)
    2. It Cheers Us (19:8)
    3. It Changes Us (19:9-10)
  B. God's Word Is Powerful (19:11-14)
  It has the power to:
    1. Convict Us (19:11)
    2. Cleanse Us (19:12)
    3. Correct Us (19:13-14)
      a. It will Keep Me from Folly (19:13)
      b. It Will Keep Me in Fellowship (19:14)

DAVID WROTE THIS PSALM. But when? Did he write it as a shepherd boy on the Judean hills, lying on his back on a dark night and staring up into the star-spangled splendor of the sky? Or did he write it as a fugitive with Saul's bloodhounds baying on the distant hills? Or was it when he fled from Absalom to seek refuge in the wild wastes of the mountains? Or was it at some quieter moment when, pacing the roof of his palace, he once again lifted his eyes from the darkened streets of the slumbering city to the blazing pinpoints of light that studded the black velvet sky?

On a winter's night, David could gaze up into the heavens and see the constellation Orion—Orion, the mighty hunter with three bright stars in his belt and another group of stars for a sword. He could see the mighty club in Orion's hand used to ward off Taurus the charging bull. He could see hard on the hunter's heels the two dogs Canis Major and Canis Minor and he could see how bright was the larger dog's eye and perhaps would know that star by its name Sirius, the "dog star." Down in Egypt, Hebrew ambassadors paid court to Pharaoh. Perhaps David knew how much stock the Egyptians placed on

Sirius. The star's appearance, just before the sun in the predawn sky, heralded the flooding of the Nile.

So as a boy, as a hunted fugitive, or as a powerful king David wrote this great hymn and handed it to the chief musician for the edification and instruction of the people of God.

The psalm tells us how God has revealed Himself both in the sky—in worlds, infinite *worlds*—and in the Scriptures—in words, infallible *words*. God has revealed Himself in what He has *wrought* and in what He has *written*. He is the God of *creation* and He is the God of *revelation*.

I. GOD'S REVELATION OF HIMSELF IN THE SKY (19:1-6)

David's astronomy was probably very primitive, but he knew full well that the heavens were:

A. An Unmistakable Witness to God (19:1)

"The heavens declare the glory of God; and the firmament sheweth His handywork." The stars are God's *oldest testament*.

We picture Adam after the fall as he stands with Eve, clothed in animal skins, his shoulders drooping, wretchedness written in every line of his form. The gates of the garden of Eden have closed upon him and the cherub with flaming sword stands there to bar the way back to paradise. On the hills can be heard the savage roar of a lion and the high scream of an antelope as its death agony comes. Adam sees thorns and thistles already marching forward to curse the earth. The message of salvation through shed blood has been vividly portrayed for him by God but his memory and his intellect have already been impaired by sin. The evening shadows come and night descends—a night filled with fear, by beasts of prey. Adam shivers with fear and cold.

God draws Adam's attention to the stars. The heavens were to declare the glory of God in a new and significant way—in signs. Adam had named the animals; God had named the stars and in those names had written the gospel. Long before He wrote the gospel in the Scriptures He wrote it in the sky, in plunging planets and in blazing stars—the whole story of man's ruin and redemption. So Adam lifts his head and gazes upward to the sky. And lo, there it is, a vast volume filled with hope, written into the names and groupings of the stars.

Perhaps David knew something about the gospel of the stars, written in the twelve great books we call the signs of the zodiac. The twelve books make up an encyclopedia of prophecy in which was foretold the coming of the Redeemer. The twelve signs begin with the sign of the virgin and end with the sign of the lion. Some have suggested that the Egyptians invented the sphinx to preserve the truth; the sphinx has a human head and a lion's body. Christ's two

comings are thus immortalized in the sky—His first coming to redeem, and His second coming to reign; His first coming as the promised Seed of the woman, His second coming as the great Lion of God.
Prophecy commences with the virgin: "The seed of the woman shall
bruise the serpent's head." It goes on from sign to sign and from
constellation to constellation—the gospel, written larger than life and
in the constellations of space: "The heavens declare the glory of God;
and the firmament sheweth His handywork." There in the sky is
God's *unmistakable* witness to Himself.

B. An Untiring Witness (19:2)

"Day unto day uttereth speech, and night unto night sheweth
knowledge." David may not have known that the gospel was written
in the stars, but the very fact that they were there, great shining
worlds marching across the heavens, was an unmistakable witness to
God. And they were always there. They never grew tired of declaring
"the hand that made us is divine." They never tire! For stars are hot
and burning fires with massive stores of energy to consume. Our sun,
for instance, which is only a star of moderate temperature, bright-
ness, and size, is a vast powerhouse of ceaseless energy, a huge ball
of very hot hydrogen fired by an extremely complicated chain of
events. Astronomers report that the sun is capable of burning for
billions of years without noticeable reduction of heat or mass.

David knew nothing of proton-neutron reactions. He knew nothing
of galaxies which give off energy at such prodigious rates that scientists postulate the collision of galaxies as a possible explanation for
their energy output. David knew nothing of thermonuclear fires, of
hydrogen clouds and solar flares, of radio waves and cosmic rays. He
simply knew the stars were tireless in their testimony: "Night unto
night sheweth knowledge."

If the stars could speak with an audible voice they would borrow
the language of the poet:

> Gaze on that arch above;
>   The glittering vault admire.
> Who taught those orbs to move?
>   Who lit their ceaseless fire?
>
> Who guides the moon to run
>   In silence through the skies?
> Who bids the dawning sun
>   In strength and beauty rise?

The answer they compel is God, an omnipotent, eternal God. They
have an unmistakable and an untiring witness.

C. An Understandable Witness (19:3-6)

"There is no speech nor language, where their voice is not heard. Their line is gone out through all the earth, and their words to the end of the world." Scholars have had trouble with that! In the King James version three words are in italics, signifying they have been supplied by the translators and are not in the original text. They were inserted to help bridge the gulf between the Hebrew and English languages: "*There is* no speech nor language *where* their voice is not heard." Strip off these three words and you get a totally different sense, the sense of the original Hebrew text. Instead of a positive statement you get three negative statements: "No speech! No language! Their voice is not heard!" In other words, the starry hosts of Heaven do not speak in the tongues of men for they have no speech and no language. Their voice, though loud and clear, is inaudible to the human ear. Nevertheless those burning pinpricks in the sky communicate powerfully to all mankind.

The Psalmist draws special attention to the sun: "Up there is a tabernacle for the sun." He had watched it often. He knew just where on the horizon the sun entered its tent at night, just where it would emerge next day. He had watched it dissolve the darkness, chase the shadows from the hills, and fill the earth with light. He had watched it mount the sky and race across the meridian. He had watched it sink in fiery splendor to its nighttime rest. He had pondered its *coming,* its *career,* its *character.* The sun spoke to all men everywhere without uttering a single word in the languages of men.

In one of the world's backward countries a missionary had been trying to impress a chief with the nature and character of God. The chief pointed to his idols: "There are my gods. Now show me your God and perhaps I shall believe in Him." The missionary explained as patiently as he could that God is invisible, He can be seen by no human eye. To see Him would be to be blinded, so God veils himself from the prying eyes of men. The chief was unimpressed. "I can see my gods," he said, "show me yours." The missionary replied: "I cannot show you my God, but I can show you one of His messengers. Let me blindfold you here in your hut. Then I will lead you into the presence of the great minister of my God." The chief agreed. The missionary bound his eyes, led him from the hut, and told him to turn his face toward the sky. When he tore the blindfold away, the chief staggered back, blinded by the blazing light of the noonday sun. "That," said the missionary, "is but one of the *servants* of my God. That's why you cannot see *Him.*" The sun spoke a language even the chief could understand.

So David thrills to *God's revelation of Himself in the sky.* But there's an even greater revelation. The stars have their place, but God places no great stock in stars. In Genesis 1 He dismisses the creation of all the suns and stars and satellites of space in five brief words: "He made the stars, also."

II. GOD'S REVELATION OF HIMSELF IN THE SCRIPTURES (19:7-14)

By a process of reasoning man can learn about the stars. All he needs is time and patience and the necessary sophisticated instruments. So God doesn't spend much time in His Word on stars. Their size and weight, density and orbits, magnitude and behavior can be measured, plotted, and explained by man. That is what astronomy is all about.

There is, however, a realm beyond the ability of man to explore, beyond human reasoning, a realm in which man must grope in eternal night apart from the initiative of God. The witness of the stars tells us something *about* God, but if we are ever to know God Himself—what God is like as to His *nature,* His *person,* and His *personality* —then God must reveal Himself in spoken Word. The stars say: "God is almighty, He is eternal, He is omniscient, He is a God of infinite order and immeasurable power. The Scriptures tell us God is a *Person* who loves and feels, who knows and cares and rules. So David turns from what God has *wrought* to what God has *written.*

A. God's Word Is Precious (19:7-10)

God's Word speaks to life's greatest areas of need. It speaks with more authority and with greater insight than can the social scientist or the behavioral psychologist, the materialistic philosopher or the world's religious systems. For it speaks with the voice of God.

1. It Challenges Us (19:7)

"The law of the LORD is perfect, converting the soul: the testimony of the LORD is sure, making wise the simple." The verb for *converting* literally means "bringing back." As the sun returns in the heavens, so God's Word returns the sinner to God. He is brought back— converted! Wisdom replaces folly. The great function of God's Word in conversion is to enlighten a mind darkened by the world's philosophies and religions. It opposes all man-made theory with an authoritative, "Thus saith the Lord." It cuts right through to the marrow of the soul. The unconverted man rambles down all kinds of religious, philosophical, and ideological blind alleys. He has his own notions about sin, self, and salvation. God's Word has the power to challenge all that. It convicts and brings men back to the point of departure from divine truth. Then it converts the soul and makes wise the simple.

2. It Cheers Us (19:8)

"The statutes of the LORD are right, rejoicing the heart: the commandment of the LORD is pure, enlightening the eyes." God's Word cheers us, it rejoices the heart. Imagine having to face death and eternity without God's Word, without even so much as John 3:16 or

Romans 10:9. The Word of God takes away all uncertainty. It provides us guidance for today and promises glory for tomorrow.

Martin Luther tells us that when the words: "The just shall live by
faith" first dawned upon his darkened soul it was "like entering into
paradise." The words are his. "Before those words broke upon my
mind, I hated God and was angry with Him because, not content with
frightening us sinners by the law and by the miseries of life, He still
further increased our torture by the gospel. But when, by the Spirit
of God, I understood those words 'the just shall live by faith'—then
I felt born again, like a new man. I entered in by the open doors *into
the very paradise of God.* In very truth this text was to me the *true gate
of paradise.*" As the hymnwriter put it:

> Heaven above was deeper blue,
>   Earth around was brighter green,
> Something lived in every hue.
>   Christless eyes had never seen.

So God's Word challenges us and it cheers us. No wonder it is
precious!

3. It Changes Us (19:9-10)

"The fear of the LORD is clean, enduring for ever: the judgments
of the LORD are true and righteous altogether. More to be desired are
they than gold, yea, than much fine gold: sweeter also than honey
and the honeycomb." God's Word has a *cleansing* effect upon us and
it has a *consecrating* effect upon us. The man who once craved for gold
now craves for God.

Take the case of Zaccheus. What a covetous old sinner he was. For
financial gain he had sold his soul to Rome by purchasing the right
to collect taxes. His job was to turn in to his imperial masters a fixed
amount. Caesar didn't care how much extra he collected. Indeed, the
extra was his pay. So Zaccheus waxed rich by squeezing money out
of the poor. But then Zaccheus met Christ and Zaccheus was changed.
Then and there he pledged away half his estate to the poor, and in
addition determined to restore to every person he had wronged 400
percent. Clean and consecrated, Zaccheus beamed into the face of
Jesus, the living Word of God. That is the change God can effect in
a man's life.

B. God's Word is Powerful (19:11-14)

The Bible is not like any other book. J. B. Phillips confesses in the
introduction to his *Letters to Young Churches* that when he first began
to translate the New Testament he did not believe in the plenary
verbal inspiration of the Scriptures. But in the process of translating
it he received so many shocks from the New Testament that he
changed his mind. The material he was handling had power. He said

that translating it was like trying to rewire a house without pulling the main switch. God's Word is powerful.

1. Power to Convict Us (19:11)

"By them is Thy servant warned." As one translator renders that, "even thine own servants find warning in them." The Word of God has an uncanny way of confronting us with our sin. The Holy Spirit uses it like a surgeon's knife to slice away all surface things and reveal the cancers of the soul. As someone has said: "This book will keep you from sin, or sin will keep you from this book."

2. Power to Cleanse Us (19:12)

"Who can understand his errors? cleanse Thou me from secret faults." If a person reads a dirty book it will sully his mind; if he reads anti-Semitic literature he will soon come to hate the Jews. This is the principle behind all propaganda. If a person reads the Bible it will cleanse him.

There are two kinds of cleansing. There is a *radical cleansing* from sin that depends on the blood of Christ. There is also a *recurrent cleansing* from sin that depends on the Word of God. This recurrent cleansing was centered in Old Testament times in the laver, first in the Tabernacle and then in the Temple. The laver was made of the mirrors of the women and filled with water. Thus it both *revealed* defilement and it *removed* defilement. It symbolized the cleansing function of the Word of God. We need to spend time daily reading God's Word so that its convicting and cleansing action might act upon our souls.

3. Power to Correct Us (19:13-14)

Here David underlines two facts about the Word. It will keep us *from folly:* "Keep back Thy servant also from presumptuous sins; let them not have dominion over me: then shall I be upright, and I shall be innocent from the great transgression." Think of it—*washed* from unwitting sins and *withheld* from presumptuous sins!

A lady once asked a captain if he knew where all the rocks and shallows were in the sea. "Oh no!" he said, pointing to his chart, "but I know where the deep water is." God's Word is a chart which will steer us clear of the rocks. David knew about presumptuous sins. They had all but wrecked his life.

God's Word has the power to correct us. It will keep us *in fellowship:* "Let the words of my mouth, and the meditation of my heart, be acceptable in Thy sight, O LORD, my strength, and my redeemer." What a prayer to pray every day! Such a prayer must bring joy to the heart of God.

"There!" says David, "Send that one to the chief Musician."

Psalm 20

WHEN A NATION GOES TO WAR

I. The People Want Help From Their Leader (20:1-5)
They want their leader to be one who is:
A. Looking to God (20:1-3)
One who is:
1. Prayerfully in Touch with God (20:1)
2. Powerfully in Touch with God (20:2)
3. Properly in Touch with God (20:3)
B. Listening to God (20:4-5)
So that he might:
1. Plan the Battle Aright (20:4)
2. Pursue the Battle Aright (20:5)
II. The Prince Wants Help From The Lord (20:6-9)
A. The Truth He Expressed (20:6)
B. The Trust He Exercised (20:7)
C. The Triumph He Expected (20:8-9)
1. Total Deliverance (20:8)
2. Total Dependence (20:9)

WAR IS A TERRIBLE THING. It is the scourge of mankind. Every right-minded man would prefer peace to war but there are times when war is inevitable and the only possible answer to circumstances that have no other solution.

Throughout history God has frequently used war as His whip with which to chastise rebellious nations. Indeed, as we read through the Old Testament, we cannot help but see how frequently God's people, Israel, were at war. The pages of Hebrew history ring with the din of strife.

When God emancipated Israel from Egyptian bondage, He led them straight into battle. He smashed, for them, the flower of the Egyptian army. He swept Amalek away before the edge of Joshua's sword. He made it clear that Canaan was to be theirs only as the prize of battle. God told Israel He was using the edge of their sword as a surgeon uses a knife—to clear out from the human race the great festering cancer of the Canaanites.

151

The books of Judges, Samuel, Kings, and Chronicles tell of a nation constantly at war. David, Israel's greatest king, was a warrior king. The great events in the histories of even the godly kings of Judah descended from David—men like Jehoshaphat and Hezekiah and Josiah—were all connected with war.

In the New Testament, Jesus clearly foresaw an end to the Roman peace which held the world in a state of precarious rest in His day. As His vision expanded to take in the end of the age, He prophesied a new kind of "total war"—nation rising against nation and kingdom against kingdom. The book of Revelation resounds with battle from end to end, and it goes on until at last the book ends with a city of peace coming down from on high, where they study war no more.

Psalm 20 is a *prelude* to war; Psalm, 21 is a *postscript* to war. Psalm 20 tells how a nation should prepare for war.

In the New Testament, of course, Jesus teaches men to turn the other cheek, to be peacemakers, to choose rather to suffer affliction than to wage war. Such teachings are not for the world at large, but for those who are saved and in the kingdom of God. Many people have misunderstood this and have adopted a position toward war which is superficial and suspect. They espouse a philosophy of nation-al peace—peace at any price. They preach appeasement, pacifism, the surrender of the nation to those who would destroy its cherished liberties. They adopt these positions because they fail to make a difference where God makes a difference.

The Sermon on the Mount was not addressed to Great Britain or the United States. It is not a Magna Charta of government for a great world power. The Sermon on the Mount is a charter for the Church, a statement of ethical conduct for the Christian. Even at that, some of its clauses are of a millennial character and refer not so much to the Church as essentially to the coming kingdom of God.

To expect a Gentile world power, even if it is a nation nourished on the Christian ethic, to face the harsh reality of Russian expansion into the vital oil lands of the Middle East by turning the other cheek is irrational and irresponsible, and not at all what is meant by the Sermon on the Mount. There comes a time in the history of every great nation when, faced with the aggression of others, it must say: "That will be enough. One step more and we fight."

What the individual Christian does at that point becomes one of the more interesting and involved issues in the practical application of the Christian ethic to the problems of life in a sin-cursed world. Many Christians become conscientious objectors; others feel that it is their responsibility to "render unto Caesar the things which are Caesar's" even to the extent of bearing arms. That is a study outside the scope of this psalm. We are considering a nation, faced with the imminent possibility of war, preparing its heart for what lies ahead.

The psalm, of course, is concerned with Israel and probably with one of the wars which were so marked a feature of David's reign. By application, its message can relate to the nation in which we live in a time of world crises when at any moment like it or not, for the sake of its own survival the nation might have to fight.

The psalm divides into two parts. First the voice of the people is raised, probably through their representatives, the Levites and the priests. Then the king responds. In the first half of the psalm the people want help from their leader (20:1-5) In the second half the prince wants help from the Lord (20:6-9). In a time of national crisis the people turn to the nation's leaders and say: "This is what we are expecting from you!" Challenged, and awed by the responsibility of committing the people to the horrors of conflict, the leaders turn to God and say: "Lord, this is what we need from you in this time of national emergency."

I. THE PEOPLE WANT HELP FROM THEIR LEADER (20:1-5)

The people tell their king just what kind of leader they want him to be in this time of crisis and impending conflict.

A. Looking to God (20:1-3)

"The LORD hear thee in the day of trouble: the name of the God of Jacob defend thee; send thee help from the sanctuary, and strengthen thee out of Zion; remember all thy offerings, and accept thy burnt sacrifice; Selah." There can be no doubt that when war looms on the horizon people tend to become more religious. Even though they may have a double standard for themselves, they expect their leaders to be devout. With war clouds gathering on the horizon, the people of Israel looked to their king.

1. They want a leader who is Prayerfully in Touch with God

"The LORD hear thee in the day of trouble: the name of the God of Jacob defend thee" (20:1). In other words, You may be skillful, you may be successful, but are you spiritual? That is what matters in this hour of national emergency. Are you in touch with God? Are you able to pray?

Three times in this psalm the name of God is introduced: "The name of the God of Jacob" (20:1), "the name of our God" (20:5), "the name of the LORD our God" (20:7). It is the key to the psalm.

"The name of the God of Jacob" implies *practical trust.* "The God of *Jacob"* is a God of compassion and care. There was nothing deserving about Jacob. He was a scheming, crooked arm-twister, a crafty cattle-man not a bit above lying and cheating if it served its turn. Yet God met Jacob, mastered Jacob, molded Jacob, magnified Jacob, and multiplied Jacob. The God of Jacob is the God who loves us in spite of our faults and failings.

To call on the "name of the God of Jacob" implies a practical trust in God. It is saying, "Here we are Lord; we need You desperately. We are weak and wayward by nature. But we are looking to You to meet us where we are."

"The name of our God" implies *personal trust.* It is not just the name of God. So often, in national life, a leader will acknowledge "God" but he will use a term that is general, vague, indefinite. He is a politician, he does not want to offend Jews, so he will not pray "in the name of the Lord Jesus Christ"; he does not want to offend the atheists, so he addresses himself to "Providence." That will not do. We must make it personal. "The name of our God." God does not want our patronage; He wants our *prayer* based on personal trust.

"The name of the LORD our God" implies *perfect trust.* The name of Jehovah our Elohim! That is, He is the God of covenant as well as the God of creation. He is the God who has revealed Himself; who has given His Word; who has spoken in specific, understandable, moral, and spiritual terms. He is the God who is not only there; He is known. And because He is known, He can be trusted. Perfectly!

It is a great thing for a nation when its leaders are men who have this practical, personal, and perfect trust in God and who are not afraid to let it be known. In an hour of international crisis nothing else will do. The people of Israel wanted their king to be *prayerfully* in touch with God.

2. They want a leader who is Powerfully in Touch with God

"The LORD . . . send thee help from the sanctuary, and strengthen thee out of Zion" (20:2). The sanctuary was the place from which one could expect an infusion of spiritual power: Zion, the great citadel of David, the military stronghold of Jerusalem. The one could not be divorced from the other. The nation's military and strategic power was essentially linked with the nation's moral and spiritual power.

3. They want a leader who is Properly in Touch with God

"The LORD . . . remember all thy offerings, and accept thy burnt sacrifice; Selah" (20:3). In this hour of crisis the people did not want a king who made vague gestures of a religious nature. They wanted a king who knew the power of the cross in his own life.

We don't see much of that in public life today. We have leaders who attend church and pay token allegiance to God. We have yet to hear them stand up and say to the people: "We are faced with crisis after crisis in our nation. We are going to give our report, then we are going to lead the nation in prayer, calling upon the Lord Jesus Christ to send a spiritual and national revival to this land." It would not be the politically expedient thing to do.

B. Listening to God (20:4-5)

Unless a leader is a man listening to God, his strategies and decisions will be based on mere human reasoning. The people of Israel were definite about what they wanted in this regard: they wanted their king to be listening to God.

1. Plan the Battle Aright (20:4)

"The LORD . . . grant thee according to thine own heart, and fulfill all thy counsel." The only way they could reasonably expect God to fulfill the war counsels of the king would be if those military plans were made in the presence of God.

There is a famous painting depicting George Washington at Valley Forge after his defeats at Philadelphia and Germantown. His soldiers had little food, hardly enough clothing. The weather was cruelly cold. The Continental Congress could not supply adequate supplies. The army lived in crude huts. Some of the men were barefoot. Many soliders died of the harsh conditions and others were too sick to fight because of a smallpox epidemic. The picture shows George Washington kneeling in prayer.

But times have changed for the United States. The New York state public schools had a simple, nonsectarian, voluntary prayer banished from its classrooms by a decision of the United States Supreme Court that it was unconstitutional. The prayer consisted of just twenty-two words: "Almighty God, we acknowledge our dependence upon Thee and we beg Thy blessings upon us, our parents, our teachers, and our country."

The American Civil Liberties Union, which helped the five parents which brought the suit against the use of this prayer, cheered its success and went on to say there is nothing wrong with public school children singing *Jingle Bells* at Christmas time, but the First Amendment is violated if Christmas carols are sung as part of a nativity scene!

The Chicago *American* carried a cartoon showing a sneering youngster wearing a tee-shirt pointing a derisive thumb at a picture of George Washington kneeling in prayer at Valley Forge. The cartoonist labeled the boy's shirt: "Future American." The boy was saying: "What's that Square doing down on his knees with his eyes closed?"

How can a nation plan the battle aright if its leaders and lawmakers refuse even to acknowledge any kind of dependence on God? The people of Israel told their king they wanted him to be listening to God so that he could plan the battle aright.

2. Pursue the Battle Aright (20:5)

"We will rejoice in Thy salvation, and in the name of our God we will set up our banners: the LORD fulfil all thy petitions." The word for "banner" here is one which occurs only in this psalm and in Song of Solomon 5:10, where it is translated "the chiefest": "My beloved is . . . the *chiefest* among ten thousand." It really means: "The standard bearer among ten thousand."

This psalm in its prophetic dimension has to do with the Messiah going forth to battle against His foes. Historically, this was the banner that the leaders were to lift up as they prepared the nation for war. The people were to rally around the Standard Bearer, the Chiefest among ten thousand, the living Lord Himself. That's how to pursue the battle aright.

Now the psalm changes. The Psalmist shows how the king, impressed by this challenge and awed by a fresh sense of responsibility, turns to God in prayer.

II. The Prince Wants Help From the Lord (20:6-9)

The speaker is no longer the people but the prince. We note three things about his prayer.

A. The Truth He Expressed (20:6)

"Now know I that the LORD saveth His anointed; He will hear him from His holy heaven with the saving strength of His right hand." The people look to the king; the king looks to the King of kings. Interestingly enough, the word for "saveth" is in the past tense. David expressed the truth that the victory was already won! The actual deployment of the army on the battlefield was a mere formality. The war had already been won the moment the people expressed a sense of their need of God, the moment the king composed himself to pray.

B. The Trust He Exercised (20:7)

"Some trust in chariots, and some in horses: but we will remember the name of the LORD our God." The pronouns are important. David says: "They are trusting in their armaments and in their mobility; we are trusting in the name of Jehovah our God."

America has come a long way from the early days when its leaders were quick to express their trust in God. Now the nation trusts in its armaments. The United States keeps over two million men and women in uniform, and that in time of peace. It maintains a worldwide military establishment valued in the hundreds of billions of dollars. It is constantly developing, testing, and deploying new and ever more expensive weapons. The list could go on and on. The experts assure us that American armed forces could sweep the seas clear of all enemy surface ships within a matter of hours with so-called "smart" bombs which can sink any ship anywhere with a single shot.

So we trust in our twentieth century horses and chariots. David trusted in the name of the Lord his God. It would be better for

America and the world if we had spiritual giants leading the West instead of politicians, scientists, and military chiefs of staff.

In today's world, a country which did not have a powerful arsenal with which to confront aggressors would be acting foolishly. David did not disband his armies simply because he had faith in God. But neither did he put his trust in his troops as his first and main line of defense. He had some able generals. There were Joab, as tough a trooper as ever took an army into the field. There were Asahel and Shammah and Benaiah and Abishai. But David's trust went far beyond men like that; his trust was in the name of the Lord his God.

C. The Triumph He Expected (20:8-9)

"They are brought down and fallen: but we are risen, and stand upright. Save, LORD: let the king hear us when we call." The Septuagint renders the phrase, "Save, LORD," as "God save the king!"

"God save the king!" It was from that familiar phrase that Great Britain developed her national anthem. But Britain, like America, has come a long way down the road to degeneration and disaster since those days when faith in God was the first line of defense.

"They are brought down . . . we are risen. . . . God save the King." Such *total deliverance* because of *total dependence* is what we need today.

But before we close our meditation on this psalm and send it off to the Chief Musician, let us remember that these principles apply to our individual life as much as to our national life. Only our enemies are spiritual, unseen, demonic. If we want total deliverance from the problems and powers which beset us, we too must have total dependence.

"Save Lord!" Let the King—the King eternal, immortal, invisible— let the King hear us when we call.

Psalm 21

CROWN HIM LORD OF ALL

I. THE SECRET OF THE KING'S STRENGTH—
   EXPOSITIONAL (21:1-7)
   A. The Secret Is Disclosed (21:1-2)
      1. The Publication of the Secret (21:1)
      2. The Proof of the Secret (21:2)
   B. The Secret Is Discussed (21:3-7)
      The king's secret strength results in—
      1. Sovereignty (21:3)
      2. Salvation (21:4-6)
      3. Security (21:7)
II. THE SUFFICIENCY OF THE KING'S STRENGTH—
    EXPERIENTIAL (21:8-13)
    A. A Kingdom Based on the Power of God (21:8-12)
       1. God's Power to Discover His Foes (21:8)
       2. God's Power to Destroy His Foes (21:9-12)
          a. In a Passionate Way (21:9)
          b. In a Permanent Way (21:10)
          c. In a Purposeful Way (21:11-12)
    B. A Kingdom Based on the Preeminence of God (21:13)

THIS INTERESTING PSALM is a sequel to Psalm 20. Psalm 20 is a *prayer before the battle*. Psalm 21 is *praise after the battle*. The din and noise of strife is over, the drums of war are stilled, the dust of conflict has settled, the foe has been vanquished. Now comes the coronation of the King. The title tells us this was a psalm of David; the contents tell us that the psalm looks far beyond David to great David's greater Son. It anticipates the coming and coronation of the Lord's true Anointed.

According to the subscription of the psalm, it was sent to the chief musician for public use, along with the note: *Upon Aijeleth Shahar.* Scholars tell us that this Hebrew expression means "hind of the morning." This gives us the key to the psalm. The hind of the morning! The expression is also rendered "The day-dawn." The first rays of the rising sun, slanting upward on the horizon, are likened to the horns of a deer appearing above the rising ground before the rest of the creature can be seen.

158

Psalm 21 rejoices in victory after battle. It is a national anthem, a coronation hymn, a song of thanksgiving for victories won. It may perhaps have been sung at the coronation of David. It looks forward to the day when the Lord Jesus will return, put down all His foes, cause every knee to bow, and wear the diadem of the world empire, swaying His scepter from the river to the ends of the earth. There are three ways we can handle our exposition of this psalm: as *Davidic* —the triumph of David over his foes; as *Messianic*—the triumph of Jesus over the world; as *sermonic*—the way to victory for God's people in all ages over the foes that rise against them on the journey home. For the most part, we are going to focus on the Messianic overtones in the psalm and rejoice in the prospect of the soon-coming of our Lord.

The psalm divides into two parts: *expositional* and *experiential*. In the first part we have seven things the Lord *had done* for the *king*, in the second part we have seven things the Lord *will do* for the *King*.

I. THE SECRET OF THE KING'S STRENGTH—EXPOSITIONAL (21:1-7)

A. The Secret Is Disclosed (21:1-2)

Everyone would like to know the secret of victory. How the Philistines longed to find out the secret of Samson's greath strength! They found it out at last because poor Samson, strong as the sun shining in its strength where men were concerned, was weak as water spilt upon the ground where women were concerned. Delilah soon drew the secret out of him.

The secret of the king's strength is an open secret.

1. The Publication of the Secret (21:1)

"The king shall joy in Thy strength, O LORD: and in Thy salvation how greatly shall he rejoice!" The King has already visited the planet, He has lived here. He stayed here for thirty-three and a half years, lived life on human terms. He had innate, inherent strength of His own, He drew daily on God for strength. He refused ever to act in independence of God His Father.

We see that clearly brought out in Gethsemane. There alone He fought out the issues of Calvary. After His first outpouring of agonizing prayer, "there appeared an angel unto Him from heaven, *strengthening* Him" (Luke 22:42-43). The word means "to establish, to fix firmly." After that, Jesus "being in an agony . . . prayed more earnestly: and His sweat was as it were great drops of blood falling down to the ground." Our Beloved found His strength in God—strength to go right through with it—all the way to Calvary. We have, then, the publication of the secret: strength is from God—strength for anything. The Hebrew word for "strength" here means "prevailing strength."

2. The Proof of the Secret (21:2)

"Thou hast given him his heart's desire, and hast not withholden the request of his lips. Selah." The request referred to is the one found in the previous psalm, the request for victory in the hour of battle.

We know how gloriously Jesus triumphed on the tree. "Having spoiled principalities and powers, He made a show of them openly, triumphing over them in His cross" (Colossians 2:15). J. B. Phillips paraphrases that: "And having drawn the sting of all the powers ranged against us He exposed them shattered, empty, and defeated in His own triumphant act."

Jesus went into death in seeming weakness and defeat. But He went committing His spirit to God, confident that all His foes were vanquished. He proclaimed it in his departing cry: *"Tetelestai! It is finished!* So then, the secret of the King's strength is disclosed.

B. The Secret Is Discussed (21:3-7)

David sees three things resulting from the King's secret of strength.

1. Sovereignty (21:3)

"For Thou [camest to meet] him with the blessings of goodness: Thou settest a crown of pure gold on his head." Two words are used in the New Testament for "crown." There's *stephanos*—a woven garland of parsley, oak, olive, or sometimes of gold. This was the victor's crown, given as a token of public honor for distinguished service or military victory. Perhaps this is the crown that David prophetically has in mind. The first and the last time that the Holy Spirit uses the word *stephanos* in the New Testament it is in connection with the Lord Jesus: "They platted a crown [*stephanos*] of thorns" (Matthew 27:29). The last time the word is used John sees the Son of man coming on a cloud to reap the harvest of the earth wearing a golden crown (*stephanos,* Revelation 14:14). The *stephanos* of thorns given to Him by mocking men in ribald tribute to His prowess in war, to His distinguished service, and as a token of public shame has been replaced now by a golden *stephanos* given to Him by God. For who else has indeed such prowess in war? Who else has rendered such distinguished service? Who else is so worthy of public honor?

> Sinners in derision crowned Him
> Mocking thus the Saviour's claim—
> Saints and angels crowd around Him,
> Own His title, praise His name.

The other word for crown is *diadema,* a word reserved solely for the crown of a king. Probably that is the crown David has in mind. This occurs only three times in the Bible. On the first occasion the great red dragon with the seven heads and the ten horns is wearing it (Revelation 12:3). He has seven diadems—one for each of his fiendish heads and showing him as the one who has usurped the kingship of the earth. It is a kingship he stole from Adam in paradise.

On the second occasion, the beast, the devil's messiah has the diadems (Revelation 13:1). He, too, has seven heads and ten horns and wears ten diadems—one on each of his horns. Those ten horns with their diadems depict the ten-nation confederacy he will head, for he will take from Satan's hand the kingdoms, the power, and the glory which Jesus contemptuously refused.

But when Jesus comes back to reign, riding His white horse to the battle of Armageddon, He will be wearing *many* diadems (Revelation 19:12). Absolute, omnipotent sovereignty is to be His and His alone. David is looking forward to this: "Thou settest a crown of pure gold upon His head."

2. Salvation (21:4-6)

The King's secret of strength results not only in sovereignty but in salvation, everlasting, ennobling, exciting salvation. "He asked life of Thee, and Thou gavest it him, even length of days for ever and ever." Everlasting salvation! As our Lord hung upon the cross the mockers shouted: "He saved others, Himself He cannot save." How wrong they were! Those iron bolts of Rome could have become thunderbolts in His hands, He could have come down from the cross, He could have ushered in Armageddon then and there. How right they were! He could not save Himself and save us, too. That issue had been settled in a past eternity.

Yet God *did* save Him, for He brought Him back in triumph from the tomb and gave Him life, even length of days forever and ever. Eternal life! It's all bound up with the crown-rights of Jesus.

Think of the way they crown an English king as an illustration of the crowning of the King of kings. After the king has been invested with the royal robe, after the orb has been delivered into his hands, after the ring has been placed on the fourth finger of his majesty's right hand to symbolize the marriage of the king with his kingdom, after the scepter with the cross and the scepter with the dove have been delivered into the hands of the king—*then* they crown him. As soon as the crown is placed by the archbishop upon the king's head the people in the abbey shout, "God save the king!" and they keep on shouting, "God save the king!" The peers and those officiating put on their coronets, the trumpets sound, the great guns at the Tower of London boom out so that all England knows that the new king is crowned. Then the king is presented with a copy of the Bible and is enthroned.

The princes and peers of the realm present their homage and swear their allegiance. Then, when the homage is ended, when the archbishop, the princes of the blood royal, and all the members of the nobility have solemnly touched the crown upon the head of the king and knelt down before him and sworn their fealty to their king—and after the choir has sung a selection of Scriptures, then the drums beat and the trumpets sound and the people shout again: "God save the king!" "Long live the king!" "May the king live forever." How long? Who could think of assigning a limit? As long as God wills! Loyalty declines to assign a limit.

What is mere symbolism with a human king is glorious truth with Heaven's King: "May the King live forever!" As David put it: "He asked life of Thee, and Thou gavest it Him, even length of days for ever and ever."

Everlasting, ennobling salvation! "His glory is great in Thy salvation: honour and majesty hast Thou laid upon him." Yes, and exciting salvation: "For Thou hast made him most blessed [happy] for ever: Thou has made him exceeding glad with Thy countenance."

Not just life. Not just everlasting life. But life filled with honor, majesty, happiness, and bliss. Life on God's terms! The years when Jesus reigns on this planet will be the most exciting years in all the history of mankind.

3. Security (21:7)

"For the king trusteth in the LORD, and through the mercy of the most High he shall not be moved." The king's trust in God is twofold: it is in God as *Jehovah* and in God in His character as *Elyon*. His trust is in God as the God who *redeems His Word* and as the God who *rules the world.* It is in Jehovah, the God of promise, the God of covenant, the God who never fails to redeem His given Word. His trust is in Elyon, the God of possession, the possessor of Heaven and earth, the One who alone has the ultimate right to divide up the nations.

No wonder Jesus turned down Satan's offer! "All these," Satan promised, "All these kingdoms, with their glitter, glamor, and government—all these will I give Thee if Thou wilt fall down and worship me." The whole offer was a gigantic fraud; Satan could give no guarantee that the kingdom he offered would be secure. But God does, and it is from Him that Jesus receives the throne. So there it is—the *secret* of the King's strength is rooted and grounded in God Himself.

II. THE SUFFICIENCY OF THE KING'S STRENGTH—EXPERIENTIAL

The scope of the psalm reaches beyond anything David had experienced, for its ultimate focus is on the coming of God's King. The coming kingdom of Christ is to be founded on two great facts.

A. The Power of God (21:8-12)

The coming kingdom is to be brought in by force.

1. The Power of God to Discover His Foes (21:8)

"Thine hand shall find out all Thine enemies: Thy right hand shall find out those that hate Thee." What do we see in that hand? We see a scepter. We look again, we look deeper, we see a mark there, the mark of the cross.

That is how the Lord will discover His foes. He will put a mark on all those who belong to Him, and the devil will put a mark on all those who belong to him. When the Lord separates the sheep from the goats in the Valley of Jehoshaphat the process will be simple—each one will already bear the appropriate mark.

2. God's Power to Destroy His Foes (21:9-12)

We have anemic views of God today, having lost sight of the righteousness and holiness of God. We have forgotten that God's holiness is outraged at man's sin, that the Bible says that God is angry at the wicked every day. The psalmists and the prophets of the Old Testament never lost sight of that side of God's character.

We must always remember the dispensational character of the Bible. What we have in these next few verses was true in Old Testament times—God executed vengeance on His foes; it will be true in a coming day. But it is not true today. God is not acting openly and publicly as He *did* and as He *will*.

a. God is Going to Destroy His Foes in a Passionate Way (21:9)

"Thou shalt make them as a fiery oven in the time of thine anger: the LORD shall swallow them up in His wrath." We are not living in the day of wrath today, but in the day of grace. However, there is to be a day of wrath. After the rapture of the Church the age of judgment will begin and God will passionately destroy those that destroy the earth and persecute His people. War, famine, pestilence, persecution, earthquake—these are all weapons ready to His hand. The man who refuses the forgiveness of God will have to face the fury of God.

b. God is Going to Destroy His Foes in a Permanent Way (21:10)

"Their fruit shalt Thou destroy from the earth, and their seed from among the children of men." The coming age of judgment will see earth's population greatly reduced by one disaster after another. Those who finally assemble in the Valley of Jehoshaphat will be a mere handful, all the rest will be dead. Under the seal judgments alone millions will be killed; a quarter of the world's population will perish of the plague. Under the trumpet judgments two hundred million men will be involved in one single battle. The greatest single feature of the years when the word is *readied* for the beast and the years when the world is *ruled* by the beast will be the constant reduction of the world's population by judgment, as David says: "Their fruit shalt Thou destroy from the earth, and their seed from among the children of men."

c. God is Going to Destroy His Foes in a Purposeful Way (21:11-12)

"For they intended evil against Thee: they imagined a mischievous device, which they are not able to perform. Therefore shalt Thou make them turn their back, then Thou shalt make ready Thine arrows upon Thy strings."

The world will be united over one thing—to get rid of God and every person on the planet who dares to acknowledge Him in any way. The beast will inaugurate the great tribulation, a planned attempt to exterminate believers once and for all.

This is the "evil device" planned against God which the beast, for all his authority and power, will be unable to finish. God will intervene. The armies of the earth will be drawn to Armageddon by demonic power and while they are assembled there to decide the fate of the world, *Jesus will return.* All the time, God has been making ready His strength.

So then, the coming kingdom of Christ will be founded on the *power of God*—the power of God to discover and to destroy His foes.

B. The Preeminence of God (21:13)

"Be Thou exalted, LORD, in Thine own strength; so will we sing and praise Thy power." For Jesus will reign at last in His own strength: "All power [*dunamis,* absolute, unhindered, unequalled power] is given unto Me in heaven and earth." He is the only Person who can be trusted with such power and He will wield it in such a way that the *sobbing* planet will be transformed at last into the *singing* planet. "There!" says David, "'Send *that* to the chief Musician!'"

Psalm 22

DARK CALVARY

NO OLD TESTAMENT INDIVIDUAL suffered the agonies expressed in this psalm, certainly not David. We scour his story in vain for an occasion when his trials were such that they even so much as approximated the sufferings described here.

This psalm might have been written when David was cornered by Saul in the wilderness of Maon. Persecution by Saul had been fierce and David, scrambling from place to place to keep out of his reach, was in desperate straits. David could easily have thought that even God had abandoned him, but he soon learned otherwise, for a providential Philistine invasion of Israel at the other end of the country distracted Saul in the nick of time and forced him to call off the hunt (1 Samuel 23:25-29).

The intense personal note in this psalm shows it was wrung out of David in some bitter experience, but the statements really go far beyond anything David personally experienced. He described the situation graphically. He was pinned to one spot, his enemies gathered all around, deprived of his clothing, subjected to at least one form of torture (for his hands and feet have been wounded), absolutely friendless. Somewhere in the background were many friends but even so his enemies were many and strong, his sufferings prolonged, and his mental and spiritual anguish intense. His chief pain, however, lay in the fact that God seemingly had abandoned him.

Christians have seen a vivid and realistic portrait of the Lord Jesus Christ in this psalm. The sufferer is evidently enduring the horrors of crucifixion. David never suffered any such thing—possibly never knew there was such a way to die.

Some of the hyperbole is really inspired prophecy as we can see when we compare what is written with the story of the crucifixion. Indeed, the Psalmist gives a more vivid description of the sufferings of Christ on the cross than do the authors of the gospels, none of whom dwell on the horrors of crucifixion, which were too well known in their day to need elaboration.

All this continues to verse 21. Then there is a sudden silence as though death intervenes, an interruption which Rotherham likens to a broken column in a cemetery. In verse 22 the psalm begins again, but this time with a shout. A resurrection has taken place! The psalm began with a cry of despair, going down, down, down for 21 agonizing verses; then suddenly the mood changed and it goes up, up, up until it ends with a triumphant cry.

Notice how the psalm begins: "My God, my God, why hast Thou forsaken me?" Now note how it ends: "They shall come, and shall declare His righteousness unto a people that shall be born, that He hath done this." Our English text does not do that justice. The expression, "He hath done this" is one word in the Hebrew, *asah, finished!* When Jesus died He uttered one single word, a Greek word, *tetelestai, finished!* So the psalm begins with one word Jesus uttered on the cross and it ends with another. "My God, my God why hast Thou forsaken me! . . . Finished!"

From verse 22 on the psalm marches triumphantly down the present age of grace and into the millennial age when the Lord will come and set up His kingdom on earth. Jesus might well have quoted the whole of this psalm on the cross. If He did, the dying thief, saved by the grace of our Lord Jesus Christ, certainly had much truth upon which to hang his faith in his last, pain-wracked hours.

We approach this psalm like Moses at the burning bush, feeling we should, as it were, remove our shoes for the place whereon we stand is holy ground.

I. THE TERRIBLE REALITY OF CALVARY (22:1-21)

This psalm contains thirty-three distinct prophecies which were fulfilled at Calvary. Yet it was written a thousand years before the birth of Christ. It is a most convincing example of the divine inspiration of the Scriptures, for only God can prophesy with such unerring accuracy.

We learn that Christ was to be:

A. Abandoned by God (22:1-6)

The great Sufferer realized there was a gulf that isolated him.

1. The Holiness of God (22:1-3)

Note that significant word "but." It occurs twice in verses 1-6. The sufferer begins with the well-known words: "My God, my God, why hast Thou forsaken me? Why art Thou so far from helping me, and from the words of my roaring?" The Hebrew word rendered "roaring" is often used for the roar of a lion, or the noise of thunder, or the cry of an animal in distress. When that dreadful midday-midnight darkness swept over Calvary it was rent by a dreadful cry, a God-abandoned cry, Emmanuel's orphan cry. The Lord Jesus was abandoned by God: "O my God, I cry in the daytime . . . and in the night season, and am not silent. But Thou art holy." He was abandoned because of the holiness of God.

But surely Jesus was holy Himself, the only truly holy Person who ever lived upon this planet. Did He not say, "I do always those things that please the Father?" Did not God open Heaven and call down to earth and say, "This is My beloved Son in whom I am well pleased"? Oh yes! Why then did Jesus cry in agony, "But Thou art holy"? Because there on the cross "He who knew no sin was *made sin* for us." A great gulf separated Him from the holiness of God. God was holy and Jesus had become—not sinful—never that! He had become *sin* for us. No wonder He was abandoned by God, no wonder He roared out like a lion in pain. He was tasting death for us, experiencing what every lost soul will experience in hell for all eternity, what it meant to be God-abandoned in the dark.

2. The Holiest of Men (22:4-6)

Others have cried to God in their distress and God has heard them. Moses cried, Abraham cried, David cried. Jesus cried and was left unanswered. Here the Psalmist brings in his second significant *but*. "But I am a worm and no man." The word "worm" is used for the crimson crocus from which scarlet was obtained to color the robes of kings. To yield that royal dye the lowly worm had to be crushed. "I am a worm!"

On the cross the Lord Jesus died—was crushed—beneath the load of our sin and under the wrath and curse of God. That crimson death of His made possible our royal robes of state. But, at the moment, He was a worm and no man—think of it! The eternal Son of God, Creator of every star, a worm and no man! So then, the Lord Jesus was to be *abandoned by God.*

B. Abhorred by Men (22:7-18)

1. The Contempt of Men (22:7-10)

"All they that see me laugh me to scorn: they shoot out the lip, they shake the head, saying, He trusted on the Lord that He would deliver him: let Him deliver him, seeing He delighted in him."

One of the most significant features of this prophecy lies in the fact that it foretold exactly what the Lord's enemies would say to Him. One can conceive an imposter playacting prophecies to make them seem to come true. But how could such a one make his *enemies* playact the fulfillment of prophecy too? The priests and people assembled at Calvary knew Psalm 22 well enough. But they had no desire to prove the claims of Jesus to be Messiah to be true. On the contrary they did everything they could to disprove those claims. Yet, despite themselves, they used the very language of Psalm 22 when taunting Him, thus fulfilling prophecy. "He trusted on the Lord!" The prophetic words of the psalm fell from the lips of Christ's foes. In the Hebrew Old Testament there are seven distinct words for trust but the one used here occurs nowhere else in the Hebrew Bible: "Roll it on Jehovah!" they cried. "Roll it on Him!"

2. The Cruelty of Men (22:11-12)

The Lord's enemies would be like "bulls of Bashan." Bashan was a wide and fertile farming district stretching from the Jabbok to the spurs of Mount Hermon. It included Gilead and was famous for its pasturelands. Bulls will often gather in a circle around any new or unaccustomed object which they will charge upon the slightest provocation. The Lord's enemies were like that, standing strong and menacing around His cross. They were not only bulls with ready horns, they were roaring lions, tearing, rending, devouring. They were "dogs" too. "For dogs have compassed me." The dogs were not tame household pets but the ravenous, unclean packs which roamed the streets of eastern cities. Bulls! Lions! Dogs! That's how cruel were the Lord's enemies—possessed of the strength of the bull, the self-sufficiency of the lion, and the savagery of wild dogs.

3. The Callousness of Man (22:18)

"They part my garments among them, and cast lots upon my vesture." The Roman soldiers fulfilled this prophecy. We can easily picture the scene and imagine what was said: "Here, Marcellus, you take the sandals; Marcus, you take the girdle; Antonius, you can have this head covering; Quintus, why don't you have the tunic? What shall we do with this vesture? It's too good to tear. Tell you what, we'll throw dice for it." Alongside them, the greatest tragedy in all the annals of time and eternity was being enacted. God's beloved Son was suffering physical, emotional, and spiritual anguish. He was dying for their sins, He was dying for the sin of the world. It meant nothing to them.

The great redemptive work went on: "I am poured out like water, and all my bones are out of joint: my heart is like wax; it is melted within me. My strength is dried up like a potsherd; and my tongue cleaveth to my jaws; and Thou has brought me into the dust of death .... They pierced my hands and my feet. I may count all my bones." He who had created every mountain stream, every babbling brook, every river, every lake, every well was consumed with thirst. He who began His public ministry by being *hungry,* ended it by being *thirsty*.

As for men: "They look and stare upon me" (22:17), or as some have rendered it, "They gaze." The original suggests the malicious delight with which His enemies feasted their eyes on the sight. There they were—the priests, the elders, the Scribes. We can hear them gloat: "There you are Annas. He'll never trouble us again. Messiah! Come down from the cross and we'll believe in You." The contempt, the cruelty, the callousness of men was all foretold in this psalm.

But He was not only to be abandoned by God and to be abhorred by men.

C. Abused by Satan (22:19-21)

"O LORD: O my strength, haste Thee to help me. Deliver my soul. ... Save me from the lion's mouth." This is not physical suffering now, it is soul-suffering. The *lion* is there, that roaring lion who goes about seeking whom he may devour. The powers of the pit were present at Calvary, the principalities and powers of whom Paul speaks— the rulers of this world's darkness. The wicked spirits in high places of whom Paul writes—all hell gathered around the cross to gloat.

"Thou hast heard me from the horns of the unicorns," says the King James text. Moffat puts it much more vividly: "O Thou Eternal. O Strength of mine . . . save my life from these curs, pluck me from the lion's jaws, pluck my unhappy soul from these wild oxen's horns." "This is your hour, and the power of darkness," Jesus said (Luke 22:53).

Then comes that broken column in the graveyard, the sudden close of the first section of the psalm, the *Terrible Reality of Calvary*.

II. The Tremendous Results of Calvary (22:22-31)

The song is suddenly transposed into another key. The music is lifted an octave higher. The whole tenor of the words is changed. There is a sudden silence as death intervenes and then the psalm begins again on resurrection ground. The cross gives way to the crown; the tree to a throne.

The Lord Jesus now appears before us in His twofold character of *Priest* and *Prince*. It is as *Priest* He reigns today at God's right hand in Heaven. It is as *Prince* He is coming again to earth to reign. These are the tremendous results of Calvary!

He was a prophet during His earthly life. It was as a prophet that He suffered at the hands of man. That was yesterday. Today He is a priest; ministering on our behalf in Heaven. Tomorrow He will be king. The first section of this psalm dealt with Christ's yesterday. This section deals with today and tomorrow.

A. The Lord as Priest (22:22-26)

1. His Resurrection (22:22)

"I will declare Thy name unto my brethren: in the midst of the congregation will I praise Thee." The risen, ascended Lord Jesus is seen here gathering around Himself a special, unique company of people he calls "My brethren." David of course knew nothing about the Church but we have no difficulty in seeing it here. This is exactly what the Lord Jesus is doing today. He is praising God in the midst of His brethren.

2. His Return (22:23-26)

The thought of priesthood and mediation is still here, but now the focus is on the end times.

There are three classes of people who are going to be affected by the Lord's return. First there is the *Nation of Israel* (22:23-24). Israel is depicted here as she will be at the end of the great tribulation, beset on every hand, facing extermination, desperate, ready at last to acknowledge Christ. Right on time the Lord will come back to redeem His ancient people. Note how the Jews are urged to acknowledge *Him,* the One of whom the whole psalm speaks and the very One they have rejected so long: "Ye that fear the LORD, praise Him; all ye seed of Jacob, glorify Him: and fear Him, all ye seed of Israel. For He hath not despised nor abhorred the affliction of the afflicted; neither hath He hid His face from him; but when he cried unto Him He heard." This perfectly describes the Lord's coming priestly ministry to Israel. He will bring them to acknowledge Him at last! This is the necessary foundation upon which all Israel's other blessings will rest.

Then there is *the Church* (22:25). The Church is going to benefit too from the Lord's return to the earth at the end of the tribulation: "My praise shall be of Thee in the great congregation: I will pay my vows before them that fear Him."

God has many congregations: the angelic hosts make up one, the nation of Israel another, the 144,000 saved and sealed and ministering with power during the great tribulation yet another. The multitude of saved Gentiles won to Christ during this same period make up still another.

But He has one *great congregation,* the Church! It stands apart from all others by virtue of its special, unique, and glorious relationship to the Lord Jesus and by its special destiny in eternity. The Church is the Lord's great congregation and He has vowed to show her off before all other congregations! At His coming He will pay that vow along with many others He has made to His Church.

Finally there are *the nations* (22:26). The Lord has no priestly ministry to the world as such today, but in a coming day He will act in a priestly capacity towards those Gentiles who enter the millennial kingdom: "The meek shall eat and be satisfied: they shall praise the LORD that seek Him: your heart shall live for ever."

Here is the first tremendous result of Calvary. The Lord is seen as *Priest.*

B. The Lord as Prince (22:27-31)

1. He is Acclaimed as King (22:27-29)

Calvary has insured that the Lord Jesus will not only be a *Redeemer;* He will be a *Ruler* too. When Jesus comes back to earth He will do three things: He will *convert the nations:* "All the ends of the world shall remember and turn unto the LORD: and all kindreds of the nations shall worship before Thee" (22:27). He will *control the nations:* "For the kingdom is the LORD'S: and He is the governor among the nations" (22:28). He will *content the nations:* "All they that be fat upon earth shall eat and worship: all they that go down to the dust shall bow before Him: and none can keep alive his soul" (22:29). The very ones who stood on the edge of the grave, about to die from want, misery, and trouble at the end of the great tribulation, now gain new life. They sit down in the kingdom as the guests of the great King Himself.

2. He is Proclaimed as King (22:30-31)

"A seed shall serve Him: it shall be accounted to the Lord for a generation. They shall come, and shall declare His righteousness unto a people that shall be born, that He hath done this." As the golden years of the millennium unfold the story of the Lord's work will be told from generation to generation. People will remind each other just how much the world owes to His *redemption* and to His *rule.* "He hath done this!" they will say. "He hath done this!" The same word is used in 2 Chronicles 4:11: "And Huram *finished* the work," i.e., of building the Temple. "Finished!" "The Lord hath done this!"

Psalm 23

THE SHEPHERD PSALM

I. THE SECRET OF A HAPPY LIFE (23:1-3)
It has:
A. Its Roots in a Magnificent Spiritual Relationship
B. Its Results in a Magnificent Spiritual Reality (23:1-3)
The Good Shepherd:
1. Shares His Life *with* Us
2. Gives His Life *for* Us
3. Puts His Life *in* Us
II. THE SECRET OF A HAPPY DEATH (23:4-5)
David talks about:
A. The Tomb
We have the assurance of:
1. The Lord's Presence
2. The Lord's Protection
B. The Table
III. THE SECRET OF A HAPPY ETERNITY (23:6)

DAVID WROTE THIS PSALM, but we cannot be sure when. Some think he wrote it as an old man, approaching the end of life's journey, looking back over his life and rejoicing in the goodness of God. Others think he wrote it as a youth, out there on the Judean hills, his father's flock around him, his harp in his hand, and his soul aflame with the great thought which had just come to him—*The Lord Is My Shepherd!* I like to think that, when David faced the Valley of Elah and the threats of Goliath of Gath, as he ran to meet his foe, he sang:

> Yea, though I walk in death's dark vale
> Yet will I fear no ill:
> For Thou art with me, and Thy rod
> And staff me comfort still.

The psalm divides into three parts. First David takes us into *the glen,* then he takes us down into *the gorge,* and finally, on into *the glory.* In the first part of the psalm he introduces us to One who can take care of *our frailty;* then to One who can take care of *our foes;* and finally to One who can take care of *our future.* But of all the ways we can divide this psalm, I like best the one I found in my mother's open Bible, there beside her bed, the day after she died. Alongside this psalm she had written: "The secret of *a happy life, a happy death, a happy eternity.*"

I. THE SECRET OF A HAPPY LIFE (23:1-3)

A happy life is not the result of chance.

A. Its Roots in a Magnificent Spiritual Relationship

David says, "The LORD is my shepherd." The word translated "LORD," of course, is the regular word for Jehovah, one of the primary names for God in the Old Testament. According to Thomas Newberry the name *Jehovah* combines the three tenses of the Hebrew verb "to be": *Yehi,* "He will be" (the future); *Hove,* "being" (the present); and *Hahyah,* "he was" (the past). We take the first three letters of Yehi (Yeh), the middle two letters of Hove (Ov), and the last two letters of Hahyah (Ah) and we have YEH-OV-AH (JEHOVAH)! The name signifies God as the One who is, who was, and who is to be, the eternal One—the One who is becoming and becoming and becoming to His own all that they need until, at last, the Word becomes flesh.

The Jews well knew the significance of this great Name. When Jesus stood before them and said, "Before Abraham was I AM," they knew He was claiming to be God, in the absolute sense of the word. He was claiming that the *Jesus* of the New Testament was the *Jehovah* of the Old Testament.

It is a great thing to be able to say "the *Lord* is *my* Shepherd." It is not enough to own Him as *a* shepherd, for that only equates Him with the founders of the world's religions. It is not enough to own Him as *the* Shepherd, for that simply sets Him apart from everyone else. We must establish a *personal relationship* with Him. We must be able to say He is *my* Shepherd, for the secret of a happy life has its roots in a magnificent spiritual relationship.

B. Its Results In A Magnificent Spiritual Reality (23:1-3)

1. This Good Shepherd Shares His Life with Us

"I shall not want. He makes me lie down in green pastures, he leadeth me beside the still waters." His own resources, His own restfulness is shared with His own people. They need have no worries. He undertakes to look after everything. That is something the world cannot give and something it cannot take away.

Someone once said to a friend of mine that the devil has no happy old men. He decided to put it to the test and for a week asked every old man he met if he was happy. He found it was true—the devil has no happy old men. He helped one old man carry a suitcase up a hill. The man thanked him but when my friend asked him if he was a happy old man the man swore at him. He found only one happy old man. He helped an old blind man across a street and half way across he asked him if he was happy. The man said he was and, sure enough, he was a Christian!

The Lord Jesus *shares His life with us,* puts His illimitable resources at our disposal, puts His inimitable restfulness at our disposal. He is the Great Shepherd of the sheep. He cares for us as though we were the sole care and concern He had in the universe.

2. This Good Shepherd Gives His Life for Us

"He restoreth my soul." The word "restoreth" is a far stronger word than it seems on the surface. In Hebrew it literally means *He brings back my soul.* That is the point of the Lord's story of the lost sheep. A sheep is not *smart* like a lion; it is not *swift* like an antelope; it is not *smart* like a dog. The outstanding characteristic of a sheep is that it is *stupid.* When a sheep goes astray it does so for no reason, and once it has gone astray, it cannot find its own way back home. That is why the Good Shepherd had to leave the ninety and nine sheep in the wilderness and go after the one that was lost. But:

> None of the ransomed ever knew
> How deep were the waters crossed;
> Nor how dark was the night that the Lord passed through
> E're He found His sheep that was lost.

He gave His life for us and bears to this day the scars of Calvary. But His quest has been successful:

> Up from the mountain thunder riv'n,
>   And up from the rocky steep;
> There comes a glad cry to the gates of Heaven
>   "Rejoice! I have found My sheep."
> And the angels echo around the throne
>   "Rejoice! for the Lord brings back His own."

3. This Good Shepherd Puts His Life in Us

"He leadeth me in the paths of righteousness for His name's sake." There can be no true happiness apart from true holiness. Moreover, there can be no walking the paths of righteousness in our own strength. So He puts His life in us. As Paul put it: "He was made sin for us, who knew no sin, that we might be made the righteousness of God in Him."

II. The Secret of a Happy Death (23:4-5)

A. The Tomb

"Yea, though I walk through the valley of the shadow of death, I will fear no evil: for Thou art with me; Thy rod and Thy staff they comfort me."

1. The Lord's Presence

"Thou art with me." So far, David has been using the third person singular to describe the journey. *"He* leadeth . . . *He* makes me lie down . . . *He* restoreth my soul . . . *He* leadeth in the paths of righteousness for *His* name's sake."

Suddenly death looms on the horizon and instantly David drops the third person for second person singular: *Thou! Thou! Thou!* He is no longer talking *about* the Shepherd. He is talking *to* the Shepherd: "Yea, though I walk through the valley of the shadow of death, I will fear no evil: for Thou art with me." We note that this is only the valley of the *shadow* of death. The shadow of a dog cannot bite, the shadow of a sword cannot kill, the shadow of death cannot harm the child of God.

Where we have a shadow we have two other things—a substance, and a light. David has already talked about the valley of the *substance* of death in Psalm 22: "My God, my God, why hast Thou forsaken me?" That is what Jesus cried at Calvary. The very substance of death is to be forsaken of God. That is the essence of a lost eternity—to die, God-abandoned. That is what awaits those who die without the Shepherd.

Where there is a shadow, there must not only be a substance; there must also be a *light*. It is the light shining on the substance that casts the shadow. This is what makes the difference between the death of a believer and the death of an unbeliever. The unbeliever goes out into the dark. There is reserved for him "the blackness of darkness forever." It would be hard to imagine a greater horror than to be lost and alone in eternal darkness.

The believer, however, goes out into the light. Some years ago a medical missionary came to the end of life's journey. He had served the Lord for many years and was dying of leukemia. Being a doctor, he knew just how far the disease had progressed, knew just about how long he had life to live. He wrote a letter to the circle of churches with which he had fellowshiped for many years. "Brethren, David speaks of the valley of the shadow of death. I have now come to the valley, but I find no shadows there. On the contrary, I have found that the path of the just is as a shining light that shineth more and more unto the perfect day."

"I will fear no evil: for Thou art with me." There we have the assurance of the *presence* of the Shepherd when we come face to face with the tomb.

2. The Lord's Protection

"Thy rod and Thy staff they comfort me." I often wondered how a rod and a staff could comfort the sheep in the valley. The commentaries say that the staff was for the shepherd and the rod to chastise a wayward sheep. That did not sound like a comforting thought—to think that the Shepherd was waiting in the shadows rod in hand to beat the wayward sheep. That sounded rather like a Protestant purgatory—to think that, at death, punishment was in store.

That is one of the tragedies of Roman Catholicism. When a devout Catholic dies, dies in what his church calls a "state of grace," all he can look forward to is *fire*—to the flames of purgatory. According to Roman Catholic theology, the unrepentant sinner goes to hell, the good Catholic goes to purgatory. Both go into the fire.

Some years ago Kenneth Opperman was granted an interview with Pope Paul VI. During the course of the interview, Opperman asked the pope if he was saved and the pontiff related some mystical experience he had received as a boy. It wasn't much to go on, but at least it was a start. The visitor rephrased the question: "Sir, when you die, will you go to Heaven?" The pope's answer was most revealing. "Ah! Mr. Opperman, you have asked me a very hard question." It certainly was a hard question. If he had said "Yes!" he would have demolished the Catholic Church then and there because the Catholic Church does not believe that people die and go to Heaven. According to Roman dogma they die and go to purgatory. Then the pontiff brightened. "Ah, but Mr. Opperman, when I die I shall have seven hundred million Roman Catholics praying for my soul." What darkness!

The Bible teaches something better than that. We can say with David: "Yea, though I walk through the valley of the shadow of death, I will fear no evil: for Thou art with me." Look again now at that rod and staff. David was thinking of his *exodus* and his mind goes back to Moses and the great exodus of Israel from Egypt. He visualizes Moses with two things in his hands—a rod and a staff. The children of Israel come to the Red Sea. Behind them Pharaoh's chariots are being deployed in preparation for a thunderous attack upon the helpless multitudes; before them are the unyielding waters of the sea. Then Moses takes his rod, He uses that rod to part the waters and the Hebrews march over dry-shod. Pharaoh's chariots come hurtling down and straight into the opened path through the sea. Moses again takes his rod to summon back the banked up waters of the sea, and Pharaoh's hosts are swept away to be seen no more.

That *rod* was not for the Hebrews, it was for the foe! That *staff* in Moses' hand was a pilgrim's staff. Israel was not to stay there, in the bed of the sea; they were simply passing through. "Thy rod and Thy staff they comfort me," says David, thinking of the inevitable hour of death.

Eventually, we all must come to the waters of death. We shall look up and see our Shepherd there, rod and staff in hand. He will see us safely over the sea; no foe can daunt us even in the hour of death. It is simply a case for the believer of being *absent from the body, present with the Lord.*

B. The Table

"Thou preparest a table before me in the presence of mine ene-mies: Thou anointest my head with oil; my cup runneth over." That is what God did for Israel in the wilderness—He spread a table for them in defiance of their foes. There was the table in the Tabernacle, there was manna to carpet the desert sands. The *table* was to sustain and satisfy on their journey home to the Promised Land.

III. The Secret of a Happy Eternity (23:6)

"Surely goodness and mercy shall follow me all the days of my life: and I shall dwell in the house of the LORD forever." We are given two glimpses of what lies ahead. We are given a glimpse of *the king's highway.* We are on a journey. Hard on our heels come God's two great ambassadors—goodness and mercy. Goodness takes care of *my steps;* mercy takes care of *my stumbles.*

C. H. Spurgeon used to call "goodness and mercy" God's footmen. In his day, when a wealthy man traveled, two footmen took their place behind him on his coach. Their task was to smooth the way for him. Where he went, they went, always there. When his coach stopped they jumped down to open the door for him. They would hurry into the inn to make sure his room was ready and his supper served. God's two footmen are goodness and mercy and they follow us just like those footmen to smooth our journey home.

Then we have a glimpse of *the King's home:* "And I shall dwell in the house of the LORD for ever." There it is!—a happy eternity!

In 1572 John Knox died. As he lay dying his friends gathered around him and one of them begged him that, if all was well as he crossed the river of death, he would give them a sign. The poet tells us what happened:

> Grim in his deep death anguish the stern old champion lay,
> And the locks upon his pillow were floating thin and gray:
> And visionless and voiceless, with quick and labored breath
> He waited for his exit through life's dark portal death.
>
> "Hast thou the hope of glory?" They bow to catch the thrill,
> That through some languid token might be responsive still;
> Nor watched they long nor waited for some obscure reply,
> He raised a clay-cold finger and pointed to the sky.
>
> Thus the death angel found him, what time his bow he bent
> To give the struggling spirit its last enfranchisement;
> Thus the death angel left him, what time earth's bonds were riv'n,
> The cold, stark, stiffening finger *still pointing up to Heaven.*

Psalm 24

THE KING COMES HOME

I. The Lord's Claim (24:1-2)
II. The Lord's Call (24:3-6)
    A. The Question Asked (24:3-4)
    B. The Question Answered (24:5-6)
III. The Lord's Coming (24:7-10)
    A. The First Challenge (24:7-8)
    B. The Further Challenge (24:9-10)

THIS PSALM WAS WRITTEN to commemorate the return of the sacred ark of God to Jerusalem. For seven months the Philistines had kept it under lock and key until finally, deciding it was too hot to hold, they returned it to Israel. It had resided at Kirjath-jearim on the western border of Benjamin in the rugged wooded highlands during the days of Samuel and Saul.

David himself had made one disastrous attempt to bring it to Jerusalem after he had wrested the fortress of Zion from the Jebusites. But now the time had come and the ark began its journey home. The historian tells us of the music and dancing, of the shouting and sacrifices which marked the triumphal entry of the ark into Jerusalem. Psalm 24 gives us the anthem which heralded the ark along the way.

When the temple came to be built in Jerusalem various psalms were sung as part of the daily liturgy. On Monday it was Psalm 48, Tuesday Psalm 82, Wednesday Psalm 94, Thursday Psalm 81, Friday Psalm 93, and on the Sabbath Psalm 92. On the first day of the week they sang Psalm 24. The very day that Jesus tore away the bars of death and marched in triumph from the tomb the temple choir was scheduled to sing this victorious psalm.

I. The Lord's Claim (24:1-2)

"The earth is the LORD's and the fulness thereof; the world, and they that dwell therein." The Lord's territorial claims in space embrace much more than that. All the vast stellar empires of space are His, the countless stars and their satellites traveling at inconceivable velocities on prodigious orbits. All are His! One amid a hundred

178

million galaxies is the Milky Way, one hundred billion stars spinning around a center in the form of a giant disc, an enormous disc of stars. One hundred thousand light years from rim to rim, an inconceivable 600 *million billion* miles of stars—all His! Some thirty thousand light years from the center of that disc of stars is a moderate star. We call it the sun. That sun, hurrying around the hub of its universe, carries with it a family of baby planets. They too are scurrying across intangible space, holding tight to their mighty mother's skirts. That sun and its family make their orbit around the center of the galaxy once every two hundred million years.

One of the planets, Earth, C. S. Lewis has called *The Silent Planet.* Lewis pictures the stars, the galaxies, and the planets making merry music as they swing around the throne of God. All except one. One planet has no song. It is quarantined, diseased. It is the planet Earth. The silent planet! Perhaps it might be better to call it the sobbing planet, for this world is not silent at all. It is filled with screams and cries of agony. The Lord's all-seeing eye passes over the galaxies and supergalaxies and focuses on Earth, the rebel planet, the sobbing planet, the sin-cursed Earth: "The earth is the LORD's and the fulness thereof, the world, and they that dwell therein."

But why Earth? Why not Mars? Mercury? Venus or Saturn or Neptune? Why *Earth?* Because nowhere else in the universe does God have any need to assert His claims!

But He has His ninety and nine obedient orbs, why should He bother about the one that has gone astray? This Earth, after all, is such a puny place, just a microscopic speck of dust in terms of all the suns and stars and satellites of space. But this Earth is important to God because of what happened here.

Let us consider an illustration. Prior to Sunday, June 18, 1815, hardly anyone had heard of a place called Waterloo. It was just a tiny village in the vast empire of France, but it was there that the "Iron Duke" of Wellington on that fateful Sunday in June met and mastered the armies of Napoleon and changed the course of history for all the rest of time. Waterloo! It has assumed an importance in our thinking out of all proportion to its size.

Just so with the Earth. Sin had already assumed a cosmic significance in the universe long before God made man in His own image and placed him on a lonely island-planet in a far-off corner of space, long before that old serpent came into Eden, his heart filled with malice and hate against God, to drag this planet into sin.

What Satan had not realized, when he tempted Eve and dragged a race into ruin, was that God had already decided that the planet Earth should become the battle theater of the universe. Satan had fallen into an ambush planned from eternity. Earth was to be the spot for two invasions. Satan would be allowed to invade, and then God's own *Son* would invade. Here, on earth, the mystery of iniquity would be brought to a head and settled forever at a place called Calvary.

So this planet spins through space, chasing around the sun, carrying its human load of guilt and sin, one colossal graveyard. It has been invaded. The first mighty battle has been fought. Earth has been *chosen,* not abandoned. Help is on the way: the Earth is the Lord's! Thus we have the Lord's *claim.*

II. The Lord's Call (24:3-6)

A. The Question Asked (24:3-4)

Now it is true that the Earth is the Lord's, that every nook and cranny is His,

> He owns the cattle on a thousand hills
> The wealth in every mine:
> He owns the rivers and the rocks and rills,
> The sun and stars that shine.

But there is one spot on earth to which He lays special claim—the land of Israel. The Palestinian Arabs and the PLO say it belongs to them and are prepared to perpetrate any act of terrorism to advertise their claim. It doesn't belong to them at all! It belongs to God. It is called *His Land* and He has deeded it to Abraham, Isaac, and Jacob—to Isaac, not Ishmael; to the Jew, not the Arab. No world conference is ever going to change that—no summit meeting of the superpowers. The land of Israel is God's land.

There is one spot in the land which the Lord has singled out—the city of Jerusalem. The United Nations can declare Jerusalem an "International City" but God says that Jerusalem is *His.* He calls it "the city of the Great King."

In Jerusalem there are two special spots: *the hill* and *the holy place.* The "hill" is Mount Zion, crowned in David's day by the great Jebusite fortress, sometimes called "the citadel of David." The "holy place" is Mount Moriah, where later the Temple was to stand. God claims both these places in Jerusalem for Himself.

Now these are significant locations so far as this psalm is concerned. Mount Zion was Israel's "Tower of London," the military stronghold of the city. He who held Zion held Jerusalm. It stands for *secular power.* Mount Moriah was Israel's "Westminster Abbey," a place of sacred memories even in David's day before ever the Temple crowned it. It was there on Mount Moriah that Abraham and Isaac, nearly two thousand years before, had enacted Calvary. The name "Moriah" means "foreseen by Jehovah." It stands for *spiritual power.*

Now we are ready to look at the Lord's *call.* The scene moves down the ages to the millennial reign. In that day Israel will be the heartland of a vast world empire stretching to the ends of the earth, and Jerusalem will be the capital city of the world. All nations will come to Jerusalem to pledge their allegiance to the flag of the King of kings.

In Jerusalem all secular power will be centered on the hill—Mount Zion, and all spiritual power will be centered in the holy place—Mount Moriah. These two mountains will be the most important centers of power in the universe.

The Lord now throws down the challenge! "Who wants to ascend to the hill of the Lord? Who wants a lofty place in the kingdom? Who wants a share in all that is going to be controlled from Mount Zion? Who wants a share in the dynamics of secular power during the coming kingdom? Who wants to stand in the holy place?" In David's day only the high priest of Israel could stand in the holy place and then only briefly once a year. The Lord, however, throws wide the temple gates and rends the veil: "Who wants a share in all that goes on in the holy place?"

What a call! It was to try to attain just such a dual throne of power that Lucifer fell.

B. The Question Answered (24:5-6)

Such positions of eminence during the coming golden age are not for everyone, just for those who earn them. The essential qualification will be Christlikeness!

Christlikeness of Life. "Who shall ascend . . . Who shall stand . . . ? He that hath clean hands, and a pure heart." Clean hands—that's the outward life, pure heart—that's the inward life. God brings the hands and the heart together because we do what we do because we are what we are.

Christlikeness of Longings. "Who shall ascend . . . Who shall stand . . . ? He that hath not lifted up his soul into vanity." That word "vanity" became the text for Ecclesiastes, a sermon about the emptiness and shallowness of this world. Solomon went in for this world and threw away a crown, a throne, and an empire. He set his heart and his affections on the wrong world and lost everything. Which world are we living for? Where are our longings? Are they set on things above, where Christ sits at the right hand of God?

Christlikeness of Language. "Who shall ascend . . . Who shall stand . . . ? He that hath not sworn deceitfully." God is looking for people who are trustworthy and dependable—whose word is their bond, who do what they say they will do and do it promptly and cheerfully and conscientiously for the simple reason they would not dream of doing anything else.

III. THE LORD'S COMING (24:7-10)

Five times in these closing verses the Holy Spirit speaks of Christ as the King of Glory! Twice the challenge goes forth to the Gates of Glory that they be lifted up. The challenge goes forth the first time and the answer to the question "Who is the King of glory?" is given as: "The LORD, strong and mighty, the LORD mighty in battle." The challenge goes forth the second time and now the answer is: "The LORD of hosts. He is the King of glory."

A. The First Challenge (24:7-8)

"Lift up your heads, O ye gates; and be ye lift up, ye everlasting doors; and the King of glory shall come in. Who is the King of glory? The LORD, strong and mighty, the LORD, mighty in battle."

We must put things in perspective. The Lord Jesus had been on earth for thirty-three and a half years and had won victory after victory over the world, the flesh, and the devil. Every form of temptation had been presented to Him, He was tempted by Satan after being weakened by a forty-day fast in the wilderness. The lust of the eye, the lust of the flesh, the pride of life—the three great primeval temptations, the three great prevalent temptations—were presented to Him. But Satan was defeated every time. The Lord was always triumphant.

Then Satan had Him betrayed, had Him scourged to the bone, crowned with thorns, taunted, crucified, mocked. He tempted Him to come down from the cross. He had him sealed in a tomb to make a final end of Him.

It was all in vain. He was "the LORD strong and mighty, the LORD mighty in battle." Not once in thought or word or deed—as a babe, a child, a teen, a man; in the home, in the classroom, in the synagogue, at the workbench—not once did Satan win even the slightest victory. Jesus triumphed gloriously everywhere and all the time. Then, to crown all His other triumphs, He rose in triumph from the tomb.

He was "the LORD strong and mighty; the LORD mighty in battle." For forty days He came and went, appearing here, appearing there. Then, He gathered His little band of disciples, marched with them out through the city gates, down across the Kedron, past Gethsemane, and on to Olivet's brow. Then He lifted His hands in parting benediction and rose majestically to the skies. So significant is *that* event that there are twenty distinct references to it in the Gospels and in Acts 1. Moreover the Holy Spirit uses thirteen different words and expressions to describe it, each one reflecting a different shade of meaning.

The stunned disciples stood watching as the clouds swept Him up and hid Him from their view. The disciples saw Him go into the cloud but they did not see what happened afterward: but David, writing a thousand years before, *did* see what happened next. The Lord Jesus mounted the star-road and demanded entrance into Glory: "Lift up your heads, O ye gates; and be ye lift up, ye everlasting doors; and the King of glory shall come in."

The demand was challenged by a sentinel: "Who is this King of glory?" Back came the answer as the Lord raised His nail-scarred hands, mute witness to the nature of the war in which He had been engaged: "The LORD strong and mighty, the LORD mighty in battle." The gates swung open and in He went to take His place at God's right hand. That was the first challenge.

B. The Further Challenge (24:9-10)

"Lift up your heads, O ye gates; even lift them up, ye everlasting doors; and the King of glory shall come in. Who is this King of glory? The LORD of hosts, He is the King of glory."

Between verses 8 and 9 the long centuries of this present age of grace come and go. The Lord, by His Spirit, has been busy here on earth—calling out a people for His name, gathering a Church from every kindred and tribe, people and tongue. Now it has become "a multitude that no man can number"! It is a glorious Church; heaven-born and heavenbound, a Church rooted in eternity, spread out through all time and space, terrible to Satan as an army with banners.

And now the time has come. Rejoicing as a strong man to run a race, the Lord steps off His throne. The trumpet sounds and He swoops down the spangled splendor of the sky. "Arise my love, my fair one, and come away!" He cries. The day of the rapture has dawned.

Instantly the graves are emptied of the believing dead; they leap boldly to the clouds. Not a single believer is left behind. The mighty host arises. The hordes of hell, blinded and dazzled, fall back in disarray. The Church is there. The Old Testament saints are there. The angel escort is there. The Lord is there!

At last the enormous multitude, led by the King, arrives at the gate of Heaven. Again and for the second time, the mighty shout goes forth: "Lift up your heads, O ye gates; and be ye lift up, ye everlasting doors; and the King of glory shall come in."

Again the sentry gives the ceremonial response: "Who is the King of glory?" and *this time* the Lord points to those who have been saved by His blood, to that enormous multitude, the redeemed of all ages and He cries: "The LORD of hosts! He is the King of glory." Thus *we* get the same triumphal entry into Heaven that He had Himself. So shall we ever be with the Lord.

Then comes the judgment seat of Christ. Then is decided who shall ascend into the holy hill and who shall stand in the holy place during the millennial reign. And on that high note this majestic psalm ends.

Psalm 25

GUIDE ME OH THOU GREAT JEHOVAH

I. DAVID'S PLEA (25:1-14)
  A. David's Concern as a Believer (25:1-7)
    1. Lord, Protect Me (25:1-3)
    2. Lord, Pilot Me (25:4-5)
       a. He Was Wanting to Be Led (25:4)
       b. He Was Willing to Be Led (25:5a)
       c. He Was Waiting to Be Led (25:5b)
    3. Lord, Pardon Me (25:6-7)
  B. David's Confidence as a Believer (25:8-14)
    1. The Priorities of Guidance (25:8-9)
       a. A Person Must Be Saved (25:8)
       b. A Person Must Be Submissive (25:9)
    2. The Principles of Guidance (25:10-11)
       a. Consecration (25:10)
       b. Confession (25:11)
    3. The Prerequisites of Guidance (25:12-14)
       a. A Right Attitude Toward the Lord (25:12-13)
       b. A Right Attitude Toward the Word (25:14)
II. DAVID'S PLIGHT (25:15-22)
  A. How He Proceeded to Evaluate His Plight (25:15-19)
    1. His Difficulty (25:15)
    2. His Desolation (25:16)
    3. His Distress (25:17)
    4. His Disgrace (25:18)
    5. His Danger (25:19)
  B. How He Planned to Evade His Plight (25:20-22)
    1. As a Person (25:20-21)
    2. As a Prince (25:22)

IN THIS PSALM we come down from the mount. In Psalms 22, 23, and 24 we are occupied with "no man save Jesus only." We follow Jesus to *Golgotha* in Psalm 22, through the *glen* in Psalm 23, and on up to the *glory* in Psalm 24. In Psalm 24 the Lord Jesus is seen *claiming* the world, *calling* out those who are to be joint heirs with Him in His kingdom, and *coming* to summon to His home on high all those who

184

belong to Him. But now, in Psalm 25, we come down from the mount.

This is one of nine acrostic psalms in the Hebrew hymnbook (9, 10, 25, 34, 37, 111, 112, 119, and 145). The acrostic of this psalm is incomplete for, although the psalm contains twenty-two verses, it reflects only twenty-one letters of the Hebrew alphabet. This artificial arrangement makes verse 11 the central verse: "For Thy name's sake, O LORD, pardon mine iniquity; for it is great"—the first confession of sin in the psalms. Another peculiarity of the psalm is the double use of *aleph* (A) in verse 1 and at the beginning of verse 2, and the double use of *resh* (R) in verses 18 and 19. These two verses are thus structurally linked together. In verse 18 we have David looking up to God; in verse 19 we have God looking down at David.

We do not know when this psalm was written but the best conjecture is that it was written sometime during the Abaslom rebellion. The writer, of course, was David. It is a psalm which belongs as much in the prayer book as in the hymnbook. There are three prayers in the psalm. It begins with prayer (25:1-7); there is prayer in the middle (25:11); and there is prayer at the end (25:15-19). The closing prayer is not nearly so bright and full of faith and hope as the opening prayer. But, after all, that's the way it is in our experience. Often we end up on a note of discouragement even in our brightest moments of spiritual exercise.

The underlying theme of this psalm is *guidance*. David's circumstances are dire, he hardly knows which way to turn, so he turns to God. Was it not Abraham Lincoln who said, "I have often been driven to God by the overwhelming sense that I had nowhere else to go." A good title for this psalm would be: "Guide Me, Oh Thou Great Jehovah."

The psalm divides into two main parts.

I. DAVID'S PLEA (25:1-14)

The psalm begins with a prayer in which David expresses:

A. His Concern as a Believer (25:1-7)

"Lord, I want you to *protect* me, I want you to *pilot* me, and I want you to *pardon* me."

1. Lord, Protect Me (25:1-3)

"Unto thee, O LORD do I lift up my soul. O my God, I trust in Thee: let me not be ashamed, let not mine enemies triumph over me. Yea, let none that wait on Thee be ashamed: let them be ashamed which transgress without cause." He appeals to *Jehovah* and to *Elohim*—to the God of covenant and to the God of creation. He wants to make sure that the God of promise and of power is on his side.

As Martin Luther's clash with the Roman church approached its climax we see the shabby monk, staff in hand, striding toward the city of Worms. There the might of the holy Roman emperor was arrayed against him, hand in hand with all the pomp and power of Rome. The hearts of his own friends were filled with doubt and despair. As he approached the city, where the great debate was to take place, his well-wishers sent urgent messages: foul play was intended, his books had already been burned by the hangman, he was condemned already, if he entered the city he would never leave it alive. "I trust in God Almighty!" was the bold warrior's reply. Thus David prayed: "I want You to *protect* me! Never let me or any of Your friends be ashamed."

2. Lord, Pilot Me (25:4-5)

Here we first strike the note so characteristic of this psalm—the note of guidance. The next three verses give us three basic principles.

a. He was Wanting to Be Led (25:4)

"Shew me Thy ways, O LORD; teach me Thy paths." Many of us *say* we want to be led but we don't *really* want God to show us His will; we simply want Him to confirm our will.

David's prayer here echoes a prayer of Moses in a like hour of perplexity. Six times Moses had been up into the mount of God, six times he had come back down again. At the time of his fifth ascent he had taken with him the seventy elders of Israel who had been given a vision of the glory of God. Moses himself had received detailed instructions for the building of the tabernacle while on the mount. God, in all His glory, was going to come down, move in with His people, and pitch His tent among them. Then Moses had come down from the mount only to find that the people had lapsed into idolatry and were dancing naked around a golden calf. God told Moses to stand aside so that He could pour out His wrath upon this faithless people but Moses played the part of a mediator and God's wrath was turned aside.

Moses then went up into the mount the sixth time, alone, to plead with God to blot *him* out of His book rather than blot out Israel. God told Moses that his prayer was heard but from henceforth God, instead of coming to camp with Israel, would let the people get along as best they could without Him. He would send an angel. For if He, the living, holy God, were to come among His people now it would be as a flaming fire of vengeance. Moses came down from the mount the sixth time with these tidings.

It was an hour of great perplexity for Moses. He took the tent of testimony, the place where God was wont to meet with him, and carried it outside the sinful camp. There God, in grace, talked to him: "The LORD spake unto Moses face to face, as a man speaketh with his friend." Moses poured out his perplexity to the Lord: "Show me now Thy way" (Exodus 33:13). He did not dare make a move without God. No angel, no matter who that angel might be, not Gabriel the messenger angel, nor Michael the martial angel, would do. It had to be *God* guiding and leading or there was no point in going on.

Thus David prayed. He was wanting to be led. When God sees that we really want to be led, then He will lead.

b. He Was Willing to Be Led (25:5a)

"Lead me in Thy truth, and teach me: for Thou art the God of my salvation." Whenever I am in my travel agent's office I like to look at the colorful advertising books he has on display. Here is one that offers a safari in Africa, promising exciting encounters with lions and elephants in the great game parks of Kenya or exotic experiences among the warlike Masai. Here is a brochure that promises a cruise of the Caribbean—moonlight nights, native bazaars, romance beneath the stars, and meals to tempt a king.

But God does not hand out brochures. God does not say, "Follow Me and I'll give you an exotic and an exciting experience; follow Me and I'll guarantee you good health and money in the bank." God says: *"Follow Me no matter what!"* until we are *willing* to be guided God will not reveal His will to us. And notice, David says, "Lead me *in Thy truth,* and teach me." Guidance begins with the Word of God: "You see this book? Get into it and I'll lead you." David was wanting to be led and he was willing to be led.

c. He Was Waiting to Be Led (25:5b)

"On Thee do I wait all the day." An important principle of guidance is that God is never in a hurry. Often He will make us wait and wait before finally making the path clear. That is where most of us break down; we are impatient so we act without God's guidance and then complain when things go wrong.

Often when facing an important decision we will find that everything is cloudy at first. Guidance will come only as we wait. It is Satan who says: "Hurry! Act now! It's now or never! If you miss this you'll miss God's will." Satan guides by impulse; God guides us as we wait. We can liken guidance to a glass filled with cloudy water. If we wait, the sediment will sink to the bottom and the water will become clear. God cannot lead us if we are rushed and hurried, dashing here, there, everywhere—always responding to pressure. David was wanting, willing, and waiting to be led. "Lord, *protect* me! *Pilot* me!"

3. Lord, Pardon Me (25:6-7)

David knew better than many that sin in the life makes it impossible for God to lead and direct. "Remember, O LORD, Thy tender

mercies and Thy lovingkindnesses for they have been ever of old."
That is the essential of pardon—God's mercy. "Remember not the
sins of my youth, nor my transgressions: according to Thy mercy
remember Thou me for Thy goodness' sake." God warns: "If I regard
iniquity in my heart, the LORD will not hear me." So David, with that
tender conscience of his, prays: Lord, *pardon* me!

But David not only expresses his *concern* as a believer.

B. David's Confidence as a Believer (25:8-14)

These verses are not part of David's prayer, but a meditation on
this great subject of guidance. David was an authority. In his early
days he knew how to follow the Lord's leading in his life. All down
those fugitive years, David had learned just how and when God
guides. There are few people more fitted to instruct us in this subject
than David.

1. The Priorities of Guidance (25:8-9)

There are two of them. The number one priority is:

a. A Person Must Be Saved (25:8)

"Good and upright is the LORD: therefore will He teach sinners in
the way." Guidance begins with a saving knowledge of the Lord Jesus
Christ. David is occupied here with God's goodness. Paul tells us that
"the *goodness* of God leads to repentance." So a person must be saved
if he is to be guided by God. Therefore the first thing God reveals is
the need for salvation.

b. A Person Must Be Submissive (25:9)

"The meek will He guide in judgment: and the meek will He teach
His way." If we have our minds made up there is no point in asking
God to guide us. We will rebel when God's will is made known: "A
man convinced against his will is of the same opinion still." If we are
to be guided we must be submissive, or as David puts it, we must be
meek.

A young believer comes to a counselor for guidance as to whether
she should marry Sammy. The counselor asks: "Is he a Christian?"
She says: "Oh yes. He's a wonderful Christian. He never goes to
church or reads his Bible but he's a wonderful Christian." The counselor says "If he's not a born-again believer God says you should *not*
marry him. The Bible says you are not to be unequally yoked together with an unbeliever." But that is not what Maggie wants to hear,
so she goes off and marries Sammy anyway. Maggie might be saved
herself but she certainly was *not* submissive to the Word of God. Any
guidance in her case is not only useless, it is incriminating.

So David sets forth the *priorities* of guidance: a person must be saved by the Lord and submissive to the Word of God if he is to know anything at all of God's leading. God refuses to play games with us in this area, and He is much too wise ever to be conned.

2. The Principles of Guidance (25:10-11)

There are two basic principles.

a. Consecration (25:10)

"All the paths of the LORD are mercy and truth unto such as keep His covenant and His testimonies." Unless one is committed to keeping the Lord's commandments there is little point in asking for guidance. When we think of finding out God's will we tend to think primarily in terms of a career or of some complication which has arisen; God thinks primarily in terms of character. He has given us many specifics along this line. If we get our characters in line with God's Word then our questions regarding careers and our complications will soon be resolved.

b. Confession (25:11)

"For Thy name's sake, O LORD, pardon mine iniquity; for it is great." David's whole life came apart after his sin with Bathsheba. God says He will not even hear the person who cherishes iniquity in his heart. If we want God to lead us, confession is of prime importance. If we don't get unconfessed sin out of the way, it will be impossible for us to hear what God is saying.

3. The Prerequisites of Guidance (25:12-14)

a. A Right Attitude Toward the Lord (25:12-13)

"What man is he that feareth the LORD? Him shall He teach in the way that he shall choose. His soul shall dwell at ease; and his seed shall inherit the earth." The Bible says that "the fear of the Lord is the beginning of wisdom." A right attitude toward the Lord is essential.

This was the great prerequisite of Israel's guidance in the wilderness. God led His people by means of the Shekinah glory cloud. Any Israelite could know he was exactly in God's will simply by looking toward the cloud. When it moved, he moved; when it halted, he halted. The *stops* as well as the *steps* of the people of God were thus daily and divinely directed. Their guidance was conscious, conspicuous, and continuous. The Lord is willing to lead us, too, just as clearly if we get our eyes firmly fixed upon Him. *That* is the first great prerequisite.

b. A Right Attitude Toward the Word (25:14)

"The secret of the LORD is with them that fear Him; and He will shew them His covenant." God's covenant with Israel, of course, was contained on the tables of stone laid up within the ark. God's covenant with us is likewise contained in His Word. Nobody can hope to have any real guidance unless willing to spend time with the Word of God, seeking out the great secrets of the Lord which are contained in Scripture. There is no situation we can face in life which is not covered by some specific word of God.

So we have *David's plea*—his *concern* as a believer and his *confidence* as a believer. But David has not yet finished his psalm.

II. DAVID'S PLIGHT (25:15-22)

When David was writing this psalm he was in trouble, in desperate need of guidance from God. His whole world had collapsed. This discussion of the priorities, principles, and prerequisites of guidance was no mere academic exercise. David needed help. In the closing verses he makes that clear.

A. How He Proceeded to Evaluate His Plight (25:15-19)

Note the five things he says about this.

1. His Difficulty (25:15)

"Mine eyes are ever toward the LORD; for He shall pluck my feet out of the net." Absalom's plots were cleverly and cunningly laid. He had succeeded in winning the hearts of the men of Israel and David's plight was real.

2. His Desolation (25:16)

"Turn Thee unto me, and have mercy upon me; for I am desolate and afflicted." One translator renders that last phrase as "lonely and humbled." David, long used to being the national hero, had discovered in the Absalom rebellion just how much his sin with Bathsheba and the murder of Uriah had alienated the goodwill of his people. He had lost the respect of the youth of the land.

3. His Distress (25:17)

"The troubles of my heart are enlarged: O bring Thou me out of my distresses." Adultery and murder had stalked his steps, breaking out again and again in his own family circle. The rebellion of his beloved and favorite Absalom broke his heart. It was, as Shakespeare would have said, "The most unkindest cut of all." The troubles of David's heart were enlarged. He had sinned with his heart and now he must pay with his heart.

4. His Disgrace (25:18)

"Look upon mine affliction and my pain; and forgive all my sins." David cannot get the terrible, tragic past out of his mind. Although he was long since forgiven by God, yet his guilt still haunts his mind. When God forgives He forgets; we cannot forget.

5. His Danger (25:19)

"Consider mine enemies; for they are many; and they hate me with cruel hatred." The whole nation, except for Joab and a handful of loyalists, had joined the rebellion. David must have felt like the Shah of Iran when, almost overnight, subversive forces ran him out of the country and would have lynched him had they been able to.

That is how David evaluated his plight. It was serious. But not for a moment does he lose sight of God. *That* helps him keep his sanity and his soul.

B. How He Planned to Evade His Plight (25:20-22)

First he views his plight:

1. As A Person (25:20-21)

"O keep my soul, and deliver me: let me not be ashamed; for I put my trust in Thee. Let integrity and uprightness preserve me; for I wait on Thee."

No matter how dark and desperate his situation, no matter, even, that its roots could be found in his own sin—he would trust God. God had forgiven his sin, so God's integrity and uprightness would now be his preservation as once it had been his peril. The very attributes of God which seem to frown upon us when we are in our sins actually fortify us when we are standing upon salvation ground. So David planned to evade his plight, as a person, simply by taking refuge in the integrity and uprightness of God.

But David was more than an ordinary citizen. David was a king, so his plight involved not only himself but his kingdom. He tells us in closing how he planned to evade his plight:

2. As a Prince (25:22)

"Redeem Israel, O God, out of all his troubles." There are two Hebrew words translated "redeem" in the English Bible. There is the word which means to redeem from bondage by *purchase*—the way Boaz redeemed Ruth.

There is the word which means to redeem from bondage by *power* —to release, to liberate. That is the word David uses here. The kingdom had fallen into the hands of a rebel. The popular movement against the establishment had been swift and strong. God would have to redeem Israel by power.

Thus David finds himself driven back on God as the only solution to his embarrassments and to the nation's embroilments. On this note he closes the psalm. There are times when the consequences of our own behavior involve other people, those given to us by God as a sacred trust. There are times when we fail miserably in this trust and the disobedience in our own lives is reproduced in theirs—often in a more arrogant and aggressive way.

Then what are we to do? Fly back to God and weep out our confession in His ears and ask Him to redeem those enslaved because of our failures—to redeem them *by His power.*

Psalm 26

SEARCH ME, OH GOD

I. A Divinely Open Life (26:1-2)
II. A Divinely Obedient Life (26:3)
III. A Divinely Overcoming Life (26:4-6)
    A. The Principle of Separation (26:4-5)
    B. The Principle of Sanctification (26:6)
IV. A Divinely Overflowing Life (26:7-8)
    Overflowing in the direction of:
    A. Praising the Lord (26:7a)
    B. Preaching the Lord (26:7b)
    C. Pursuing the Lord (26:8)
V. A Divinely Obstructed Life (26:9-10)
VI. A Divinely Ordered Life (26:11-12)

D AVID WROTE THIS PSALM but we do not know exactly when. The psalm quite clearly reflects a time of national crisis when people were dying under the judgment of God. The national calamity was such that there seemed to be no discrimination between saint and sinner, but as to what calamity it was, scholars are not agreed.

Some have thought that perhaps the great plague which broke out toward the end of David's reign might be the occasion. David had ordered Joab to number the children of Israel. It was an act outside of the will of God. Numbering, apart from paying a redemption price, was absolutely forbidden under the Mosaic law and nothing but pride could have prompted David to such an act. Even Joab seemed to have had more sense, but David's will was law, so the numbering was done—and the judgment of God fell. A terrible plague broke out. David, in utter repentance, asked God's forgiveness and pleaded for the people. On that occasion he accepted full blame and responsibility. But in this psalm he declares his innocence. So, on textual grounds, we must rule out that occasion.

There is a more likely occasion. When David was about fifty-eight years of age, with the prime of life well behind him, a famine broke out in his kingdom. It went on for three dreadful years. David did what he had so often done in his fugitive years, he inquired of the Lord. He was told that the famine was a punishment on Israel because of Saul's massacre of the Gibeonites many years before. The

Gibeonites were covered by a treaty which they had tricked Joshua into signing, but Saul, in his carnal zeal, had broken the treaty and had put the Gibeonites to the sword.

Nothing happened, though time passed and the nation did nothing to redress the wrong. God expects a nation to honor its treaties. Therefore, when even David did not make restitution to the Gibeonites, God acted. David, and most of the nation of Israel, was innocent of Saul's sin. Probably most of the people involved were already dead. But God was treating Israel as a *nation,* not as a collection of individuals. National sin called for national punishment. One can see why David was perplexed at the time, especially when the famine went on and on, becoming progressively worse as year succeeded year. Probably Psalm 26 was written at some time during these years of famine.

The psalm is interesting because it gives a rare glimpse of David's personal spiritual life. There are six simple movements to the psalm and as we move from one to another we see a soul under the searchlight of the Almighty. The psalm tell us six things *we* should ever bear in mind as we journey through life.

I. A DIVINELY OPEN LIFE (26:1-2)

The expressions in the first two verses could well be summed up in the words of that lovely hymn:

> Search me, O God, and know my heart today;
> Try me, my Saviour, and know my thoughts I pray—
> See if there be some wicked way in me;
> Cleanse me from every sin and set me free.

But David does not feel he has anything to confess. What a delightful state of soul! To be able to open up the heart to the all-seeing eye of God confident that God Himself will be satisfied with what He sees. Notice what David says: "Judge me, O LORD; for I have walked in mine integrity: I have trusted also in the LORD; therefore I shall not slide. Examine me, O LORD, and prove me; try my reins and my heart." Not many of the Lord's people would care to put their lives on the line like that! Let us examine a little more closely some of the words David uses.

Judge me. Examine me. Put me to the test. There were not many subjects in school at which I achieved much more than a passing grade. But there was one subject at which I excelled—English history. I dreaded the final exams for math and French and chemistry. But history! I would march into the examining room with an eager pen in my hand. My whole attitude was "examine me!" That exam was no ordeal, it was an opportunity. Thus David prays, examine me!

Prove me. Assay me. Test me for reality. It is the language of the smelter. The gold has been purified in the fire, purged of its dross. It is now ready for the assayer. It is ready for the acid test. Thus David prays, prove me!

Try my thoughts and feelings. Try my heart and mind. Probe down into the innermost recesses of my being. You will find integrity! I have trusted you without wavering. Vindicate me. Thus David prays. With disaster abroad in the land, David comes and stands before God and cries: "I am innocent!" In reality, of course, only the Lord Jesus could talk like that.

An Israelite brings an offering to the priest. The animal is slain and the priest takes a sharp knife and flays it. Next he brings to light the inward parts and subjects each one to the most careful scrutiny. What is he doing? He is making sure that the offering is without blemish. Thus the Lord Jesus could open up His entire life to the probing inspection of His Father. God's verdict on the life of Jesus was: "This is My beloved Son in whom I am well pleased."

But how could David pray the way he did? Perhaps the hymnwriter put it best. He was writing for saints of another dispensation, but the principle was true even back in David's day:

> Oh God of matchless grace,
> We sing unto Thy name.
> We stand accepted in the place
> That none but Christ could claim.

II. A DIVINELY OBEDIENT LIFE (26:3)

"For Thy lovingkindness is before mine eyes: and I have walked in Thy truth." Love is the most powerful motive in the world. A man will do things for love he will not do for fear, hate, or gain.

Let me tear a page out of the history of British India to illustrate the power of love. One of the government's greatest problems was the vileness and moral uncleanness of the Hindu religion. But beyond that, there were some tribes in India more ignorant, more sunk in vileness than the rest. They were known as Criminal Tribes for they lived solely for and by crime. Sir John Hewett, the British governor of the United Provinces of India, had tried everything. The tribes had been harassed by the police. They had been punished with severity. Yet still they roved the land in lawless bands, scarcely human. Moslem, Hindu, and British government influence had failed. Then Sir John had an idea. Why not try kindness? He had heard of the Salvation Army's success in reclaiming the broken ones of Europe.

So the governor paid a visit to General Booth in England. The old Salvationist's attitude could be summed up in a sentence: "You cannot make a man clean by washing his shirt." Only one power is known in all the long experience of human history by which a bad man can become a good man. That power is the gospel.

The government agreed to provide territory; the Salvation Army undertook to provide men. The Criminal Tribes were to be brought into the territory, and the Salvationists would appeal to them with the love of Christ. The great statesman who governed a sizeable slice of empire for Britain, bowed to the argument of General Booth that love and kindness could do more for the wicked than an army of police-men and troops.

The experiment was tried. It was so successful that it infuriated the Hindus, but the governor stood firm. As a result, story after story has been told of lives transformed by the power of love—the love of God in Christ as seen in the lives of the Salvation Army missionaries, which won large numbers of the Criminal Tribes to saving faith in Christ, to lives of usefulness and industry.

These vicious tribesmen had come under what Henry Drummond called "the expulsive power of a new affection." David knew some-thing of it: "For Thy lovingkindness is before mine eyes: and I have walked in Thy truth." His was a divinely obedient life, a life made obedient not by the compulsion of *law* but by the compulsion of *love*.

> Love never faileth,
> Love is pure gold—
> Love is what Jesus
> Came to unfold.

III. A DIVINELY OVERCOMING LIFE (26:4-6)

David states two principles which make any person an overcomer in a world which hates the things of God.

A. The Principle of Separation (26:4-5)

David deliberately separated himself from people who had no use for God: the disdainful man, the deceitful man, the degenerate man. "I have not sat with vain persons, neither will I go in with dissemblers. I have hated the congregation of evil doers; and will not sit with the wicked."

The *vain person* is a person whose character is essentially false or worthless. The *dissembler* is the out-and-out hypocrite. The *evil doer* is the man who is set to destroy all that is good, as the Hebrew word suggests. (The corresponding Greek is the word from which we get our English word pornography). In view is the lewd, lustful person. The *wicked man* is the lawless man, who is driven by the restlessness of his fallen human nature. David separated himself from these kinds of people.

This is something often forgotten today. There is a place for saying a polite but a positive "No!" to certain friendships, associations, or partnerships. There comes a time when the only sensible thing to do, if we are to remain true to the Lord, is simply to walk away from such entanglements. That is what Joseph did. When Potipher's wife set her eyes upon him he ran from her as fast as he could.

VI. A DIVINELY ORDERED LIFE (26:11-12)

"My foot standeth in an even place: in the congregations will I bless the LORD." Or, as someone has put it:

> When my foot rests on the temple floor,
> Then will I bless the Eternal in the choir!

The word translated "congregations" is an unusual one. It is not so much the idea of many congregations that is in mind. The plural is what we call "the plural of majesty." When the Queen of England speaks, she does not use the first person singular; she uses the first person plural. She does not say, "I am happy to be here." She says, "We are happy to be here." She is referring to one person (herself) but, because she is a queen, she speaks for the nation. So she uses the plural of majesty.

Sometimes the Holy Spirit uses this kind of plural. He uses it, for instance, when He wants to add dignity and majesty to the thing He is mentioning, as He does here: "In *the congregations* will I bless the LORD!" The expression can be rendered, "the *great* congregation." That is what God thinks of the assembly of His people: He bestows upon it that which belongs to a king—the plural of majesty!

A divinely ordered life will be a life which takes stand there. In a world filled with snares and pitfalls: "My foot standeth in an even place [in a level place]: in the congregations will I bless the LORD."

Psalm 27

A MERCURIAL TEMPERAMENT

I. TRUSTING ON THE HIGHLANDS OF FAITH (27:1-6)

    A. David's Intelligent Delight in the Lord (27:1-3)
    Based on:
      1. The Lord's Personal Dealings (27:1)
      2. The Lord's Past Dealings (27:2)
      3. The Lord's Promised Dealings (27:3)
    B. David's Intense Desire for the Lord (27:4-6)
      1. Wanting to Enjoy the Presence of the Lord
        in His House (27:4)
        a. A Deliberate Passion
        b. A Daily Passion
        c. A Discerning Passion
      2. Wanting to Enjoy the Protection of the Lord
        in His House (27:5-6)
        He wanted the Lord to:
        a. Hide Him (27:5)
        b. Help Him (27:6)

II. TREMBLING ON THE LOWLANDS OF FEAR (27:7-14)

    David wanted a fresh experience of—
    A. The Grace of God (27:7-10)
    Note:
      1. How Repentant He Was (27:7-8)
      2. How Rejected He Was (27:9-10)
        Rejected, so he felt, by:
        a. His Father in Heaven (27:9)
        b. His Family on Earth (27:10)
    B. The Guidance of God (27:11-12)
    He needed:
      1. Direction (27:11)
      2. Deliverance (27:12)
    C. The Goodness of God (27:13-14)
      1. What Saved Him: the Trust Element
        in Focus (27:13)
      2. What Strengthened Him: the Time
        Element in Focus (27:14)

IF YOU HAVE EVER JOURNEYED across the prairies you know what a dull experience it can be. I remember once traveling by train from Montreal to Vancouver, straight across Saskatchewan, Manitoba, and Alberta. Hour after hour, day after day, the train thundered westward and all there was to see was the open plain. To me it was the most uninteresting scenery on earth.

In contrast, recently I was back in my homeland of Wales, a country of mountains. You climb up one hill, never knowing what's around the next corner. You top the rise, and there behind you is a valley and before you is another. It's a country of constantly changing points of view: a field of yellow broom, a flock of mountain sheep, a little Welsh village with its terraced cottages clinging to the side of a hill, a coal mine with its ugly profile and black slag heaps, a storm breaking upon a green-clothed mountain.

People who are prairie born and prairie bred can doubtless see beauty in the plains, but give me the mountains every time. They are more perilous to cross, it is true, but they are never dull. In Psalm 27 we are in the mountains.

The psalm clearly divides into two parts. The first half we see David *trusting on the highlands of faith* (27:1-6). In the second half we see him *trembling on the lowlands of fear* (27:7-14). Indeed, so great is the contrast between the two sections that some expositors insist that the psalm is a composite, the work not of one man but of two. They argue that no man could switch so suddenly from faith to fear, from trust to trembling, from confidence to cowardice. However, we only have to look at our own deceitful hearts to see that such a switch is not only possible, it happens all the time, often within the same prayer. Faith and fear very often fight each other for mastery of the soul.

So I for one am content to leave the authorship with David. *When* he penned it is another matter. Some have suggested he wrote it during his struggle with Absalom, when a minor victory gave cause for elation but when the over-all strategic situation still left the odds with Absalom. Others think the psalm was written during the fugitive years when David fled from Saul.

I. TRUSTING ON THE HIGHLANDS OF FAITH (27:1-6)

The psalm opens with David voicing his confidence in God. He displays two aspects of his faith in God.

A. David's Intelligent Delight in the Lord (27:1-3)

David's confidence in God was no mere whim, no passing religious fad. It was based on three things.

1. The Lord's Personal Dealings (27:1)

"The LORD is my light and my salvation; whom shall I fear? the LORD is the strength of my life; of whom shall I be afraid?" Mark the personal pronouns. David's confidence is based on *personal* experience. Over the years David had put God to the test in many a trying situation. He never found Him wanting!

Picture the prodigal with his pig-pail in that farmer's lonely field in the country far from home. When he came to himself he came to his father as well. "My father's servants are better dressed, better housed, better paid, better treated than I am here in this pagan land. I'm going home. I'm going to say to my father: 'Father I have sinned . . . please give me a job. I don't expect to be your son any longer. Just put me on the payroll as one of your hired hands.' " The prodigal dredged up from his memory long-forgotten thoughts of his father. Experience told him that his father would treat him with at least the gentleness and generosity he showed to his hired hands.

So David, in his hour of trial, based everything on his personal knowledge of God.

2. The Lord's Past Dealings (27:2)

"When the wicked, even mine enemies and my foes, came upon me to eat up my flesh, they stumbled and fell." That was David's past experience. His enemies, for all their ferocity, had never been able to do him harm. Time and again God had stepped in and delivered him.

We can see the same thing in our own personal history. Had I ever kept a diary its pages would record countless examples of God's unfailing goodness and grace. How He met me as a ten-year-old boy and saved by soul; how He met me again on a train, thundering through the night to the north of England as a youth of eighteen bound for induction into the British army; how He met me again and again as a youth, as a young man, in middle age.

We could all recount stories of the Lord's dealings with us if we have anything like an intelligent delight in the Lord. Like David we can take our stand, trusting on the highlands of faith. We can point to the Lord's *personal* dealings with us and we can point to the Lord's *past* dealings with us. We can say: "Hitherto hath the Lord helped us!" We can say with David: "When the wicked, even mine enemies . . . came upon me to eat up my flesh, they stumbled and fell." The angel of the Lord has mounted guard round about us time and time again.

3. The Lord's Promised Dealings (27:3)

"Though an host should encamp against me, my heart shall not fear: though war should rise against me, in this will I be confident." Rotherham puts it: "In spite of this I am trustful."

David's assurance that he was on the victory side had its roots in the fact that Samuel had anointed him king. The holy oil had been secretly poured upon his head. God had promised him the throne, so not all of Saul's army, nor any amount of hostility could prevent him from sitting on that throne. The future was in good hands. And so is ours! Let us never forget that.

B. David's Intense Desire for the Lord (27:4-6)

There are two things which David wanted with all his heart.

1. The Presence of the Lord in His House (27:4)

"One thing have I desired of the LORD, that will I seek after; that I may dwell in the house of the LORD all the days of my life, to behold the beauty of the LORD, and to enquire in His temple."

Now, of course, David wanted the impossible. David in those days was truly "a man after God's own heart." He was God's model man, a warrior, a born leader of men, a courageous, compassionate conqueror. And he was a worshiper, with a passion for God and for the things of God. He was a prince, a poet, and a prophet. But by no stretch of the imagination was he a priest, nor ever could be. Privileges such as being allowed access into the inner sanctuaries of the Tabernacle were reserved for men born of the tribe of Levi of the family of Aaron, not to men born of the tribe of Judah of the family of Jesse. What David wanted was impossible. Yet *that* is what he desired. This was the daily passion of his heart: "That I may dwell in the house of the LORD all the days of my life." Not just on the Sabbath. He did not attend the services in the Temple out of a sense of duty; he haunted the place because it was where his treasure was, and his heart was there also. "All the days of my life!"

In Psalm 23 he expands that to "I shall dwell in the house of the LORD for ever." If we are going to dwell in the house of the Lord forever then, it follows that we should want to dwell there all the days of our life. If we have no love for the meeting place of God's people, no passion to be there, then there's something radically wrong with our belief.

David had *a deliberate passion* and *a daily passion,* he had also *a discerning passion.*

"To behold the beauty of the LORD, and to enquire in His temple [palace]." If we could just once catch a glimpse of the beauty of the Lord we would lose sight of all beside. It was David's intense desire to enjoy the presence of the Lord in His house.

2. The Protection of the Lord in His House (27:5-6)

David was far from the house of God so far as his physical circumstances went; in actual fact he was a fugitive on the mountains of

Judah. But in heart and soul, in spirit and desire he was in the house of the Lord. The thought of God's house controlled him. He desired, spiritually, that which he could not have physically. He desired sanctuary!

It was the custom in medievel times for a man under the active displeasure of a king or a lord to flee to the nearest church for sanctuary. The custom had its roots in Old Testament times when cities of refuge were set up into which the fugitive could flee. None of them could shelter David from Saul, so he sought sanctuary in the house of God—not physically, for that was impossible, but spiritually.

a. Lord, Hide Me (27:5)

"For in the time of trouble He shall hide me in His pavilion [dwelling]: in the secret of His tabernacle shall He hide me; He shall set me up upon a rock."

That English consumptive, August Toplady, seeking refuge from a violent storm in the cleft of a rock, thereafter wrote one of the greatest hymns of the Christian church:

> Rock of Ages, cleft for me
> Let me hide myself in Thee.

Some such spirit animated the robust soul of that tough young outlaw David as he wrote these words: "LORD, let me hide myself in Thee."

b. Lord, Help Me (27:6)

Not only hide me, but help me: "And now shall mine head be lifted up above mine enemies round about me: therefore will I offer in His tabernacle sacrifices of joy; I will sing, yea, I will sing praises unto the LORD." This is the high point of the psalm. David sees all his enemies routed and he himself bringing triumphant sacrifices to the sanctuary in Shiloh. Thus we see David climbing higher and higher up the mountain. He stands now on its glorious summit gazing across the vistas of the future to the coming moment when total and complete victory will be his. He lifts up his soul in song! Most of us, in times of great trouble, occasionally have found ourselves at some such point of spiritual ecstasy.

But suddenly David falls. From the mountaintop he tumbles headlong down the steep slopes and ends up far below in the deep, dark valley of doubt. As we have said, the transition is so startling, so sudden, that some have tried to argue for another author for the second half of this psalm. Not so! Most of us have tumbled down that same steep place ourselves—and just as quickly.

II. TREMBLING ON THE LOWLANDS OF FEAR (27:7-14)

We must never forget that fear lives right next door to faith. Those who have a problem and who are facing it right now hardly need to be reminded of that. We ride the roller coaster from faith to fear over and over again. One moment we say: "Everything's going to work out fine." The next moment we are looking at our circumstances in absolute despair. How did David handle the situation when he found himself at the bottom of the mountain? First, we see that he recognized his need for a fresh experience of grace.

A. The Grace of God (27:7-10)

Let us plumb the depths with David and see how far he had fallen and how despondent he had become.

1. How Repentant He Was (27:7-8)

"Hear, O LORD, when I cry with my voice: have mercy also upon me, and answer me." "Lord, I'm sorry! I shouldn't be down here in the dumps. Can you hear me, Lord?"

2. How Rejected He Was (27:9-10)

There is nothing more desolate than the feeling of being rejected by those we love or admire. One of our strongest psychological and spiritual needs is for acceptance and it is astonishing to what lengths we will go to get it. The feeling of rejection is a dreadful one, which Satan exploits to the full.

a. His Father in Heaven (27:9)

"Hide not Thy face far from me; put not Thy servant away in anger; Thou hast been my help; leave me not, neither forsake me, O God of my salvation." Of course, God never leaves us nor forsakes us, but sometimes it may seem that He does. Everywhere we turn in Scripture we seem to find just the angry passages, the dire warnings, the pages overcast with judgment and wrath. Christian fellowship seems to fail. Those we love in the Lord let us down. The pressures of life and its problems abound as never before. We pray and nothing happens. Worse, we have no desire to pray. God seems to have withdrawn into His high Heaven and left us to ourselves.

David had the feeling that he had been rejected by His Father in Heaven.

b. His Family on Earth (27:10)

"When my father and mother forsake me, then the LORD will take me up."

We do not know what prompted this statement. There was a time, when he was in the cave of Adullam, that Saul's persecutions became so indiscriminate that David felt, for his parents' safety, he would have to remove them from the farm and bring them to the relative safety of the cave.

But even the cavernous cave of Adullam was not to be safe for long. So David approached the king of Moab with the request that his parents be allowed political asylum down there—after all, Jesse's own grandmother was a woman of Moab so in a sense the family would be coming for a visit to their ancestral home (1 Samuel 22:1-3). Incidentally, this is the last historical reference we have to David's parents. We never read of their coming back from Moab so we presume they died there.

Perhaps David had just heard of their death in Moab. Perhaps his parents were not understanding about David's difficulties and reproached him for the loss of their farm, for the hardships of their old age, for their exile to Moab. All we know is that David had a feeling of being forsaken even by his family. "When my father and my mother forsake me, then the Lord will take me up!"

When Israel marched through the desert, in the days of the Exodus, God provided a rearguard. Its duty was to pick up the stragglers, the weak, the children, the old folks, and carry them forward with the rest. David felt like one of those stragglers. He had fallen by the wayside. He prayed that God would play the part of the rearguard to him, and tenderly, lovingly pick him up.

This, of course, is just what God delights to do. He loves to be the Good Samaritan. He will indeed pick us up when we kneel, forsaken by everyone, and gather us into His arms.

B. The Guidance of God (27:11-12)

In the dark valley of doubt and fear David prayed earnestly for guidance along two lines.

1. Direction (27:11)

"Teach me Thy way, O Lord, and lead me in a plain path, because of mine enemies."

"A plain path!" Hebrew scholars tell us that the word translated "plain" here simply means a level or even path. David has just been speaking of his "enemies," a word which means "watchful foes." The thought seems to be that of enemies lying in ambush, waiting to catch him unawares. David did not pray for an *easy* path. He simply prayed that God would show him what steps to take in the difficult circumstances which surrounded him.

2. Deliverance (27:12)

"Deliver me not over unto the will of mine enemies: for false witnesses are risen up against me, and such as breathe out cruelty." If Satan cannot destroy a person with weapons he will try to destroy him with words. David feared the tongues of his enemies as much as he feared their swords, so he felt his need for the Lord's grace and for the Lord's guidance.

C. The Goodness of God (27:13-14)

In the closing verses of the psalm David is once again coming out of the valley, up from the lowlands of fear.

1. What Saved Him (27:13)

"I had fainted, unless I had believed to see the goodness of the LORD in the land of the living." He brings the *trust element* back into clear focus. You will notice that the words "I had fainted" are in italics, indicating that the translators had trouble here. "I believe I shall yet see," is one translator's effort. David's faith soars again. The trust element is what saved him from utter despair. He deliberately took his stand upon the goodness of God. We can do the same. We can open our hymnbooks and sing:

> How good is the God we adore,
> Our faithful, unchangeable Friend;
> Whose love is as great as His power
> And knows neither measure nor end.

2. What Strengthened Him (27:14)

"Wait on the LORD: be of good courage, and He shall strengthen thine heart: wait, I say, on the LORD." In other words, he brings the *time element* back into focus. Wait! Wait on the Lord. Our times are in His hands. God is never in a hurry, He can never fail. What He has promised He will most certainly perform. The great thing is to be patient and wait. "Wait on the LORD . . . wait, I say, on the LORD."

That was the one thing King Saul could not do. His failure to wait cost him his crown. David learned a lifelong lesson from that. His parting word to us, in our desperate need, is *wait*. We are not to wait fretfully, fitfully, or fatalistically; but we are to *wait on the Lord.*

Psalm 28

THE LORD'S MY ROCK

I. THE REQUEST (28:1-5)
  A. David's Invocation (28:1-2)
  He invokes:
    1. The Word *of* God (28:1)
    2. The Word *with* God (28:2)
  B. David's Invitation (28:3-5)
  He invites the Lord to:
    1. Deliver Him (28:3)
      a. No Rest
      b. No Rules
      c. No Restraint
    2. Destroy them (28:4-5)
      a. Righteously (28:4)
      b. Reasonably (28:5)
II. THE RESULT (28:6-9)
  A. A Note of Praise (for himself) (28:6-7)
    1. He Has Been Heard (28:6)
    2. He Has Been Helped (28:7)
  B. A Note of Prayer (for others) (28:8-9)
  That they might know:
    1. The Strength of God (28:8)
    2. The Salvation of God (28:9a)
    3. The Satisfaction of God (28:9b)

THIS SHORT PSALM was probably written by David during a time of national crisis—the Absalom rebellion when the country was torn apart by civil war, spurred on by the fierce ambition of David's best-loved son. Because of the language of verses 4 and 5 this psalm is regarded as imprecatory, one which calls down curses or wrath upon those who are doing wrong. Such imprecations are never motivated by personal passion and vindictiveness. We know from David's treatment of such a wretch as Shimei that he was not a vindictive person. These imprecations are inspired by the Holy Spirit and give us a solemn view of God's hatred of sin.

The great burden of this psalm is the wicked. David prays that he might be kept from their doom and pleads that they might receive fitting retribution from the hands of God.

I. THE REQUEST (28:1-5)

In view of his circumstances, David turns to the Lord.

A. The Invocation (28:1-2)

1. The Word of God (28:1)

He prays that God will speak directly to him: "Unto Thee will I cry, O LORD my rock; be not silent to me."

Jehovah my rock! That is an interesting way to address God. The name Jehovah may be rendered as "the becoming One," the concept can be expressed thus: "I am becoming what I am becoming." Campbell Morgan suggests: "the ever changeableness of the unchanging one." Throughout the Old Testament era the Lord was becoming and becoming to his people just what they needed until the Word became flesh. The Lord my Rock! The becoming One (Jehovah) is the changeless One (the Rock). God is so addressed by David, and addressed in such a way that the term "rock" becomes a proper name for God. Jehovah, as a *rock,* is God in all His glorious changelessness and immutability. The hymnwriter puts it thus:

> Change and decay in all around I see
> Oh Thou who changest not, abide with me.

David's world was falling apart. His own son, his beloved, handsome Absalom, had stolen the hearts of the men of Israel. David's throne, which had seemed so strong and invincible, had been snatched from him. The nation had turned against him. The fickle crowd had hailed Absalom as though he were a messiah. David's world collapsed and he turned to Jehovah—the One who is always becoming and becoming that which His people need. He appeals to Him as "my Rock."

It is a lovely name for God. There is something permanent, massive, and immutable about a rock. In the Old Testament the figure of a rock is never used of a man, only of God. God is as changeless as creation's rocks. Behind the symbol is the substance: Jesus Christ *the same,* yesterday and today and forever!

As the earthquake of civil war rumbled and shook the very ground on which he stood, David cast himself upon the Rock. I like the story of the open-air preacher in Ireland at the time of the Shamrock races, who was constantly interrupted by a heckler in the crowd: "Hey mister! What do you know of the shamrock?" After a while the preacher had enough. "Well sir," he said, "on Christ the solid Rock I stand. All other rock is shamrock!"

Jehovah my Rock! An old lady lay dying. Her friends gathered around her bed. "She's sinking fast!" one of them said. But the old lady opened her eyes and said: "Oh no, I'm not sinking. You cannot sink through Rock!"

David was taken up with the Word of God, praying that Jehovah his Rock might speak to him: "Be not silent to me: lest, if Thou be silent to me, I become like them that go down into the pit." The pit, the sepulcher—a hewn tomb. If God did not speak to him he was as good as dead. Do we have such a passion for hearing from God? "Lord, speak to me! For if you don't I am already dead." Such an attitude would surely revitalize our daily quiet time! If we really believe that the most vital and necessary thing in life is to hear from God we will have no trouble finding time to get alone with Him. It's a matter of life and death.

2. The Word with God (28:2)

"Hear the voice of my supplications, when I cry unto Thee, when I lift up my hands toward Thy holy oracle." The sanctuary in Jerusalem was in enemy hands, so all David could do was lift up his hands and stretch them out toward it. It was a passionate gesture of yearning and longing for the house of God. The oracle was the innermost place in the sanctuary, the holy of holies in the Tabernacle where God sat enthroned in the Shekinah cloud upon the mercy seat between the cherubim. David's heart yearned after God. Out there on the distant Judean hills, he turned back in his headlong flight from Absalom to look toward Jerusalem. He reached out his hands in longing, not for *his* throne, but for God's throne.

It was an expressive gesture. Paul tells us in Romans 8 that the Holy Spirit makes intercession for us with groanings which cannot be uttered, or as J. B. Phillips renders it: "His Spirit within us is actually praying for us in those agonizing longings which cannot find words."

So we have the *invocation*.

B. The Invitation (28:3-5)

1. David Asked the Lord to Deliver Him (Romans 28:3)

"Draw me not away with the wicked, and with the workers of iniquity, which speak peace to their neighbours, but mischief is in their hearts."

The three important words here are "wicked," "iniquity," and 'mischief." David prayed first that he might not be drawn away with "the wicked." The word has to do with the restless activity of fallen human nature. It denotes those who have *no rest,* for sin makes us restless. "The wicked are like the troubled sea, when it cannot rest, whose waters cast up mire and dirt." That is why people cannot sit still, why they have to be up and doing.

David prayed that he might not be drawn away with "the workers of iniquity." The word "iniquity" is especially connected with idolatry because an idol is really nothing but a vanity, an emptiness, a course of bad action flowing from evil desires. It refers to those who have *no rules,* who are going to do what they want to, controlled by their own vain, evil desires.

Then David spoke of those who have "mischief" in their hearts. The word means "wicked," "the breaking up of all that is desirable, that which is injurious to others." The equivalent Greek word is *ponoros,* from which we get our English word pornographic. Thus the word stands for moral depravity, corruption, and lewdness. Absalom's rebellion brought into the open the pornography that was in his vile heart. He put on a public display of immorality in Jerusalem which has no parallel in the Bible. This word denotes those who have *no restraint.*

The three words put together summarize the spirit of the Absalom rebellion. It was sponsored by men who had no *rest,* no *rules,* and no *restraint.* David prayed that he might not be drawn away with such people. The word translated "drawn away" is a strong word used of condemned criminals being dragged away for execution. "Drag me not off with the ungodly" is the way one translator has rendered the prayer.

David prayed that he might not share the doom of men exposed to God's wrath. No wonder Absalom's rebellion failed when a man like David prayed like this.

2. David Asked The Lord to Destroy Them (28:4-5)

Now comes the imprecation, a marked feature of a number of psalms. C. S. Lewis says of these imprecations, "If the Jews cursed more bitterly than pagans it was because they took right and wrong more seriously."

There is a *righteous* tone to David's imprecation: "Give them according to their deeds, and according to the wickedness of their endeavours: give them after the work of their hands; render to them their desert" (28:4). That prayer was simply the prayer of a man living in the days of the law, applying the standards of the law to the lawless: "An eye for an eye and a tooth for a tooth."

There is a *reasonable* tone to David's imprecation: "Because they regard not the works of the LORD, nor the operation of His hands, He shall destroy them, and not build them up" (28:5). This was no wild, wrathful curse, but the plea of a man who knew God's Word, knew something of the rights and wrongs of human life and society, and who saw the law of cause and effect in God's moral government of the world.

It is no wonder that there could be no hope for Absalom. David's prayers to the Lord were answered fully and dreadfully within a few weeks. Absalom, hanging by his hair in a tree with Joab's darts through his heart; Absalom dead and damned and his grave an object of national execration upon which every passer-by contemptuously flung a stone—was simply Absalom reaping the due reward of his deeds as David had prayed. "Deal gently with the young man, with Absalom!" David had urged, but Absalom was beyond the reach of any such plea. David had invoked the judgment of God and had invited God to act righteously and reasonably. And so He did.

So we have the first part of the psalm, *the request.*

II. THE RESULT (28:6-9)

A. A Note of Praise (28:6-7)

1. He Had Been Heard (28:6)

David lifted up his heart in gratitude and praise to God. His circumstances had not changed, but he thanked God because *he had been heard.* "Blessed be the LORD, because He hath heard the voice of my supplications" (28:6). How did David know that? There was no sudden rending of the heavens, no mysterious voice booming over the mountains saying: "Message received and understood. Help is on the way." No angel came with a special mandate to minister to the royal fugitive. No prophet loomed upon the horizon arrayed in camel's hair to perform a miracle, to make the sun stand still, or cause the earth to shake. No, there was nothing like that. But David knew he had been heard.

How did he know? How do we know? We pray, we besiege the throne of God with some urgent need, we fling ourselves beside the bed, we pour out our hearts. We rise from our knees and nothing has changed. The sun still shines, the kettle continues to boil upon the stove, the dog still barks at the bird in the trees, the children still squabble over whose turn it is to ride the bike. Nothing has changed, yet deep within, we feel that we have been heard. It is subjective, perhaps, but satisfying.

Even when we do not have the *feeling* we still have the *fact.* God has pledged Himself in a hundred ways to hear His people's cry. He hears, He says so, and that's enough: "When thou prayest, enter into thy [secret place], and when thou hast shut thy door, pray to thy Father which is in secret; and thy Father which seeth in secret shall reward thee openly" (Matthew 6:6). We have the Lord's word for it. What more could we want than that? As David Livingstone once said: "It is the word of a gentleman of the strictest and most sacred honour. And that's the end of it."

2. He Had Been Helped (28:7)

"The LORD is my strength and my shield; my heart trusted in Him, and I am helped: therefore my heart greatly rejoiceth; and with my song will I praise Him."

Notice the important order here: "My heart trusted"—past tense; "I am helped"—present tense; "I will praise"—future tense. Thus we grow in grace and increase in the knowledge of God. Supplicating, seeing, singing. Based on his personal experience with God, David resolved that henceforth his soul would be filled with song. We do not live our Christian lives in a vacuum. Where we are today is the result of where we were yesterday; where we will be tomorrow is being determined by where we are today.

B. A Note of Prayer (28:8-9)

Praise for himself, prayer for others. David prayed that others might know:

1. The Strength of God (28:8)

"The LORD is their strength, and He is the saving strength of His anointed." Saving strength! Hebraists tell us that this could be rendered "great saving strength," literally "strength of salvations." The word *salvation* is in the plural, the plural of majesty. David knew that ultimately Absalom could not win. In taking up arms against the throne the foolish young man was taking up arms against God Himself. Israel's throne was the earthly symbol of God's throne, and Israel's king was the Lord's anointed. All his life David had held both throne and king in high, holy regard—even when the king was Saul. Down through the long fugitive years when Saul hounded him from pillar to post, David resolutely refused to lift a hand against him or attempt to seize the throne, even when it was within his grasp. The Lord's anointed was inviolate. David prayed that others might come to know how impregnable was a position rooted and grounded in the pledged Word of the living God.

2. The Salvation of God (28:9a)

"Save Thy people, and bless Thine inheritance." God's inheritance was Israel. The people had fallen into the hands of a scoundrel—handsome, charming, with a persuasive tongue, good manners, and strong support. But he was a scoundrel. The people needed to be saved from him. He had them utterly deceived.

David having prayed for himself and received the assurance that his prayers had been answered now prayed for others. Prayer needs to have a strong note of intercession in it. It is amazing how selfish we are even in our spiritual exercise. We can wax eloquent over our own plight, but can we wax as eloquent over the needs of others?

3. The Satisfaction of God (28:9b)

"Feed them also, and lift them up for ever." "Feed them," literally, "shepherd them." The people had fallen into the hands of a wolf, and David, with true instinct of a shepherd-king, cried to God to take over the shepherding of His people. David, that great shepherd of the sheep, back out on the hills again, had his mind filled with memories of his boyhood days when he tended his father's flocks on the slopes outside Bethlehem, leading the sheep beside the still waters and into the green pastures. How often he would stoop down and bear up in his arms a little lamb or a wounded or frightened sheep.

"Oh Lord," he prayed, "look at your people. They have no shep-herd. They are blindly following one who is not interested in their welfare. Lord, be Thou a shepherd to them. Feed them! Lift them up forever!"

What a heart David had! The people had gone over to Absalom, but David did not lash out at them. He saw them as lost sheep, and prayed that they might know the strength, the salvation, and the satisfaction to be found in God alone. No wonder he is called a man after God's own heart.

Psalm 29

HE RIDES UPON THE STORM

———————————————

THIS IS A VERY SIGNIFICANT PSALM for it mentions the *Lord* eighteen times. If we add to that the use of pronouns and the mention of *God* and *King* we have God mentioned no less than twenty-five times in eleven short verses.

The psalm was written by David and seems to be a sequel to the preceding one where David expressed his fear that he might perish with the ungodly in some sweeping national disaster. Now he expresses his faith that God will abundantly save His own.

There are a number of ways in which we can look at this psalm. First, we can see in it *a present thunderstorm*. David is out in it and feels its fury.

He describes *the first rumblings of the storm over the Mediterranean* (29:3-4): "The voice of the LORD is upon the waters: the God of glory thundereth . . . the voice of the LORD is full of majesty." The storm sweeps eastward, in from the sea. From the west come dark clouds and the rumble of thunder.

He describes *the fierce raging of the storm* as it *breaks over Lebanon and Hermon* (29:5-6), making the mighty cedars bend like reeds: "The voice of the LORD breaketh the cedars. . . . He maketh them [the very mountains] also to skip like a calf; Lebanon and Sirion [the old Sidonian name for Hermon] like a young unicorn."

He describes *the final results of the storm* as it bursts over the desert (29:7-9). Sweeping southward, shaking forest and hill, pouring down

rain in torrents, it hurries out to the desert in the far south toward
Kadesh, toward the borders of Edom (a place famous in the history
of Israel's wanderings). The lightning flashes. Even the animals are
affected: "The voice of the LORD maketh the hinds to calve."

Beneath the storm clouds there is a great convulsion of nature, but
above, everything is at peace. David hears the voice calling to the
angelic hosts to ascribe glory to God: "The LORD sitteth upon the
flood; yea, the LORD sitteth King for ever." Some have graphically
rendered verse 9: "In His temple everything saith, Glory!"

But we can come back and look at this psalm another way. We can
see in this psalm *a powerful throne,* for this psalm is clearly a prophecy.
David was not only a patient sufferer; he was a perceptive seer, a
prophet. The psalm looks ahead to the coming of Christ at the end
of the age to rescue Israel. The very cedars are broken—cedars, the
noblest and strongest of trees, symbolic of worldly magnificence. The
mountains themselves—used symbolically for world powers—are
shaken; Babylon was a destroying mountain.

There is a clear reference in this psalm to the Flood: "The LORD
sitteth upon the flood." The Hebrew word for "flood" is found
thirteen times in the Bible (an ominous number in Scripture, being
used in connection with rebellion and apostasy) and all other uses of
the word are in connection with the flood of Noah in Genesis 6—10.
God was then executing His judgment upon a people so corrupt that
only Noah and his family were saved.

Prophetically this psalm looks forward to the day when the Lord
Jesus will come as King and sweep His enemies away in a mighty
outpouring of His wrath. There will be fearful convulsions on the
earth and the powers of the earth and of the heavens will be shaken.
Above it all, enthroned in glory, will be the Lord. And the very last
word is *peace!*

There is still another way we can view this psalm, *a practical theme,*
for it clearly pictures the storms of life. Nobody is exempt from them.
They sweep in, in their fury and power, and tear at us, breaking,
destroying, sweeping away family, fortune, friends.

The godly Israelite saw all the phenomena of nature in a religious
mirror. He did not admire the beauty of nature just for its own sake.
It mirrored to him the greatness of God's power, beneficence, glory,
and wrath. The sun, the storm, the seasons all supplied him with
symbols whereby to express God's attributes and ways. A number
of psalms (e.g., Psalms 19, 8, 104) deal with nature as a revelation of
God.

It is appropriate then to see in the thunderstorm a pictorial unfold-
ing of a practical theme. It is a theme which finds its way into many
of our hymns:

> When the storms of life are raging,
> Tempests wild on sea and land,

I will seek a place of refuge
In the shadow of God's hand.

Enemies may strive to injure,
Satan all his arts employ,
God will turn what seems to harm me
Into everlasting joy.

So, while here the cross I'm bearing,
Meeting storms and billows wild,
Jesus for my soul is caring
Naught can harm His Father's child.

God would have us dwell in Him, above the storm. In His temple everything saith, "glory!" Things may look very black down here at times, but nothing can disturb the serenity of God's throne and "all things work together for good to them that love God, to them who are the called according to His purpose" (Romans 8:28).

There is one more way we can look at this psalm—*a profound theology,* as we are going to develop it in this study.

Undoubtedly David was not thinking along the lines of this application but there are depths to God's Word far beyond anything the writers ever fathomed, deeper than we can reach even with all the magnificence of New Testament revelation to guide us. Let us look at the profound theology which lies beneath the surface of the song of the storm and relate its spiritual application to ourselves.

I. THE LORD'S PREEMINENCE (29:1-2)

"Give unto the LORD, O ye mighty, give unto the LORD glory and strength. Give unto the LORD the glory due unto His name; worship the LORD in the beauty of holiness." The psalm begins in Heaven. The word translated "mighty" is rendered "sons of God" in the margin of the Revised Version. The Targum bluntly reads "angels." The angels—the sinless sons of light who surround the throne of God—are called to pour out their praises to the *Lord,* Jehovah, the covenant God of Israel. They are to worship Him in "the beauty of holiness" or, as the Revised Version margin renders it, "in holy array." The priests in the earthly tabernacle arrayed themselves in holy garments, "garments for glory and beauty" (Exodus 28:2) when they ventured into the holy place. What they did on earth illustrated what takes place in Heaven. The psalm begins with the Lord's preeminence.

II. THE LORD'S POWER (29:3-9)

As we have already seen, this power is primarily expressed in a thunderstorm. Spiritually, it is expressed in the way God deals with men. We see the thunderstorm over the sea, over Lebanon, over the wilderness—places we can express in spiritual terms.

A. Over the Sea

The Lord's dealings with *the Natural Man* (29:3-4)

"The voice of the LORD is upon the waters." The waters are often used symbolically in Scripture for the unregenerate masses of mankind. "The wicked are like the troubled sea" (Isaiah 57:20). In the closing book of our Bible the great Babylonian system is seen sitting upon "many waters": "The waters which thou sawest . . . are peoples, and multitudes, and nations, and tongues" (Revelation 17:15).

In this psalm "the voice of the Lord" is referred to seven times, three in connection with the waters: that is, in connection with the natural man. "The voice of the LORD is upon the waters . . . the voice of the LORD is powerful; the voice of the LORD is full of majesty." Thus God speaks to the sinner. He speaks widely, powerfully, majestically. The scope, the strength, the splendor of God's voice is thus described. There is nobody who can escape the sound of His voice.

Nowadays God speaks to men through His Word, the Scriptures. But what about those who do not have His Word? Dan Crawford, a pioneer missionary in the early days of African exploration, related an interesting story:

> Coming out of the long grass I met a band of solemn-looking men with a curious old-world look in their faces. They were "a dream embassy," they said; had traveled a long way afoot on a kind of missionary journey from one great chief to another. . . . God had spoken to their chief in a great dream, and the solemnity of it all had so sunk into his soul that he sent off these missionaries of his dream to warn his dear friend, a brother-king, of the ways of God with men. . . . Picture me there a dazed missionary listening to these dream tellers—listening and wondering—as with uplifted hands they point skywards and paint it all so vividly. . . ."

Dan Crawford gives some description of the dream, indeed an interesting, compelling dream until, at last, the chief they represented cried out, "All kingship is Thine and all power." Then Dan Crawford said:

> In our zeal for God's written record we are too apt to treat all this as a weird and doubtful business—mere, misty dream. Forgetful of the fact that God's own Book it is that declares, "in a dream . . . He openeth the ears of men." Forgetful . . . that *God may speak to those to whom He does not write.*[1]

God speaks through His Word, He speaks in dreams to those who do not have His Word, He speaks in the stars, in the storms. He speaks when a babe is born, when death visits a home. He speaks sometimes with a still, small voice. He speaks sometimes, as depicted in this psalm, in thunderous tones, hammering at sin-deafened hearts. It is the voice of God upon the waters.

---

[1]Dan Crawford, *Thinking Black* (New York: George H. Doran Company, 1912) pp. 57-58.

As in the dawn of time, the Spirit of God brooded upon the face of the waters and began a series of ten almighty words that brought light into darkness, loveliness and order out of chaos, life out of death—so God's voice is heard upon the waters today.

B. Over Lebanon

The Lord's dealings with *the Spiritual Man* (29:5-6)

The phrase "the voice of the Lord" occurs only once here. The Lord does not have to speak so often to the spiritual man to get his attention, but at times He speaks with equal force and power to bring him to his knees.

Mount Hermon is here called *Sirion*, derived probably from the glistening snow on its summit. Lebanon and Hermon are the noblest mountains in the Holy Land, marking its northernmost boundaries. The snowcapped summits of the Lebanon range (the very place where some think the Lord was transfigured before His disciples—where the splendor and glory of His deity burst through the veil of His humanity), suggest to us the spiritual heights to which God would have us aspire.

Then too there are the cedars. The cedar is truly a noble tree, standing straight and tall, of necessity planted in the earth but reaching toward Heaven. It is an incorruptible wood, with beauty of grain and color, warm and mellow.

Years ago we started a small assembly in Prince George in northern British Columbia. When we had enough in fellowship we decided to put up a building. We all donated what we could. One brother in the lumber business said: "My cash situation is poor right now but I do have half a carload of cedar at the mill. You can have that." We ran those roughhewn planks through the planer. Then we covered the inside walls and ceilings of the building with cedar and rubbed it down with oil. The place was a joy to behold. No wonder they used this noble tree in building the temple in Jerusalem. Like the mountains of Lebanon, like Hermon, the cedars point symbolically to the spiritual man. God would have us be straight and tall, ever reaching heavenward, noble and of a beautiful grain.

How does all this come about? God tests us in the storm. The psalmist looked at the Lebanon range. He saw the storm at work there. The very hills shook beneath the mighty blast of the wind. Everything he thought *stately* was humbled: "The voice of the LORD breaketh the cedars." Everything he thought *stable* was shaken: "He maketh them [the hills] to skip like a calf."

That is what God does to the spiritual man. The storm comes and God puts him to the test as He did when He tested Abraham: "Take now thy son, thine only Isaac and offer him up as a burnt offering upon one of the mountains I will tell thee of." He never tested Lot, there was no need, it was a foregone conclusion what Lot would do.

According to the Talmudic treatise *Sopherim,* this particular psalm is the psalm for Pentecost and in the synagogue it is still used on the first day of that festival. At Pentecost the Holy Spirit came down like a mighty, rushing wind. He appeared like forked lightning in that upper room. The Church was born in spiritual circumstances which answer to the natural phenomena of this psalm. God was bringing into being a new man, a spiritual man, He was creating a Church out of wind and flame.

C. Over the Desert

The Lord's dealings with *the Carnal Man* (29:7-9)

The phrase "the voice of the Lord" occurs three times here. God has to speak more urgently, more persistently to the carnal man and the natural man than He does to the spiritual man. "The voice of the LORD divideth the flames of fire. The voice of the LORD shaketh the wilderness. . . . The voice of the LORD maketh the hinds to calve, and [strippeth] the forests."

Here we have three graphic pictures. There is a picture of *danger:* "The voice of the LORD divideth the flames of fire" or "cleaveth the flames of fire," or as in the RV margin, "heweth out flames of fire." It is a poetic way of describing forked lightning darting out of a cloud. The carnal believer is in danger. He is spoiled for both worlds. He cannot enjoy *this* world because *that* world won't let him. So there he stands, like Lot in Sodom, waiting for God to come in and shake him to pieces for his wretched way of life. If you don't think the carnal man is in danger, just read the book of Jonah. God had a wind, a whale, and a worm waiting for him.

There is a picture of *desolation.* The voice of the Lord "shaketh the wilderness." Nothing grows in the wilderness except worthless scrub. It is a barren place. When I was in the British Army I was stationed for six months at El-Ballah on the Suez Canal. As far as the eye could see there was nothing but sand—rolling, endless dunes of sand. I remember catching a train for Palestine when I was transferred there. For hour after hour the train hurried on through the wilderness. I went to sleep and woke up in Palestine. Instead of sand I saw hills with olive trees and vines. The contrast was as sharp as night and day. The life of the backslider is a wilderness. It is of little value either to God or man the way it is, so God has to shake the carnal believer out of his complacency. "The voice of the Lord shaketh the wilderness." The Lord is prepared to do whatever he must to shake us out of our barrenness, bleakness.

There is a picture of *deliverance.* "The voice of the Lord maketh the hinds to calve." Out of fright! God wants us to be fruitful. Oh, that He would shake us out of our lethargy and complacency and bring us to the point where we become fruitful for Him.

So then, we have the Lord's Preeminence (29:1-2) and the Lord's Power (29:3-9).

III. THE LORD'S PEOPLE (29:10-11)

First of all they recognize:

A. His Sovereignty In All This (29:10)

"The LORD sitteth upon the flood; yea, the LORD sitteth King for ever." That's the place to which He would bring us, where we acknowledge that He really and truly is *King*. Not just a constitutional monarch, such as they have in some countries—where the monarch makes no decisions, is a mere figurehead. No, nothing like that—although all too often that's just the way we treat the Lord. He must be King indeed, "Lord of every thought and action."

B. His Sufficiency In All This (29:11)

"The LORD will give strength unto His people; the LORD will bless His people with peace." The storm is raging but we have peace. The closing word of this psalm is like a rainbow arching over all. That is what God offers us—peace in the midst of storm.

Psalm 30

JOY COMETH IN THE MORNING

THE PLACE IS HOLLAND. The country is overrun with Spanish troops led by the notorious and cruel Fernando Alvarez de Toledo, Duke of Alva, secular arm of the Papacy and the Spanish Inquisition. His mission, to bring the country back under the yoke of Spain and back into the arms of the mother church. His dreaded courts have already sentenced thousands to torture, to imprisonment, and to the stake. The Hollanders call it the Council of Blood. They fight back, cutting the dikes to drown his troops and putting up a resistance for the right to worship God without the interference of pope or priest or prelate.

In one of the duke's dungeons is a notable prisoner, John Herwin. He is a man of like passions as we are, yet strong in faith and filled with the Spirit of God. In his dreadful prison, like Paul and Silas of old, he simply sings. Sings! Sings so that the people flock to hear him.

222

er (30:4)

Lord, O ye saints of His, and give thanks at the
His holiness." That is a new note for many of us.
hanks to God for His love, compassion, and grace.
spiritual insight, gave thanks to God for His *holiness.*
iness which is the basis of all *punishment,* for God is
n to behold iniquity. His holiness is a consuming fire,
that makes even the shining seraphim hide behind
chant, "Holy, holy, holy is the Lord." But God's
the basis of all *pardon.* God does not say: "*You're* sorry
I'm sorry you've sinned. So let's just forget the whole
policy would erode the very foundations of His throne.
d a righteous way to pardon men, the way of the cross:

> God will not payment twice demand,
> First at my Saviour's pierced hand,
> And then again at mine.

se He is holy! So David urges us to praise God for His
'e should also give praise for:

ompassion (30:5)

are on more familiar ground. It is a compassion which is
ne and generous. Behind God's mercy is His holiness;
holiness is His compassion: "For His anger endureth but
in His favour is life: weeping may endure for a night, but
h in the morning." Sorrow is but a passing wayfarer who
es for a night; with the dawn he leaves and joy takes his

nificant, surely, that God's day begins with an evening and
a morning. Thus all the way through that creation chapter
is we read: "The evening and the morning were the first day
vening and the morning were the second day. . . ." Right now
hurrying through the nighttime of our experience. The shad-
en are dark and menacing; but the morning comes, and with
that will never end! The night through which we are passing
temporary. When the morning comes there will be no more
, no more sadness, no more suffering, no more sickness, no
separations. "One glimpse of His dear face all sorrows will
, Joy cometh in the morning!

III. DAVID'S PRESUMPTION (30:6-7)

e of the remarkable things about the Bible is that its characters
k with astonishing honesty about themselves. People in ordinary
do not tend to be so candid about their own secret faults.

But that defeats the purpose of the Council of Blood. So away with
him! At the place of execution he lifts his head high and sings! An
angry priest interrupts him, tries to make him stop. The martyr
gestures to the crowds. They lift their voices and join him in his song!
And what does he sing? Psalm 30!

> Hear Lord, have mercy, help me, Lord.
>   Thou hast turned my sadness
> To dancing; yea, my sackcloth loos'd
>   And girded me with gladness
> That sing Thy praise my glory may
>   And never silent be.
> O Lord my God, for evermore
> I will give thanks to Thee.

Scholars are divided as to when and where David wrote this psalm.
The title says it is "a psalm and song at the dedication of the house
of David."

Some say this is clearly a reference to the dedication of David's
palace in Zion. We know from the sacred historian that Hiram, king
of Tyre, considered it good politics to keep in with David. He sent
messengers and cedar trees and carpenters and masons, and they
built David a house (2 Samuel 5:11). It was a great occasion for David,
for it meant that the wilderness years were over. He had come into
the good of the promised land. Even those who would normally have
been his enemies made haste to be at peace with him. The building
of his house might, indeed, have been seen by David as a pledge of
the security and prosperity of his kingdom. It would be just like David
to sing:

> Lord I will Thee extol, for Thou
>   Hast lifted me on high,
> And over me Thou to rejoice
>   Mad'st not mine enemy.

Other commentators are equally convinced that the dedication has
nothing to do with David's palace but with the house of God; even
though that house was not actually built by David, it was as good as
done in David's mind. Others have suggested that the psalm was
written after David's second attempt to bring the sacred ark of God
up to Jerusalem (2 Samuel 6:13-14). Some even insert the psalm
between verses 13 and 14 of 2 Samuel 6.

David's first attempt to bring the ark to Jerusalem ended in disaster, in the judgment of God upon Uzzah, and in general dismay
among all those involved. The project was abandoned for the time
being, but later David tried again—only this time he resorted to the
Scriptures for God's mind on how the ark should be carried. This time
all went well. "And it was so," says the historian, "that when they that
bare the ark of the Lord had gone six paces, he [David] sacrificed
oxen" (2 Samuel 6:13). Then, some think, came Psalm 30.

> For but a moment lasts His wrath,
> Life in His favour lies:
> Weeping may for a night endure
> At morn doth joy arise.

The historical narrative continues: "And David danced before the LORD with all his might; and David was girded with a linen ephod. So David and all the house of Israel brought up the ark of the LORD with shouting and with the sound of the trumpet" (2 Samuel 6:14-15). It would be just like David to write a psalm about the whole wonderful and instructive story. We know that he did compose other psalms in connection with the bringing up of the ark. So perhaps these commentators are right.

There have been some other suggestions. We know that in the days of his prosperity, David acted presumptuously by numbering Israel without paying the required shekel of the sanctuary for each person included in the count. We know, too, that God sent a great plague upon Israel as a consequence, and that David pleaded for his people, asking God to hold him solely accountable. We know how the plague was stayed and how David, in his gratitude and in obedience to the command of God, offered up a sacrifice on the threshing floor of Araunah the Jebusite in Jerusalem on Mount Moriah. David refused Araunah's kingly offer of the place, the oxen, the threshing instruments, everything for David's use, and bought the entire site, which later became the site of the Temple. Some think that Psalm 30 was written to commemorate that. It may well be. Especially if, as some think, David himself fell grievously ill—perhaps even being touched by the plague itself which raged in the city as a result of his folly in numbering the people.

We can well picture David writing:

> O Thou who art my Lord my God
> I in distress to Thee,
> With loud cries lifted up my voice
> And Thou hast healed me.
> O Lord, my soul Thou hast brought up
> And rescued from the grave;
> That I to pit should not go down,
> Alive Thou didst me save.

Still others abandon all attempt at trying to locate the occasion when the psalm was penned. In the words of Rotherham: "We may at least feel satisfied that we are within the charmed circle of psalm-production."

One is, indeed, tempted to leave the historical for the prophetical when studying this psalm, it fits so well the coming history of Israel—Israel's dreadful night of weeping, followed by the joy that cometh in the morning of the millennial age. But we will content ourselves with looking for some practical lessons as we explore the dozen verses that make up this psalm.

David begins by
ing him from *scornfu*
he had been in dang
from:

A. Scornful Men (30:

"I will extol Thee, (
not made my foes to r

David had plenty of e
fled from Saul. He had e
the days when all went w
in his own family, among
ed for a while in driving
would exult over his defea

God, however, had lifted
the Lord.

He thanked God for prote

B. Serious Malady (30:2-3)

The maladies he mentions
thanks God for healing him *in b*
Elohim], I cried unto Thee, and
narratives do not tell us that
indicate that upon occasion he w

In his sickness David cried unto
of covenant and the God of creati
thanked God for healing him *in sou*
my soul from the grave," or more
my soul from Sheol." Sheol was th
Hades, the place of departed souls. I
ness was serious enough that he had b
God had brought him back. The ga
against him.

He thanked God for healing him *in s*
me alive, that I should not go down to
dead. His spirit had congregated with th
departing this life, but, from the very mids
reached down and lifted him up. He thar
well again—in body, in soul, and in spir
protection.

II. DAVID'S PRAISE (30:4

At once he strikes the note of song.

A. God's Charact

"Sing unto the
remembrance of
Usually we give
David, with rare
It is God's ho
of purer eyes tha
a blazing qualit
their wings an
holiness is also
you've sinned,
thing." Such a
God had to fir

Why? Becau
character.

B. God's C

Here we
both genu
behind His
a moment
joy comet
only tarr
place.
It is sig
ends wit
of Genes
... the
we are
ows oft
it a day
is only
sorrow
more
erase!

Or
spea
life

A. His Spiritual Pride Remembered (30:6-7a)

1. What He Had Felt (30:6)

"And in my prosperity I said, I shall never be moved." Uninterrupted good fortune is a peril to our souls. It is doubtless what we would choose if we could sit down before a great smorgasbord of life and pick the things we would like to have—and we would make ourselves thoroughly unhappy.

"In my prosperity I said, I shall never be moved." As soon as things go our way we tend to become careless of spiritual things. *This* world is the sworn enemy of *that* world. Solomon, the wise man of Israel, prayed that God would give him neither wealth nor poverty. But that was after he was wealthy beyond the dreams of avarice and had already laid the foundations of his own spiritual ruin. Things had gone well with David too, and in his prosperity he said, "I shall never be moved." It was a mistake, for then came the rough awakening. In David's case it came through a sickness that brought him down to the doors of death and taught him not to trust in circumstances. He tells us, then, what he had *felt*.

2. What He Had Forgotten

"LORD, by Thy favour Thou hast made my mountain to stand strong" (30:7a). He had forgotten that his strength lay in God. David's victorious troops had taken the dizzy heights of Zion. They had planted his banners upon the ancient Jebusite fortress. The hill country of Judah was all in David's hands. The whole land was at peace. There was not a nation on the horizon which dared to take up arms against him. He was strong. The Lord had made him strong. He had forgotten that.

We might well sing:

> Tell me the story often,
> For I forget so soon;
> The early dew of morning
> Has passed away at noon.

We have such treacherous memories. That is why we have the Lord's Supper. It is His constant voice saying to us, "Remember Me!"

Thus David tells us how his spiritual pride was remembered. He tells us just as honestly how:

B. His Spiritual Pride Rebuked (30:7b)

"Thou didst hide Thy face, and I was troubled." The word "troubled" is a strong one which expresses confusion, helplessness, and terror.

That is all the Lord needs to do—just hide His face and at once our

world will fall apart. For God to hide His face, of course, is a figure
of speech. It suggests God looking the other way, leaving us prey for
the bullies of life to get at us, but held back because of God's watchfulness.

IV. DAVID'S PRAYER (30:8-10)

He has learned his lesson. He realizes now that his safety lies in
keeping in constant touch with God, and the way to do this is through
prayer. David was a great man of prayer. We can learn much about
its secrets from him.

A. His Approach (30:8)

"I cried to Thee, O LORD, and unto the LORD I made supplication."
What a wonderful God we have! Some people are very quick to take
offense. Slight them or snub them, even unintentionally, and off they
go in a huff. Forget to invite them to something, or fail to make
sufficient fuss of them if you do invite them, and they get their backs
up. To mollify them will take years, and even then they will scarcely
forgive and be doubly watchful lest you should treat them so again.

Suppose God were like that! Suppose that if we slighted Him,
ignored Him, forgot to consult Him, or even deliberately planned
something apart from Him—suppose He was touchy, quick to take
offense, harder to be propitiated than the offended brother of Solomon's proverb. What a blessing we do not have a touchy God!
Suppose He snubbed us when we came back saying, "I'm sorry."
Thank God He is not like that! "I cried to Thee, O LORD." David knew
that God was a wonderful God.

B. His Appeal (30:9)

"What profit is there in my blood, when I go down to the pit? Shall
the dust praise Thee? Shall it declare Thy truth?" Walk through an
old graveyard. How many corpses can you hear praising God? Can
the dust speak? "Lord, I'm more use to you living than dead!" That's
David's argument.

The Old Testament saints had a gloomy view of death. Death to
them was seen as an interruption in their communion with God, even
for God's *saints*. They saw death as a continuation of existence, but
on terms which robbed it of all that deserves to be called life. David
shared the common view, and he uses it as part of his appeal to God.

C. His Application (30:10)

"Hear, O LORD, and have mercy upon me; LORD, be Thou my
helper." It's a great idea to use the power of persuasion with God.
Not because He needs to be convinced, but because we do. George
Mueller was a master of the art. He would besiege the throne of grace

But that defeats the purpose of the Council of Blood. So away with him! At the place of execution he lifts his head high and sings! An angry priest interrupts him, tries to make him stop. The martyr gestures to the crowds. They lift their voices and join him in his song! And what does he sing? Psalm 30!

> Hear Lord, have mercy, help me, Lord.
> Thou hast turned my sadness
> To dancing; yea, my sackcloth loos'd
> And girded me with gladness
> That sing Thy praise my glory may
> And never silent be.
> O Lord my God, for evermore
> I will give thanks to Thee.

Scholars are divided as to when and where David wrote this psalm. The title says it is "a psalm and song at the dedication of the house of David."

Some say this is clearly a reference to the dedication of David's palace in Zion. We know from the sacred historian that Hiram, king of Tyre, considered it good politics to keep in with David. He sent messengers and cedar trees and carpenters and masons, and they built David a house (2 Samuel 5:11). It was a great occasion for David, for it meant that the wilderness years were over. He had come into the good of the promised land. Even those who would normally have been his enemies made haste to be at peace with him. The building of his house might, indeed, have been seen by David as a pledge of the security and prosperity of his kingdom. It would be just like David to sing:

> Lord I will Thee extol, for Thou
> Hast lifted me on high,
> And over me Thou to rejoice
> Mad'st not mine enemy.

Other commentators are equally convinced that the dedication has nothing to do with David's palace but with the house of God; even though that house was not actually built by David, it was as good as done in David's mind. Others have suggested that the psalm was written after David's second attempt to bring the sacred ark of God up to Jerusalem (2 Samuel 6:13-14). Some even insert the psalm between verses 13 and 14 of 2 Samuel 6.

David's first attempt to bring the ark to Jerusalem ended in disaster, in the judgment of God upon Uzzah, and in general dismay among all those involved. The project was abandoned for the time being, but later David tried again—only this time he resorted to the Scriptures for God's mind on how the ark should be carried. This time all went well. "And it was so," says the historian, "that when they that bare the ark of the LORD had gone six paces, he [David] sacrificed oxen" (2 Samuel 6:13). Then, some think, came Psalm 30.

For but a moment lasts His wrath,
    Life in His favour lies:
Weeping may for a night endure
    At morn doth joy arise.

The historical narrative continues: "And David danced before the
LORD with all his might; and David was girded with a linen ephod.
So David and all the house of Israel brought up the ark of the LORD
with shouting and with the sound of the trumpet" (2 Samuel 6:14-15).
It would be just like David to write a psalm about the whole wonderful and instructive story. We know that he did compose other psalms
in connection with the bringing up of the ark. So perhaps these
commentators are right.

There have been some other suggestions. We know that in the days
of his prosperity, David acted presumptuously by numbering Israel
without paying the required shekel of the sanctuary for each person
included in the count. We know, too, that God sent a great plague
upon Israel as a consequence, and that David pleaded for his people,
asking God to hold him solely accountable. We know how the plague
was stayed and how David, in his gratitude and in obedience to the
command of God, offered up a sacrifice on the threshing floor of
Araunah the Jebusite in Jerusalem on Mount Moriah. David refused
Araunah's kingly offer of the place, the oxen, the threshing instruments, everything for David's use, and bought the entire site, which
later became the site of the Temple. Some think that Psalm 30 was
written to commemorate that. It may well be. Especially if, as some
think, David himself fell grievously ill—perhaps even being touched
by the plague itself which raged in the city as a result of his folly in
numbering the people.

We can well picture David writing:

O Thou who art my Lord my God
    I in distress to Thee,
With loud cries lifted up my voice
    And Thou hast healed me.
O Lord, my soul Thou hast brought up
    And rescued from the grave;
That I to pit should not go down,
    Alive Thou didst me save.

Still others abandon all attempt at trying to locate the occasion
when the psalm was penned. In the words of Rotherham: "We may
at least feel satisfied that we are within the charmed circle of psalm-
production."

One is, indeed, tempted to leave the historical for the prophetical
when studying this psalm, it fits so well the coming history of Israel—
Israel's dreadful night of weeping, followed by the joy that cometh
in the morning of the millennial age. But we will content ourselves
with looking for some practical lessons as we explore the dozen verses
that make up this psalm.

I. DAVID'S PROTECTION (30:1-3)

David begins by celebrating the good hand of the Lord in protecting him from *scornful men* and from *serious maladies*. It would seem that he had been in danger from both. He thanked God for protecting him from:

A. Scornful Men (30:1)

"I will extol Thee, O LORD; for Thou hast lifted me up, and hast not made my foes to rejoice over me."

David had plenty of enemies. He had enemies during the days he fled from Saul. He had enemies, hidden enemies like Shimei, even in the days when all went well. He had enemies in his own household, in his own family, among his own sons. He had enemies that succeeded for a while in driving him off his throne. David knew how they would exult over his defeat, his downfall, his death.

God, however, had lifted David on high. He in turn would lift up the Lord.

He thanked God for protecting him from:

B. Serious Malady (30:2-3)

The maladies he mentions were both physical and spiritual. He thanks God for healing him *in body*. "O LORD my God [O Jehovah my Elohim], I cried unto Thee, and Thou hast healed me." The historical narratives do not tell us that David was sick, but several psalms indicate that upon occasion he was brought low by sickness.

In his sickness David cried unto the Lord, Jehovah-Elohim, the God of covenant and the God of creation, and evidently not in vain. He thanked God for healing him *in soul*. "O LORD, Thou hast brought up my soul from the grave," or more literally, "Thou hast brought up my soul from Sheol." Sheol was the Old Testament equivalent of Hades, the place of departed souls. It would seem that David's sickness was serious enough that he had been right at the point of death. God had brought him back. The gates of hell had not prevailed against him.

He thanked God for healing him *in spirit* (30:3b). "Thou hast kept me alive, that I should not go down to the pit." David was almost dead. His spirit had congregated with the spirits of those who were departing this life, but, from the very midst of that company, God had reached down and lifted him up. He thanked God for that. He was well again—in body, in soul, and in spirit. So David speaks of his *protection*.

II. DAVID'S PRAISE (30:4-5)

At once he strikes the note of song.

A. God's Character (30:4)

"Sing unto the LORD, O ye saints of His, and give thanks at the remembrance of His holiness." That is a new note for many of us. Usually we give thanks to God for His love, compassion, and grace. David, with rare spiritual insight, gave thanks to God for His *holiness*.

It is God's holiness which is the basis of all *punishment,* for God is of purer eyes than to behold iniquity. His holiness is a consuming fire, a blazing quality that makes even the shining seraphim hide behind their wings and chant, "Holy, holy, holy is the Lord." But God's holiness is also the basis of all *pardon*. God does not say: "*You're* sorry you've sinned, *I'm* sorry you've sinned. So let's just forget the whole thing." Such a policy would erode the very foundations of His throne. God had to find a righteous way to pardon men, the way of the cross:

> God will not payment twice demand,
> First at my Saviour's pierced hand,
> And then again at mine.

Why? Because He is holy! So David urges us to praise God for His character. We should also give praise for:

B. God's Compassion (30:5)

Here we are on more familiar ground. It is a compassion which is both genuine and generous. Behind God's mercy is His holiness; behind His holiness is His compassion: "For His anger endureth but a moment; in His favour is life: weeping may endure for a night, but joy cometh in the morning." Sorrow is but a passing wayfarer who only tarries for a night; with the dawn he leaves and joy takes his place.

It is significant, surely, that God's day begins with an evening and ends with a morning. Thus all the way through that creation chapter of Genesis we read: "The evening and the morning were the first day . . . the evening and the morning were the second day. . . ." Right now we are hurrying through the nighttime of our experience. The shadows often are dark and menacing; but the morning comes, and with it a day that will never end! The night through which we are passing is only temporary. When the morning comes there will be no more sorrow, no more sadness, no more suffering, no more sickness, no more separations. "One glimpse of His dear face all sorrows will erase!" Joy cometh in the morning!

III. DAVID'S PRESUMPTION (30:6-7)

One of the remarkable things about the Bible is that its characters speak with astonishing honesty about themselves. People in ordinary life do not tend to be so candid about their own secret faults.

A. His Spiritual Pride Remembered (30:6-7a)

1. What He Had Felt (30:6)

"And in my prosperity I said, I shall never be moved." Uninterrupted good fortune is a peril to our souls. It is doubtless what we would choose if we could sit down before a great smorgasbord of life and pick the things we would like to have—and we would make ourselves thoroughly unhappy.

"In my prosperity I said, I shall never be moved." As soon as things go our way we tend to become careless of spiritual things. *This* world is the sworn enemy of *that* world. Solomon, the wise man of Israel, prayed that God would give him neither wealth nor poverty. But that was after he was wealthy beyond the dreams of avarice and had already laid the foundations of his own spiritual ruin. Things had gone well with David too, and in his prosperity he said, "I shall never be moved." It was a mistake, for then came the rough awakening. In David's case it came through a sickness that brought him down to the doors of death and taught him not to trust in circumstances. He tells us, then, what he had *felt.*

2. What He Had Forgotten

"LORD, by Thy favour Thou hast made my mountain to stand strong" (30:7a). He had forgotten that his strength lay in God. David's victorious troops had taken the dizzy heights of Zion. They had planted his banners upon the ancient Jebusite fortress. The hill country of Judah was all in David's hands. The whole land was at peace. There was not a nation on the horizon which dared to take up arms against him. He was strong. The Lord had made him strong. He had forgotten that.

We might well sing:

> Tell me the story often,
> For I forget so soon;
> The early dew of morning
> Has passed away at noon.

We have such treacherous memories. That is why we have the Lord's Supper. It is His constant voice saying to us, "Remember Me!"

Thus David tells us how his spiritual pride was remembered. He tells us just as honestly how:

B. His Spiritual Pride Rebuked (30:7b)

"Thou didst hide Thy face, and I was troubled." The word "troubled" is a strong one which expresses confusion, helplessness, and terror.

That is all the Lord needs to do—just hide His face and at once our world will fall apart. For God to hide His face, of course, is a figure of speech. It suggests God looking the other way, leaving us prey for the bullies of life to get at us, but held back because of God's watchfulness.

IV. DAVID'S PRAYER (30:8-10)

He has learned his lesson. He realizes now that his safety lies in keeping in constant touch with God, and the way to do this is through prayer. David was a great man of prayer. We can learn much about its secrets from him.

A. His Approach (30:8)

"I cried to Thee, O LORD, and unto the LORD I made supplication." What a wonderful God we have! Some people are very quick to take offense. Slight them or snub them, even unintentionally, and off they go in a huff. Forget to invite them to something, or fail to make sufficient fuss of them if you do invite them, and they get their backs up. To mollify them will take years, and even then they will scarcely forgive and be doubly watchful lest you should treat them so again.

Suppose God were like that! Suppose that if we slighted Him, ignored Him, forgot to consult Him, or even deliberately planned something apart from Him—suppose He was touchy, quick to take offense, harder to be propitiated than the offended brother of Solomon's proverb. What a blessing we do not have a touchy God! Suppose He snubbed us when we came back saying, "I'm sorry." Thank God He is not like that! "I cried to Thee, O LORD." David knew that God was a wonderful God.

B. His Appeal (30:9)

"What profit is there in my blood, when I go down to the pit? Shall the dust praise Thee? Shall it declare Thy truth?" Walk through an old graveyard. How many corpses can you hear praising God? Can the dust speak? "Lord, I'm more use to you living than dead!" That's David's argument.

The Old Testament saints had a gloomy view of death. Death to them was seen as an interruption in their communion with God, even for God's *saints.* They saw death as a continuation of existence, but on terms which robbed it of all that deserves to be called life. David shared the common view, and he uses it as part of his appeal to God.

C. His Application (30:10)

"Hear, O LORD, and have mercy upon me; LORD, be Thou my helper." It's a great idea to use the power of persuasion with God. Not because He needs to be convinced, but because we do. George Mueller was a master of the art. He would besiege the throne of grace with his arguments, telling the Lord that the orphans he had in his care were not his orphans at all—they were God's responsibility. *He* had declared Himself to be a "Father to the fatherless." God loves to hear us approach Him thus.

IV. DAVID'S PROCLAMATION (30:11-12)

He tells us what God had done in his life. As a result,

A. His Life Had Been Greatly Changed (30:11)

There is evidence of this *within*. "Thou hast turned for me my mourning into dancing." The transformation has taken place in his heart. God has taken away his inner gloom and given him instead an inner glow. Sighs have given way to songs, songs which set his feet in motion, that make him want to dance.

There is evidence *without*. Not just dancing, but "Thou hast put off my sackcloth, and girded me with gladness." The expression "put off" is a vivid one. The word is literally, "torn open," thus "Thou hast torn off my sackcloth." The gods of the heathen delight to see their worshipers in sackcloth, with long faces. Even Martin Luther used to think that God, even the true God, was like that. But God wants to tear off our sackcloth.

B. His Life Had Been Gloriously Channeled (30:12)

"To the end that my glory may sing praise to Thee, and not be silent. O LORD, my God, I will give thanks unto Thee for ever." John Bunyan in *Pilgrim's Progress* tells us of a man with a muckrake in his hand, forever grubbing in the muck and mire of earth, not knowing that over his head there hovered a crown of glory, because he never looked up. David suddenly looked up, dropped the muckrake with which he had been turning over and over his fears and failures, and saw that crown. He seized it with both hands.

His life was gloriously channeled: "I will give thanks unto Thee." Forever! What a way to end!

Psalm 31

LIFE'S UPS AND DOWNS

I. SALVATION AND STRENGTH (31:1-4)
  A. David's Desire (31:1)
  B. David's Defense (31:2-3)
  C. David's Danger (31:4)
II. SURRENDER AND SONG (31:5-8)
  A. The Redeemed Man (31:5)
  B. The Righteous Man (31:6)
  C. The Rejoicing Man (31:7-8)
    1. God Is Merciful (31:7a)
    2. God Is Mindful (31:7b)
    3. God Is Masterful (31:8)
III. SORROW AND SHAME (31:9-13)
  A. The Completeness of David's Grief (31:9-10)
    1. Encompassing Grief (31:9)
    2. Endless Grief (31:10a)
    3. Exhaustless Grief (31:10b)
  B. The Cause of David's Grief (31:11-13)
    1. He Was Forsaken (31:11)
    2. He Was Forgotten (31:12)
    3. He Was Fearful (31:13)
IV. SUPPLICATION AND SCORN (31:14-18)
  A. The Prayer for Victory (31:14-16)
  B. The Prayer for Vengeance (31:17-18)
V. SAFETY AND SYMPATHY (31:19-22)
  A. The Goodness of God (31:19)
  B. The Greatness of God (31:20)
  C. The Graciousness of God (31:21-22)
    1. How Wonderful He Is (31:21)
    2. How Wicked I Am (31:22)
VI. SWEETNESS AND STABILITY (31:23-24)
  A. Love for the Lord Urged (31:23)
  B. Loyalty to the Lord Urged (31:24)

THE SCHOLARS CANNOT AGREE about this psalm. Some point to incidents in David's life when he fled from Saul as being the time when it was written. Others maintain it was when David was crowned king in Hebron over the tribe of Judah. Some think Hezekiah wrote it. Others suggest Jeremiah as its author. Perhaps David wrote this psalm at some time after the Absalom rebellion, going back, as it were, over some of his life's experiences, reliving them, putting himself back in one situation after another.

Rotherham says this psalm is a mosaic of misery and mercy. Clarke sees faith fighting with feelings. Scroggie pictures David riding now the crest, now the trough of the wave. Hull reminds us that the psalm ultimately speaks of Jesus and urges us to read it in the light of that.

There can be no doubt that it is important. It is quoted by Jonah, by Jeremiah, and by Jesus, which would suffice to make it significant.

We creep up Calvary's hill just as the sufferings of Jesus are about to end. For six long hours the Holy One has suffered beyond our ability to comprehend. For the past three hours He has been the sin offering, alone with God and our sins in the darkness. Now it's all over. He is about to utter *His very last words* and he turns to this psalm: "Father, *into Thine hand I commit My spirit.*" That quotation alone embalms this psalm with fragrance and significance. The psalm divides into six parts, half a dozen pairs of contrasting or complementary ideas. We have salvation and strength; surrender and song; sorrow and shame; supplication and scorn; safety and sympathy; sweetness and stability.

I. SALVATION AND STRENGTH (31:1-4)

This scene is cast first in 1 Samuel 23:1-13. Keilah, a city on the Judean plain, was under attack by the Philistines and, even though it was a strong city consisting of two strongholds separated by a valley, the situation was desperate. David, following the clear leading of the Lord, took his men to the relief of Keilah and delivered it from the enemy. Nevertheless, the men of the city entered into treacherous correspondence with King Saul to betray David into his hand. David, warned by God, hastily pulled his men out of the place and headed once more for the hills. This is what seems to be in David's mind in the opening stanza.

David's Desire; "In Thee, O LORD, do I put my trust; let me never be ashamed" (31:1).

David's Defense: "Deliver me in Thy righteousness. Bow down Thine ear to me; deliver me speedily. Be Thou my strong rock, for an house of defense to save me . . . lead me, and guide me" (1b-3).

David's Danger: "Pull me out of the net that they have laid privily for me; for Thou art my strength" (31:4). Perhaps David had hoped to settle down in that Judean city, fortify it against Saul, and enjoy some relief from constant persecution. If so, he was disappointed. Salvation and strength were in God, not in a man-made fortress.

II. SURRENDER AND SONG (31:5-8)

The scene changes—so does the time and so do the circumstances. Saul is dead and David, still looking to the Lord for guidance, moves to Hebron, an important city in the Judean mountains midway between Beersheba and Jerusalem. Hebron was sacred to the memory of Abraham, Isaac, and Jacob, as well as to Joshua and Caleb. David was thirty years of age when the men of Judah came to Hebron and crowned him king. There was still to be desultory civil war between his forces and the rest of the nation, but David's fortunes were now improving and those of Saul's house were on the wane.

A. The Redeemed Man (31:5)

"Into Thine hand I commit my spirit; Thou hast redeemed me, O LORD God of truth." The word for redeemed here is the Hebrew word which means to redeem not by *payment,* but by *power.* It is first used in connection with the law's demand that the firstborn of an ass either be redeemed or else slain (Exodus 13:13). The context demanded that the first child of every Israelite had to be redeemed as well: "And it shall be," said Moses, "when thy son asketh thee in time to come, saying, What is this? that thou shalt say unto him, By strength of hand the LORD brought us out of Egypt, from the house of bondage" (Exodus 13:14).

David did not ascend the throne by subtlety and strength but by surrender: "Into Thy hand I commit my spirit." Because he was such a surrendered man, such a submissive man, God saw to it that he ascended to the throne—and by power. But not by his own power! God had long ago promised David he would be king and God redeemed His promise. *He* put David on the throne: "Thou hast redeemed me, O LORD God of truth." It was God's power that preserved David during his fugitive years and God's redeeming power that raised him to the throne.

B. The Righteous Man (31:6)

"I have hated them that regard lying vanities: but I trust in the LORD." Jonah had this very thing in mind when he cried to God from the belly of the fish. Lying vanities are things which come between the soul and God and, in particular, the false idols people worship. Jonah had allowed his own fanatical patriotism to come between him and God. He confessed that he had forsaken his own mercy. But in his desperation he put his trust in the Lord and the moment he did so God set him free.

C. The Rejoicing Man (31:7-8)

"I will be glad and rejoice in Thy mercy: for Thou hast considered my trouble; Thou hast known my soul in adversities; And hast not shut me up into the hand of the enemy: Thou hast set my feet in a large room" [or, as one translator suggests, "Thou hast set me at liberty"]. *God is merciful. God is mindful. God is masterful.* These are the three great themes for praise here. Well might David thus sing, as he stood at Hebron with the mighty tribe of Judah at his back. No longer would he be a weary fugitive with only outlaws for supporters and friends.

III. SORROW AND SHAME (31:9-13)

The scene shifts again. Now David is reliving the terrible months that followed his sin with Bathsheba and the murder of her husband. During those days his conscience lashed him unmercifully and the hand of God was heavy upon him. Several psalms suggest that, during this period, David not only suffered from remorse but actually became a leper. This psalm adds credence to this conclusion. David could never think back to this period in his life without a shudder.

A. The Completeness of David's Grief (31:9-10)

When will we learn that sin inevitably brings sorrow and shame? Sin is a killer. It destroys health, homes, happiness. It seems to promise freedom and fun and for a few tantalizing moments it seems to make good on its promise. But then come the regrets, the remorse, the ruin.

1. How Encompassing Was His Grief

"Have mercy upon me, O LORD, for I am in trouble: mine eye is consumed with grief, yea, my soul and my [inner man]" (31:9). Body and soul were being racked with pain.

2. How Endless Was His Grief

"For my life is spent with grief, and my years with sighing" (31:10a). What has happened to that happy David whose songs could charm away the evil spirits from the soul of Saul, who could go singing to meet the giant of Gath? Where is "the sweet singer of Israel" now? Day merged into night; night dragged on until daylight came. What difference did it make?

3. How Exhausting Was His Grief

"My strength faileth because of mine iniquity, and my bones are consumed" (31:10b). We note the completeness of David's grief.

B. The Cause of David's Grief (31:11-13)

The days following the murder of Uriah were almost unbearable to a man with a tender conscience like David. The period which followed David's public denunciation by Nathan is ignored by the historian for God takes no pleasure in our shame. But with David it was different, he does not hesitate to tell us what the historians conceal. That is one of the capital values of the psalms. They shed light on certain areas touched only lightly by the historian's pen, baring the emotions and unveiling the secrets of the heart, revealing the cause of David's grief.

1. He Was A Forsaken Man (31:11)

"I was a reproach among all mine enemies, but especially among my neighbours, and a fear to mine acquaintance: they that did see me without fled from me." This is one of the hints that David actually became a leper. Several of the psalms describe a grief and a horror so hopeless, and a physical condition so dreadful that leprosy seems to be the only way to account for the extravagance of David's despair and grief. Little did David think that the stolen waters of lustful passion would sweep him into such a quagmire of horror. He was a forsaken man.

2. He Was A Forgotten Man (31:12)

"I am forgotten as a dead man out of mind: I am like a broken vessel." David had always been a companionable man. But those friends of his who had so often sat down at his table for a meal, for a hearty laugh, and for a round of lively conversation—where were they now? It wasn't that they liked David less but he was socially dead. Such are the wages of sin. He was forsaken, a forgotten man.

3. He Was A Fearful Man (31:13)

"For I have heard the slander of many: fear was on every side: while they took counsel together against me, they devised to take away my life." Assassination was a quick and handy way to get rid of him and clear the throne for Absalom or for another of his sons, or even for someone else entirely. The air was full of rumor and plot.

The expression, "fear on every side," is especially significant. They called David by a nickname: *"magor missaviv"*—"terror round about." The expression became a favorite phrase of the great prophet Jeremiah (6:25; 20:3-4; 46:5). Probably nobody ever suffered so much as he in Old Testament times. Yet even the weeping prophet had to go to David for the fitting phrase to describe his griefs—*magor missaviv.*

IV. Supplication and Scorn (31:14-18)

Now David puts himself back in the time of Absalom's rebellion. The foes are gathering and David sees himself fleeing from Jerusalem with his bodyguard. As he went his heart had been lifted up by prayer and this psalm tells us how he prayed.

A. The Prayer for Victory (31:14-16)

David knew where His strength lay, even though his kingdom was in ruins. We note three themes in this part of his prayer. He wants *conscious victory:* "But I trusted in Thee, O LORD: I said, Thou art my God" (31:14). He calls upon the two appropriate names for God: Jehovah, the God of *covenant,* and Elohim, the God of *creation.* His kingdom may have fallen apart but he still had God, whose *promise* set him on the throne and whose *power* can set him back there—all circumstances to the contrary notwithstanding.

He wants *continuous victory:* "My times are in Thy hand: deliver me from the hand of mine enemies, and from them that persecute me" (31:15). My times are in Thy hand! It is a wonderful statement. Almost instinctively we take it up and make it our very own. Dan Crawford, that great pioneer African missionary, once said that if he wanted to quote these words to a native, "My times are in Thy hands," he would be forced to translate it: "All my life's ways and whens and wheres and wherefores are in God's hands!" What more could we want than that?

He wants *conspicuous victory:* "Make Thy face to shine upon Thy servant: save me for Thy mercies' sake" (31:16). Our thoughts fly instantly to a greater King than David, suffering an even greater rejection in that selfsame city, wending His way toward Gethsemane with similar words. But if on David's lips there was a prayer for *victory,* there was something else on his lips, something that was not heard on the lips of his so very much greater Son.

B. The Prayer for Vengeance (31:17-18)

"Lord!" David cries, "Shame them! Silence them!" "Let me not be ashamed, O LORD; for I have called upon Thee: let the wicked be ashamed, and let them be silent in the grave. Let the lying lips be put to silence; which speak grievous things proudly and contemptuously against the righteous." There can be no doubt that David was under great pressure and extreme provocation. We only need to think of Shimei, that reptile of the house of Saul, and his venomous words to understand why David pleaded thus for God to shame and silence his foes. And in his day a cry to God for righteous retribution was in order.

V. SAFETY AND SYMPATHY (31:19-22)

The dark days are over. The throne is once again David's and he sits upon it in peace with no clouds upon the horizon.

A. The Goodness of God (31:19)

"Oh how great is Thy goodness, which Thou hast laid up for them that fear Thee, which Thou hast wrought for them that trust in Thee before the sons of men!" The word translated "laid up" is sometimes rendered "treasured up." God's goodness is an inexhaustible treasure stored up for the use of His own.

B. The Greatness of God (31:20)

"Thou shalt hide them in the secret of Thy presence from the pride of man: Thou shalt keep them secretly in a pavilion from the strife of tongues." David suffered much in his life from gossipers. Undoubtedly he provided some fuel for the fire, but his critics were unmerciful, malicious, and persistent. David discovered that he could hide in God's presence from what one translator calls "the scourge of slander." It is no use answering such people. Anything you say will simply be twisted and distorted. Get into the presence of God, let Him pour His balm into your soul, and let Him answer those who would maliciously wound with their tongues.

C. The Graciousness of God (31:21-22)

Ah, says David, *how wonderful He is!* "Blessed be the LORD: for He hath showed me His marvellous kindness in a strong city." That "strong city," of course, was Jerusalem. As David headed for the Jordan and then on up toward the land of Gilead with his ragged band of fellow fugitives; as he heard the daily news of further defections and of the strengthening of Absalom's might; as he heard how Ahiphothel, the crafty, had joined the conspiracy; as he looked at his own meager forces and weighed his chances against the growing might of the usurper; David must have despaired of ever seeing Jerusalem again.

But there he was! Back in the strong city. Reveling in the graciousness of God. How wonderful He is! That is what David thought.

How worthless I am! "For I said in my haste, I am cut off from before Thine eyes: nevertheless Thou heardest the voice of my supplications when I cried unto Thee." He confesses in the hour of triumph his wavering faith; how he had thought himself cast out of God's sight. It had been a black moment. And it had been a thought so unworthy of God. No wonder he speaks now of the graciousness of God. How wonderful He is! How wicked I am! We have all had similar thoughts.

VI. SWEETNESS AND STABILITY (31:23-24)

The scene changes for the last time, only now David is no longer thinking of the vicissitudes of his own checkered career; he is thinking of the people of God. He has two things to urge as he brings his song to a close.

A. Love for the Lord (31:23)

"O love the LORD, all ye His saints: for the LORD preserveth the faithful, and plentifully rewardeth the proud doer." It seems incredible that we should have to be urged to love the Lord! We only have to look within our own wicked hearts, however, to see how little love we really have for Him. We sing!

> My Jesus, I love Thee, I know Thou art mine;
> For Thee all the pleasures of sin I resign.

But we really don't love Him very much. He says: "If ye love Me keep My commandments!" That's the acid test! It's easy for us to sing about how much we love Him—especially when everything is going our way. The real test is whether or not we do what He says. So David urges love for the Lord.

B. Loyalty to the Lord (31:24)

"Be of good courage, and He shall strengthen your heart, all ye that hope in the LORD." There may be times when circumstances frown, when things to wrong, when all looks black. The tempter may come and whisper words of discouragement, doubt, and defeat.

John the Baptist knew about that. There he was in Herod's dungeon facing certain death—just for speaking the truth of God with the fearless courage of a prophet. He had denounced Herod for stealing his own brother's wife and, in so doing, he had earned the malicious hate of the woman involved. He sends a message to Jesus: "Have I made a mistake? Where is this messianic kingdom I have so fearlessly and faithfully preached? Are you really the Messiah? Why am I in prison? Nothing seems to be working out the way it should."

Be loyal! That was the essence of the Lord's message back to John. All is well, the kingdom's on the way! But it is going to take time. It has to begin in the hearts and lives and souls of men. "Be of good courage, and He shall strengthen your heart, all ye that hope in the LORD."

Psalm 32

THE SIN QUESTION

I. SIN AS SEEN BY THE SINNER (32:1-7)
   A. The Pleasure We Feel When Sin Is Cleansed (32:1-2)
      1. Sin Is a Defiance (32:1a)
      2. Sin Is a Defect (32:1b)
      3. Sin Is a Distortion (32:2a)
      4. Sin Is a Deception (32:2b)
   B. The Penalty We Face When Sin Is Concealed (32:3-4)
      David had once been:
      1. A Healthy Man (32:3)
      2. A Happy Man (32:4a)
      3. A Hearty Man (32:4b)
   C. The Pardon We Find When Sin Is Confessed (32:5)
   D. The Path We Follow When Sin Is Conquered (32:6-7)
      1. The Power of Prayer (32:6a)
      2. The Power of Position (32:6b-7a)
      3. The Power of Peace (32:7b)
      4. The Power of Praise (32:7c)
II. SIN AS SEEN BY THE SAVIOUR (32:8-11)

   We need to be:
   A. Guided (32:8)
   B. Governed (32:9)
   C. Guarded (32:10)
   D. Gladdened (32:11)

IF ONE REALLY WANTS TO KNOW the intricacies of a subject the best thing is to find an expert, someone who has had wide experience of it. Ask him! David is such a help to us in this prevalent and personal matter of sin because he, himself, was such a great sinner. For although David was one of the greatest *saints* of Scripture and one of the greatest *sages* of Scripture and one of the greatest *sovereigns* of Scripture, he was also one of the greatest *sinners* of Scripture. He sinned with a high-handed rebellion and with a depth of cunning and duplicity which would astonish us did we not know the wickedness of our own hearts.

Three times he uses that significant word, *selah!* "There! what do you think of that?" "When I kept silence, my bones waxed old . . . my moisture is turned into the drought of summer. *Selah.*" "I said, I will confess my transgressions unto the LORD, and Thou forgavest the iniquity of my sin. *Selah.*" "Thou shalt compass me about with songs of deliverance. *Selah.*" Conviction! Confession! Confidence! Think about that!

David was a haunted man after he had seduced the wife of his most loyal soldier, and arranged with Joab for the murder of the man himself. For the best part of a year David put up a bold front and tried to brazen it, haunted at night, haughty by day. Then God sent Nathan the prophet to publicly accuse and condemn the king—and then to promise forgiveness when he saw the tears of repentance flow. Like the lancing of a boil it brought immediate relief.

At once David wrote Psalm 51 in which he promised he would teach transgressors God's ways. He did so by writing Psalm 32. This is a *maschil* psalm, the first of thirteen such teaching psalms in the Hebrew hymnbook. From his own bitter experience David intends in Psalm 32 to set forth a sermon in song on the nature of sin, what happens when it is concealed, and what happens when it is confessed, cleansed, and conquered. So then Psalm 32 is both a sermon and a song. If, as Augustine said, "The beginning of knowledge is to know thyself to be a sinner," then here we have the place where all true knowledge begins.

I. SIN AS SEEN BY THE SINNER (32:1-7)

David looks at his sin from four different points of view. He does not begin, however, at the beginning. He begins with a tremendous shout of joy!

A. The Pleasure We Feel When Sin is Cleansed (32:1-2)

Sin is so radical an offense against God that the Holy Spirit uses fifteen different Hebrew words to describe it in the Old Testament. In the first two verses of this psalm alone David uses four of them: transgression, sin, iniquity, and guile.

Sin is a defiance. That is what the word "transgression" means. Sin is rebellion, revolt against lawful authority. It is what a child manifests when he says "No!" to a parental command. It is what makes a child test every regulation, rule, and restriction placed upon him.

Sin is a defect. The word David uses for "sin" comes from a Hebrew root that means "to miss the mark" or "to fall short." It indicates something missing in one's life, a defect, a coming short of the glory of God.

Sin is a distortion. The word for "iniquity" denotes "perverseness," coming as it does from a Hebrew root meaning "bent" or "crooked." Human nature is warped, bent, and twisted instead of being straight, perfect, and true.

Sin is a deception. The word "guile" needs no explanation. It stands for the insincerity, cunning, and duplicity of human nature.

David in his sin with Bathsheba and in his murder of Uriah had acted in revolt against divine authority. He had fallen short of the law's minimum demands. He had expressed the perversity and crook-edness of his heart. He had craftily sought to hide his sin and, when that failed, to pretend that nothing was wrong. All this he confesses in his opening comments.

No wonder he begins with a happy shout of joy. "Blessed [Happy] is he whose transgression is forgiven, whose sin is covered. Blessed is the man unto whom the LORD imputeth not iniquity, and in whose spirit there is no guile." David begins his psalm with a beatitude. His sin is forgiven! It is covered! It is no longer imputed! It is *forgiven!* The word means literally, "to be taken up and carried away!" The *burden* of it has been lifted. Just as Bunyan's Pilgrim came at length with his back-breaking load of sin to the cross and suddenly felt the burden roll away, so David's burden was lifted and carried away.

Covered! The *blemish* of his sin has been put out of sight. Nothing, so long as time lasts, will put it out of sight of the gossips, we can be sure of that, but it has been covered in God's sight and that's what matters.

Not imputed! That is an accounting expression meaning that the debt is not reckoned. The *bankruptcy* of his sin has been taken care of. There's a source of joy enough for any poor sinner. God is willing to carry his sin away, cover it, cancel it. God is the only One able to deal thus with sin. Only the eternal, omnipotent God who controls all the factors of time and space could ever remove sin and its conse-quences and even He can do it only because of Calvary. Well might the cleansed sinner sing:

> My sin! Oh the bliss of this glorious thought,
> My sin, not the part but the whole
> Is nailed to His cross and I bear it no more,
> Praise the Lord, praise the Lord, O my soul!

B. The Penalty We Face When Sin Is Concealed (32:3-4)

Before David made a complete breast of his sin and openly con-fessed it, he tried to hide it; but sin is very hard to conceal. Too many people knew about what he had done, knew of the visit of Uriah to Jerusalem, his dedicated refusal to take his ease at home when the army was fighting furiously in the field, and his convenient death. Bathsheba's stealthy visits to the palace or David's nocturnal visits to her home would have been hard to hide, not to mention the letter— that compromising letter containing his own death warrant that Uriah had carried so unsuspectingly to Joab. We can be sure Joab still had that letter. Tool turned tyrant—that was Joab from that moment on.

But David tried to conceal his sin and paid the penalty. He had always been a *healthy man,* for he had lived an active, busy, outdoors life. But no more. Sin and conscience sapped his physical strength, his "bones waxed old." That's one of the prices of concealing sin. It takes a physical toll.

David had always been a *happy man,* known as "the sweet singer of Israel." But no more! Horror at his sin and the fierce fires of conscience drove him to sobs and groans, "roaring all the day long. For day and night Thy hand was heavy upon me."

David had always been a *hearty* man, the kind of person who attracted men—and women. But no more. Now we see him listless, unhappy, and wretched. "My moisture is turned to the drought of summer." His vitality was sapped, he was utterly spent.

It is always that way when we have something on our conscience. We conceal it and have it well hidden, so we think. But it cannot be hidden from God. If it is not confessed and cleansed then God will deal with it Himself. There is a high price tag on sin. *Selah!*

C. The Pardon We Find When Sin Is Confessed (32:5)

"I acknowledged my sin unto Thee, and mine iniquity have I not hid. I said, I will confess my transgressions unto the LORD; and Thou forgavest the iniquity of my sin."

One of the curious things in recent history is the pardoning of President Richard Nixon by President Gerald Ford. It began on June 17, 1972 with a seemingly minor crime—a bungled burglary. Two years later it blossomed into a national scandal. People in the highest offices in the land were found to be involved and their names were forever tarnished. Close associates of the president went to jail. The press, like hounds after a fleeing fox, bayed and barked at the heels of the president. At length the House Judiciary Committee approved three articles of impeachment and pressure for the president's resignation mounted. What had begun with a scrap of tape on a basement lock ended with an all-time first—the resignation of a president of the United States.

But again clamor was raised—this time for Mr. Nixon's arraignment before the courts. Gerald Ford faced the dismal prospect of the whole set of dirty political linen being once more washed in public, before the courts, in the face of the world for months and years to come. He did an astonishing thing: He pardoned Richard Nixon. Before the former president could be arraigned, tried, and condemned—he was pardoned! Then the public outcry turned against President Ford—and with some justification. After all, you cannot pardon a man who says that he is *not guilty,* and Mr. Nixon, to the last, refused to acknowledge guilt.

Said David: "I acknowledged my sin unto Thee, and mine iniquity have I not hid. I said, I will confess my transgressions unto the LORD." Anyone crushed in heart by a knowledge of guilt and sin can come and find the pardon God offers when sin is confessed. Sin does not need to be confessed to a man, unless it involves that man. There were hundreds of priests in Israel in David's day, but David took his sin straight to the Lord.

D. The Path We Follow When Sin Is Conquered (32:6-7)

It is one thing to get out of the condemned cell; it is something else to live a godly life. Unless sin in the life is conquered, a pardon is just a license to go on sinning. David tells us four things that mark out the way of victory over sin.

The power of prayer: "For this shall every one that is godly pray." That is the first thing to do when tempted—pray! Sin is too big a thing to be handled alone.

When the *Titanic* struck that massive iceberg things were suddenly different in the wireless shack. When the *Californian* broke in at 11:00 P.M. with the sixth ice warning, the *Titanic's* wireless operator had simply told her to shut up and hadn't bothered sending the warning to the bridge. When the frantic SOS signals were sounding over the radio waves, it was too late! Don't wait until you strike! Send up your SOS now! Realize the power of prayer.

The power of position: "For this shall every one that is godly pray unto Thee in a time when Thou mayest be found: surely in the floods of great waters they shall not come nigh unto him. Thou art my hiding place." David found a hiding place from the dreadful storm near to the heart of God.

That was the best that could be said in the Old Testament: a man could draw near to God. In the New Testament our life is hid with Christ in God. Here, for instance, is a valuable deed. You put that deed in your safety deposit box and then you put that safety deposit box in the vault at the bank. Here is a redeemed human life, something very valuable to God, purchased at infinite cost. He puts that life in Christ; then he enfolds Christ in Himself. *That* is the power of position. As Toplady the hymn writer put it:

> Rock of Ages, cleft for me,
>   Let me hide myself in Thee;
> Let the water and the blood
>   From Thy riven side which flowed,
> Be of sin the double cure,
>   Save me from its guilt and power.

The power of peace. "Thou shalt preserve me from trouble." The believer is not exempt from troubles. Satan will often use them to worry and weaken us. God wants to use them to strengthen us. David had his fair share of trouble, and he had more to come. His whole family was yet to dissolve in ruins as adultery and murder would break out again and again among his own sons. Yet David would be preserved. What a wonderful peace! Come what may, God will not change.

> Peace, perfect peace,
>   In this dark world of sin?
>   The blood of Jesus whispers
>   Peace within.

The power of praise: "Thou shalt compass me about with songs of deliverance." David saw himself completely circled with song! This was the man who, moments before, had been talking about his "roaring"—his irrepressible anguish. Praise is a wonderful thing; it disarms the enemy! What can he do to a person who turns every experience of life into an opportunity for praise?

Look at Paul and Silas in prison with their backs torn to shreds by a Roman scourge and their hands and feet bound fast with chains of iron. The whole prison rings with harmony as two mutilated missionaries sing praises to God. Their songs lead to the conversion of the jailer and all his house. How could they sing under such circumstances? They believed in the truth of Romans 8:28. "Thou shalt compass me about with songs of deliverance. *Selah!*"

II. Sin As Seen by the Saviour (32:8-11)

Even when we have been forgiven and been received into the family of God, sin still lurks as a lion in the way.

A. We Need To Be Guided (32:8)

"I will instruct thee and teach thee in the way which thou shalt go: I will guide thee with Mine eye." The speaker is now the Lord Himself, who begins by putting us in the classroom. The textbook is the Bible. The teacher is the Holy Spirit. Often when we think of guidance we have our *careers* in mind; God usually has our *character* in mind. The Bible is full of principles which, if heeded, will keep us from making foolish and sometimes fatal choices.

A thorough knowledge of the Psalms, the Proverbs, the Gospels, and the Epistles will often be sufficient to guide us. Where God has spoken on a subject, there is no need to look any further for guidance. For instance, a believing Christian man, who is contemplating business expansion, wonders if he should take a partner. Someone comes along with plenty of capital, great ideas, and a charming personality, but he is not a believer. He offers to come into partnership. What should the believer do? Well, God has spoken: "Be not unequally yoked together with unbelievers." That should be the end of it.

But note! God wants to guide us with His eye! He did that for Peter, when Peter was in trouble, warming his hands at the world's fire, getting deeper and deeper into a situation too big for him to handle, denying his Lord, cursing and swearing. He was arrested by the crowing of the cock. At that critical moment the Lord "turned and looked on Peter." That was all. Just a look. He did not speak to him, simply guided His erring disciple with His eye: "Remember, Peter! Remember! Satan hath desired to have you but I have prayed for you. You're in the wrong place, Peter; you're with the wrong people." It was all that Peter needed.

If the Lord is to guide us with His eye, it means that we must stay close to Him. A person cannot give another person a *warning* look or a *warm* look or a *welcoming* look if he is in Chicago and the friend in Atlanta. They must be within sight of each other. Nor can he guide with his eye if his friend is not looking at him. How desperately we need guidance in our journey through this world! Let us see to it that we allow our Lord to guide us by keeping our Bibles open and our eye ever looking to Him. He will make it plain what we ought to do.

B. We Need to Be Governed (32:9)

"Be ye not as the horse, or as the mule, which have no understanding: whose mouth must be held in with bit and bridle, lest they come near unto thee," or, as some have rendered that: "else they will not come near unto thee." The horse has a nature which makes it want to run away; the mule has a nature which makes it refuse to move. The Lord does not wish to handle us like a dumb beast with a wild and willful nature. He does not want to have to bridle us. The only way to govern a beast of burden is to put a bit in its mouth and a bridle on its head; then it has to do what its master wants. God would have us show more sense than that!

C. We Need To Be Guarded (32:10)

"Many sorrows shall be to the wicked: but he that trusteth in the LORD, mercy shall compass him about." Graham Scroggie suggests that the wicked man is surrounded by a swarm of *wasps* which will sting him and drive him before them. They have many sorrows in store for him. The saved man is surrounded by a swarm of *bees,* busy storing honey for him. The word translated "sorrows" signifies calamities. They are all around us and the wicked will fall prey to them. We need to be guarded so that they might not harm us even if they come our way.

D. We Need To Be Gladdened (32:11)

"Be glad in the LORD, and rejoice, ye righteous: and shout for joy, all ye that are upright in heart." What a lot we have to sing and shout about! We have salvation, sanctification, and security! We have the best of this world and the best of the world to come! We have more than heart can desire! We have freedom to meet with the people of

God, and answers to every problem we could possibly face in God's Word. Yet often we look gloomy, as though we were friendless and forsaken.

Let us try *singing,* for a change! Ira Sankey, the great song leader who accompanied D. L. Moody on his campaigns, used to sing:

> My life flows on in an endless song;
> Above earth's lamentation;
> I hear the sweet, not far-off hymn
> That hails the new creation;
> Through all the tumult and the strife
> I hear the music ringing;
> It finds an echo in my soul—
> How can I keep from singing?

"Shout!" And remember, this is not David who is the speaker here, but the Lord Himself: *"Shout for joy* all ye that are upright in heart."

Psalm 33

FROM EVERLASTING THOU ART GOD

I. THE LORD AND HIS PRAISE (33:1-3)
We Are To Praise Him:
   A. Thankfully (33:1)
   B. Thoroughly (33:2)
   C. Thoughtfully (33:3)
II. THE LORD AND HIS POWER (33:4-9)
   A. The Moral Power of His Word (33:4-5)
   B. The Manifest Power of His Word (33:6-7)
   C. The Moving Power of His Word (33:8)
   D. The Matchless Power of His Word (33:9)
III. THE LORD AND HIS PROVIDENCE (33:10-19)
   A. The Nations and Their Decisions (33:10-12)
      1. Those That Rebel at God's Word (33:10-11)
      2. Those That Respond to God's Word (33:12)
   B. The Nations and Their Destinies (33:13-19)
   The Lord looks at:
      1. Their Communities (33:13-14)
      2. Their Characteristics (33:15)
      3. Their Conflicts (33:16-17)
      4. Their Calamities (33:18-19)
IV. THE LORD AND HIS PEOPLE (33:20-22)
   A. The Help of the Saved (33:20)
   B. The Happiness of the Saved (33:21)
   C. The Hope of the Saved (33:22)

PSALMS 32 AND 33 are organically linked together, so much so that some commentaries treat them as one. In the first book of Psalms (Psalms 1–41) all have a title or a caption with only four exceptions: Psalms 1, 2, 10, and 33. All the others have some sort of a heading. Often it is simply the expression "A Psalm of David," sometimes there is more.

The first two psalms are organically linked together by their *situation*. They stand shoulder to shoulder at the beginning of the book, one to introduce us to the *law* and the other to the *prophets*. The entire book revolves around these two centers. Similarly, Psalms 9 and 10 are linked by their *structure,* in the form of a continuing but irregular acrostic. Psalm 32 and 33 are linked by their *subject*—the mercy and majesty of God. Together they set Him forth as a God of infinite grace and greatness. One deals with God as Redeemer, the other with God as Creator.

We do not know who wrote Psalm 33 but it seems to have been written in a time of national crisis; nor do we know who linked it to Psalm 32. Psalm 33 reveals that the God of Heaven is the God of history, for His hand can be seen just as clearly in the way He controls the destinies of men as in the way He creates empires in space. Souls and stars alike bend ultimately to His will.

I. THE LORD AND HIS PRAISE (33:1-3)

The psalm begins with praise. In fact, praise is commanded along three distinct lines.

A. Thankfully (33:1)

"Rejoice in the LORD, O ye righteous: for praise is comely for the upright." It is here that the structural link with the preceding psalm is evident. It is not so evident perhaps in the King James text, but it is evident when we get behind the English translation to the Hebrew. Rotherham translates the very last line of Psalm 32: "Ring out your joy all ye upright in heart." He translates the opening line: "Ring out your joy ye righteous in Jehovah," one psalm leading to the other.

There are some basic differences between the two psalms, but the organic link between them is real. Psalm 32 is impassioned, Psalm 33 is impersonal; Psalm 32 is emotional, Psalm 33 is logical; Psalm 32 is experiential, Psalm 33 is expositional; Psalm 32 deals with God's pardon, Psalm 33 with God's power; Psalm 32 shows us the throne of God's grace, Psalm 33 the throne of God's government; Psalm 32 deals with the heart, Psalm 33 deals with Heaven.

Here then is the vital connection between the two psalms. We can ring out our joy in Psalm 32 because our sins are forgiven. But sin contaminates the whole universe. We can ring out our joy in Psalm 33 because the God who forgives our sins in Psalm 32 is the God who controls the factors of space and time. No wonder we can praise Him thankfully.

B. Thoroughly (33:2)

"Praise the LORD with harp: sing unto Him with the psaltery and an instrument of ten strings." Tune up the orchestra! Pull out the stops! Bring all the musical skills you have and use them to sound forth the praises of our God. God is not displeased with instrumental music in our meetings. In the Old Testament it was commanded again and again. In the New Testament, music begins in the heart, but it can be expressed with the hands as well as with the voice. We are to praise Him thoroughly.

C. Thoughtfully (33:3)

"Sing unto Him a new song; play skilfully with a loud noise." A new song but an old theme! A new song calls for thought and exercise, for skill and careful composition. There are seven new songs in the Old Testament—six of them are in the Psalms (33:3; 40:3; 96:1; 98:1; 144:9; 149:1) and one in Isaiah 42:10. The word for "a new song" in the original text suggests a song never heard before. That calls for thought. Our thoughts about God should ever be exploring new frontiers of wonder and awe and should ever be expressing themselves in new paeans of praise. The psalm begins with the Lord and his praise.

II. THE LORD AND HIS POWER (33:4-9)

At once our thoughts are directed to the Word, for the Lord expresses His power in His Word. "In the beginning was the *word* and the word was with God and the word was God." When the Lord Jesus came to earth that Word was translated for us into something we could comprehend and understand, for "the word was made flesh and dwelt among us." The Psalmist has four things to tell us about the word—the "word of His power," as Hebrews 1:3 phrases it.

A. The Moral Power of His Word (33:4-5)

"The word of the LORD is right; and all His works are done in truth. He loveth righteousness and judgment: the earth is full of the goodness of the LORD." The world today has lost its moorings. We have cast the ship of state adrift upon the tides of time without sail, anchor, rudder, chart, or compass. We have abandoned the objective standards of morality taught, for instance, in the Ten Commandments, and as a result people are bewildered. Children come into our classrooms without any knowledge of right and wrong and are an easy prey for the dope pusher, the pervert, the sensualist.

Some time ago I found it necessary to fly out of Boston to Presque Isle, Maine. I was booked aboard a Bar Harbor plane (one of those little planes that hold about a dozen people). The weather was foggy with low-lying clouds. I wished I had found some other way to go when the plane took off and we plunged at once into a dense bank of clouds and began to pitch up and down almost as much as we lurched forward.

We hadn't been in the air two minutes before I began to wonder whether those two fellows up front knew what they were doing. I couldn't see a thing with the fog, the clouds, and the turbulence. Moreover, it was very late afternoon and night was coming on. I had only one ray of comfort. I could *see* those two fellows and they didn't seem to be the least bit worried! In front of them they had a big dashboard of instruments—clocks, dials, and gauges. They didn't look at the clouds outside, but at their instruments. They were not flying by sight, but by faith, guided not by their feelings, but by their instruments.

Without those instruments the pilot has to rely on his feelings or his senses. In blind flying, a pilot is deprived of visual references and he also loses his ability to distinguish between the usual forces of gravity and the "g-forces" of turning, diving, or climbing. Instrument flying is based on the principle that the pilot must have an accurate standard of reference outside of himself. He must obey it whether he feels like it or not. That is why I survived the trip from Boston to Presque Isle. Those two pilots on that little plane had faith in their instruments and those instruments brought them safely through the clouds, the fog, and the darkness to a pinpoint landing on an airstrip at our destination.

In the area of the moral and the spiritual, modern man has decided he needs no outside standard of reference. He has given birth to a permissive society which has no absolute standards of right and wrong. Everybody does his own thing. As a result homes are smashing up at an alarming rate; children in school experiment with dangerous drugs; men and women live promiscuously, ignoring the inevitable consequences of divine judgment; the most horrible forms of perversion are allowed to express themselves openly; pornography is allowed to propagate itself; crime goes very largely unpunished.

The arguments of those who espouse these things sound reasonable but that is only because society has abandoned the objective standards God has provided. For, like it or not, there *are* absolutes of morality. They are contained in God's Word: "For the word of the LORD is *right;* and all His works are done in *truth.* He loveth righteousness and judgment." People who abandon the objective standard of the Word of God will inevitably come crashing down. It's as much a law of the soul and of the state as instrument flying is a law of the sky. Such is the moral power of God's Word.

B. The Manifest Power of His Word (33:6-7)

"By the word of the LORD were the heavens made; and all the host of them by the breath of His mouth. He gathereth the waters of the sea together as an heap: He layeth up the depth in storehouses." The same almighty Word that breathes through the pages of the Bible is the very Word that spoke the stars into being in the early morn of time.

Astronomers have been aware for some fifty years that we are living in an expanding universe—that is, all the galaxies are traveling away from us at fantastic speeds up to one hundred million miles an hour. Moreover, the further away from us the galaxies are, the faster they are traveling. Some of the distances are beyond our understanding. In recent years astronomers have photographed quasars (galaxy-like objects of exceptional brilliance) at distances of fifteen billion light years away from the earth. One light year is six trillion miles.

This discovery of an expanding universe has upset the old theory of a steady-state universe—one in which the universe was believed to have been eternal and without beginning. That theory is no longer tenable because it fails to accommodate all the facts. The universe *did* have a beginning and a very remarkable beginning it was. These new discoveries in astronomy were anything but welcome to many scientists.

The crux of their problem was simple—if the universe simply exploded into existence at a given moment in time, *what caused that prodigious effect?* It certainly had to be a cause commensurate with the result. Many simply did not want to face the implications of that for it confronted them with God. To the materialist, these discoveries in astronomy are like a bad dream. The theologians were right all the time—"In the beginning, God." The Psalmist puts it thus: "By the word of the LORD were the heavens made; and all the host of them by the breath of His mouth." No scientist can argue with that on scientific grounds at least.

C. The Moving Power of His Word (33:8)

"Let all the earth fear the LORD: let all the inhabitants of the world stand in awe of Him." That is the counsel of sound common sense. Behind the universe is a God who is at once both omniscient and omnipotent. Well might the world stand in awe of Him. Men should be moved to the depths of their beings by the thought of such a God—not just try to thrust away such thoughts.

One Princeton University professor, a scientist who has made important contributions to the theory of the expanding universe, said: "What the universe was like at the day minus one, before the big bang, one has no idea. The equations refuse to tell us. I refuse to speculate." That is illogical. Driven by the sheer logic of facts right back to the morning of creation, he digs in his heels and refuses to take one step more because he knows full well that one step more will bring him face to face with God—as though refusing to take that step makes any difference to the fact. "I refuse to speculate."

There is no need for speculation. The God who was there has revealed Himself. The name the Psalmist uses for God, interestingly enough, is not *Elohim,* the God of *creation,* but *Jehovah,* the God of *revelation.* There is therefore no excuse. God *has* revealed Himself and the motivating power of His Word should drive us to worship.

D. The Matchless Power of His Word (33:9)

"He spake, and it was done; He commanded, and it stood fast." Just like that! "Light be," he said, and light was. One word from Him and the universe rushed out some fifteen billion light years into space. Just one word!

We have, then, the Lord and *His praise* and we have the Lord and *His power*. The psalmist, however, is only warming up to his theme. He is reveling in the God of Psalm 32, the infinitely compassionate and forgiving God who, as Psalm 33 declares, controls all the factors of space and time. Because He does He can will our sins into oblivion.

III. THE LORD AND HIS PROVIDENCE (33:10-19)

The nations are in His hands. The psalmist looks at the nations, their decisions, and their destinies and he concludes that God is in control.

A. The Nations and Their Decisions (33:10-12)

He looks, first, at *the nations that rebel at God's Word:* "The LORD bringeth the counsel of the heathen [the nations] to nought: He maketh the devices of the people of none effect. The counsel of the LORD standeth for ever, the thoughts of His heart to all generations" (33:10-11). For instance, God is not impressed by the atheism and militarism of the Soviet Union, a nation of some two hundred million people which has officially embraced atheism as a national creed. For the past several score of decades it has been zealously spreading atheism to nation after nation and, on the surface, it seems to have met with tremendous success. It is tireless in its zeal, crafty in its policies, global in its ambitions, awesome in its armed might. But it is not going to win! Its total and devastating overthrow has already been decreed; the place has been chosen and the time set. God has pledged Himself to bring the counsels of this nation to nothing. The Psalmist says: "The LORD bringeth the counsel of the [nations] to nought."

Then the Psalmist looks at *the nations that respond to God's Word:* "Blessed is the nation whose God is the LORD; and the people whom He hath chosen for His own inheritance" (33:12). In its full Biblical context that nation is Israel, but the principle has wider application. In the heyday of empire, for instance, Britain was governed by a succession of godly men, or at least men who owned and acknowledged God. That is why the nation was so singularly blessed; the same is true of the United States. The decline both of Britain and America is in step with their growing independence of God.

B. The Nations and Their Destinies (33:13-19)

The Psalmist looks at *their communities:* "The LORD looketh from heaven; He beholdeth all the sons of men" (33:13-14). He looks at *their characteristics:* "He fashioned their hearts alike; He considereth all their works" (33:15). Each nation has its own characteristics, yet at heart they are all the same. Whether it be the arctic Eskimo or the African Zulu; whether it be the Afghan peasant or the American physicist, each is different—yet each has the same basic needs.

The Psalmist looks at *their conflicts:* "There is no king saved by the multitude of an host: a mighty man is not delivered by much strength. An horse is a vain thing for safety: neither shall He deliver any by his great strength" (33:16-17). No matter how powerful a nation might be, no matter how great its armaments, no matter how mobilized for war—God is not impressed.

The Psalmist looks at *their calamities:* "Behold, the eye of the LORD is upon them that fear Him, upon them that hope in His mercy; to deliver their soul from death, and to keep them alive in famine" (33:18-19). He sees and saves His own. The destinies of the nations are in His hands. World affairs are not, ultimately, decided in the Kremlin or in Washington. The economic fate of the nations does not lie in the hands of the oil-rich Arabs. God is on the throne. The God who guides the paths of the stars, who brings into being countless stars and their satellites, who tosses them into intangible space, who keeps them whirling and plunging at inconceivable velocities on prodigious orbits with such mathematical precision that we can foretell, years in advance, the visit of a comet or the occasion of an eclipse—*that* God also holds the destinies of the nations in *His* hands.

The men in the Kremlin may think they can outplay God on the great chessboard of time, but God has overthrown nations just as belligerent as Russia. Nobody ever checkmates Him! His *King* is always in control.

IV. THE LORD AND HIS PEOPLE (33:20-22)

A. The Help of the Saved (33:20)

"Our soul waiteth for the LORD: He is our help and our shield." Waiting seems to be the agelong lot of God's people. It often seems as though our prayers go unanswered, that God takes a long time to act. But help is on the way! God works to His own mysterious timetable. He has not forgotten us, we can be sure of that. His interference in history, when He sent His Son to *redeem,* was right on time. We can see that quite clearly now as we look back over the Old Testament Scriptures. His interference in history when He sends back His son to *reign* will also be right on time. Help is on the way! Often, even in the scaled-down affairs of our little lives, it comes in the nick of time.

B. The Happiness of the Saved (33:21)

"For our heart shall rejoice in Him, because we have trusted in His holy name." The secret of happiness is in *Him!* Our circumstances frown upon us at times but He never changes. He cannot let us down. How happy we should be!

C. The Hope of the Saved (33:22)

"Let thy mercy, O LORD, be upon us, according as we hope in Thee." That word "hope" means "to wait." Hoping and waiting go together. Nor is our hope unfounded; it is not just some vague pious wish. Our hope is anchored within the veil to the eternal verities and certainties of the universe. Yes, indeed! God is still on the throne—a throne around which all the galaxies parade, a throne which decides the destinies of the nations. For us it is a *throne of grace.*

Psalm 34

THE GOLIATHS OF GATH

I. DAVID'S PRAISE (34:1-10)
 A. What He Resolved (34:1-3)
 B. What He Remembered (34:4-6)
  1. His Danger
   a. "I was lost" (34:4)
  2. His Discernment
   a. "I looked" (34:5)
  3. His Deliverance
   a. "I was liberated" (34:6)
 C. What He Realized (34:7-10)
  1. God Protects (34:7)
  2. God Provides (34:8-10)
II. DAVID'S PROCLAMATION (34:11-22)
 A. The Summons (34:11)
 B. The Subject (34:12)
 C. The Sermon (34:13-20)
  1. Listen to My Exposition (34:13-16)
   a. Watch Your Words (34:13)
   b. Watch Your Walk (34:14)
   c. Watch Your Works (34:15)
  2. Learn from My Example (34:17-20)
 D. The Summary (34:21-22)

THE SUPERSCRIPTION on this psalm tells us it was written by David when the Philistines seized him in Gath. Let us remind ourselves of his situation.

He had killed Goliath of Gath, in the battle of the Valley of Elah. Goliath was a monster of a man who stood some ten and one-half feet tall. His strength was prodigious. For forty days he terrified Israel, roaring out his challenges and cursing and deriding the living God. Then came the young Hebrew boy, stooping down at the brook, picking up some stones. And before the Philistines could shout "Long live Dagon!" Goliath was down and David had cut off his head with his own sword.

The slaying of Goliath not only spelled *triumph* for David, it spelled *trouble* as well. It meant trouble with King Saul, for Saul was instantly jealous of David, wished him ill, and began a campaign of persecution which lasted to the day of his death.

First Saul eyed David with a resentful, envious eye. Then twice he cast a javelin at him. He plotted against David, sought to embroil him in fights with the Philistines hoping he would be killed. He set a gang of bullies to murder David in his bed, he hounded him all over the country. And so it went until David, for all his trust in the Lord, began to weary of this deadly game of hide and seek in and out of the cities and strongholds of Israel.

At last, David's faith failed. He went to Ahimelech the priest and told four lies in a single breath, conning the priest into giving his men shewbread to eat and into giving him the sword of Goliath. Then he made a momentous decision, he would go where Saul would never reach him, he would go down to Gath and seek asylum with Achish, one of the great Philistine lords.

After the slaying of Goliath we can be sure that the people of Gath longed to get their hands on that unknown but famous Bethlehem youth whose name had been cheered and sung throughout Israel. So when David showed up in Gath seeking political asylum one does not need to be a prophet to guess what happened. David was clapped in irons as soon as his identity was known. We do not know what David told Achish but any story he might have contrived must soon have been discredited by the sight of *Goliath's* sword!

Too late David realized his mistake: "David was sore afraid of Achish the king of Gath." So he pretended to be mad, and he did it so well that the disgusted Achish had him released and flung out of the land.

Once safely back in Israel David went to the famous cave of Adullam in the hill country of Judea southwest of Jerusalem. There he waited while his band of fellow outlaws assembled. There he picked up his harp and converted the cave into a cathedral, echoing to the strains of Psalm 34.

This is an interesting psalm. In the first place it is an acrostic, that is, in the original Hebrew text every verse begins with a different letter of the alphabet. In those days books were scarce and the acrostic was a popular device to aid the memory. David wanted his experience and his escape, and above all the lesson he had learned, to be remembered, so he cast his song into this easily memorized form. First David lifted up his heart in gratitude to God, then he gathered his outlaws around him and told them on what principles henceforth he was going to govern his camp. Part one of this psalm is a *song*, part two is a *sermon*. The first part is *devotional*, the second is *doctrinal*. Part one shows us the *grace* of God, part two the *government* of God.

I. DAVID'S PRAISE (34:1-10)

A. What David Resolved (34:1-3)

He resolved that he would henceforth praise the Lord no matter what happened to him: "I will bless the LORD at all times: His praise shall continually be in my mouth." What an effective antidote to the poison of doubt, depression, and despair. How often we fail right here!

God has said that "all things work together for good to them that love God, to them who are the called according to His purpose." How quickly we forget that. Jacob forgot it. When one thing after another went wrong in his life he wrung his hands: "Joseph is not, and Simeon is not, and ye will take Benjamin away: all these things are against me" (Genesis 42:36). But at that very moment Joseph was exalted to the right hand of the majesty of Egypt; God was working all things together for the good of Benjamin and Simeon and Jacob and all.

B. What David Remembered (34:4-6)

David's mind goes back over the ordeal in Gath when he first observed the Philistines eyeing him and muttering: "This is the fellow who killed Goliath." "I sought the LORD, and He heard me, and delivered me from all my fears" (34:4). We read in 1 Samuel 21 that David was "sore afraid of Achish, the king of Gath." Here was the man who could slay a lion, a bear, a giant; the man who could say confidently to King Saul: "The Lord that delivered me out of the paw of the lion and out of the paw of the bear, He will deliver me out of the hand of this Philistine." But he knew his *danger* there in Gath was greater than any he had ever known. He had taken matters into his own hands and was lost.

"I looked," he says. "They looked unto Him, and were lightened: and their faces were not ashamed" (34:5). The force of that statement is changed, in some versions, to the imperative: "Look unto Him!" David had been looking at Goliath's sword, he had been looking at Achish. He had been looking everywhere except to the Lord. "Look unto Him," David says, "look expectantly!"

"I was liberated," he says. "This poor man cried, and the LORD heard him and [*delivered*] him out of all his troubles" (34:6). Even while pretending to be mad, even while acting insane, David was praying in his soul: "Have mercy, Lord! Help me, Lord! Save me, Lord!" That's what David remembered. And, instead of rubbing David's nose in the dirt, the Lord stepped in and set him free!

C. What David Realized (34:7-10)

Looking back over that dreadful experience David came to a full and fresh realization of two wonderful truths.

1. God Protects (34:7)

"The angel of the LORD encampeth round about them that fear Him, and delivereth them." If we had other, larger eyes than ours we would see all about us, in the air, the mighty, countless hosts of hell—those fearful "principalities and powers, those rulers of this world's darkness, those wicked spirits in high places" of which Paul speaks. But we would see, too, the resplendent ranks of the shining ones, the mighty angels of God drawn up in battle array to preserve and protect the saints of God. Above and beyond them all is the glorious angel of the Lord Himself.

The "angel of the Lord" mentioned by David was the Lord Jesus in one of His pre-incarnate roles. He is mentioned in this guise only twice in the book of Psalms—here and in Psalm 35 where David, speaking of His many enemies, said: "Let them be as chaff before the wind: and let the angel of the LORD chase them" (Psalm 35:5). In Psalm 34 the angel of the Lord is seen *protecting* the saint. In Psalm 35 he is seen *pursuing* the sinner. David was brought into fresh realization that God protects.

2. God Provides (34:8-10)

"O fear the LORD, ye His saints: for there is no want to them that fear Him. The young lions do lack, and suffer hunger: but they that seek the LORD shall not want any good thing." David is remembering, perhaps, the callous way he was thrown out of Gath. It is not likely that the indignant king and his hostile court were mindful of David's physical needs. They probably escorted him to the border and gave him a count of twenty to get out of arrow range. And there he was, facing the hostile wilderness alone, defenseless, without food or drink.

But God had cared for him, provided for him, seen him safely to Adullam. David does not tell how the Lord took care of his needs, but there in the cave surrounded by his faithful men, with great hunks of venison hanging from the roof and with the tribute from a dozen farms stacked in a corner, David assures us that the Lord provides. He hears the angry growl of a hunting lion out there on the hills ("The young lions do lack," he mused, "and suffer hunger") and comments, "But they that seek the LORD shall not want any good thing." The first half of this psalm is full of praise.

Now David looks at his men. It is time he enforced some of the lessons he had learned. He must turn them to good account. He must come up with some rules for the camp.

II. David's Proclamation (34:11-22)

A. The Summons (34:11)

David gathers his men around him: "Come, ye [sons], hearken unto me: I will teach you the fear of the LORD." Because they loved him and admired him and would follow him to the ends of the earth they gathered around.

B. The Subject (34:12)

"What man is he that desireth life, and loveth many days, that he may see good?" What man is there that doesn't want to live to a ripe old age? That doesn't want "the good life" with all its rich rewards? It was a subject calculated to grip the attention of every one of his ruffians, cut off from the comforts of home and living always with the hangman's noose over their heads.

C. The Sermon (34:13-20)

It was a very good sermon, good enough for the Holy Spirit to pick up and quote at some length in the New Testament a thousand years later (1 Peter 3:10-12).

In the first part of his sermon David urges his men to:

1. Listen to His Exposition (34:13-16)

"Based on my recent experience I should like you to take heed of three things":

a. Take Heed to Your Words (34:13)

"Keep thy tongue from evil, and thy lips from speaking guile." "I don't know how many of you know this, but down there in Gath I disgraced myself and I disgraced the Lord. I said a lot of very foolish things. I wish I could relive the last few weeks but I can't. I can only pray that *you* will never relive them. I pretended to be mad. I am ashamed of some of the things I said. I didn't know my tongue could employ such evil nor my lips speak such guile. And so I beg you, take heed to your words."

b. Take Heed to Your Walk (34:14)

"Depart from evil, and do good; seek peace, and pursue it." "My real troubles began, not when King Saul set his dogs of war upon my tracks, but when I lied to Ahimelech the priest. I've got that on my conscience, because it led to the murder of Ahimelech. My troubles came to a head when I went to Gath. I wish I had never been near the place. I failed to take heed to my walk. There are some places in life where a believer ought not to go, there are some doors a child of God ought never to darken. My friends, I beg of you, depart from evil, and do good; seek peace, and pursue it. Take heed to your walk."

c. Take Heed to Your Works (34:15-16)

"The eyes of the LORD are upon the righteous, and His ears are open unto their cry. The face of the LORD is against them that do evil, to cut off the remembrance of them from the earth." "God sees what you do and He hears what you say. *That* is a terrific truth to everyone who is doing and saying the things that please the Lord, but it is a terrible truth to those who are displeasing Him. So, my friends, take heed to your works."

Thus David urged his fellow wanderers to listen to his exposition.

2. Learn from His Example (34:17-20)

"The righteous cry, and the LORD heareth, and delivereth them out of all their troubles. The LORD is nigh unto them that are of a broken heart; and saveth such as be of a contrite spirit. Many are the afflictions of the righteous; but the Lord delivereth him out of them all." Says David, "I am living proof of what I have been telling you. Down there in Gath I was a broken and contrite man, bitterly sorry for what I had said and done. I still don't know why Achish let me go. I can only say that the Lord delivered me. Get right with God, and He will see you through."

D. The Summary (34:21-22)

"Evil shall slay the wicked: and they that hate the righteous shall be desolate. The LORD redeemeth the soul of His servants: and none of them that trust in Him shall be desolate." In effect, "I am going to practice what I preach. From now on I am going to leave my case in God's hands." And so David did, as far as Saul was concerned. He refused to slay him even when he was delivered providentially into his hands—even though urged by some of his men to make a full and final end. "No," he said, "Evil shall slay the wicked. It is not for me to slay Saul. God will take care of him."

Some years ago a preacher watched some rabbits flying in terror from a strange brown creature which began to follow one of them with slow, serpentine movements. It was a weasel. The preacher was puzzled how so slow a creature as the weasel could make a much faster animal its prey. Later he read that a weasel has an insatiable thirst for blood. It singles out a particular rabbit for destruction and persistently follows its trail, never losing the scent of its victim. It is generally a long chase. The rabbit makes a dash ahead, then a double or two, and halts at the mouth of the hole. The weasel follows. Although the bank is tenanted by fifty other rabbits past whose hiding place the weasel must go, they scarcely take notice. They seem to know it is not their turn. So the chase goes on, for the weasel never allows himself to be turned aside. The stricken rabbit rushes from field to field and from hedgerow to hedgerow, but still his pursuer follows. The rabbit, tired to the death, at last hides in the grass, but across the meadow, stealing along the furrow, comes the weasel.

"Evil shall slay the wicked," says David. Evil is God's weasel on the trail of the rabbit. Nothing but intervening grace can turn it aside.

"None of them that trust in Him shall be desolate," concludes David. His point is illustrated by an Englishman named Archibald Brown, who experienced a wild night on the southern shore of the Isle of Wight. The wind had been blowing all day and the sea had risen mightily. It was near time for high tide, and Brown and his wife came out and stood on the balcony of their home, watching the inrushing sea. Between them and the sea was but a narrow strip of roadway. The waves broke in fury on the sea wall, fell back, and came on again. Far away in the moonlight they could see line after line of advancing billows.

After a while, Mr. Brown turned to his wife and said, "Well, we can go to bed now!" What? Go to bed with those wild waves still thundering on the shore? Go to rest with destruction so near? Yes! For he had taken a look at his watch and realized that high tide had come and gone. "The waves will come no further," he said. "We can go to bed now."

What perfect faith in a simple law of nature to dare to stand within a few yards of a roaring sea and say: "We can go to bed now, the tide has turned." What faith in the law of the tide! Yet behind those crested waves there was a power mightier than the storm. Behind them stood God with His infallible decree: "Thus far and no further: and here shall thy proud waves be stayed" (Job 38:11). Thus too runs this infallible decree: "The Lord redeemeth the soul of His servants."

Here, then, is David's summary. For the sinner it is *the law of the weasel,* the law of the relentless trail. For the saint it is *the law of the wave,* the law of the obedient tide. "Evil shall slay the wicked: and they that hate the righteous shall be desolate. The LORD redeemeth the soul of His servants: and none of them that trust in Him shall be desolate."

> The soul that on Jesus has leaned for repose,
> He will not, He will not, desert to its foes;
> That soul, though all hell should endeavor to shake,
> He'll never, no never, no never forsake.

Psalm 35

WHEN FRIENDS BECOME FOES

I. IN THE CAMP: DAVID AS A WARRIOR (35:1-10)
   A. What He Wants for His Foes (35:1-8)
   He wants them to be:
   1. Defeated (35:1-3)
   2. Destroyed (35:4-8)
   B. What He Wants for His Fears (35:9-10)
   He wants them dissolved by:
   1. The Joy of the Lord (35:9)
   2. The Justice of the Lord (35:10)
II. IN THE COURT: DAVID AS A WITNESS (35:11-17)
   A. David's Plight (35:11-12)
   B. David's Plea (35:13-17)
III. IN THE CLOISTER: DAVID AS A WORSHIPER (35:18-28)
   A. A Praising Man (35:18)
   B. A Praying Man (35:19-27)
   1. Informing the Lord (35:19-21)
   2. Invoking the Lord (35:22-27)
   C. A Proclaiming Man (35:28)

K ING SAUL nurtured a deadly jealousy against David. In some ways it was natural enough for Saul was a giant of a fellow and a grown man whereas David was a youth, hardly more than a boy. Yet David had been willing to go down and fight Goliath, the giant of Gath. That must have been humiliating enough for Saul but, when the jubilant songs of the Hebrew women extolled David above Saul, the king's envy knew no bounds.

But there was more to it than that. Jonathan went out one day to where David was hiding in the hills and "strengthened his hand in God" (1 Samuel 23:16). It was only a brief visit, but it was long enough for Jonathan to fill in some of the missing pieces for David. Not only did Saul resent David but David had powerful enemies at court. There was Doeg the Edomite, for instance, and others.

We can picture the two young men sitting there together, the courtly Jonathan and the outlaw David. "David," says Jonathan, "you have other enemies." He names people that David had always counted

261

as his friends. David had such a guileless, generous nature he could hardly believe such treachery. People he had thought were his friends, people he had helped, loved, and trusted were actually poisoning the mind of Saul with malicious lies about him. That seems a suitable background for this psalm. In spirit David takes up three positions and puts on three mantles. He takes up positions *in the camp, in the court,* and *in the cloister.* We see him as *a warrior, a witness,* and *a worshiper.*

I. IN THE CAMP: DAVID AS A WARRIOR (35:1-10)

David puts on, as it were, the whole armor of God. He realizes that you can do little against slander, that it is almost impossible to fight gossip. A man can be destroyed by a malicious tongue far easier than by a bullet or a knife. So David picks up the only weapon he has against gossip, the spiritual weapon of communion with God.

A. What He Wants For His Foes (35:1-8)

He enlists God in his cause, asks Him to do what he cannot do for himself. For how can he fight slander, especially when it is picked up, repeated, embellished, and pumped into the ears of a person already inflamed with jealousy? David tells the Lord what he wants his foes to be.

1. Defeated (35:1-3)

"Plead my cause, O LORD, with them that strive with me: fight against them. . . . Take hold of shield and buckler, and stand up for mine help." What a bold and daring way to speak to the Lord! Only a person convinced of his innocence could so charge the Lord.

2. Destroyed (35:4-8)

It is here we run into one of the great exegetical problems of the psalms for this is the first real imprecation in the book. David prays that his enemies might be confounded, that they might be put to shame: "Let their way be dark and slippery: and let the angel of the LORD persecute them." Whatever are we going to make of a statement like that?

The angel of the Lord was the Jehovah angel. In the preceding psalm we have the only other reference to Him in the entire book of Psalms. There David prayed concerning the godly: "The angel of the LORD encampeth round about them that fear Him, and delivereth them." It was the Jehovah angel who met Hagar when she fled from the abuse she had received in Abraham's home, met her on the very threshold of Egypt, and ministered love and compassion, comfort and promise to her wounded soul. It was the angel of the Lord who met Joshua when he was contemplating the formidable fortress of

Jericho and took matters out of his hands. "Don't worry about a thing, Joshua!" was what He said, in effect.

Imagine praying that a man's path might be not only dark, but slippery! It was a deliberate prayer that his enemies might come to a disastrous end. All kinds of suggestions have been made about these imprecatory psalms—and Psalm 35 is by no means the most vehement. Some have pointed to the fact that the Old Testament Scriptures offset these imprecations. "If thou see the ass of him that hateth thee lying under his burden . . . thou shalt surely help with him. . . . If thou meet thine enemy's ox going astray, thou shalt surely bring it back to him again" (Exodus 23:4-5). "Thou shalt not hate thy brother in thine heart. . . . Thou shalt not avenge, nor bear any grudge against the children of thy people, but thou shalt love thy neighbor as thyself" (Leviticus 19:17-18).

Others have pointed out that these fierce outcries and imprecations are not a reflection of God's heart, but of the imperfect hearts of his people. Some have switched the imprecation from the lips of the Psalmist to the lips of the foe, the Psalmist, in other words, simply reminding the Lord of what the ungodly are saying against him. Others have claimed that the implications are not personal but prophetic and that they belong to the end of the age. Still others have said that they belong not to the age of grace but to the age of the law. Some have excused them on the grounds of the intense provocation being suffered by the Psalmist. Others have taken the position that the imprecations reflect the Hebrew viewpoint—the Psalmist's enemies were the *Lord's* enemies and therefore it was up to Him to vindicate His own righteous cause.

Some have underlined the passionate zeal for righteousness which gave birth to such expressions of vehemence. Others have argued that, since the Old Testament saints did not have such a well-developed eschatology as we have and knew little about a final judgment, they therefore believed that the righteous *had* to be rewarded in this life that the wicked and *had* to get what was coming to them in this life too. No doubt all these arguments have a measure of truth.

But here, in this first imprecation, David, a man of very large sympathy and a great capacity for forgiveness, gives his reasons for the curse he invokes. Having prayed that his enemies might be *driven, doomed, dismayed,* and *damned,* he says that such an expression of divine wrath would be an expression of *perfect justice:* "For without cause have they hid for me their net in a pit, which without cause they have digged for my soul" (35:7). It was right that they should reap what they sowed, their malicious gossip was without cause, he had been their friend.

David says that such an expression of divine judgment would also be a fitting expression of *poetic justice:* "Let destruction come upon him at unawares; and let his net that he hath hid catch himself: *into that very destruction* let him fall."

That poetic justice was later going to pursue David himself. After his sin with Bathsheba and his murder of Uriah, both murder and adultery broke out again and again in his own family. This kind of poetic justice is clearly seen in the Bible. David, here in Psalm 35, was praying that his enemies might get what they were giving him. If that is not in accordance with the Sermon on the Mount, or the kind of prayer Jesus would have prayed, it is because David lived a thousand years before New Testament truth was revealed. It is not so much a matter of perfection as of perspective.

B. What He Wants For His Fears (35:9-10)

He wanted them to be dissolved by:

1. The Joy of the Lord (35:9)

"And my soul shall be joyful in the LORD: it shall rejoice in His salvation." David never knew from one day to the next when or where Saul would strike. He was always on the run, often with fear gnawing at his heart. He has now discovered, however, that joy in the Lord is the best antidote to fear.

2. The Justice of the Lord (35:10)

"All my bones shall say, LORD, who is like unto Thee, which deliverest the poor from him that is too strong for him, yea, the poor and the needy for him that spoileth him?" He wanted what we call fair play. We get a great deal of satisfaction, for instance, in seeing a bully meet his match.

Richard Llewellyn illustrates that in *How Green Was My Valley.* Young Huw had been sent to the school on the other side of the mountain. The schoolmaster took an instant dislike to his new pupil. He bullied him, held him up to ridicule, and finally thrashed him to within an inch of his life. Young Huw dragged himself home. Two of his older brothers, tough young colliers, their muscles hardened in the coal mines, decided to teach the bully a lesson he would never forget. Over the mountain they went and into the school. Having dealt with others who tried to intervene, Huw's brother Dai seized the schoolmaster around the neck, bent him over his knee, took off his belt, and gave him the thrashing of his life. When he had finished, the young coal miner pitched the wretched schoolmaster head over heels through the open trap of the coal cellar and shut the lid. Young Huw never had to fear that schoolmaster again.

Our very bones, as David puts it, thrill within us when we see justice being done and the fearful injustices of life being corrected. That is what David wanted done to his fears!

Now comes a change of pace. We have been looking at David in the camp, appealing to the Lord as a warrior. There were foes he could not fight, foes too sly for him, so he turns them over to the Lord.

II. IN THE COURT: DAVID AS A WITNESS (35:11-17)

He is pleading his case now before the Lord, taken up with the wrong his supposed friends have done to him. There is no indignation here, no passion, no imprecation. Here we have not so much the dust of battle as the impassive calm of a court. David is both plaintiff and witness.

A. His Plight (35:11-12)

"False witnesses did rise up; they laid to my charge things that I knew not. They rewarded me evil for good to the spoiling of my soul." David depicts himself a fallen warrior whose finery has all been stripped away, his valuables stolen, and he has been left a prey to the wild beasts. The slanderers have stripped him of his honor and his character, surely one of the most dastardly things a person can do to another—to lie and so misrepresent a person that his good name is gone, his reputation ruined. And to do it all secretly and behind his back! Such was David's plight. He lays the facts before the Judge of all the earth.

B. His Plea (35:13-17)

"But as for me, when they were sick, my clothing was sackcloth. . . . I behaved myself as though he had been my friend or brother . . . But in mine adversity they rejoiced. . . . Lord, how long wilt Thou look on? Rescue my soul from their destructions." Thus David sets before the Lord his innocence, his injuries, and his indignation, asking the Lord to redress the wrongs that have been done, and to vindicate him.

The Lord, of course, did vindicate David by raising him up to the throne, and setting him over all his foes. It says much for the character of David that never once do we read that he used power to punish those who had so terribly slandered him. Perhaps they were already dead. Perhaps they had already been summoned before that very throne at which David so effectively pleaded his case.

We can be sure we never assassinate a person's character with impunity. The damage we do may be irreparable in this life, but we will have to answer for it at the judgment seat of Christ. Let us think twice before we engage in this terrible sin.

Some time ago I was ministering in a church where there was a telephone in the foyer anybody could use. A little text had been put up next to it, a quotation from Ephesians 4:32: "Be ye kind one to another." What a good text that would be to engrave on *every* telephone in the country.

III. IN THE CLOISTER: DAVID AS A WORSHIPER (35:18-28)

A. A Praising Man (35:18)

"I will give Thee thanks in the great congregation: I will praise Thee among much people." David would have delighted in that little chorus so popular some few years ago:

> I believe the answer's on the way
> I believe that night will turn to day.

Nothing has changed outwardly, but David's spirits have received a tremendous boost. He *knows* that he will one day be vindicated. He gives thanks for that.

B. A Praying Man (35:19-27)

He comes back to his original theme and prays again that his secret enemies might not be allowed to triumph. How human that is! How often we pray through to victory, only to come back almost in the next breath, certainly in the next prayer, to the same petition all over again! It is a blessing that the Lord is infinite in His patience.

1. Informing the Lord (35:19-21)

David tells the Lord of the malicious glee of his foes: "Let not them that are mine enemies wrongfully rejoice over me: neither let them wink with the eye that hate me without a cause." What a graphic picture. We can see it as though it happened today. There sits King Saul, glowering upon his throne, while Doeg, or somebody else, fills his ears with lies about David: "Yes, my lord king! I have it on good authority that he has been plotting with Ahimelech, down there in Gath. He intends to raise insurrection in the country and join with the Philistines in an attack upon your throne." "There!" shouts the king. "I knew it all the time! He's a treacherous dog."

Perhaps Jonathan speaks up: "My father, be fair. David is as loyal as I am. He's not planning any such thing. I was talking to him only a few days ago. . . ." "There!" shouts the king again. "You're in it too. You are the son of a perverse, rebellious woman, Jonathan. I've half a mind to put this javelin through you." And behind the throne, secretly stirring up the strife, are other courtiers once counted by David as friends.

So here David is seen informing the Lord of the *malicious glee* of his foes and also of the *malignant guile* of his foes: "For they speak not peace: but they devise deceitful matters against them that are quiet in the land" (35:20-21)

2. Invoking the Lord (35:22-27)

David wanted the Lord to awaken, to answer, to acknowledge, and to act: "O LORD; keep not silence. . . . Stir up Thyself, and awake to my judgment. . . . Judge me, O LORD my God, according to Thy righteousness. . . . Let them not say . . . We have swallowed him up." He goes on and on, spelling it out, restating his case, urging the Lord to do something. It is all so very human.

C. A Proclaiming Man (35:28)

"And my tongue shall speak of Thy righteousness and of Thy praise all the day long." When God answers a prayer like this it is impossible to keep quiet about it.

Several years ago a man borrowed some money from my mother, a widow, promising to invest it safely and at good interest. The borrower not only badly invested the money but defaulted on the interest, gave my mother worthless security, and lied about his intentions. We made it a matter of urgent prayer. The matter dragged on for several years. One day another businessman in town asked me if we were having trouble with this individual. I said, "Yes, we are." "Come down to my office," he said. "I doubt if you'll ever see that money again, so I am going to buy the entire indebtedness from you and I will try to collect it. If I don't succeed, I'll write it off as a business debt." He was as good as his word. His kind and generous act filled us with delight in the goodness and faithfulness of God. During the long months we went through this trouble we prayed and prayed. At times the Lord gave us assurance and peace that all would be well. Then we would have another disappointment, another string of broken promises, and we seesawed like David, up and down. Yet the Lord was as good as His word. My mother's estate recovered every penny of that bad debt thanks to the kindness of a wealthy Christian brother. Omnipotence has its servants everywhere!

Like David I can take my place as a proclaiming man. Like David I must say: "My tongue shall speak of Thy righteousness and of Thy praise all the day long."

"There," says David, "Send *that* to the chief musician. That's something to sing about."

And so it is!

Psalm 36

A STUDY IN CONTRASTS

I. THE SINFUL MAN (36:1-4)
   A. The Sinful Man's Persuasion (36:1)
   B. The Sinful Man's Pride (36:2)
   C. The Sinful Man's Policy (36:3a)
   D. The Sinful Man's Past (36:3b)
   E. The Sinful Man's Plans (36:4a)
   F. The Sinful Man's Path (36:4b)
II. THE SAVED MAN (36:5-12)
   Rests in the lovingkindness of God, which is backed by:
   A. The Righteousness of God's Throne (36:5-6)
      1. It Cannot Be Matched (36:5)
      2. It Cannot Be Moved (36:6a)
      3. It Cannot Be Measured (36:6b)
   B. The Resources of God's Throne (36:7-9)
      We can be:
      1. Wonderfully Sure (36:7)
      2. Wonderfully Satisfied (36:8)
      3. Wonderfully Saved (36:9)
   C. The Responsibilities of God's Throne (36:10-11)
      1. To Justify the Saint (36:10-11)
         a) Permanently (36:10)
         b) Practically (36:11)
      2. To Judge the Sinner (36:12)

THIS PSALM BEARS THE TITLE, "A psalm of David, the servant of the Lord." The only other psalm entitled this way is Psalm 18, written by David when the long, terrible outlaw years had ended. Saul was dead at last and David was free with the kingdom, the power, and the glory before him.

We know just when Psalm 18 was written, but by contrast we do not know when Psalm 36 was written. Indeed, despite the Davidic title, some argue for a composite authorship. There is no need for that. Psalm 18 was written to commemorate deliverance from foes *within*. One set of foes was *martial,* another *mental;* one was *Saul's dragoons,* the other *the soul's doubts.* We can date, easily enough, David's conquest of the *warriors of a Saul;* we cannot so easily date the conquest of the *worries of a soul.* The one can be defeated decisively, once for all; the other is not nearly so easily nor so permanently slain.

This psalm divides into two parts.

I. THE SINFUL MAN (35:1-4)

David has half a dozen things to say about the sinful man. We all carry him around within us for "the heart is deceitful above all things and desperately wicked." When General Mola told his enemies in Spain that he was going to take Madrid because he had four columns without the city and a fifth column within, he expressed, in military terms, the problem we all face morally. The enemy has a fifth column within the gates. He has dark allies lurking everywhere deep down within our hearts.

A. The Sinful Man's Persuasion (36:1)

"The transgression of the wicked saith within my heart, that there is no fear of God before his eyes." Maclaren translates the first line: "The wicked has an oracle of transgression within his heart." Rotherham puts it much the same way. The word translated "saith" is far too weak. It is not the ordinary word for speaking, but means "to speak with authority," as an oracle; it is regularly used in the Old Testament for divine utterances. When we read "Thus *saith* the Lord," it is the same word.

The word translated "transgression" is the usual Hebrew word for "rebellion." The wicked man makes rebellion his inner oracle. He gives to the lawless voice of rebellion within his soul the same place that the believer gives to the Word of God. This lying voice, which appeals to all his inner bentness and lawlessness, becomes a lying spirit within his breast. This explains why wicked men go on doing what they do. They are listening to a lying oracle within. It says there is no need to fear God's punishments. God does not exist, or if He does, He does not concern Himself with men.

David found, to his horror, that there were times when he, too, was tempted to listen to the same lying oracle.

B. The Sinful Man's Pride (36:2)

"For he flattereth himself in his own eyes, until his iniquity be found to be hateful." He is flattering himself that his iniquity will never be found out. He is ruled by terrible negatives—no fear of God or accountability for his iniquity. He has persuaded himself that God will not interfere with him. To lose the fear of God is to open the door to every kind of wickedness.

Of course, in the end man pays for his folly because there *is* a God and there *are* absolute standards of right and wrong as laid down in

God's Word. Man's desires and discernments, unless checked by the rigid rules of right and wrong of the Bible, soon become blurred.

Today society at large, having abandoned the Bible, is now beginning to pay the price for infatuation with man's own ideas. According to one statistic, one out of every ten people in America can expect to spend time in a mental hospital. Murder, rape, hate, terrorism, and drugs have become norms in our society. Double standards, conflicting claims, and blurred issues all help build up tension. People have lost their sense of right and wrong and consequently are being driven to the verge of mental breakdown and insanity.

This kind of behavior and consequence has been demonstrated in controlled laboratory experiments. White rats are placed in wire cages having two openings, one at each end. One opening is square, the other round. When the rat becomes hungry he learns that when he pushes against the square hole he receives food, but when he pushes against the round hole he receives an electric shock. Naturally he goes for the square hole. So far so good. But then the experimenter gradually rounds out the square, food-rewarding hole. It begins to look more and more like the hole which administers the unpleasant experience. Before long, the rat's powers of discrimination fail. The hard, squared edges of the food-rewarding hold become increasingly blurred and the rat no longer knows what to expect when he pushes against a hole, whether he will be rewarded with pleasure or punished with pain for the choice he makes. His entire organism becomes unbalanced and out of control. In the end he dashes madly around his cage, biting and clawing, completely disoriented and upset. He has a nervous breakdown.

People today are suffering from the same thing and for the same reason. They are no longer controlled by the hard, squared edges of God's moral standards, as revealed in His Word, so they lose their orientation. The end result of blurring moral standards, watering down divine commands, and eliminating the sharp edges of God's moral code is disaster both for the individual and for the race. People are listening to the wrong voices—to the humanist, the psychologist, the socialist instead of to the Word of God. These false voices appeal directly to that inner voice that says that God does not punish sin. Thus we have become a disoriented society. "He flattereth himself" is the Holy Spirit's pungent comment.

C. The Sinful Man's Policy (36:3a)

"The words of his mouth are iniquity and deceit." This is one fruit of practical atheism from David's day and ours. Atheism is a form of self-deception. The person who opens his heart to deception and rejects absolute moral standards will see nothing wrong with lying. One of the things that staggers us today is the ease with which people lie. They will look one in the eye and tell, with the utmost seeming sincerity, the most blatant untruths.

D. The Sinful Man's Past (36:3b)

"He hath left off to be wise, and to do good." Rotherham renders that: "He hath ceased to act circumspectly." In other words, once he did but now he doesn't. His behavior is *learned* behavior adopted as a matter of deliberate choice. There was once a time when he did act in a way which showed he was aware that God had claims upon his life, but no more.

The idea behind acting "circumspectly" is best conveyed by illustration. When I was a boy in Britain many homeowners surrounded their property with brick walls. Along the top of these walls they would place a layer of cement in which they would embed pieces of broken glass to discourage intruders from trying to climb over the wall. Sometimes an alley cat would get on top of one of those walls. It was an education to watch that cat walk along the wall studded with broken glass! He did not dash blindly along it. He walked circumspectly. He watched where he was going. He put his foot out gingerly and tested each step to make sure he wasn't going to get hurt. That is how we ought to walk when our path is strewn with snares. That is how the sinful man, described by David, used to walk. But now he has grown bold in unbelief. He no longer thinks there is any danger in dashing on through life pretending there is no God. He has become the victim of his own philosophy.

E. The Sinful Man's Plans (36:4a)

"He deviseth mischief upon his bed." He lies awake at night thinking up evil things to do. He deliberately plans to pursue his own evil desires. It's not that he is suddenly overtaken in an unexpected temptation. He plans out what he is going to do.

F. The Sinful Man's Path (36:4b)

"He setteth himself in a way that is not good; he abhorreth not evil." The word "evil" is from a root which means "to break up all that is good" and is the Hebrew equivalent of the Greek word *ponoros*, from which we get our English word pornography. The word is connected with corruption, depravity, and lewdness. This man, who once knew better, having persuaded himself that God can be ruled out, finds nothing wrong with doing vile and filthy things.

David thinks about this sinful man but it is not until the last verse that he tells what happens to this kind of person.

II. THE SAVED MAN (36:5-12)

There are better things to think about than the filth and foolishness of those who delight in sin. David can see that the saved man rests in the loving-kindness of God. That loving-kindness is not capricious but rests upon three pillars—the *righteousness*, the *resources*, and the *responsibilities* of God's throne.

A. The Righteousness of God's Throne (36:5-6)

Notice three things about that righteousness.

1. It cannot be matched (36:5)

"Thy mercy [loving-kindness], O LORD, is in the heavens; and Thy faithfulness reacheth unto the clouds." God's love is as high as Heaven and His loyalty soars to the skies. In other words it cannot be matched. How high is Heaven? Where does the sky end? God would have to betray His own character if He let down one trusting in His love. That love stands alone, unique, unsurpassed. There's nothing like it in the universe.

2. It cannot be moved (36:6a)

"Thy righteousness is like the great mountains." A mountain is the very symbol of things unmovable. We could bring our picks and shovels, even our trucks and tractors and how long would it take us to shovel the Rocky Mountains to the sea? That is what God's righteousness is like. It cannot be moved.

3. It cannot be measured (36:6b)

"Thy judgments are a great deep: O LORD, Thou preservest man and beast." Go down to the ocean, take your sounding line and drop it down. Get more line! More, more, more. As the children's chorus puts it:

> Wide, wide as the ocean
> High as the Heaven above;
> Deep, deep as the deepest sea
> Is my Saviour's love.

As David discerned, it is a love backed by a righteousness just as high, just as wide, just as deep as the ocean.

The saved man, then, rests in a loving-kindness that is backed by the righteousness of God's throne.

B. The Resources of God's Throne (36:7-9)

That throne is great enough to meet our every need, no matter what that need might be. Whatever else may fail, that throne cannot fail. That is the best security we could ever have. It is better to be backed by the resources of God's throne than by the resources of all the banks in the world.

When I was little, I sometimes went to the bank where my father made his deposits. In England coins were not counted, they were weighed. Every teller had a set of scales before him. He would shovel the sixpences and the shillings, the florins and the half crowns onto one side of the scale and put weights on the other side. It was fascinating to watch him weigh the coins and flip through a pile of banknotes like lightning, counting up the total and bringing a rubber stamp down with a resounding thud on the deposit slip. It was a magic world. No wonder when I left school I went to work for that bank!

But supposing all the vast resources of that bank were to be placed as guarantee behind some great need of mine. It still would be a finite sum and it would still be subject to the financial and economic tremors that from time to time shake the business world.

When the United States froze Iran's assets, near panic shook the great banking centers of Europe. Foreign banks, which own an astronomical $750 billion of United States currency as so-called Eurodollars, were afraid that they would become enmeshed in petropolitics and that the rich oil producing countries might dump their dollars and move their funds into other currencies or gold. The financial world is so delicately balanced that the slightest tremor in one place could cause an upheaval somewhere else.

The astronomical debts piled up by countries such as Poland, Mexico, and Argentina also frighten the big banks. Default by one such country could upset the whole financial structure of the world. What a blessing our most essential needs are not backed by banks but by the resources of God's throne, that cannot fail.

1. Wonderfully Sure (36:7)

"How excellent is thy loving-kindness, O God! therefore the children of men put their trust under the shadow of Thy wings." David uses the name Elohim here, not Jehovah. *Jehovah* was the covenant name, used especially in God's pledges and promises to Israel. David uses the more universal name of *Elohim* because he wants all men to be sure.

Moreover, he has been comparing God's loving-kindness to the sea, the sky, and the towering mountain peaks. His illustrations are drawn from creation. He speaks of God as the Creator, as Elohim. The God who can create galaxies is a God of whom we can be wonderfully sure. We can trust Him implicitly. He cannot fail.

"The children of men put their trust under the shadow of Thy wings," says David. He is thinking of a mother hen. She is the biggest, kindest object in the universe to a dozen little fluffy chicks. When danger threatens they come scurrying to her and crouch beneath her wings where it is warm and safe.

How much better are the wings of the Almighty! We know only too well how feeble a mother hen is. But God! And we can be wonderfully sure if we are safely gathered beneath the shadow of His wings.

2. Wonderfully Satisfied (36:8)

"They [that is, men who are trusting God] shall be abundantly satisfied with the fatness of Thy house; and Thou shalt make them drink of the river of Thy pleasures." That word for "pleasures" is *edene,* a reference to the delights of Eden—to what men enjoyed in paradise before the fall. God wants to restore *that* for the believer. Pleasure, after all, is God's invention. The devil has never been able to invent one single pure and satisfying pleasure. The devil's formula, a characteristic of the artificial amusements and pasttimes he concocts for men and women, is a deadly one—an ever-increasing dose required for an ever-diminishing return.

But the believer can be wonderfully satisfied. "They shall be abundantly satisfied with the fatness of Thy house; and Thou shalt make them drink of the river of Thy pleasures." God is not against pleasure. He is just against sinful "pleasure"—the kind the devil supplies.

God offers us "rivers of pleasures"—pleasures invented and produced in Heaven, that flow from the paradise of God. We can be wonderfully satisfied. The resources of heaven cannot fail.

3. Wonderfully Saved (36:9)

"For with Thee is the fountain of life: in Thy light shall we see light." Life and light! These are the two essentials of a genuine spiritual experience, the exact opposites of darkness and death. Golden sayings like this anticipate the gospel. Gems of inspiration like this are the very essence from which the Gospel of John was distilled.

So then, the saved man rests in the loving-kindness of God, backed by the righteousness and the resources of God's throne.

C. The Responsibilities of God's Throne (36:10-12)

Those responsibilities, as David sees them, are twofold. If I make you a promise I am responsible to keep that promise. If I break it then I do you harm, but I also do myself harm for I do damage to my character. The same is true of God. God has a responsibility, based on His character and His Word.

1. To Justify the Saint (36:10-11)

David now asks God to justify the saint *permanently:* "O continue [the word is "prolong"] Thy loving-kindness unto them that know Thee; and Thy righteousness to the upright in heart." One of the most satisfying aspects of our salvation is that it is permanent. What assurance would there be for the believer if salvation, once bestowed, could be snatched away by God as though He were some irate parent?

The believer's rest is discussed in Hebrews 4: creation rest, into which God entered on that first sabbath morn of a newborn universe;

Canaan rest, the cessation from warfare and lasting peace into which Joshua was supposed to lead Israel; Calvary rest, the blessed rest implied in both the other two but never realized because of human sin and disobedience. We enter into all that is implied in creation rest because the work has been finished and into all that is implied in Canaan rest because the war has been fought. Certainly God will prolong his loving-kindness. Calvary guarantees it, the throne of God guarantees it, and that throne has its responsibilities clearly spelled out at the cross.

David also asks God to justify the saint *practically:* "Let not the foot of pride come against me, and let not the hand of the wicked remove me." It is a prayer for protection here and now, not just in eternity.

We are living in a dangerous world. Indeed, we are living in occupied territory. The invader is here with all the power of his might to harass the saints of God and to stir up against them all kinds of trouble. David prays that God will protect His people from all that.

2. To Judge the Sinner (36:12)

"There are the workers of iniquity fallen: they are cast down, and shall not be able to rise." David is so sure that the responsibilities of the throne will be asserted in this way that he speaks of it in the past tense as having already been done! "Yonder, they lie, the evildoers, felled to earth, unable to arise!" is one translator's graphic rendering.

The sinner and the saint! The sinner may think everything is going his way as he plunges into sin, seeking those tasteless, disappointing pleasures offered to him by the evil one. But that is because, having dethroned God from his thinking, he cannot reason aright. In the end the saint gets the best of it because he gets the best of both worlds. He has the righteousness, resources, and responsibilities of God's throne to back him up down here and then light and life for all eternity!

Psalm 37

WHEN WICKEDNESS TRIUMPHS ON EARTH

I. PROSPECTS THAT ARE FOREIGN TO THE WICKED (37:1-11)
   The righteous man's:
   A. Discovery (37:1-2)
   B. Dwelling (37:3)
   C. Delight (37:4)
   D. Dependence (37:5-6)
   E. Discipline (37:7)
   F. Deliverance (37:8-10)
   G. Domains (37:11)
II. PURSUITS THAT ARE FAVORED BY THE WICKED (37:12-22)
   The wicked man's:
   A. Plots (37:12-13)
   B. Power (37:14-15)
   C. Prosperity (37:16-17)
   D. Protection (37:18-20)
   E. Pledge (37:21-22)
III. PATHS THAT ARE FORSAKEN BY THE WICKED (37:23-31)
   The righteous man's:
   A. Walk (37:23-24)
   B. Wants (37:25)
   C. Works (37:26-27)
   D. Welfare (37:28-29)
   E. Wisdom (37:30-31)
IV. POINTS THAT ARE FORGOTTEN BY THE WICKED (37:32-40)
   He forgets that:
   A. Truth Is on the Side of the Godly (37:32-34)
   B. Time Is on the Side of the Godly (37:35-36)
   C. Trust Is on the Side of the Godly (37:37-40)
      1. A Perfect Standing (37:37-38)
      2. A Perfect Stability (37:39-40)

DAVID WROTE THIS PSALM in his old age. It deals with a perennial problem, one that has puzzled people throughout all the ages. How do we account for the fact that the lawless are often prosperous and the godly often face the greatest possible hardships?

David probably had the book of Job before him as he pondered the problem. Job shows that there are factors in God's government which are unseen by men and that things come out right in the end. But the end is sometimes so long in coming—sometimes it doesn't seem to come at all in this life.

Two other psalms wrestle with the same problem—Psalms 49 and 73, but each of them takes up the problem from a different point of view. Psalm 37 emphasizes *the Psalmist's discernment.* He sees the problem in the light of man's true worth. He is not concerned with lesser things, such as money, and the things money can evaluate.

Psalm 73 emphasizes *the Psalmist's doubts.* For the problem remains. We read Sir Robert Anderson's classic *The Silence of God* and C. S. Lewis's *The Problem of Pain,* but somehow the problem doesn't go away that easily. No wave of a wand, no matter how magic, can dissolve the problem: why does wickedness seemingly triumph and goodness so often go seemingly unrewarded?

David tackles the problem in an interesting way. He writes an acrostic psalm. The acrostic itself is almost perfect, but not quite. Most of the letters in this acrostic are developed in four lines to each successive letter of the alphabet. However, the fourth letter (verse 7), the eleventh letter (verse 20), and the nineteenth letter (verse 34) have only three lines each. Those three triplets are in structural order. One marks the seventh verse from the beginning; one marks the seventh verse from the end; and one marks the verse in the middle. In three instances (verses 14-15, 25-26, and 39-40) the acrostic consists of five lines. The last letter *(toph)* is missing, which may be a hint that the perfect answer has not been given because we have not yet arrived at the perfect state. To make the acrostic complete it is necessary to avoid the last verse as it is recorded in some versions.

David divides his subject into four parts, elaborating each; one at considerable length. To some the subject of this psalm may be an interesting exercise in philosophy, but to anyone who has found himself in the clutches of an unscrupulous man this psalm deals with very pertinent issues.

I. Prospects That Are Foreign to the Wicked (37:1-11)

The first eleven verses look at things from the point of view of the righteous man. David strikes the right note at once for the righteous man has certain prospects that are absolutely outside the realm of experience of the wicked man. These prospects are rooted both in the character and continuance of God's throne, things which are spiritual and unseen rather than seen and temporal. The righteous man has a dimension of life altogether different from that of the sinner. David begins with that.

It would be profitable to go down the psalm verse by verse but for the sake of space we are going to give a careful analysis of each section and then summarize the points being made.

Here then, is how David looks at those *prospects* which are *foreign* to the wicked man.

A. The Righteous Man's Discovery (37:1-2)

"Fret not thyself because of evildoers, neither be thou envious against the workers of iniquity. For they shall soon be cut down like the grass, and wither as the green herb." In the end the evil man's harvest is not something to be envied. He is to be pitied for his little day does not last very long.

B. The Righteous Man's Dwelling (37:3)

"Trust in the LORD, and do good; so shalt thou dwell in the land, and verily thou shalt be fed." David knew what he was talking about. For years he had lived as a hunted fugitive, yet he had not missed a meal and now Saul his enemy was dead and he himself sat upon his enemy's throne. He indeed had his dwelling in the land.

C. The Righteous Man's Delight (37:4)

"Delight thyself also in the LORD, and He shall give thee the desires of thine heart." This is good to remember, for when things go wrong we tend to get occupied with the problem. Maybe things have gone wrong at work or at home. Perhaps the children are rebellious. We must get our eyes back on the Lord. As long as we look at the problem, we shall become increasingly depressed, but if we look at the Lord we shall rise above our circumstances. After all, *He* hasn't failed. He cannot fail. Our happiness must not rest upon what happens. It must be drawn out of the wellsprings of salvation and from our experiential knowledge of the goodness, grace, and greatness of our God.

D. The Righteous Man's Dependence (37:5-6)

"Commit thy way unto the LORD; trust also in Him, and He shall bring it to pass. And He shall bring forth thy righteousness as the light, and thy judgment [i.e., thy vindication] as the noonday." That word "commit" is an interesting one. It literally means "to roll over." We should take our great burdens and roll them over on Him. Trust Him, and remember God is working on a very grand scale indeed and is not going to be hustled and hurried by our fretting.

E. The Righteous Man's Discipline (37:7)

"Rest in the LORD, and wait patiently for Him: fret not thyself because of him who prospereth in his way, because of the man who bringeth wicked devices to pass." Fret not! The word "fret" means "to blaze" or "to get hot." We could easily get into a fever of rage against those who are building pornography into a billion dollar business, against those who are destroying the moral fiber of our youth with drink and drugs, against those in our colleges who are systematically stripping young people of any faith they may have in God. Our best resource, however, is in God, for the weapons of our warfare are not carnal but spiritual and they are mighty through God for the pulling down of strongholds. Sometimes it takes greater discipline to *wait* than it does to *war.*

F. The Righteous Man's Deliverance (37:8-10)

"Cease from anger, and forsake wrath: fret not thyself in any wise to do evil. For evildoers shall be cut off. . . . For yet a little while, and the wicked shall not be: yea, thou shalt diligently consider his place, and it shall not be." There we have deliverance from the power, the penalty, and from the very presence of sin. Note again that word "fret not!" Three times we are told not to fret; three times we are told not to be envious of the wicked. We are not to be occupied with them at all—we might start wanting to be like them.

G. The Righteous Man's Domains (37:11)

"But the meek shall inherit the earth: and shall delight themselves in the abundance of peace." We need to pause here for a moment for this is one of those verses of the Old Testament which shed a flood of light on our Lord's teaching. The reason Jesus "spoke with authority and not as the scribes" was because He based *His* teaching solidly on the Scriptures whereas the scribes based *theirs* on the traditions of the elders. Jesus simply taught the Bible. We tend to think that Jesus taught a lot of new and novel things whereas in actual fact He rarely introduced anything new. His soul was so saturated with the Scriptures that they flowed out of His mouth and nearly all His teaching comes right out of the Old Testament.

Nowadays people think they can discredit the Lord if they can find some pre-Christian document (such as the Dead Sea Scrolls) and show that a Jewish sect (such as the Essenes) actually "anticipated" Christ's teaching. They did nothing of the kind. They simply went back to the same sources as He did—the Scriptures. Jesus took the Old Testament, passed it through the prism of His holy intellect, and restated it in a particularly memorable and forceful form. Thus, when we read in the Sermon on the Mount: "Blessed are the meek for they shall inherit the earth," we are not reading something new; we are reading Psalm 37:11, only it is Psalm 37:11 lifted to a new and vital plane.

For the meek *will* inherit the earth. That truth is ingrained in the Biblical concept of the coming millennial reign of Christ. The meek man's domain will extend, in that day, from the river to the ends of the earth, from sea to sea, from shore to shore, from pole to pole. In the light of that the prospects of the wicked man are somewhat tarnished after all.

II. PURSUITS THAT ARE FAVORED BY THE WICKED (37:12-22)

In this section David explores the kinds of things that loom so large in the life of the man who imagines he can get along without God and, indeed, often seems to be successful in doing so.

A. The Wicked Man's Plots (37:12-13)

"The wicked plotteth against the just, and gnasheth upon him with his teeth. The LORD shall laugh at him: for He seeth that his day is coming." There is a certain poetry in God's administration of justice, of which we can get an occasional glimpse in the Bible, but which is rarely seen in the rush and bustle of our own lives even though it is there. Perhaps in eternity God will show us how it has never failed to work in every instance of His dealings with men.

We glimpse God's justice in the book of Esther when we see Haman being hanged upon the gallows he had prepared for Mordecai. We glimpse it in the book of Jonah when we see that angry prophet experiencing for himself the "belly of hell" into which he so much wanted the people of Nineveh to fall. We glimpse it again in the life of David himself—reaping in his own family the lust and lawlessness he had sowed. The poetic justice of God is real: "With what measure ye mete, it shall be measured to you again" the Lord warns (Matthew 7:2).

B. The Wicked Man's Power (37:14-15)

"The wicked have drawn out the sword, and have bent their bow, to cast down the poor and needy, and to slay such as be of upright conversation. This sword shall enter into their own heart, and their bows shall be broken." When the wicked man has the power to do so, he commits terrible atrocities. The history of our times affords only too many examples. Indeed, the twentieth century has put out of its mind, because it can no longer cope with the enormity of the statistics involved, the crimes which have been committed against humanity during its span. Who can measure the sum total of suffering wrought by men like the kaiser, Lenin, Stalin, Hitler, Mao Tse Tung, the communist rulers of Vietnam, to mention but a few? But God has a sword for them, a sword which will enter into their own souls and twist and turn there for all eternity.

C. The Wicked Man's Prosperity (37:16-17)

"A little that a righteous man hath is better than the riches of many wicked. For the arms of the wicked shall be broken: but the LORD upholdeth the righteous." All too often in our materialistic culture we put the emphasis in the wrong place. We think that money can buy happiness. The wicked man's prosperity, however, is illusionary. It is like the pot of gold supposed to rest at the foot of the rainbow.

When General Booth asked Cecil Rhodes, the wealthiest man in the world in his day, if he was a happy man, the South African gold-and-diamond magnate replied: "Me, happy? Good heavens, no!" The Bible says, however, that "godliness with contentment is great gain."

D. The Wicked Man's Protection (37:18-20)

"The LORD knoweth the days of the upright: and their inheritance shall be forever. They shall not be ashamed in the evil time: and in the days of famine they shall be satisfied. But the wicked shall perish, and the enemies of the LORD shall be as the fat of lambs: they shall consume; into smoke shall they consume away." The wicked man, in other words, has no protection. It may look as though the *righteous* man has no protection, but God says otherwise. Viewed from *His* perspective, the wicked man's defenses against misfortune are worthless. He likens his future to smoke. We have all seen what happens to smoke coming out of a chimney. Sometimes it lies thick enough, but it soon disperses and vanishes. God has His winds which can soon blow away the defenses of the wicked man and dissipate them before his very eyes.

E. The Wicked Man's Pledge (37:21-22)

"The wicked borroweth, and payeth not again: but the righteous showeth mercy, and giveth. For such as are blessed of Him shall inherit the earth; but such as are accursed of Him shall be cut off" (Rotherham). It is terrible to fall into the clutches of a man like that, who borrows with the certain knowledge he cannot repay. It is worse still if the man calls himself a Christian—God has a different description of him in this verse.

By contrast how happy is the man who gives generously to help those in need, especially those of the family of faith. Such people are laying up treasure for eternity. As a friend of mine used to say: "If you want treasure in Heaven you had better give to someone who is going there!"

There is no treasure in the unprincipled pursuits favored by the wicked because he thinks he can get away with them, because so often it seems he does. But that is because his perspectives are warped, which is David's next great theme.

III. PATHS THAT ARE FORSAKEN BY THE WICKED (37:23-31)

David comes back now to look at the godly man and at the path that he walks through life. It is the good and the right way, the straight and the narrow path. It holds no attraction at all for the wicked man.

A. The Righteous Man's Walk (37:23-24)

"The steps of a good man are ordered by the LORD: and He delighteth in his way. Though he fall, he shall not be utterly cast down: for the LORD upholdeth him with His hand." George Mueller, who founded five great orphan houses on Ashley Down in Bristol and who knew what it was to walk close to the Lord, dependent upon Him for the daily needs of hundreds of boys and girls, and in his later years a missionary to a score of lands, used to say: "Yes, and not only the steps! Sometimes also the *stops* of a righteous man are ordered of the Lord."

B. The Righteous Man's Wants (37:25)

"I have been young, and now am old; yet have I not seen the righteous forsaken, nor his seed begging bread." David was now in his old age. His turbulent days were over. Twice he had been a fugitive and he might have said at the time that he had been forsaken and was begging bread. But he had outlived all that; he had lived long enough to get things into perspective. He had never seen the righteous abandoned by God and any temporary shifts of fortune had all been part of the wise discipline of God to make of him a true man of God.

C. The Righteous Man's Works (37:26-27)

"He is ever merciful, and lendeth, and his seed is blessed. Depart from evil, and do good; and dwell for evermore." The righteous man's works are both merciful and moral in character, the kinds of works God is bound to bless.

D. The Righteous Man's Welfare (37:28-29)

"For the LORD loveth judgment, and forsaketh not His saints; they are preserved for ever: but the seed of the wicked shall be cut off. The righteous shall inherit the land, and dwell therein for ever." Again, we must remember that the ultimate vision of the psalm is millennial and that God's purposes do not ripen in a day. In the Old Testament the believer anticipated a "heaven on earth," the glory-age when Christ will reign and when the Old Testament saints will come into their own. It is worth remembering this basic difference between the Old Testament believer and his blessing and that of the Christian today. In the Old Testament for blessing a believer had to be in a *place,* in the New Testament he has to be in a *person;* in the Old Testament he had to be in *Canaan,* in the New Testament he has to be in *Christ;* in the Old Testament God's blessing was "yea and amen" in the *land,* in the New Testament it is "yea and amen" in the *Lord.*

E. The Righteous Man's Wisdom (37:30-31)

"The mouth of the righteous speaketh wisdom, and his tongue talketh of judgment. The law of his God is in his heart; none of his steps shall slide." The ungodly man prides himself on his cleverness and cunning, but he is a fool. The righteous man draws from a well of wisdom which has its unfailing springs in the omniscience of God.

These are the paths that are forsaken by the wicked. They are steep and narrow, but they lead to life. How much better it is, after all, to go in at the narrow gate and to climb the steeps that lead to God than to enter in at the wide gate and tread the broad, downward path to destruction!

IV. POINTS THAT ARE FORGOTTEN BY THE WICKED (37:32-40)

These points are crucial to the whole argument David has been making. The wicked man forgets three things.

A. Truth Is on the Side of the Godly (37:32-34)

"The wicked watcheth the righteous, and seeketh to slay him. The LORD will not leave him in his hand, nor condemn him when he is judged. Wait on the LORD, and keep His way, and He shall exalt thee to inherit the land: when the wicked are cut off, thou shalt see it." The wicked man's designs and deceits will be rewarded by death. In the day when God settles accounts, the righteous man will see how just God is. In the meantime, it may look as though lies prosper, wicked men may unjustly condemn the righteous. But there is a great day of reckoning coming when truth will be on the side of the godly, and settled it will be.

B. Time Is on the Side of the Godly (37:35-36)

"I have seen the wicked in great power, and spreading himself like a green bay tree. Yet he passed away, and, lo, he was not: yea, I sought him, but he could not be found." David could have written such words about either Saul or Absalom. He knew from his own personal experience that time is on the side of the godly.

The communists boast that time is on their side; they claim that the inevitable laws of history guarantee their ultimate success. But they are wrong: time is God's tool; it is not the wicked man's ally, it is God's. Sooner or later time will run out for the wicked man and he will be hurried off to his grave and into a Christless eternity. Time is the friend of the people of God, bringing them safely home at last.

C. Trust Is on the Side of the Godly (37:37-40)

The godly man has something that the ungodly man does not have: he has a vital trust in God that tips the scales firmly in his favor.

1. A Perfect Standing (37:37-38)

"Mark the perfect man, and behold the upright: for the end of that man is peace. But the transgressors shall be destroyed together: the end of the wicked shall be cut off." The righteous man has his feet firmly planted on the Rock; the ungodly man builds everything on shifting sand.

2. A Perfect Stability (37:39-40)

"But the salvation of the righteous is of the LORD: He is their strength in the time of trouble. And the LORD shall help them, and deliver them: He shall deliver them from the wicked, and save them, because they trust in Him." The very character and continuance of God's throne is ultimately at stake in this issue. God would have to cease to be God, cease to be righteous and just, holy and true if He failed to come through fully, finally, and forever on behalf of the righteous man. That is a point the wicked man has forgotten.

So much, then, for David's handling of the problem. How can we apply it to the forces that are shaping society today, to those evil and lawless forces bent on enslaving the world in atheism, godlessness, and wickedness?

There can be no doubt that we are living in a very wicked world. Look, for instance, at just one fruit of the communist conspiracy in the world today—at the triumph of communism in Vietnam.

Soon after the communists unified their conquests in the south they began a program of genocide which has been bluntly called "the liquid Auschwitz." They launched the most heartless programs of human exploitation ever exhibited, even in this callous twentieth century. For a fee (over $4,000 a person) the government allowed certain of the people to leave the country. They were especially interested in getting rid of people of Chinese extraction. They stood to gain both ways. They received hard cash and they rid themselves of an unwanted minority. Hong Kong officials, who bore the brunt of the resulting horrors, say that Hanoi hoped to collect well over $3 billion before its Chinese population was completely expelled.

The officials who conducted this cold-blooded traffic in misery knew perfectly well that the majority of people leaving their shores would never make it to freedom. They were crammed into hopelessly overcrowded and often unseaworthy vessels, and simply cast adrift to make their own way, a prey to pirates on the high seas, victims of thirst, starvation, and storms, and worst of all, with no destination in mind. The other countries of southeast Asia, having absorbed all they could of these pathetic "boat people," began to turn them away, thrust them unceremoniously back out to sea.

Who can measure the guilt of men who callously plan and perpetrate atrocities like that? "The wicked," says David, "the wicked have drawn out the sword and have bent their bow to cast down the poor and needy. . . ." Well, God has promised to settle such accounts with the men responsible. "The sword," he says, "shall enter their own heart." We will have to take our stand on that, and remember that the accounting is not always in the here and now.

But let us go back a step further. What about the man whose ideas and writings, whose strategic planning and vision lies behind the communist cause in the world today? What about Lenin? To millions of people in the world he is painted as a hero. His mummified corpse lies in state in Red Square in Moscow. Millions of people file past it to worship as they gaze through the glass at his waxen features and look at his horribly shrunken face. Everybody knows that he was the mastermind behind the communist revolution. It was he who fashioned the party as a political army, who laid down its strategy, who charted its course. What about Lenin? What about this man who unleashed communism upon mankind and who had no compunction about liquidating anyone who stood in his path?

Lenin died on January 21, 1924, having just finished putting on trial some Roman priests in Moscow. The archbishop and his companions had been paraded through the streets as objects of derision, hatred, and scorn. The next night *Death* came for Lenin, passing swiftly by the triple row of guards, marching unconcernedly through locked and bolted doors. He came and stood by the bed on which the dictator lay and there he tarried for a little while, contemplating the man he would soon carry off into eternity.

From that day on Lenin became a living corpse. The autopsy performed on Lenin's body later showed that there had been terrible destruction to his brain, which had thought so incisively through the worldwide ramifications and implications of communism. One of England's newspapers, *The Daily Mail,* in its issue dated February 1, 1924, tells what happened to Lenin before the end finally came. He went mad. It was commonly reported, the paper says, that Lenin spent his last days of activity crawling on all fours like a beast around the room in his carefully guarded retreat, apologizing to the furniture for his misdeeds—the memory of which remained amid the ruins of his mind—and shouting repeatedly: "God save Russia and kill the Jews."

Then God gave the final nod to Death. And Death silenced the madman forever and took his naked and guilty soul into eternity to await judgment at the great white throne. The wicked man's plot, the wicked man's power, the wicked man's prosperity, the wicked man's protection—all reduced to nothing in a moment of time by Death.

Time is on God's side. *That* is the great message of Psalm 37.

Psalm 38

SICKNESS AND SUFFERING BROUGHT ON BY SIN

IS THERE NOT A CAUSE? The words were spoken by a fresh-faced teenager. The lad had left his employment and had come down to the front line where opposing armies were at daggers drawn. His brothers, enlisted men, accused him of idle curiosity, of shiftless irresponsibility, of all kinds of evil motives, and scarcely gave him the time of day for the fresh-baked goods he had brought to them from home. "Is there not a cause?" asked David. Of course there was! There was a cause that neither they nor he knew at that moment, but they would know it an hour later when Goliath of Gath lay dead upon the hill and Israel's victorious armies were charging upon the foe.

The cause is not always so evident, especially when it comes to sickness—which is the subject of this psalm—sickness brought on by sin.

During meetings I was having some time ago, I was fighting an infection which finally settled in my ear, making me virtually deaf. There was a young man in that particular church who believed in faith healing. He as good as told me that I was suffering because of some sin. Maybe I was. But I certainly didn't agree with him. He was very bold about it, he told me that he intended *never* to be sick. According to this young fellow there was a cause: I was sick because I had sinned and I was remaining sick because I would not confess that sin (I take it he meant confess to him) and because I did not have enough faith to be healed. I said to him: "The trouble with you healing people is that you are Job's comforters. They came along to poor old Job and they said to him: 'Job we know why you're sick, it is because you're a sinner, and the severity of your sufferings is commensurate with your guilt. Come on, Job, confess!' But Job's comforters only made him worse." The young fellow was taken aback for a moment, then he blurted out: "But Job's friends did not have all the facts. They didn't know what they were talking about." I said "Exactly. You said it! That *is* the whole point, they didn't know what they were talking about, and neither do you."

"Is there not a cause?" Of course there is. More often than not sickness is caused simply and solely by disease. It is part of the common lot of mankind in this world. God may or may not heal it in answer to prayer. Usually He sends us to a doctor. Where in the Bible did God do something for somebody that he could do for himself?

Our psalm was written by that same man who, when a lad, confidently asserted: "Is there not a cause?" It was written by David, but a David suffering under the stroke of God for his flagrant sin with Bathsheba and for his murder of Uriah, one of the most faithful of his mighty men.

In the background the Absalom rebellion is brewing and David is tortured in body and mind. He has been deserted by his friends and is being menaced by enemies. "Is there not a cause?" He knows perfectly well there is for he is reaping what he sowed. Moreover, as he writes this sad psalm, there seems to be no hope.

It is the third of the *penitential* psalms (the others are 6, 32, 51, 102, 130, 143). The title indicates that this psalm is "to bring to remembrance." How remarkable! Usually we try to forget the wrong things we have done.

The Jews, in their services, used this psalm as part of the general confession of sin on the great Day of Atonement. There is a wail of despair that haunts this psalm, but it is David's despair in *himself,* not in God.

I. DAVID'S SIN (38:1-4)

David begins at the end.

A. The Consequences of Sin (38:1-3)

We don't think of the consequences when we start playing with sin. When we first indulge in some evil habit we little think of the fearful chains it has in store for us later on. David begins with that, for he was now receiving the due reward of his deeds. He emphasizes two aspects of the consequences of sin. We should underline them in our Bibles and in our memories.

1. The Divine Anger (38:1-2)

"O LORD, rebuke me not in Thy wrath; neither chasten me in Thy hot displeasure. For Thine arrows stick fast in me, and Thy hand presseth me sore." He had no doubt that the condition in which he found himself was the direct result of God's judicial dealings with him. Underline that! We don't get away with sin. God says, for instance, that "marriage is honorable in all and the bed undefiled but whoremongers and adulterers God will judge." That is worth remembering in this day of loose morals. Nobody gets away with immorality, God sees to that. Payday may be postponed for a time, but it always comes.

In David's case it had come almost within the year. The word he uses for *God,* as he cries out under the chastening hand, is LORD (Jehovah). In other words, he recognizes the faithfulness of the promise-keeping God in the chastening he was now experiencing.

2. The Daily Anguish (38:3)

He had not thought of *that* when he so blithely sent his invitation to Bathsheba. He is thinking of that daily anguish now: "There is no soundness in my flesh because of Thine anger; neither is there any rest in my bones because of my sin."

Well might Paul write: "Flee fornication. Every sin that a man doeth is without [outside] the body; but he that committeth fornication sinneth against his own body" (1 Corinthians 6:18). God has fearful weapons He can bring against the bodies of those who refuse to listen to Him in the matter of morality. There are some twenty different sexually transmitted diseases defined in modern medicine, every one of them marked by disgusting symptoms and several of them lead to horrifying complications such as blindness, brain damage, insanity, eye-infection, damage to skin, bones, liver, teeth, consequences to unborn children, and even death. With at least ten to fifteen million Americans being struck every year, with a new infection occurring every forty-five seconds, and with the annual bill in America alone for these kinds of diseases running at over one billion dollars, it is no wonder that public health officials are at their wit's end.

Even if the immoral person somehow manages to evade disease, God has other weapons for those who break His laws. Some of them are psychological. The anguish they ultimately cause to the mind is no less real than the physical ravages in the body.

Now, there is forgiveness with God, as David discovered. However, before God showed him that, He allowed him to suffer: "There is no soundness in my flesh," David wailed, "because of Thine anger." It is not likely that David had contracted venereal disease. His affliction was much more dramatic than that. The point here is that David was suffering, not only from divine anger but also from daily anguish, and all as a result of his immorality. That was the *consequence* of his sin.

B. The Consciousness of Sin (38:4)

"For mine iniquities are gone over mine head: as an heavy burden they are too heavy for me." He hadn't thought of that, either, when he had cultivated his intimacy with Bathsheba. The word he uses for "iniquities" brings out all the wrong and crookedness of sin. The word he uses for these iniquities going over his head reminds us of the eastern porters. You can see them in an eastern city staggering along under loads so vast and heavy you are astonished that they can bear them. Their spindly legs seem as though they must surely snap under the strain. That is how his sin now seemed to David.

II. DAVID'S SUFFERING (38:5-8)

Now he delves deeper into his miseries. It is evident from the next three verses and from the special word he uses in verse 11 for his "sore" that David was severely inflicted with a loathsome disease.

We may well wonder why we don't read about this disease in those historical books of the Old Testament which describe David's sin and subsequent repentance. Both Samuel and Chronicles are silent on the subject. Perhaps no royal scribe would feel at liberty to talk about this aspect of David's sufferings. But David had no such qualms. The dishonor he had done to Jehovah's name fully merited the dreadful thing that had now overtaken him. The secret must come out, and who more fitting to confess his shame than David himself? He does so in this and several other psalms.

In fact, so thorough is his confession in this psalm, and so sincerely does he want others to learn from his own experience, that he actually adds a subscription to this psalm by addressing it: "To the chief Musician, even to Jeduthun."

In 2 Chronicles 35:15, Jeduthun is called "the king's seer." He was also one of the three chief musicians in charge of the musical side of the organized Jewish religion, so he was both a *seer* and a *singer*. Perhaps that is why David assigned this psalm to him. It is as much a sermon as a song.

In any case, David, even in the midst of his sufferings, was so convinced of the justice of what had happened to him that he had no qualms whatever about publicly confessing it and having his record included as part of the repertoire of the temple choir—to be sung out in the ears of all men. What a rare soul was David! Most of us would rather die than confess the kinds of things David confesses, and certainly we would rather die than have them become public knowledge. But not David! He can learn even from his sins and sufferings. No wonder the Spirit of God calls him "a man after God's own heart."

Now look at what he says about his sufferings. He underlines four things.

A. Disgusted (38:5)

"My wounds stink and are corrupt because of my foolishness." Whatever the malady was that afflicted him it was something foul, that filled his chambers with a nauseating stench.

B. Distressed (38:6)

"I am troubled; I am bowed down greatly; I go mourning all the day long." The physical malady that had him in its grip caused far more than pain of body; it caused him acute distress of mind.

C. Diseased (38:7)

"For my loins are filled with a loathsome disease: and there is no soundness in my flesh." The word for "loathsome" means "burning." He had a fever; he was inflamed.

D. Disturbed (38:8)

"I am feeble and sore broken: I have roared by reason of the disquietness of my heart." One Hebrew authority suggests a different rendering: "I have roared beyond the roaring of a lion" (Ginsburg). The inward anguish of his soul found utterance at times in dreadful howls. Anyone who has ever heard a lion roar knows that it is a fearful sound.

The servants in the royal palace must have whispered to themselves at the cries from David's sick room, cries out of the very depths of David's soul. David's sufferings are all written down to warn us. Sin leads us ultimately into suffering. It is in the very nature of the thing.

III. DAVID'S SORROW (38:9-14)

David describes three things about the inexpressible sorrow of his soul at this dreadful time in his experience.

A. Spiritual (38:9-10)

"LORD, all my desire is before Thee: and my groaning is not hid from thee. My heart panteth, my strength faileth me: as for the light of mine eyes, it also is gone from me." He had lost all sense of victory, all sense of vitality, all sense of vision. He was defeated, depressed, and in the dark. He was like a lost soul. Yet all his being cried out for God, Jehovah.

That is perhaps the worst thing about the hour of conviction, when one's sins come home to roost: one tends to lose all sense of the presence of God. There was a spiritual dimension even to the horrible affliction which attacked David's body.

B. Social (38:11-12)

He was deserted by his friends and derided by his foes: "My lovers and friends stand aloof from my sore; and my kinsmen stand afar off. They also that seek after my life lay snares for me: and they that seek my hurt speak mischievous things, and imagine deceits all the day long."

We have now come to the clue for which we have been searching. What kind of disease was it in Israel which set a man apart from family and friends; which drove him as a dreadful pariah outside the camp; which caused him to roar his uncleanness whenever anyone started to approach? What fearful affliction caused the Jews to flee from anyone tainted with it? What was looked upon as the very stroke of God? Surely it was *leprosy. David had become a leper!* Or so it seems.

That fact alone, perhaps, would help account for the strange silence of the historians about David's sickness. How could they record *that* about the best, the bravest, and the most beloved of all their kings? David does not hesitate, however. He says: "My lovers and my friends stand aloof from my sore." The word he uses for "sore" is the word specifically used in the Old Testament for the plague of leprosy. No wonder even his family fled from him. Had it been anyone but David, anyone but the king, he would have been driven outside the camp, forced to cover his lip, forced to cry unceasingly, "Unclean! Unclean!"

David's sorrows were spiritual—the leper could have no place in the sanctuary. David's sorrows were social—nobody wanted to come near him.

C. Silent (38:13-14)

So overwhelming was his situation that at times David simply sat deaf and dumb in the presence of God: "But I, as a deaf man, heard not; and I was as a dumb man that openeth not his mouth. Thus I was as a man that heareth not, and in whose mouth are no reproofs." He had nothing to say. What could he say? His mouth was stopped.

The sweet singer of Israel, the man who always had a ready answer, was dumb.

We can be sure David never expected anything like this when he first began to play with sin. But then, neither do we.

IV. DAVID'S SUPPLICATION (38:15-22)

He has a threefold petition:

A. Lord, Hear Me! (38:15-16)

Recovering from the dreadful admission, David first expresses *his confidence:* "For in Thee, O LORD, do I hope: Thou wilt hear, O LORD, my God" (38:15). David may be deaf and dumb in his shock but that does not prevent his whole soul from crying out to God—to Jehovah His Elohim, the Only One who could possibly help. To *Jehovah,* the God of Covenant—the gracious, merciful compassionate One who of His own free will sought out the poor sons of men in order to reveal Himself as the God of promise. To Elohim, the God of Creation, who could just as easily recover the leper as He could create a universe. "In *Thee* do I hope."

David expresses *his concern:* "For I said, Hear me, lest otherwise they should rejoice over me: when my foot slippeth, they magnify themselves against me" (38:16). In the first part of the psalm David is mostly taken up with his malady; in the second part he is mostly taken up with his maligners, his enemies so ready to capitalize upon his misfortunes. "Hear me!" He wanted his enemies to know that it was God with whom they would have to reckon. It was one thing for God to enter into judgment with his child; it was something else for others to try to take advantage of the occasion.

B. Lord, Heal Me (38:17-18)

David mentions both his contrition and his confession: "For I am ready to halt, and my sorrow is continually before me. For I will declare mine iniquity; I will be sorry for my sin." That is always a good first step; that is getting down to the root of the problem. There *are* some sicknesses caused by sin; *those* sicknesses call for a spiritual diagnosis and prescription.

This is what we have in the book of James where the sick man calls for the elders of the church and puts things right with the church in order to be healed. James is not giving a blanket prescription for healing—the sickness and the sin, the confession and the cure are too closely linked. This was certainly David's case. If he had not repented he would have died a leper.

Last of all he prays:

C. Lord, Help Me! (38:19-22)

David is aware of what is happening in his kingdom. The Absalom affair is coming to a head. He desperately needs his health back so that he can once again take over the affairs of state.

1. Consider What My Situation Is (38:19-20)

"But mine enemies are lively, and they are strong: and they that hate me wrongfully are multiplied. They also that render evil for good are mine adversaries; because I follow the thing that good is." David never ceased to be astonished at the downright malignity of men. There were the terrible curses of Shimei, for instance, which David had to face a little later. On the whole his reign had been a good one. He had been concerned for the welfare of others. However, there were those in the kingdom who hated him even for that, especially those who had once been cronies of Saul. "Lord! Consider my situation!" David prayed.

2. Consider Who My Saviour Is (38:21-22)

"Forsake me not, O LORD: O my God, be not far from me. Make haste to help me, O Lord my salvation." That is always a great argument with God: "Lord, let me remind You that in the last analysis *You are my Saviour,* the Lord of my salvation. I have nothing else to plead but that, and I need nothing else. You *must* save me, because that's the kind of God You are." Then David added a postscript: "Here you are Jeduthun. Here is a song worth singing!"

Psalm 39

ALTOGETHER VANITY

I. DAVID'S PLEDGE (39:1-3)
   A. The Importance of It (39:1)
   B. The Impropriety of It (39:2)
   C. The Impossibility of It (39:3)
II. DAVID'S PLEA (39:4-5)
   He wanted the answer to:
   A. Life's Frailty (39:4)
   B. Life's Futility (39:5)
III. DAVID'S PLIGHT (39:6-11)
   It was the plight of:
   A. The Wealthy Man (39:6)
   B. The Wicked Man (39:7-11)
      He must therefore face:
      1. The Reality of His Sin (39:7-9)
         a. He Needed a Saviour (39:7-8)
         b. He Needed a Spokesman (39:9)
      2. The Results of His Sin (39:10-11)
         a. He Had Lost His Blessedness (39:10)
         b. He Had Lost His Beauty (39:11a)
         c. He Had Lost His Bearings (39:11b)
IV. DAVID'S PLAN (39:12-13)
   To ask God to make him:
   A. Happy Again (39:12a)
   B. Holy Again (39:12b)
   C. Healthy Again (39:13)

THIS PSALM is probably a continuation of Psalm 38. David is still in the same dreadful plight of a man who has been stricken by God. However, in this psalm the mood has changed. David is no longer outraged at the dreadful thing which has seized upon his flesh. Instead, he has become more thoughtful, able to look at his plight more objectively, able even to philosophize upon his condition.

Like the previous psalm, he addresses this finished poem too to the chief musician. Ultimately, the chief musician is the Lord Jesus Himself, so in effect, David says: "Here, Lord, I have written the words,

you write the music. Tune up my heart and set my soul to singing—
even in this, Lord, even in this!"

Two other books need to be kept in mind when we read this psalm.
One of them David had probably committed to memory during the
dreadful days of physical agony and soul anguish: the book of *Job*.
There would be one notable difference, however, between Job's case
and that of David. Job could see no cause-and-effect relationship
between his life and his sufferings. Job was seventy when his world
caved in. To the best of his knowledge, his life had been one of
benevolence, uprightness, and integrity, lived in the fear of God.
Then disaster, disease, and dissension tore his world apart. Job did
not know that his life had become a stage upon which God and Satan
struggled for mastery and that he would emerge from the trial with
double for all that he had lost—even double the length of days so that
another hundred and forty years of blessing and benediction lay
before him. Job could see no reason for his sufferings.

Not so David! He knew that, if ever a man deserved to be punished
by the living God for flagrant sin, for abuse of privilege, position, and
power, for high-handed wickedness, then he was the man. Nevertheless, David probably spent much time with Job during these dreadful
days.

The other book which needs to be read in connection with Psalm
39 is *Ecclesiastes*. Ecclesiastes is a sermon written by Solomon, en-
dowed with wisdom, insight, knowledge, understanding more than
any before or since but whose light turned to darkness on account
of his sin. Solomon, in spite of all his proverbs and wise sayings and
profound insights, played the fool in Jerusalem, gave his lustful heart
to a host of pagan women, and ended by raising up altars to the foul,
false idols of Canaan in Jerusalem, the city of the living God.

With old age came remorse. Solomon looked back over his wasted
life, over the disastrous things he had done, and longed to make
amends, at least to leave some warning notice to those who might
be tempted to follow his foolish ways. But what could he do, with his
influence on the wane, with a fool for a son, and with rumblings of
rebellion abroad in the land?

We can picture Solomon in his palace brooding over the words of
divine wrath that had been delivered to him: "Forasmuch as this is
done thee, and thou hast not kept My covenant and My statutes,
which I have commanded thee, I will surely rend the kingdom from
thee, and will give it to thy servant. Notwithstanding in thy days I will
not do it for David thy father's sake: but I will rend it out of the hand
of thy son. Howbeit I will not rend away all the kingdom; but will give
one tribe to thy son for David My servant's sake, and for Jerusalem's
sake which I have chosen" (1 Kings 11:11-13).

For David's sake! For David thy father's sake! For David My servant's sake! Perhaps this word of judgment, that focused attention on
David, turned Solomon's mind to David's psalms. We can picture him

thumbing through them until at last he comes across Psalm 39. We can see him reading it carelessly, then carefully, then contritely, with tears running down his face and splashing on the page before him: "Verily every man at his best state is altogether *vanity!* Selah." Surely every man is *vanity!* That was it—that was the word that summed up his life. Solomon stared at the word. We can see him throwing himself on his knees, as David his father had so often done. We can see him pouring out his heart as David, God's servant, had done. We can see that handsome, dissipated old man, Solomon, power and pomp forgotten, wealth, wives, and works forgotten: "O spare me, that I may recover strength, before I go hence, and be no more."

Then we can picture Solomon, with a new look in his eye and a fresh set to his jaw hail his servant and call for paper and pen. With the fresh page before him he pauses for a moment then begins his task: "The words of the Preacher, the son of David, king in Jerusalem. Vanity of vanities, saith the Preacher, vanity of vanities; all is vanity." So begins the greatest book in the Bible on the pursuits, perspectives, and prospects of the worldly-minded man.

So then, we may say almost that Psalm 39 has some of its *roots* in the book of Job and some of its *fruits* in the book of Ecclesiastes.

I. DAVID'S PLEDGE (39:1-3)

It was, purely and simply, a pledge to hold his tongue.

A. The Importance of It (39:1)

"I said, I will take heed to my ways, that I sin not with my tongue: I will keep my mouth with a bridle, while the wicked is before me."

David starts out with the good intention of keeping his mouth shut, afraid that he may compound his liabilities by speaking evil against God and by murmuring because of his chastisement. He is particularly resolved not to speak against God in the presence of wicked men.

There were many whose lot he could have compared with his. There was that villain Shimei, whose venomous tongue was gossiping about David and pouring scorn upon his name and reputation. There was Absalom, his own son, plotting to seize the kingdom, even if it meant his father's murder. There was Joab, tool turned tyrant ever since David wrote that compromising letter telling him to arrange for the death of Uriah.

Why did men like Shimei, Absalom, and Joab seemingly go scot-free when he, David, was living in the very suburbs of hell because of his sin? David resolutely pledged not to say a word, not to add to his other sins by sinning with his tongue. He would bridle his tongue. It was an important pledge, one to which we all would do well to pay heed.

B. The Impropriety of It (39:2)

"I was dumb with silence, I held my peace, even from good; and my sorrow was stirred." The word translated "dumb" means "to be tongue-tied." David so clamped down upon his words that he even refrained from saying good things. But his efforts to keep silence only aggravated his sufferings. It is one thing to bridle the tongue against evil-speaking. But when we try to keep total silence we go beyond what God intended.

Thomas B. Costain in his book *The Black Rose* tells that Walter of Gurnie had the misfortune to be born out of wedlock. He was brought up by his dour old grandfather who, in his anger at his offending daughter, took an oath that he would never speak to his grandson. This pledge he kept with stubborn resolution nearly all the way through the story, even though he was secretly proud of young Walter's good looks and knightly achievements.

When the old man had something to say to Walter, he would get around his oath by addressing himself instead to his faithful old steward. For instance, when Walter arrived back from an unprecedented visit to distant Cathay and presented himself at Gurnie before his grandfather, the old man addressed his steward: "Wilderkin, he has become a man! How he has filled out! It is a pity his mother is not here to see him. She would have been proud, as proud as his grandfather is, Wilderkin." Walter likewise addressed the steward: "Tell my lord Alfagar for me, Wilderkin, that I am happy to be home with him again." And so it went on. The oath of silence had to be kept at all costs.

But the oath was too cumbersome to be kept. The day came, when in the stress of great excitement the old lord of Gurnie so far forgot himself as to speak directly to his grandson. It was a silly oath when all is said and done.

So, too, with David's oath. It had a measure of impropriety about it. He so clamped down on his tongue that he would not even speak a word of good for fear he would speak a word of ill.

C. The Impossibility of It (39:3)

"My heart was hot within me, while I was musing the fire burned: then spake I with my tongue." He might just as well have tried to cap a volcano as try to keep silence. The smouldering fires within simply had to have an outlet. We are not told all he said when finally the inward pressure blew off the cap he had so artificially fastened on his emotions. We can be sure he said plenty.

Centuries later the Apostle James takes up the theme of bridling the tongue: "If any man offend not in word, the same is a *perfect* man" (James 3:2). The word James uses means "the end." In Latin it is *finis*. There is nothing beyond. The person has attained perfection. No wonder we find it so difficult to hold our tongues! It is the mark of perfection. David was anything but a perfect man. He was a poor, erring, mortal man with a heart too full ever to be stopped up by a vow of silence.

II. DAVID'S PLEA (39:4-5)

He wanted to know the answer to two questions—the very two questions which plagued Solomon all through Ecclesiastes.

A. Life's Frailty (39:4)

"LORD, make me to know mine end, and the measure of my days, what it is; that I may know how frail I am." Since silence is impossible, David breaks it in the best possible way—by pouring out his heart to God. Poor David already knew the brevity of life. He had the prayer of Moses the man of God before him, that amazing prayer forever embalmed in Psalm 90. He knew that man's days were spanned by seventy years and that a man, blessed with unusual strength, might lengthen his days by another decade. That does not seem to be his burden. What David wanted to know was how much longer *he* had left—how much longer he must drag out his days, a living corpse, now that he had come under the punitive stroke of God. Life's frailty was very real to the afflicted king.

B. Life's Futility (39:5)

"Behold, Thou hast made my days as an handbreadth; and mine age is as nothing before Thee: verily every man at his best state is altogether vanity. Selah." A handbreadth was just four fingers wide, less than half a span. David realized that life, at best, was very brief, "like the falling of a leaf, like the binding of a sheaf." Even in his best state the whole of man's life is soon over.

This is what Lord Byron, the most colorful of the English romantic poets discovered. Popular, successful, titled, Byron lived careless of public opinion. He roamed Europe and the Middle East, became involved in Italian revolutionary politics, cast in his lot with the Greeks in their war of independence from the Turks. He died while still in his thirties. His poetry captured the imagination of his fellows. He tasted all that pleasure, popularity, and position could give. He wrote *vanity* across his life just three months before he died:

> My days are in the yellow leaf;
> The flowers and fruits of love are gone;
> The worm, the canker, and the grief
> Are mine alone.

Benjamin Disraeli, Earl of Beaconsfield, one of Britain's brilliant peers of Parliament and her most zealous empire-builder, came to much the same conclusion. He defended and advanced Britain's imperial interests in Africa and India. He thwarted Russia's bid to seize Turkey, and confined the Russian bear to the Black Sea. He made Britain the dominant power in the Middle East by buying up a controlling interest in the Suez Canal. He was not only a brilliant Jewish statesman but a novelist of repute. Yet when he was old Disraeli wrote *vanity* over it all: "Youth is a mistake, middle age a struggle, old age a regret."

Man at his best—vanity! So David thought. He pleaded with God for some answer to the problem of life's frailty and life's futility. But, as with Job, the answer seemingly did not come at once; he was left to languish in the dark, grappling with problems which seemed to have no solution.

III. DAVID'S PLIGHT (39:6-11)

It was a twofold plight.

A. The Wealthy Man (39:6)

Nobody thinks of the rich man as being in a trap, but often he is. David's sickness had sharpened his senses and brought things into clear focus: "Surely every man walketh in a vain shew: surely they are disquieted in vain: he heapeth up riches, and knoweth not who shall gather them." "Only as a phantom doth each walk to and from" is the way the revised text puts it.

There is no doubt David was wealthy. He had amassed a vast fortune for the building of the temple alone. That part of his wealth was earmarked in his will for the Lord's work and on his deathbed he charged Solomon that he must not touch it except for that purpose. But David was independently rich. The scribe tells us, in recording David's death, that "he died in a good old age, full of days, riches, and honour" (1 Chronicles 29:28). But in his sickness he saw things in a sharper focus. He saw men laboring for wealth and as a result living lives of unreality and unrest, all made worse by materialism and mortality, living for what he calls "a vain show."

Here is a traveler in the desert: he has lost his way, he is frantic with thirst. Then he sees it! Clear as can possibly be—the sparkling waters of an oasis with palm trees raising verdant heads toward the sky. He hurries toward it, arms outstretched, staggering over the burning sands, but it recedes before him and at last vanishes altogether. He has been pursuing a delusion, a mirage painted on the sands by a trick of light. He falls to the ground, spent, lost, doomed. Thus, too, as David could clearly see, was the pursuit of riches. It was a vain show. The world of comfort and command, created by wealth, was a phantom unable to satisfy a thirsty, desperate soul.

B. The Wicked Man (39:7-11)

In his sick room David thinks back over his past. There are two things he has to face.

1. The Reality of His Sin (39:7-9)

a. He Needed a Saviour (39:7-8)

"And now, Lord, what wait I for? my hope is in Thee. Deliver me from all my transgressions: make me not the reproach of the foolish." He knew that he was suffering under the hand of God for his sin but he kissed the hand that smote him. "Thank you, Lord. I needed that! But Lord, do not just smite me; save me." It is a great moment when we cast our all on Him!

b. He Needed a Spokesman (39:9)

"I was dumb; I opened not my mouth; because Thou didst it." He explains to the Lord why, before, he tied up his tongue. He knew his sufferings were what his sin deserved. But, if he had no defense, could not God find one to speak for him? His was the cry of Job when his soul yearned for a daysman, a mediator. Thank God, that Mediator has been found, that Spokesman now sits enthroned at God's right hand in glory, a great High Priest, touched with the feelings of our infirmities, an Advocate with the Father, Jesus Christ the righteous. What more could we need? A Mediator, a Priest, an Attorney in the presence of God!

2. The Results of His Sin (39:10-11)

a. He Had Lost His Blessedness (39:10)

"Remove Thy stroke away from me: I am consumed by the blow of Thine hand." The word "stroke" is the same word as in the previous psalm (38:11), a word which refers to the affliction of the leper. He had lost all sense of God's blessing; instead he felt himself accursed. That was a direct result of his sin; fellowship with God was broken, life was filled with fear. Truly we pay a high price for sin.

b. He Had Lost His Beauty (39:11a)

"When Thou with rebukes dost correct man for iniquity, Thou makest his beauty to consume away like a moth."

When mother would take our winter clothes out of the closet, when I was a boy, they always needed to be hung outside for a while to air. They had a strong, pungent odor, not very pleasant. Mother had learned by experience that to hang clothes in a dark closet for the summer without protection was to invite disaster. In those days clothes were not made of rayon or nylon but of good English wool, and moths have a great appetite for wool—at least their grubs do. When the time came for the clothes to be worn again, the damage was done. So mother would put bags of mothballs into the closet. The moths couldn't stand that!

Sin, like a moth, eats away in the dark—secretly, silently, surely. It leaves its marks not only on the human soul, but on the human body as well. David's beauty was gone: those good looks, that magnificent physique—the things that made him a born leader of men and irresistible to women, gone! Sin and sickness had consumed his beauty like a moth.

We have all seen it happen. A young girl or an eager boy leaves home, falls into bad company, and becomes a prey to sin. Soon the effects are seen, leaving indelible marks on the face and form.

c. He Had Lost His Bearings (39:11b)

"Surely every man is vanity. Selah." "Only as a vapour is a man" (Rotherham). We see vapor rising from the surface of a lake. It stands for a moment, drifts with whichever breeze happens to blow, then vanishes away. David felt his life had become like that. He was adrift on life's sea without chart or compass, rudder or sail.

These things were all the results of his sin. It was the same plight in which Solomon his son found himself at the end of his life when, haunted by the thought of death, he looked back over the wreckage of his life.

IV. DAVID'S PLAN (39:12-13)

David's plan was simply to cast himself wholly and unreservedly on the very God under whose chastening hand he writhed. He asked God to make him:

A. Happy Again (39:12a)

"Hear my [cry], O LORD, and give ear unto my cry; hold not Thy peace at my tears." "Lord, look at my tears! Are not my tears evidence of my repentance? Do something about my tears!" The rabbis used to say that there are three kinds of supplication—prayer, crying, and tears; "prayer is made in silence, crying with a loud voice, but tears surpass all." Tears have an eloquence all their own.

When our situation is so desperate that we are reduced to tears in the presence of God, we can be quite sure that we have finally found the language that persuades. Our tears melt God's heart and move His hand.

Farsighted as he was, David saw that there can be no happiness without holiness for God has joined the two together. There is pleasure without purity but there is no happiness without holiness.

B. Holy Again (39:12b)

"For I am a stranger with Thee, and a sojourner, as all my fathers were." The words "strangers and sojourners" were technical terms among the Hebrews for aliens and foreigners. His sin had made David practically an alien and a foreigner in his relationship with God.

The word for "stranger" is particularly interesting. It means "a house guest" or "one who turns aside for the night." David had been God's house guest and he had trespassed against all the laws of hospitality in his sin with Bathsheba. Behind this cry is a heart hunger for a complete restoration of that fellowship which cannot exist apart from holiness.

C. Healthy Again (39:13)

"O spare me, that I may recover strength, before I go hence, and be no more." He wanted his strength back. The words "recover strength" literally mean "brighten up," as when the clouds roll away from the overcast skies. David was staring down into the grave when he prayed that. His affliction was carrying him swiftly down to the doors of death. All around was darkness but his hand reached up waveringly through the deepening gloom toward God.

Well, David did get better. The historians actually ignore his sickness altogether. When David reread this psalm he was happy again, holy again, and healthy again, so he added a little note: "To the chief Musician!"

That means he sent it to be included in the special numbers to be sung by the temple choir. It means, on a deeper and more spiritual note, that he dedicated this psalm to the Lord Jesus Christ—He who is the true Chief Musician! It was David's way of saying, "Thank you, Lord."

Psalm 40

PAST TRIUMPHS AND PRESENT TROUBLES

THERE IS NO DOUBT that David wrote this psalm, but when he wrote it is another matter. Some place its composition during his out-law years when he was the special object of King Saul's hate, and there certainly seems to be an echo of 1 Samuel 15:22 in the middle of it.

We remember how Saul forfeited all right to reign over Israel. Having solemnly reminded Saul of his calling and coronation, Samuel the prophet sent him on a special mission from God. Amalek, the ancestral foe of Israel and Old Testament type of the flesh, was to be

utterly destroyed—Amalek, Amalek's King Agag, and all that per-
tained to Amalek. But Saul kept Agag alive and he kept also the best
of the sheep and the oxen alive; and then, when challenged by the
prophet, lamely excused himself by saying he had kept the animals
for sacrifice. "Hath the LORD as great delight in burnt offerings and
sacrifices, as in obeying the voice of the LORD?" demanded the indignant prophet. "Behold, to obey is better than sacrifice, and to hearken
than the fat of rams" (1 Samuel 15:22).

There is an echo of that in verses 6 and 7 of this psalm: "Sacrifice
and offering Thou didst not desire; mine ears hast Thou opened:
burnt offering and sin offering hast Thou not required. Then said I,
Lo, I come: in the volume of the book it is written of me, I delight
to do Thy will, O my God."

But the psalm could just as easily have been written during the time
of the Absalom rebellion. Absalom commenced his revolt by holding
a sacrificial feast. Indeed, he tried to cast dust in David's eyes by
requesting permission to leave Jerusalem in order to go to Hebron
to pay a vow he had made to the Lord (2 Samuel 15:7-8). Hebron, of
course, was the focal point of the rebellion and the meeting place of
Absalom's clans. David's words in verse 6 of the psalm might well be
an echo of David's warning to the Absalom rebels who cloaked their
insurrection under a show of religion.

The words themselves, of course, are prophetic. They are picked
up and quoted by the Holy Spirit in Hebrews 10:5 (quoted from the
Septuagint version) as speaking primarily of Christ.

The psalm divides into five sections, as can be seen from the
outline. There is a sharp break when we come to verse 11, a break
so sharp that some have suggested the psalm is a composite—that is,
that fragments of two of David's psalms were later patched together
by an editor (perhaps King Hezekiah) and welded into one. It is just
as likely that David wrote the whole psalm as it now appears in our
Bible and that in the first verses he was looking back over past
triumphs and in the closing verses he was occupied with present *troubles*.

I. DAVID'S CONVICTION (40:1-5)

It was David's unwavering conviction that sooner or later God
always came through on behalf of His own.

A. The Reason For It (40:1-3a)

His reason for this conviction is based solidly on his own personal
experience. He gives us his own testimony.

1. He Heard Me (40:1)

"I waited patiently for the LORD; and He inclined unto me, and heard my cry." The expression "I waited patiently" actually suggests "I waited and waited and waited" ("waiting, I waited" would be the literal rendering). It looked to David as though the answer to his prayers would never come. But it did!

When we were small children, my father took us with him one Sunday to a little country church where he was preaching. The opening hymns had been sung, prayer had been offered, the announcements had been made, and dad stood up to speak. Just at that moment the door opened and a latecomer slipped into the church and sat down. It was winter and, since we had come in, night had descended. My little sister was sitting with mother on the back pew, right by the door. When the door opened she looked to see what was going on. She did not notice the person who came in late but the blackness of the night outside. Suddenly she called out to father in the pulpit: "Hurry up, daddy. It's getting dark!"

That is just how it is so often with us. We can wait no longer, circumstances are closing in, it's getting dark. We think: "Hurry up, Lord! It's getting dark." God, however, is never to be hurried. He takes His time, works to an infallible schedule. He smiles at our impatience knowing that His timings are perfect and cannot fail. So, David says, the Lord heard me!

2. He Helped Me (40:2-3a)

"He brought me up also out of an horrible pit, out of the miry clay, and set my feet upon a rock, and established my goings. And He hath put a new song in my mouth, even praise unto our God."

I once found myself in a situation like that. Not far from our home in South Wales there flowed a river, not large but a tidal river. When the tide came in it was deep and broad; when the tide was out it sank lower and lower between its muddy banks to its normal size. The banks were wide, steep, treacherous expanses of deep slimy mud. Woe betide anybody who ventured out on that mud! It would either swallow him up and close right over his head or else he would slip and slide down it until he ended in the river below. We were absolutely and repeatedly forbidden to go anywhere near that river.

That was a fairly easy command to obey because the river, for the most part, was inaccessible. But about a mile from our home there was one point where a fellow could get right down to the muddy bank of the river without any trouble. Once, only once, I ventured onto that forbidden ground. I can still remember what happened. For awhile I amused myself throwing stones down the slopes of the bank and thinking how loathsome and treacherous those mudbanks looked. Then I became careless, ventured too close, slipped, felt myself going, going. . . . I cried desperately to the Lord—there was nobody else to cry to—and, in His mercy, my foot caught on a snag of some sort and I was able to pull myself back up onto some rocks above the bank. I sat there in a cold sweat, with my heart wildly beating, and whispering, "Thank you, Lord! Thank you, Lord!" over and over again. He had brought me up also out of an horrible pit, out of the miry clay, and set my feet on a rock and established my goings and put a new song in my mouth even praise unto our God!

David's mud slide was a moral one. "He heard me! He helped me!" That was David's testimony. Up from out of the miry clay! Safe on the rock! Now to sing forever the praise of God! As A. P. Gibbs used to put it: "Out of the mire, into the choir!" So there was reason for David's conviction.

B. The Result Of It (40:3b-5)

His testimony had a twofold result.

1. A Soul Winner (40:3b-4)

"Many shall see it, and fear, and shall trust in the LORD. Blessed is that man that maketh the LORD his trust, and respecteth not the proud, nor such as turn aside to lies." Salvation is really a matter of *whom* we trust. Human nature is such that we would trust almost anyone rather than the Lord.

"Blessed is he," says David, "that maketh the Lord his trust." That is what salvation is all about. It is not a matter of trusting a church or a creed, but of trusting Christ. A man once came up to D. L. Moody after one of his meetings and said, "Mr. Moody, I *can't* believe." Moody looked at him for a moment then pointedly asked: "*Whom* can't you believe?"

David's testimony was such that many became believers because of him. He became a soul-winner.

2. A Spiritual Worshiper (40:5)

"Many, O LORD my God, are Thy wonderful works which Thou hast done, and Thy thoughts which are to usward: they cannot be reckoned up in order unto Thee: if I would declare and speak of them, they are more than can be numbered." As someone has put it:

> Count your many blessings!
> Name them by the score!
> And it will surprise you
> There are millions more.

Worship is simply sitting down quietly in the presence of God and seeking to recall before Him all the countless things we have received at His loving hand, starting with the gift of His Son, and then marveling at what a wonderful God He is.

II. DAVID'S CONSECRATION (40:6-8)

Worship should always result in a fresh surrender to the Lord. This is the natural response of thankfulness—devotion results in dedication. A fresh commitment to the Lord should always result from time spent contemplating our immeasurable indebtedness to the Lord.

A. Truth Realized In His Life (40:6-7)

"Sacrifice and offering Thou didst not desire; mine ears hast Thou opened: burnt offering and sin offering hast Thou not required. Then said I, Lo, I come: in the volume of the book it is written of me, I delight to do Thy will, O my God." David realized two very important truths, rarely grasped even today.

1. The Truth Concerning Ritual

His mind ran over the sacrificial religious system demanded by the Mosaic Levitical law. He used four Hebrew words to sum it up: *zebach, mincha, olah, chatah.*

The word for "sacrifice" *(zebach)* was a general term for all the communion-type offerings such as the peace offering, where offerer and priest sat down in the presence of God to enjoy a communion meal based upon the sacrifice.

The word for "offering" *(mincha)* was used for the meal offering, which related to man's toil and which emphasized that there is no line to be drawn between the sacred and the secular. It was an offering which put the emphasis on the holy life of Christ.

The word for the "burnt offering" *(olah)* depicted the precious sweet-savor offering which spoke so eloquently of Christ's wonderful life of holiness all being offered up wholly for God in a way which brought immeasurable satisfaction to God.

The word for "sin offering" *(chatah)* spoke of those sacrifices which dealt with all the dreadfulness of the human condition—with the principle of sin and with the practice of sin.

David entered fully into the truth concerning *ritual.* He saw that, even though the sacrifices themselves spoke of Christ, they were inefficient and inadequate. Worse, these very sacrifices could be abused, for a person could come to the point where he actually believed that, because he had performed some prescribed ritual, he was therefore fully discharged of all further moral and spiritual obligation in the sight of God.

We have the same thing today. Calvary has swept away all the sacrifices and offerings of the Old Testament but we still have two ordinances which Christ left for His Church—baptism and breaking bread. There are those who imagine that, because they have been baptized or have put in an appearance at the Lord's table, they have thereby discharged all their spiritual obligations.

David saw through that, summed up all the ritualistic sacrifices of the Mosaic ritual legislation in four sweeping words, then wrote off sacrifice without sincerity and ritual without reality as worthless.

2. The Truth Concerning Reality

"Mine ears hast Thou opened" (digged, bored). That is how he himself had come to this great realization. God had opened his understanding to hear the truth of the Word. The word "opened" means to open by digging. It is the word Jacob used to describe the tomb he had bored or digged in Canaan (Genesis 50:5)—implying, indeed, that Jacob had actually had to bore or dig into the rock to hew out his tomb. In Numbers 21:18 the same word is used to describe the digging of a well. The word graphically illustrates how deaf we are! God, so to speak, actually has to dig and bore into our ears before He can get His mighty Word to penetrate our thick heads!

The truth, however, had finally penetrated David's soul. At last he understood that the sacrifices and offerings, even the burnt offerings and sin offerings, had symbolic value only. They simply pointed to Calvary and, even when that was understood, they were still of little value unless the implications of Calvary transformed the life into one of obedience.

The word for "opened" conveys another great truth. The boring of the ear was something with which every Hebrew would be familiar. On the day of Jubilee in Israel, all slaves were to be set free. Here is a slave, however, who loves his master; bondage to such a master was freedom indeed and freedom from him would be wretchedness. So he declares to the officers of the law, who come to read to him the statement of emancipation, "I love my master . . . I will not go out free." He is then taken to the priest who leads him to a post. His ear is put against the post and pierced through with an awl. From then on he is a marked man—he bears in his body the stigmata, the slavebrand of his master. He has become a voluntary slave for life— one whose ear was to listen henceforth to the master's voice and whose life was pledged to his service. This was the truth concerning *reality* to which David points. Calvary, properly understood, makes me the bondslave of Jesus Christ. I become a person with "a bored ear," with no will of my own. Thus David, in describing his consecration, tells of truth realized in his life.

B. Truth Reproduced In His Life (40:8)

"I delight to do Thy will, O my God: yea, Thy law is within my heart." The bored ear of the servant meant that henceforth that man's life was to be lived to a single end—the master's will.

The Holy Spirit picks up this whole passage and applies it all to Christ in the Epistle to the Hebrews. For Jesus was God's perfect Servant. He was the One who came expressly to do His will, who did nothing else but that will, who alone could say: "I do always those things that please the Father." He it was who prayed in dark Gethsemane: "Not My will but Thine be done." He it was who became "obedient unto death, even the death of the cross." Whatever consecration David knew was but a feeble flicker of a candle's flame when compared with the burning fire of obedience which blazed in the soul of Jesus.

III. DAVID'S CONFESSION (40:9-10)

He now boldly confesses his faith before men. There were three areas of truth to which he bore witness.

A. The Righteous Majesty of God (40:9-10a)

"I have preached righteousness in the great congregation: lo, I have not refrained my lips, O LORD, Thou knowest. I have not hid Thy righteousness within my heart." The righteousness of God is at the heart of the Bible's revelation concerning God. In Paul's great doctrinal thesis, the Epistle to the Romans, he uses the word righteousness no less than sixty-six times. The great Biblical doctrines of sin, salvation, sanctification, and service (as summarized in this Epistle) all hinge on the fact that God is righteous—that is, that God always does what is right.

David preached the righteous majesty of God. He had seen it at work during the *perilous years* when he fled as a fugitive from Saul, holding on to the promise of God that the throne would be his and steadfastly refusing to do anything to take the law into his own hands. He had seen it at work during the *prosperous years* when he first ascended to the throne and saw all his foes go down before him like corn before the scythe. He had seen that righteous majesty at work in the *punitive years* after his sin with Bathsheba, when God righteously raised up first his own kinsmen and then his entire kingdom against him as punishment for his wickedness. He would see it at work yet again in the *peaceful years* when, his throne finally restored, he would at last be able to harness all national resources for the building of the temple.

We can thank God for his righteous majesty—that God always does what is right, that God does what He does because He is what He is. He is righteous.

B. The Rich Mercy of God (40:10b)

"I have declared Thy faithfulness and Thy salvation: I have not concealed Thy lovingkindness and Thy truth from the great congregation." The righteousness of God divorced from the tenderness of God would be truth without grace. It would be cold comfort to know that God always did exactly what was just and right if we did not know that along with His *law* went His *love.* To be faced with a revelation of the *holiness* of God apart from a commensurate revelation of the *heart* of God would be a frightening thing indeed.

So David spoke of God's salvation and of God's overwhelming love—what he calls his loving-kindness, not just kindness, but loving-kindness.

This, then, is David's confession. He boldly declares before men the twin truths of God's majesty and God's mercy; His inflexible character and His infinite compassion.

IV. DAVID'S CONTRITION (40:11-13)

There is a sharp break in the psalm at this point. David is no longer musing on the past, he is facing his present troubles. David was well used to facing trouble. He faced it as a fugitive from Saul and he faced it as a fugitive from his son.

These verses lead us to the conclusion that David was hemmed in by those difficulties and disasters which followed hard upon his heels after his sin with Bathsheba. That sin led, step by inevitable step, to the Absalom rebellion.

But we hardly do justice to these verses if we apply them solely to David. Surely they really belong to the Lord Jesus. Words such as these might well have flowed like hot lava from His lips at Gethsemane. For this, above all, is a Messianic psalm. The words here could have been used by Jesus when He told His Father that it was *His* will that had to be done, when He broke His heart there in the garden as He thought of the torments which yet lay ahead. Let us reverently take this prayer and read it again as it could well have come from the lips of Jesus.

A. His Suffering (40:11-12a)

"Withhold not Thou Thy tender mercies from me, O LORD: let Thy lovingkindness and Thy truth continually preserve me. For innumerable evils have compassed me about." Judas had received the blood money from Israel's religious leaders; he had accepted the sop from Israel's rightful Lord; the devil himself had entered into his heart. Already he was marching through the dark streets of Jerusalem with a mob of men at his back. The high priest was already summoning the Sanhedrin to an extraordinary and illegal midnight session. We can hear Jesus talking here about *His* suffering as Peter, James, and John slept on, only a stone's throw away, just when He needed them most.

B. Our Sins (40:12b)

Jesus identifies Himself with those sins. Within a few short hours they were to be gathered up in one enormous load and placed upon

Him. He looked into the dark depths of the cup; He saw there the wrath of God against our sins; He identified Himself with those sins; He wept: "Mine iniquities have taken hold upon me, so that I am not able to look up; they are more than the hairs of mine head: therefore my heart faileth me." To think that Jesus, the sinless, spotless Son of God, had to become so identified with our sins as to make them His very own! Oh the *shame* of our sins—He could not lift up His head for shame! Oh the *sum* of our sins—more than the hairs of His head! Oh the *sight* of our sins—"Therefore my heart faileth me!" That mighty heart of His that never quailed before the mob, that never flinched in the presence of hostile political power, failed Him at the thought of our sins.

C. God's Strength (40:13)

"Be pleased, O LORD, to deliver me: O LORD, make haste to help me." The Lord's actual recorded words were: "If it be possible, let this cup pass from Me, nevertheless, not My will but Thine be done." Such was the deeper meaning behind David's contrition. It coined the very language for our Lord's Gethsemane agony.

V. DAVID'S CONSOLATION (40:14-17)

David always knew where to turn when his troubles overwhelmed him, he turned to God. He consoled himself in three thoughts about God.

A. God Is Mighty (40:14)

"Let them be ashamed and confounded together that seek after my soul to destroy it; let them be driven backward and put to shame that wish me evil." No matter how strong and numerous his adversaries; no matter that "the conspiracy was strong" (as the historian says concerning Absalom's rebellion); no matter that Ahithophel, the most sagacious and clever of all David's counsels, had gone over to the other side—God is mighty! One, with God, is a majority!

B. God Is Magnified (40:15-16)

"Let them be desolate for a reward of their shame that say unto me, Aha, aha. Let all those that seek Thee rejoice and be glad in Thee: let such as love Thy salvation say continually, The LORD be magnified."

Our trouble is that we have such puny, microscopic ideas about God. We scale Him down to our size or we make Him just a little bigger than ourselves. We need to think great thoughts of God. We need to magnify Him. We need to think of Him in terms of all the suns and stars of space, all of which are mere pebbles under His feet.

Magnification always glorifies God. We can take anything man has made, put it under a microscope, magnify it, and its defects and imperfections will be exposed. But put the works of God under a microscope, magnify *them,* and more and more wonders will be seen! Magnification only glorifies God. His works in creation and redemption will bear the closest scrutiny and the more they are magnified the more amazed and astonished we shall be! It is the work of the scientist to magnify God as *Creator;* it is the work of the saint to magnify God as *Redeemer.*

C. God Is Merciful (40:17)

"But I am poor and needy; yet the Lord thinketh upon me: Thou art my help and my deliverer; make no tarrying, O my God." Who else would think upon the poor and needy? That, however, is just the kind of God we have! A merciful God! On that note David ends the psalm, signs it, and sends it "to the chief Musician."

"There!" he says, in effect, "Now *that* is something to sing about!"

Psalm 41

THE CONSPIRACY

I. DAVID'S FEARS (41:1-3)
  A. His Condition Is Described (41:1)
  B. His Confidence Is Described (41:2)
  C. His Consolation Is Described (41:3)
II. DAVID'S FOES (41:4-9)
  A. They Professed Concern for Him (41:4-6)
    He contemplates:
    1. The Horror of His Sin (41:4)
    2. The Hatred of His Subjects (41:5)
    3. The Hypocrisy of His Son (41:6)
  B. They Promoted Conspiracy Against Him (41:7-9)
    1. The Strength of This Conspiracy (41:7-8)
      a. His Past Wickedness (41:7)
      b. His Present Weakness (41:8)
    2. The Sting of This Conspiracy (41:9)
III. DAVID'S FAITH (41:10-12)
  He has:
  A. A Merciful God (41:10)
  B. A Mighty God (41:11)
  C. A Marvelous God (41:12)

Psalms 38, 39, 40, and 41 were all born out of the same womb. Each of them was written around the circumstances which surrounded the rebellion of Absalom against his father David.

Many a man has a rebellious son but not many have sons who have hated them as much as Absalom hated David. No rebellion takes place in a vacuum. Behind Absalom's rebellion, and ever haunting David's conscience, was David's sin with Bathsheba and the consequent murder of her husband. These hideous crimes had been forgiven, but the human consequences pursued David through the remaining years of his life.

How could David impose the death sentence, required by the law of Moses, upon Amnon for his wicked seduction of Absalom's sister, when he himself had been guilty of the wicked seduction of Bathsheba? How could David impose the death sentence, required by the law of Moses, upon Absalom for the murder of Amnon, when he himself had been guilty of murdering Uriah? So, from that one evil seed the whole Absalom rebellion flowered, flourished, and bore fruit. Truly, what we sow we eventually reap.

Psalm 41 divides into three parts. The last verse is really a final epilogue to the entire first book of psalms.

I. DAVID'S FEARS (41:1-3)

David had good cause to fear for his circumstances were serious indeed.

A. His Condition Is Described (41:1)

"Blessed is he that considereth the poor: the LORD will deliver him in time of trouble." Rotherham substitutes the word "helpless" for the word "poor." David was referring to himself and he certainly was not poor. The word means "dangling" or "slacking" or "letting go." The margin of the Scofield Bible renders it "the weak" or "the sick." That was David's condition.

What happened to David—to the mighty man who could tackle a lion and a bear and in single-handed combat rout the giant of Gath? What happened to the warrior-king who never lost a battle and who raised the Hebrew people from a dozen squabbling tribes into an international power? As the Hebrew of the passage suggests, he had been letting things go.

That's his condition. Matters of state slipped away from him; he no longer had a firm hand on the helm of the kingdom; he was a weakling. That is what sin did for David and what sin will do for everyone. But David was a contrite and a humble man. He was letting go in another sense: "let go and let God." The Lord would deliver him in time of trouble.

B. His Confidence Is Described (41:2)

"The LORD will preserve . . . the LORD will keep alive. . . . He shall be blessed upon the earth: and Thou wilt not deliver him [into the hands] of his enemies." Matters may have gotten beyond David's control but they are well in hand with God. So David looked at his fears in that light and they were not so ominous as they first appeared.

Some time ago Vance Havner, speaking at a conference, described the homecall of his wife. Two years before her death they had been in Charleston, and he had taken a picture of her standing by the waterfront. He didn't finish the roll of film. Then one day, after her death, he thought of it, finished the roll, and had it developed. And there she was, smiling at him out of the past. He said: "Just as that roll of film had lain for a year or so in the darkness of that camera, so her body lies in a quaint little Quaker graveyard in North Carolina. But one of these days the Great Photographer is going to turn negatives into positives. This mortal will put on immortality and corruption will put on incorruption, and death will be swallowed up in victory. That is part of the unfinished work."

Now think of David. He was in the dark, everything around was black. He had lost his strength, his power was gone, and the nation was slipping from his grasp. It was one big black negative. However he looked up to the Great Photographer and said in effect, "Lord, You can change this negative into a positive and I believe you will."

C. His Consolation Is Described (41:3)

"The LORD will strengthen him upon the bed of languishing: [The Lord] wilt make all his bed in his sickness." That explains the whole thing. The historical narrative does not say so, but as a result of David's great sin and his equally great sorrow, David seems to have become dangerously ill. This is the only way to account for David's loss of control over the kingdom. His sickness explains why Absalom could accuse David of neglecting his official duties and how he could mingle with the crowds of petitioners being turned away unheard from the palace, and promise immediate redress if he were made king. David couldn't attend to the cases which thronged his court. David's sickness explains also the strange failure in his natural courage as indicated in his precipitous flight from Jerusalem when the rebellion came to a head. That was not like David. What he needed was a six-month vacation on the coast; what he got was a forced march into the barren hills. David had been sick and the psalm describes the sickness.

David tosses and turns upon his bed. In comes an attendant and wipes the perspiration from David's fevered brow, lifts up the sick man, straightens out the mattress and the sheets, fluffs up David's pillow, gives him something to drink. David sinks back gratefully and closes his eyes. "Thank you, Lord. The hands were those of my servant, but the heart was the heart of God. O God, thank You for making my bed."

II. DAVID'S FOES (41:4-9)

It is difficult for us today, brought up as we are on the hero legends of David, to imagine how many and varied were his enemies. We think of David as the giant slayer, as a charismatic figure able to transform the outcasts of society into a disciplined force of fighting men. We think of the man who inspired such loyalty that men would risk everything just to bring him a cup of water. But any man in high office, no matter how wisely he rules, will have his foes and David was no exception. After his sin, which caused a scandal in Israel, his enemies were given great leverage against him.

This psalm tells us two things about David's foes.

A. They Professed Concern for David (41:4-6)

1. The Horror of His Sin

"I said, LORD, be merciful unto me: heal my soul; for I have sinned against Thee." David knew that his troubles stemmed from his sin.

What a sweet and succulent morsel sin looks like in prospect! But once it has been swallowed it turns into acid indigestion in the soul. It burns and ulcerates and kills. "My sin," groaned David, "My sin, my sin, my sin." All through his penitential psalms it is the same; he is horrified by the memory of his sin. It was all over and done with, all in his past, it had been confessed and cleansed. But still he woke at night, groaning in an agony of shame. If only he could relive that chapter of his life! And who of us does not have some such dark memory?

2. The Hatred of His Subjects

"Mine enemies speak evil of me, When shall he die, and his name perish?" His enemies were not the Philistines, the Moabites, or the children of Ammon but his own subjects, those over whom he had been given the rule by God. What a mess he had made of things!

His enemies hoped his sickness would prove to be fatal and result in a speedy death. They hoped his name would perish. They begrudged him his fame and wanted his very name to be forgotten. Such was the hatred generated against David by those who wished him ill.

3. The Hypocrisy of His Son

"When he cometh to see me" (41:6). We are not told who the "he" is but probably it was Absalom. There is a cheery hail in the corridor outside, a gust of laughter from the men on guard. Then a sharp stamping of feet as they come to attention and a thud as they ground their arms. David has recognized the voice of his favorite son, his handsome, captivating Absalom—Absalom, with all of David's wit, charm, and charisma but with none of David's honesty and spiritual life.

In he comes, bluff and hearty, resplendent in his uniform, his arms outstretched toward his dad, his eyes alight with sympathy, expressing the right mixture of deference, concern, and hearty good fellowship. He strides over to the bed and bows to the king. "Well, dad! And how are you today? Feeling better? Does the doctor say when you can get up?" All the while his eyes are taking in the increased pallor on David's face, the feebleness of David's voice as he bravely replies: "I'm on the mend, son. I'll be back on the throne in a week." A bold bluff denied by the choking cough which racks him until the tears start in his eyes. "I'm sure you will, dad. In the meantime, don't worry about a thing. Old Joab and I are keeping things together. Then too there's Ahithophel, president of the cabinet, he's giving us his usual good advice. Everything's under control."

David knows he's a liar and a knave. Only that morning Joab, perhaps, has warned that Absalom is up to no good: "My lord king! Be it far from me to add to your troubles but I think we should put Absalom under house arrest. Pardon me, my lord, but he's a dangerous man. We have evidence that he is heading a conspiracy aimed at your life and throne." David knows it's true but, for his very life he won't believe it and won't have it. "Enough, Joab! Not another word! I'll hear nothing against Absalom. Nothing!"

So David contemplates not only the horror of his sin and the hatred of his subjects but also the hypocrisy of his son: "And if he come to see me, he speaketh vanity [the word is falsehood]: his heart gathereth iniquity to itself; when he goeth abroad, he telleth it." In his mind's eye he sees Absalom, for all his bluff assurances leaving the sick room to gather with his friends: "The old man is worse. He could hardly speak. He'll be dead in a week. It may not be necessary to turn our shock troops loose in riot. We'll wait a week."

So then we have David's foes and their professed concern for David.

B. They Promoted Conspiracy Against David (41:7-9)

1. The Strength of This Conspiracy

David was a realist after all and much as he hated to think that Absalom was nothing but a black-hearted traitor and much as he might forbid Joab to discuss it, that was the heart of the father speaking. David was every inch a king, even when down to death's door. He knew the strength of this conspiracy—perhaps not in terms that Joab would understand—men mustered on Absalom's payrolls; secret meetings attended by Joab's spies; hidden war equipment stockpiled in secret dens around the country—but in spiritual terms, in his own guilty past and present incapacity.

2. His Past Wickedness

"All that hate me whisper together against me: against me do they devise my hurt" (41:7). There was what we would call today a whisper campaign against the king. But a deliberate attempt to incriminate a person like David would get nowhere were there was nothing in his life upon which to build the fire. David knew that the lies of his foes were all the more poisonous because of the truth mixed in with them.

3. His Present Weakness

"An evil disease, say they, cleaveth fast unto him: and now that he lieth he shall rise up no more" (41:8).

David was sick but it wasn't what *they* said it was. They called it "an evil disease," meaning "a thing of Belial" or "an affliction from the abandoned one." Some foul and filthy malady supposedly from Satan was rumored to be rotting away the king's flesh. David however, recognized his affliction as coming from God and he knew God could make him better again. But in the meantime he was helpless, weak, and so ill that his foes were saying, "He'll soon be dead!"

So David mentions the strength of the conspiracy. He also mentions *the sting of this conspiracy.* It was bad enough that his friends should abuse him, but there was something worse that that: "Yea, mine own familiar friend, in whom I trusted, who did eat of my bread, hath lifted up his heel against me" (41:9). That friend was Ahithophel, one of David's best friends and certainly his most able and persuasive counselor. "He broke bread with me!" gasped David as though unable to believe the news of Ahithophel's defection. In the East, to eat of a man's bread carried sacred associations, a covenant bond was formed. One never attacked a man with whom he broke bread in good fellowship.

But Ahithophel had gone over to Absalom, and had done so with the added venom of giving David, as it were, a vicious kick. Of course, David knew why Ahithophel had gone over to Absalom—he hoped to be avenged on David for Bathsheba and Uriah the Hittite. For Bathsheba was Ahithophel's granddaughter and despite his pretended friendship for David he never forgave him for the seduction of his granddaughter and the murder of her husband.

So we read of David's fears and David's foes.

III. DAVID'S FAITH (41:10-12)

Thinking along the lines which mark the early part of this psalm would drive a man out of his mind. The endless round of remembered sin, accusing conscience, bitter remorse, and inevitable consequence would lead to depression, insanity, and suicide, so David turned his thoughts elsewhere and, being David, he did not turn them to vain abuse of his lot. He turned his thoughts to God.

He rejoiced that God was:

A. A Merciful God (41:10)

"But Thou, O LORD, be merciful unto me, and raise me up, that I may requite them." "Lord, you know I am a very sick man and the doctors cannot cure me and people are only talking about my death. but you are a merciful God. Lord, raise me up, make me well. Give me another chance to put the affairs of my kingdom in order." He cast himself upon the mercy of God. When we find ourselves trapped like David, and do the same, the sun will shine through.

Then he rejoiced that God was:

B. A Mighty God (41:11)

"By this I know that Thou favourest me, because mine enemy doth not triumph over me." So far, all his enemies had done was plot and conspire, spy upon him, and gloat over his illness. David recognized in this not their uncertainty, unpreparedness, and hesitation to strike, but the Lord's mighty, restraining hand, able and willing to protect David who could not protect himself.

That is something else for us to think about—God controls all situations and nothing happens without His permission. He has lessons to teach us in adverse circumstances and will not permit the ungodly to take advantage of our weakness when we are in His hand.

Finally, David rejoiced that God was:

C. A Marvelous God (41:12)

"And as for me, Thou upholdest me in mine integrity, and settest me before Thy face for ever." In some ways that is the most remarkable utterance in the book of Psalms.

The background of the psalm is David's unbelievable sin. Yet David could plead his *integrity* before God! We say: the man must have been mad, he must have had mental as well as physical problems. How could he speak about integrity?

We must remember that, after his great sin when Nathan the prophet came in and convicted him, David fell on his face before God and confessed his sin. Then Nathan said: "God hath put away thy sin." David believed it, and it was counted unto him for righteousness. So David says: "I have a wonderful God. He not only forgives my sin, He forgets my sin. He not only cancels it, He gives to me His own righteousness. I am not only a forgiven man, I am a justified man." So in this psalm he boldly takes his stand in the righteousness of Christ. He had made it so really and truly his own he could actually speak of "mine integrity." That is the kind of wonderful God we have! He is a God who not only forgives our sins, He blots them out of existence.

> Such deep transgressions to forgive!
> Such guilty, daring worms to spare!
> This is Thine own prerogative
> And in the honor none shall share:
> Who is a pardoning God like Thee?
> Or who has grace so rich and free?